Http://web.ask.com/redir

———ISRAEL'S LEBANON WAR

Ze'ev Schiff and Ehud Ya'ari

Edited and Translated by Ina Friedman

SIMON AND SCHUSTER

NEW YORK

Published by Simon and Schuster
A Division of Simon & Schuster, Inc.
Simon & Schuster Building
Rockefeller Center
1230 Avenue of the Americas
New York, New York 10020
SIMON AND SCHUSTER and colophon are registered trademarks of
Simon & Schuster, Inc.
Maps by Elad Dan
Manufactured in the United States of America

10   9   8   7   6   5   4   3   2   1

Library of Congress Cataloging in Publication Data
Schiff, Ze'ev, 1932–
  Israel's Lebanon war.
  Translation of: Milhemet sholel.
  Includes index.
  1. Lebanon—History—Israeli intervention, 1982–
I. Ya'ari, Ehud.   II. Friedman, Ina R.   III. Title.
DS87.53.S3513   1984   956.92'044   84-13941
ISBN: 0-671-47991-1

Contents

The violence done to Lebanon will overwhelm you.
—HABAKKUK 2:17

Foreword

ALTHOUGH ISRAEL'S WAR IN LEBANON is not yet over, its true character and consequences are already painfully clear. That is precisely why we, as journalists, have chosen to write and publish this book now, rather than leave the work of research and analysis to future historians. We do so in the hope that drawing the lessons and conclusions of this still-unfinished war may help our country chart its course in the immediate future.

As Israelis, we found ourselves dealing with a kind of war unprecedented in the history of the State of Israel, a war attended by many highly charged issues and questions that have never before arisen in this country. We have tried to approach our subject with emotional detachment but are keenly aware that in this case there is no such thing as complete detachment or objectivity. Like all our countrymen, we have been touched by the pain of this war, and that is sure to be reflected in these pages.

Israel's war in Lebanon was first and foremost a political venture; rather than concentrate solely or even mainly on the military moves in the field, therefore, we have chosen to focus most of this book on the political drama that went on before and behind them: how the Israeli Cabinet and General Staff were led into a war they did not want, how the Phalange became partners in the collusion, how Israel got a green light from the United States for one operation and pursued another, how the PLO knew what was coming, and how all these circumstances came together as events unfolded in the field.

In our initial research we sifted through hundreds of unpublished documents and soon learned that not everything which affects the course of events is recorded in the minutes of official meetings, and that even such minutes have a way of distorting and obscuring the truth. We therefore supplemented written sources with over 150 interviews in Israel, Lebanon, and the United States. We were surprised (and heartened) by the degree of cooperation we received from Israelis (in and out of uniform) who believe, as we do, that revealing as much as possible about the real motives and manipulations behind this war is a necessary and therapeutic measure for Israel. We were also greatly aided by Lebanese and American figures who were personally involved in events and displayed a keen interest in contributing to the record of this war. In drawing on such a wealth and variety of sources, we often came upon conflicting versions of the same reality and decided between them only after a rigorous examination of the issue at hand.

Not all of what we intended to publish in this book was cleared by the Israeli military censor, to whom we were obliged to submit the manuscript. The excisions have not, in our view, changed the gist or spirit of the final product, though occasionally they cut deeply into the substance of our argument. We are convinced, however, that in the course of time a reappraisal of what does and does not prejudice the true interests of national security will result in the release of the presently classified material.

Finally, this edition, adapted from the original Hebrew, represents the combined effort of three people who complement each other in their perspectives, disciplines, and temperaments. To the degree that the analyses and conclusions of this work are judged either too mild or too harsh, we would merely point out that they have passed through the prism of three separate sensibilities, and we believe that this is one of the book's main strengths.

Our gratitude goes to Deborah Harris of The Domino Press, who has shepherded this project from its inception with unflagging devotion and skill. Don Hutter of Simon and Schuster has contributed a keen eye, deft hand, and much patience with the trials of managing an international triangle. The maps were drawn by Elad Dan; Hanni Saul and Belle Lerman typed parts of the manuscript; and the staff at Yozma, Jerusalem, cushioned the plunge into word processing. We thank them all for their help.

Ze'ev Schiff
Ehud Ya'ari

March 1984
Jerusalem, Washington

1

The Covenant

BLUE WITH COLD AND DRENCHED TO THE BONE, a burly figure climbed out of the darkness onto the deck of the Israeli missile boat, hands held high over his head. A ring of sailors closed round him, weapons poised, while others stood tense at their firing positions, peering into the night at the small pleasure craft that had just brought him. For the better part of an hour they had followed the small boat as it struggled in the rough seas, signaling its approach with a weak searchlight. They had suspected the maneuver to be a trick to get within firing range of their vessel, which was stationed off the Lebanese coast to prevent Palestinian terror squads from reaching Israel by sea.

"I am Abu Halil, a leader of the Lebanese Phalange party," the shivering figure said in English as he wrapped his body in a coarse woolen blanket. "Please take me to Israel. I am on an urgent mission."

The date was March 12, 1976, and within a few days the savage Lebanese civil war, pitting Christians, Moslems, and Palestinians against each other, would be a year old. Yet this was the first time a representative of the Maronite Christian community had directly approached the Israelis.

No sooner had Abu Halil stepped onto the dock in Haifa a few hours later than he began to lecture exuberantly about the common fate shared by the Lebanese Maronites and the Jews, about the Palestine Liberation Organization as their common enemy, about the mutual benefits to be derived from a bold alliance that would cut across national and religious boundaries. The envoy from the Phalange claimed he was on a mission of mercy; time would show that he had come to plant the seeds of war.

On the previous morning, Abu Halil had left the Phalange offices in Beirut and made off for the village of Bekfaya, home of Sheikh Pierre Gemayel, the party's leader. On the way he stopped in to see Gemayel's elder son, Amin, a district commander of the Phalange militia, hoping that Amin would help persuade his father to ask for Israeli assistance. Drastic steps had to be taken if the Christian forces were to retain any hope of prevailing over the coalition of Palestinian and leftist Lebanese factions that were crushing the Maronites in a merciless struggle for control of Lebanon. "We have nothing left to lose," Abu Halil despaired, reflecting the gloom that pervaded the Maronite camp. Amin agreed and offered Abu Halil his blessing. But persuading Pierre Gemayel was another matter.

His face drawn with age and frozen, as usual, in an inscrutable expression, the seventy-one-year-old leader listened to Abu Halil's brief in silence. All the while, reports were coming in of shellings in the Mount Lebanon region, the bastion of the Lebanese Christian community, along with word that more units of the Lebanese army were deserting to the enemy. The television continued broadcasting the harangue of a Moslem officer claiming to have pulled off a coup, under covering fire from the PLO, and demanding that Lebanese President Sleiman Frangieh, a Maronite, resign forthwith or face being turned out of his palace.

Even against that grim background, Gemayel was not enthusiastic about the idea of appealing to Israel. For forty years he had steered his Phalange movement well clear of the Arab-Israeli conflict, and certainly of any traffic with the Israelis. He was aware that for quite a while Israel had been helping the Maronites acquire weapons, but none of the leading Maronite figures was directly involved in this activity, and most pretended to know nothing about it. Yet when Gemayel finally broke his silence, it was to stress the need for total secrecy, thus according the venture his tacit approval. Soon afterward, Abu Halil was in Haifa, begging for help from Israeli Prime Minister Yitzhak Rabin and Foreign Minister Yigal Allon.

Gemayel's radical departure from Phalange policy was perhaps inevitable, and had been for many months, as increasingly the Maronite community found itself at a critical point in its history and panicked by a sense of impending disaster. The Lebanese state teetered on the brink of collapse, with the regular Lebanese army disintegrating rapidly and the nation's president, Sleiman Frangieh, finding himself a political cripple forced to work out of a bomb shelter as shells hailed down around his residence. Forces of the Palestinian-Druse-leftist Moslem alliance were poised to overrun the Maronite-dominated Mount Lebanon range between Tripoli and Beirut. The city of Zahle below the eastern slope of this range was already surrounded, Beirut itself was divided by barricades, all the Christians had fled Tripoli in the north, and defenseless Maronite villagers in remote settlements were being sadistically slaughtered—dismembered with welding irons before receiving the mercy of the coup de grace—while envoys from the Vatican, France, and the United States intoned noble sentiments about compromise and reconciliation. The American ambassador to Beirut, Dean L. Brown, had even quipped, with a perfectly straight face, that as far back as the civil war of 1840 one proposed solution to the communal strife in Lebanon was to ship all the local Christians to Algeria as colonists.

Camille Chamoun, the former Lebanese president and patriarch of the Maronite community, had already resolved to turn to Israel. The seventy-six-year-old statesman was less concerned than Gemayel about burning bridges with the Arab world; as president during the previous round of the civil war in 1958, he had considered appealing to David Ben-Gurion, but then thought better of the idea and turned to Eisenhower instead. Now he consulted with an old friend, King Hussein of Jordan, who bolstered his resolve by telling him plainly, "If you want to continue to exist, go to Israel."

Prior to the spring of 1976, Gemayel and Chamoun both believed that Syria, acting in a big-brother role, would manage to impose an acceptable solution on the two sides. Gemayel had gone to Damascus personally and received explicit assurances from President Hafez Assad that he would not allow the PLO to bring the Maronites to their knees. But within a few weeks of that reassurance, it became clear that even the Syrians could not stem the tide. In an effort to mediate the conflict, Syria had hammered out a "constitutional document" with President Frangieh providing for a more equitable division of power between the various Lebanese factions and sects. Almost immediately, Kamal Jumblatt, the Druse leader who doubled as the head of Lebanon's leftist alliance, scuttled the plan by announcing that it was too late to settle for perfunctory changes in the country's political makeup. The collapse of the Syrian mediation effort augured a long and bitter fight in Lebanon. Thus the Maronites' appeal to Israel through Abu Halil's mission came after they had played what was presumably their last card—the Syrian card—and it too had failed.

The notion of a Jewish-Maronite partnership was not a new one, nor was it born of Lebanon's latest civil unrest. In essence it went back as far as the beginnings of Zionism, though each time the Maronite leadership was forced to choose sides it preferred to edge away from the Jews and confirm its association with the Arab world. Nevertheless, the vision of what one Zionist leader described as "a Jewish-Christian front in the Arab ocean" never quite perished. In 1955 Israel's foreign minister, Moshe Sharett, had to fight tooth and nail to scotch a plan conceived by David Ben-Gurion and Moshe Dayan to "buy" a Maronite officer who would then "invite" Israeli intervention in Lebanese affairs and enable Israel to establish its control over Lebanon. "A vain fantasy," Sharett wrote in his diary. "We'll get bogged down in a mad adventure that will only bring us disgrace." The Maronites, he saw even then, "have no one who will dare risk taking a chance or can serve as a genuine ally. A broken reed," was his prophetic assessment of them.

Like any manifestation of political turbulence in the region, the Lebanese civil war was followed closely by Israel, especially as it neared the point of a crisis suggesting several unsavory possibilities: the fall of most of Lebanon to the PLO and its allies; a puppet government resulting from Syrian intervention; or, alternatively, a continuation of the bloodletting that would spread instability throughout the region. But most of all, the Israelis feared that a Maronite defeat would bring Lebanon into the so-called Banana Front that Syria was trying to create in the crescent extending from the Jordanian Red Sea port of Aqaba to Naqura on the Mediterranean coast, just over the Israeli border. Foreign Minister Yigal Allon was the main advocate of taking steps to counteract this scenario, and after listening to Abu Halil plead the Maronite case he suggested that he go to Lebanon to pursue the matter personally. But Prime Minister Yitzhak Rabin inclined toward caution in dealing with all matters Lebanese; he would not become involved so precipitously or at such a high level. He was, however, prepared to conduct a thorough investigation of the Maronite plight.

The two high-ranking Israeli intelligence officers chosen to enter Lebanon as an advance team set to work within days. It was on another Israeli missile boat, this one anchored outside of Junieh, that they first met Bashir Gemayel, Sheikh Pierre's younger son. Bashir came on board with his face concealed by a mask, spoke fretfully about recent Maronite setbacks, and left the two Israelis with the feeling that they were talking to "a child" who could scarcely be taken seriously. When they expressed interest in meeting his father, Bashir became evasive. His older brother, Amin, turned up at a second meeting on the boat—without mask and wearing a proper khaki uniform and hat—but he too made a negative impression. "Amin is not to be trusted," one of the envoys later remarked. Upon returning to Israel, the intelligence officers recommended that the contacts continue but that no direct military assistance be considered until a detailed investigation of the Maronite needs and prospects had been completed. More than a year later, Rabin had a team of four army and intelligence men put together to return to Lebanon and formulate a comprehensive report. Led by Col. Benyamin Ben-Eliezer, they left on an Israeli gunboat dressed in civilian clothing and armed only with Smith and

Wessons. As the vessel passed Beirut, the skies above the capital glittered with the explosion of shells and illumination bombs. To the dull thud of artillery beating arhythmically in the distance, the ship cut its engines at midnight opposite the bay of Junieh. Soon a luxury yacht approached, holding closely to a predetermined course. The exchange of identifying signals went on for close to an hour while two blacked-out Israeli missile boats observed the rendezvous from behind, lurking deep in the darkness.

When the four Israelis transferred to the pitching yacht, they were greeted with hearty handshakes and a broad smile by a Maronite soldier of a different breed from the Gemayels. Danny Chamoun, the younger son of former Lebanese president Camille Chamoun, was the commander of a non-Phalange militia group known as the Tigers. A handsome, ruddy young man who dressed in a fashionably cut uniform and spoke fluent English without a trace of accent, the young Chamoun set the yacht full speed ahead, and at 2:00 A.M. the Israeli team came ashore under the neon Mercedes sign of the Casino du Liban, where a convoy of cars awaited their arrival. After an honor guard of Maronite fighters saluted smartly, the convoy set out through the deserted streets of Junieh to a remote villa, while the Israeli gunboat weighed anchor and sailed for home. The two missile boats remained on silent guard over the horizon.

In the garden of the lavish villa, one of the Israelis stumbled in the dark and fell into an empty swimming pool, but within a few minutes it became clear that he had suffered only a bad bruise and despite some pain would be able to continue. A young woman came forward to lead him to the upper story of the house to recover his wits. "This is Eva, our hostess," Danny Chamoun introduced her. "She is Jewish," he added, knowing that such attention to detail would impress his guests. Indeed, the Israelis were very taken by their reception. Not only had their hosts attempted to put them at ease with the aid of a local Jewish woman, but alongside each bed, with its crisply ironed and perfumed sheets, they found a cleaned Kalashnikov rifle, a flashlight, a penknife, and stationery.

"I'm dying of hunger!" Ben-Eliezer roared, switching from English to Arabic to further ease the atmosphere, and was led to a table laden with delicacies.

Danny Chamoun began their first work session by summing up the state of affairs on the fronts, yet even when speaking of the gravity of the situation he never lost his air of self-confidence. His speech was peppered by unselfconscious expletives and easy repartee. There was something convincing, even endearing, about Chamoun that the Gemayel brothers lacked. He came across naturally as "one of the boys," and to add to his self-assurance he displayed an aristocrat's familiarity with wines and hunting rifles. He seemed the embodiment of the rich and undoubtedly spoiled playboy who had abandoned a sybaritic life to take up arms in the defense of his people. Yet Danny Chamoun had no pretensions of being a serious military man. He spoke candidly about his volunteer fighters needing training and assistance in a war that was fast outstripping their amateur capabilities. And his message was straight and to the point, uncluttered by diplomatic nuance or niceties: "Give us arms and we'll slaughter the Palestinians!" Ben-Eliezer plied him with questions, burrowing down to the most minute details of the situation. The Israelis took in Chamoun's every word but volunteered nothing themselves.

Next morning representatives from the Phalange militia arrived at the villa. The Israelis already understood from Chamoun that the two Maronite factions were operating in completely distinct sectors with minimal coordination, and they were particularly curious as to whether the Phalangists would display the same candor as the Chamounists. Danny Chamoun's militia was only a few years old, its improvised organization based largely on family ties; the Phalange had developed out of a sports-cum-military youth movement founded by Pierre Gemayel back in 1936. Built on the fascist model of the day, it boasted disciplined cadres, a long-range training program, and a dedicated group of activists. Every branch of the Phalange party was run like a military unit, with members going out on patrols and serving guard duty. Gemayel had ostensibly surrendered the compromised name Phalange in favor of the less offensive Social Democratic party, but no one ever used the new label. During the civil war the movement's ranks swelled with young volunteers—refugees from abandoned Christian villages and children of the middle class—and the Phalange clearly became the backbone of the Maronite camp, even though Camille Chamoun enjoyed a large measure of personal support and popularity.

Once again Pierre Gemayel's two sons made a poor impression on the investigating Israelis. Bashir Gemayel, then twenty-eight, and Amin, thirty-two, were both American-educated lawyers fashioned in their father's image: reticent, aloof, and schooled in the arts of circuity. Bashir, just then embarking on his political career, spoke in a thin voice and suffered from a bad case of shyness. "We had the feeling that he might burst into tears at any moment," was how one of the men in Ben-Eliezer's group described him. Both brothers joined in Danny Chamoun's request for urgent assistance, but the Israelis had the distinct feeling that, while Danny was prepared to fight until victory, the Gemayels seemed tired and would not balk if a ceasefire were arranged.

The first time the Israelis went out for a tour of the area, on their way to Camille Chamoun's residence, they were appalled by the local savagery.

Corpses of Palestinians were being dragged through the streets of Junieh tied to the backs of vehicles, their heads smashing up against the curbs in full view of the unfazed citizenry. Such barbarity was all the more shocking for its stark contrast with the charmed atmosphere within the villa. Now as they left Junieh and stopped alongside the Dog River, Maronite youngsters were hurling the bodies of two uniformed Palestinians into the gorge as drivers along the highway tooted their horns in delight. Suddenly the ferocity of the hatred between the two sides struck the Israelis like an epiphany. "I suggest that you burn the corpses quickly," Ben-Eliezer mumbled to his host, "before you have an epidemic here."

When they arrived at Camille Chamoun's residence, another lesson in the ways of the Lebanese war awaited the Israeli delegation. "I want you to see our girls," the elderly leader said without the slightest trace of salacious meaning. In the courtyard stood four young women in combat fatigues sporting hand grenades in their belts. "One of them is a Christian Palestinian," Chamoun explained, "another has a Russian mother. They are all veteran fighters."

"What have they managed to accomplish?" Ben-Eliezer asked skeptically. Immediately, the first girl produced a transparent plastic bag containing amputated fingers. "She takes a finger as a trophy from each of the men she's killed," Chamoun explained steadily, informatively. The second girl took a small bag of earlobes out of her knapsack. Suddenly stricken with nausea, Ben-Eliezer barely muttered some polite sounds of admiration before ducking back into the house.

During the final meeting of their stay, the Israelis summed up their initial impressions for their hosts. Ben-Eliezer spoke of the need to define clear objectives, to map out how to achieve them, and to build their forces accordingly. His most insistent point was that the Lebanese would accomplish very little if they continued to operate out of separate commands; it was imperative to unite their headquarters so they could transfer troops from one sector to another. The militiamen heard him out but made no reply. Even at the height of the fighting, the enmity between their various factions and clans did not abate, and in the coming months the Israelis would uncover layer after layer of obdurate rivalry and malice.

Suddenly Ben-Eliezer began to talk about the contacts that Israel had already made with a few Christian villages in South Lebanon, and before his companions could stop him he got carried away with musing aloud about organizing, training, and equipping the southern villages and, when the time came, enabling these battalions to help the Maronites in the north. Finally one of his associates cut him off by pointedly reminding him, "We'd need approval from home for that!" Yet this was to be the pattern for years to come: strict circumspection by the politicians in Jerusalem while envoys in the field exercised far less control over their tongues and gave insufficient consideration to what their Lebanese listeners were being led to believe and expect. On one level it was possible to understand such behavior: with the start of peace negotiations with Egypt in 1977, it may well have seemed to the men being treated with such munificence in Lebanon as if suddenly the whole of the Middle East was beginning to open up to Israel. Their sense of breakthrough, the prospect of air to breathe and room to move, and their consequently careless verbal largesse inflated expectations that Jerusalem would have to rein in time and again.

A case in point was the first high-level meeting between Israeli and Maronite officials in August 1976.

"Will you intervene?" Camille Chamoun asked flat out, staring Yitzhak Rabin straight in the eye through his thick lenses.

"Will you ask us to?" Rabin quickly retorted.

The two men were closeted on an Israeli missile boat anchored just outside Haifa harbor. In dealing with Chamoun, Rabin was drawing upon Ben-Eliezer's essentially mixed report. On the one hand it spoke of the fragmentation of the Christian ranks and of glaring military shortcomings, but it also stressed their uncommon dedication to the struggle against the PLO and the extent of popular support for the militias. The greatest problem was that the Maronites were spottily armed. They did not even have proper communications equipment, and under the circumstances, Ben-Eliezer concluded, it was hard to imagine how they could win any fight.

"Our guiding principle is that we are prepared to help you help yourselves," Rabin explained to his Lebanese guest, and proceeded to give Chamoun assurances that arms supplies would be increased. Indeed, the Maronites soon began to receive American M-16 rifles, LOW antitank rockets, and antiquated Sherman tanks. Within a few months, responsibility for funding the venture was transferred from the Mossad, a branch of Israeli intelligence, to the Defense Ministry, and under Shimon Peres's tutelage the aid package burgeoned. It was later estimated that during the three-year term of Yitzhak Rabin's government, close to $150 million was invested in building up the Maronite militias in Lebanon.

After two more meetings with Chamoun, Rabin invited Pierre Gemayel and his sons to join the talks still being held offshore in the austere setting of the missile boat's mess. Pierre Gemayel made no effort to hide the fact that he was unhappy about having to shake Rabin's hand. "I want to walk in Lebanon with my head held high as a Christian and as an Arab," he began. "I have been forced to turn to you, but I am filled with shame and dismay." When Rabin chose not to reply to this insult, Gemayel took his silence as an invitation to pursue an aggressive line. "It's Israel's fault that the Palestinians have settled in Lebanon and taken up arms," he lectured his host. "Lebanon's tragedy is that her fate is bound up with the conflict over Palestine." If Israel were to display more flexibility toward the Palestinians, he argued, a solution could be found to ease the pressure on Lebanon as well. The Israelis must soften up and woo the Arabs into accepting their state. In the meanwhile, Gemayel fairly scolded Rabin, they couldn't deny what they had brought upon their neighbors to the north.

The mounting tension in the room was allayed only when attention was abruptly diverted to an even more unpleasant incident. Sickened by the incessant tossing of the boat, Bashir turned pale, could contain himself no longer, and retched right next to the table. Mortified, the elder Gemayel viciously upbraided the stricken young man and then stonily apologized for his son's behavior. Bashir retreated into silence for the rest of the conversation as Rabin and his aides managed understanding smiles and tried to put the unfortunate interlude behind them. None of them imagined that within less than a year this queasy young man would turn out to be the most talented and ruthless military leader the Lebanese Christians had yet produced.

Several months later the Lebanese civil war took a sharp turn with the introduction of Syrian troops into the country to impose order—and Syrian hegemony. If in January 1976 the patriotic Pierre Gemayel was promising to "fight to the last man" in the event that the Syrians invaded his country, by May he had thought better of the matter and was arguing that "it would be pigheaded to oppose the entry of foreign forces that can save the homeland from disintegration"—especially since the objective of those forces was to quash the ascendant PLO. When a Syrian armored division actually entered Lebanon on June 1, 1976, it did so with the blessings of the Maronite elders.

Yet while praising the Syrians for the bold initiative that would "save the homeland," the Maronites were shrewd enough to keep themselves covered against all contingencies and continued to cultivate the nascent Israeli connection. Even as Syrian forces deployed within artillery range of Beirut, a small delegation of Israeli officers, again headed by Benyamin Ben-Eliezer, was invited back to Lebanon. Escorted to the Gemayel family seat in Bekfaya, they were promptly treated to a shower of complaints about the slow pace and the content of the arms shipments—the implied threat being that Israeli foot-dragging would push the Maronites even deeper into the arms of the Syrians. Yet, despite the salutary effect of the Syrian invasion on the morale and military position of the Maronites,

Bashir portrayed their situation in apocalyptic terms. "We can't go on any longer. We're on the brink of collapse!" he wailed to the Israelis in what would soon come to be recognized as his theme song. Ben-Eliezer returned to the subject of establishing a united command and working together with the Christian communities farther north, around Tripoli, where the Frangieh family had established a new militia called the Marada (after the legendary giants said to have stalked the land before the dawn of history). Bashir's response was trenchantly negative. Tony Frangieh, the president's son, was serving simultaneously as commander of the new militia and as the most corrupt minister of posts in the country's history. He had extensive business dealings with Rifat Assad, symmetrically enough the brother of Syria's president and commander of that country's most elite commando force, and together they ran a flourishing trade in hashish. When the Israelis still advocated an alliance with the Marada, Bashir decided to let them see and decide for themselves. "We're planning a little surprise for you," he announced coyly.

The next evening, at a cocktail party hosted by the junior Chamouns in a plush seaside villa, Tony Frangieh showed up in a chic denim suit and kept himself well watered with scotch as the Israelis cornered him for about half an hour. Ben-Eliezer urged him to close ranks with the Phalange and the Chamounist Tigers in fighting the leftist alliance, but the breezy Frangieh made it clear that he was not at all so inclined. He spoke vaguely of ties with the Arab world and gave the impression of being quite unconcerned about the war. The Frangieh family and its supporters had placed their trust in the Syrians and had no interest in playing longer odds.

It was also during this visit in July that Ben-Eliezer was taken to the Christian command post overlooking Tel Zatar, a Palestinian refugee camp in East Beirut that commanded the road from the capital to the Mount Lebanon region and Lebanon's main industrial area. The Christian siege of the camp had been going on for months by then. It had been conducted by a small and radical militia known as the Guardians of the Cedars, and only recently had the Phalange joined in the battle. Seated in the upper command post, Ben-Eliezer watched as the Phalangist gunners fired quantities of shells into the camp, while the few dozen Palestinian defenders sat in subterranean shelters and weathered the barrage. As he followed the progress of this heavily lopsided exchange, he was astounded by the waste. Ben-Eliezer spent two hours in that upper command post watching as the shells—many of which had come in Israeli aid shipments—poured into the camp to no discernible effect.

Ben-Eliezer and company visited Lebanon for a third time in September 1976, after which Bashir Gemayel and Danny Chamoun were invited on a

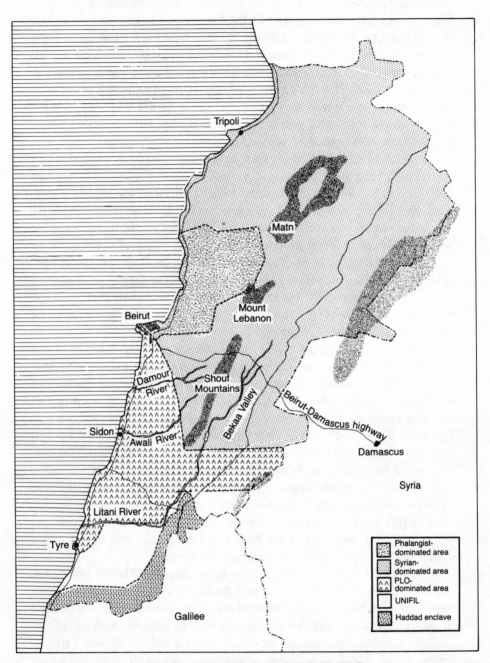

LEBANON ON THE EVE OF THE WAR

reciprocal visit to Israel. Again Bashir drew a bleak picture of the situation. He was irked by the fact that the battered PLO was still claiming a high toll in Christian lives while the Syrians held back from mounting a decisive assault on the remaining Palestinian strongholds. What Bashir wanted was Israeli intervention, and he wanted it now. He demanded to know Rabin's intentions, within forty-eight hours! The Israeli prime minister dismissed the notion as preposterous, but he did take note that the bashful young man who had shriveled under his father's scowl a few months earlier was becoming altogether brash.

On September 28 the Syrians finally launched their long-awaited attack on the remaining PLO bases, and by mid-October the civil war seemed over. Egypt, Saudi Arabia, Syria, and Lebanon drew up the Riyadh Agreement recognizing the Syrian contingent in Lebanon as a peacekeeping force, and the Syrians conveniently failed to confiscate the heavy weapons of the Christian militias, as one of the clauses required, concentrating instead on disarming the PLO and Lebanese leftists. This was the heyday of the Syrian-Maronite alliance, but even then Bashir Gemayel's keen eye foresaw the coming crisis; his lone, sad voice warned that "history is rife with examples of armies that came to aid their neighbors in distress and stayed on as immovable occupiers."

In the course of the next year Bashir Gemayel found himself all but isolated within the Maronite camp. He alone wanted to prevent the Syrians from becoming comfortably entrenched in Lebanon, while the majority of the Phalange Political Bureau regarded the Syrian presence as an opportunity to reach an accommodation with the PLO and the Lebanese left. The party elders sniffed at the tie with Israel as a brief and aberrant episode, yet Bashir, foreseeing another round of fighting just around the corner, would not hear of severing contact. Indeed, it was during the relative calm of 1977, when the sense of desperation had lost its edge, that the Israeli relationship with Bashir Gemayel began to solidify. The chief medium at this stage was a representative of the Mossad who developed an honest affection and respect for Bashir as he watched him bloom into a daring and talented leader with enormous charisma.

He wasn't the only one to appreciate these qualities. The Phalange rank and file adored their commander, and Bashir was adept at cultivating camaraderie with his men in the fortified positions. His message was tailored to their youth: there could be no return to the old Lebanon with its corruption and factionalism; instead they must build a "new Lebanon" free of stifling feudal traditions and open to modernization in all areas. No longer would their country be ruled by old men who had led their people into strife and ruin. "We have not spilled the blood of thousands of young men in order to move backward," he announced as the self-styled spokesman of the generation that had manned the barricades in the civil war. In long talks late into the night with his Mossad contact, now making regular secret visits to Beirut, Bashir would give vent to his frustrations, ranting against his father's old ways. He had even begun to flirt with the idea of the Phalange striking south toward Israel to establish a Maronite state in the lower part of Lebanon. "We must act as you did in 1948," he mused aloud, "and take over most of the country by force!"

Even more than his own new magnetism, a growing discontent with the behavior of the Syrian army was working in Bashir's favor. With the rising incidence of pillage and rape, arbitrary arrests, and confiscation of property, the country's Christian population was finding itself increasingly disenchanted with the Syrians. The grumblings in response to the imperious treatment they suffered at the hands of the Syrian troops grew louder as the Lebanese reminded themselves how superior they were to their interlopers in education, social status, and wealth. In fostering the dream of a free Lebanon, Bashir Gemayel was fast turning into a symbol of hope. But the Gemayels were not naive idealists: just to keep all bases covered, while Bashir confided in his Mossad contact Amin pursued the opposite course, cultivating close relations with Syrian officers and even publicly holding Israel responsible for the civil war.

Bashir's power base was the Phalange militia, and with Israel's support he decided to reinforce its units, reorganize the command structure, and place his young loyalists in key positions while having a small group of older intellectuals continue to serve as his brain trust. It was during this dormant period, as he devoted himself to building up his cadres, that the balance of power within the Maronite camp began to shift in Bashir's favor. At the end of 1977 he got a significant boost from Camille Chamoun, who had also come to the conclusion that a confrontation with Syria was inevitable. From then on Chamoun would champion Bashir's line, and soon a coalition had formed behind the scenes pitting Bashir and Chamoun against the old majority in the Phalange party leadership. The single but striking advantage of the Bashir-Chamoun faction was that it embraced most of the armed elements in the Christian camp.

When Bashir took stock of the ratio of forces in the field, he became convinced that only Israeli intervention would enable the Maronites to emerge from the present impasse with the upper hand. Openly he began to visit Israel, and in every talk with representatives of the Israeli Defense Forces (IDF) and the Mossad he relentlessly pressed for an Israeli move against the Syrian garrison troops in Lebanon—always in vain. Then came the electoral turnabout of May 1977 that brought the Likud party to power in Israel. Bashir's instincts told him that the scales were going to tip in his favor, that Menachem Begin's government would be more likely to take a forceful position on the Lebanese question. He prepared to impress his case on the new gallery of Israeli leaders.

Naturally they understood what he was getting at, but during the first years of his term Menachem Begin disappointed Bashir's expectations by holding fast to the rule set down by his predecessor: help the Maronites help themselves, and no more. If anything, Bashir's conduct during the Begin government's first military venture, "Operation Litani," actually heightened Israeli misgivings. The objective of this incursion into South Lebanon in March 1978 was twofold: to destroy the PLO bases that were the continuing source of harassment to settlements in the Galilee and of terrorist raids farther inland; and to extend the territory under the control of Lebanese Maj. Saad Haddad and the local militia he had recruited among the Christian population of the area—Israel's surrogate and client force in South Lebanon. After contact had been extended between Israel and the Maronite leaders in 1976, Haddad had been posted back to his native village just over the Israeli border and set about building a local force to counter the aggressive tactics of the PLO. Being a Greek Catholic made him something of an outsider to the militant Christian establishment, and his demeanor as an unassuming, almost uncouth military man further heightened the disdain of the worldly, refined Beirutis. At the start of Operation Litani Bashir was asked to send down some 800 men to reinforce Haddad's troops. Though he reluctantly complied, most of his fighters deserted shortly after arriving, and Bashir absolutely refused to express open support for Haddad. The episode raised some question in Israeli defense circles about the Phalange's reliability as an ally.

Yet there was more than internal Lebanese rancor behind the misfire of Operation Litani. Bashir's attention had been centered not on the south but on the confrontation brewing between the Phalange and the Syrians in Beirut. The Phalange instigated the friction by laying mines and sniping at the Syrians from ambushes. Their aim was to rattle the garrison troops, lest they begin to feel too comfortable in Lebanon, and to impress upon the Lebanese, the Arab states, and the world at large that the Syrian contingent was in fact an occupying army and not, as President Assad claimed, a peacekeeping force serving in Lebanon at the invitation of Lebanese President Elias Sarkis and with the approval of the Arab League. Bashir told his Israeli contacts that he knew he was taking an enormous risk. With only a few thousand fighters and a handful of tanks and artillery, the Phalange was effectively taking on a regular army of 35,000 soldiers equipped with more than 200 tanks and 300 pieces of field artillery.

To whatever degree these provocations were calculated to impress a point on Israel as well, the fact remains that the attitude in Jerusalem slowly began to shift. First the Israelis stepped up the shipment of arms to Junieh; then members of the Phalange and the Chamoun militia were invited to train in Israel. Prime Minister Begin was genuinely moved by Chamoun's and Bashir's unabashed patriotism and declarations of appreciation of Israel as the only party that cared about the Lebanese Christian minority. Neither would he be dissuaded by warnings about them. At one point after Camp David, where Cyrus Vance told Anwar Sadat that he had seen letters written in Jerusalem in Chamoun's own hand, Sadat candidly advised Begin, "Let Chamoun be. He is a despicable human being. He was an agent of the British, the French, the Americans, the Syrians, and now he's your man." Begin's former associates recall today how the prime minister savored the idea of being able to influence events in a neighboring state. But beyond that, he regarded himself as bearing the responsibility for the fate of the Maronites and believed his involvement with their plight to be a moral duty no less than a matter of national self-interest. Well before Begin expressed such sentiments outright, however, Bashir Gemayel and Camille Chamoun had sensed intuitively that the Israeli government was edging toward commitment: simply put, Begin would not permit the Maronite community in Lebanon to be destroyed. When Begin spoke in terms of preventing "genocide," the Lebanese leaders believed that he would act to forestall any significant threat to the community's political standing. No more would the relationship be limited to discreet aid without further obligation; rather, it was moving inexorably toward a pledge that Israeli forces would come to the assistance of the beleaguered Maronites in their hour of need.

Perhaps because of this palpable change of mood in Israel, Bashir Gemayel now set his sights on extending the Phalange sphere of influence northward into the rural precincts around Tripoli. His objective was to eat away at the territory traditionally under the sway of the Frangieh family, which continued to take strong exception to Bashir's anti-Syrian policy. At the end of May 1978, after Sleiman Frangieh walked out of a session of the Lebanese Front (the umbrella organization of all Christian factions in Lebanon) over this very issue, violence erupted between Tony Frangieh's militia and the Phalange. The friction escalated when a local Phalange commander was murdered, and on June 13 the showdown came: hundreds of armed Phalangists surrounded Tony Frangieh's home, where the killer was purportedly hiding, and demanded his surrender. When Frangieh refused to surrender anyone, the Phalangists assaulted the house and slaughtered everyone within: Frangieh, his wife, his daughter, his bodyguards, and the entire domestic staff.

Whether Bashir intended it or not, the murder of Syria's chief Christian ally in Lebanon precipitated a crisis that quickly spiraled out of control. The Syrians rushed commandos to Beirut by helicopter while Bashir Gemayel and Camille Chamoun instigated strikes and demonstrations that soon escalated into gunfire aimed at Syrian soldiers and the retaliatory shelling of the city's Christian quarters. Finally Assad delivered an ultimatum to the Maronites to lay down their arms and permit the deployment of Syrian troops in East Beirut or he would take their strongholds by force.

As might have been expected, Bashir's reaction was to remind Begin pointedly of his earlier promise to save his people from genocide and convince the Israelis that he was facing apocalypse *now*. "We can't stand up to a Syrian division or more!" he wailed. But Israeli military intelligence confirmed that Bashir's men had provoked the Syrians and warned Begin of further provocations calculated to draw Israel into a war with Syria. Fearing that intervention of any sort might sabotage the delicate negotiations going on with Egyptian President Anwar Sadat, Begin tried to soothe the agitated Bashir. At the same time, Defense Minister Ezer Weizman and Chief of Staff Mordechai Gur, considerably less susceptible than Begin to the Phalangists cri de coeur, ruled out the use of the Israeli air force to silence the Syrian artillery surrounding Beirut. Nor would they respond to entreaties to land troops at Junieh, though Bashir assured them that the very presence of Israeli soldiers would work as a deterrent; they wouldn't have to fight at all. Bashir's effort ended up a complete waste—or so it seemed from his position in Beirut.

But Menachem Begin was not at ease with his conscience, and on the morning of July 6 Israeli-built Kfir jets were sent to make a show of force over Beirut. The planes shrieked in from the sea, breaking the sound barrier and sending sonic booms crashing through the city, shattering windows and daunting faint hearts—though the Christians who climbed onto the rooftops to watch the spectacle from East Beirut were bitterly disappointed to see the jets bank out to sea again without dropping any bombs. Meanwhile the IDF was concentrating reinforcements of armor on the Golan Heights, bordering Syria, in a way that could not go unnoticed. And just in case it did, Begin, Weizman, and other prominent Israeli officials made public statements warning that Israel would not stand by idly and watch the massacre of a neighboring people with indifference. Under pressure from Chamoun, Lebanese President Sarkis added his voice to the deterrent effort by threatening to resign if the Syrians did not stop shelling the Christian neighborhoods.

The intricate maneuver succeeded—Syrian artillery ceased its fire—and Bashir Gemayel made no attempt to conceal his satisfaction at having badgered the Israelis into taking these first overt steps. It was a short-lived satisfaction, however: within two weeks, having had his men renew their harassment of the Syrian troops in Beirut, Bashir found himself outsmarted by Assad when the Syrians struck back in the remote Christian provinces well north of the capital. The maneuver caught Bashir off guard and left him almost frantic, for the Maronites had always regarded the Mount Lebanon region as their "fortress." Now the Syrians were both calling the shots and shattering that last illusion of invulnerability.

On the brink of tears, his voice choked with anger, Bashir confronted the Israeli liaison in Junieh and demanded immediate and forthright Israeli intervention. The Syrians, he claimed, were closing in on Junieh from the north, and if the city fell the Maronites would lose their outlet to the sea. "And then how will we get arms?" he cried out. This time, however, Menachem Begin would not be moved. The Camp David conference lay just ahead, and he would do nothing—but nothing—to imperil it. Anyhow, he reasoned, the Syrians were clever enough not to try to break into the heart of the rugged mountain district.

Piqued at not getting his way, Bashir grumbled that he was severing all ties with Israel and bitterly inveighed against the Israelis for deceiving him with promises and then abandoning him to his fate. In September, under the pressure of renewed shelling, he agreed to Saudi mediation and a new truce was achieved.

The price of the intermittent fighting with the Syrians in 1978 was a high one for the Christian community. Tens of thousands lost their homes, many of these subsequently emigrated, and territory was lost in the north. But at least the Phalange and its allies had managed to evade abject surrender to a Syrian diktat.

If that was a victory of sorts, Bashir Gemayel did not have much time to savor it before tragedy struck him personally. In February 1979 his one-and-a-half-year-old daughter, Maya, was killed in an ambush meant for her father. The loss shook Bashir to the core and changed him, aged him somehow. He was sure that the Frangieh family was behind his child's murder, yet even in his shock and grief he rose above the craving for revenge. Standing over her grave, he called for an end to the vicious cycle of bloodletting within the Christian community. Then he closed himself away with his wife, Solange.

When he emerged from his solitude almost a week later, Bashir renewed his contact with Israel and drew up a plan for the IDF to conduct a thorough survey of the Maronites' military needs so that the two sides could agree on future lines of cooperation. There was no point in continuing with the old arbitrary system of assistance—with "crumbs," as Bashir put it. Although it took a while to convince the new Israeli chief of staff, Rafael

Eitan, to sanction the idea of stepping up assistance, eventually he was won over. Israeli officers were sent to Lebanon to concentrate on two endeavors: building up the arsenal of the Maronite forces while reinforcing the obstacle system and fortifications surrounding the militias so they could exploit their resources to the maximum. Beyond that, the combat ability of the Phalange units was to be upgraded by training in Israel. Soon hundreds of militiamen were being sent to Israel for maneuvers.

Now, however, a price tag was attached: Bashir was informed that in the future he would have to bear the full cost of the arms he received. The liaisons argued, not without reason, that it was unjust for Israel to continue providing him with weapons and equipment gratis and ask its taxpayers to defray these costs when Lebanon was "bursting at the seams with money" and every second family seemed to be careening around the countryside in a Mercedes. Bashir seemingly accepted the new decree, but in fact sought every opportunity to evade it. In one case, faced with having to cough up $2 million for a shipment of ammunition, he approached Eitan and asked for a 50 percent discount. Despite his initial aversion to the "Lebanese connection," the chief of staff had a soft spot in his heart for the young militia leader and acceded to his request. Then Bashir appealed to Begin, complaining that Israeli officials were making life difficult by nagging him for $1 million. With characteristic magnaminity, Begin exempted him from the payment. When Begin's generosity became known to the captains of the Israeli arms industry, they let out a howl of protest, and the prime minister had to promise to be stricter in the future.

The Israelis continued to press relentlessly on the subject of merging the rival Maronite militias into a single standing force. Such a union would do more than just streamline operations. Every so often the tenuous relations between the Phalange and the Chamounists, or between both camps and the smaller militias, got strained to the point of bloody clashes over disputed areas of influence or tax collection. There were even periods when wholesale terror raged within the Christian enclave, replete with the demolition of offices and the kidnapping of notables. Finally, the Israelis' impatience with the inveterate factionalism must have registered—at least so Bashir would later rationalize—for on July 7, 1980, as Danny Chamoun was on his way to a tryst with his mistress, Bashir and his men mounted a consummate surprise attack on the Tigers' headquarters and in a single, savage stroke liquidated the second largest Maronite force in Lebanon. Eighty of Chamoun's men were killed during the brief action. Bashir proclaimed a "merger" of all the Christian fighting forces under his command, within a new framework known as the "Lebanese Forces."

Danny Chamoun managed to escape to Europe, where he would later complain bitterly that the Israelis were responsible for his abrupt ruin—while in fact they were chagrined by Bashir's putsch and put him on notice that they would not make a single move without first consulting Camille Chamoun. Some of the remaining Tigers joined the Phalange; others abandoned the field and returned to their civilian affairs. Georges Adwan and Etienne Saqre, the leaders of two small militias—the Organization and the Guardians of the Cedars—quickly announced that they would integrate their forces into the united army. The surprising thing was how readily Camille Chamoun reconciled himself to his son's downfall. Rumor had it that he felt a special affection for Bashir and regarded him as his political heir. For public consumption the rapprochement between the elder Chamoun and the younger Gemayel was depicted as a political necessity, but in reality another factor was involved: Bashir had paid the Chamoun family $1 million in reparations!

Within a few months, whether by menace or cajolery, Bashir Gemayel had established his hegemony over the entire Maronite enclave. His erstwhile opponents had fled or were cowed into silence; even his brother, Amin, had been squeezed out of most of his positions of influence. Some parties within the Israeli intelligence community continued to feel uneasy about Bashir and pointed to his penchant for double-talk, his poorly concealed desire to drag Israel into a war, and the Phalange's chronic military weakness. Yet they soon found themselves isolated. Begin did not want to hear their plaints; as far as he was concerned, the Christians in Lebanon were a persecuted minority, and that was that. More adamantly than ever, he shut his ears to tales of atrocities committed by the Phalange in the sincere belief that sitting opposite him were civilized men. Bashir further charmed him by immediately acceding to every one of his requests—"How can I possibly refuse such a venerable old man?" he would say with a smile to Begin's aides—though afterward he would begin to backtrack, stipulate conditions, or break his word altogether.

Since Begin was proving so pliant, Bashir kept pressing him for whatever he could get, and in December 1980 he secured another Israeli pledge guaranteeing the safety of the Lebanese Christian community. As tensions once again flared up with the Syrians, this time centering on the city of Zahle in the Bekaa valley, Bashir asked Israel to provide an aerial umbrella in the event that the Syrian air force attacked his positions in the next round of fighting, as he believed it would. Begin agreed, thereby propelling Israel into the third stage of its deepening involvement in Lebanon and the establishment of a fatal covenant between Israel and the Maronites. For this latest undertaking was a far cry from the promise not to permit the annihilation of the Christian minority, and way beyond Rabin's policy of helping the Christians to help themselves. Step by step, piece by piece, Bashir Gemayel had jockeyed the prime minister of Israel into defending Lebanese Christian interests. It was agreed that this latest extension of the Israeli commitment should be kept secret, yet all too soon it was making headlines—as Bashir knew it would, and Begin should have expected.

2

The Grand Design

TWO EVENTS OCCURRED IN APRIL that would prove milestones on the road to war in Lebanon. Although there was no manifest connection between them, in the minds of Prime Minister Menachem Begin and then Agriculture Minister Ariel Sharon they had a direct bearing on one another and set in train a policy shift that, over the next thirteen months, would exploit the Begin-Gemayel covenant and plunge Israel toward disaster.

By sheer coincidence, as tension began to simmer between the Phalange and the Syrians in the city of Zahle, U.S. Secretary of State Alexander Haig arrived in the Middle East to sound out America's friends on the notion of establishing an anti-Soviet regional alignment. Begin's people took to Haig from the start. He espoused, practically embodied, a tough-minded, trenchant approach that struck them as a refreshing change from the Carter administration's wobbly line on the Middle East. In terms of Israel's immediate neighbors, Haig spoke of President Assad's regime in biting language and left his hosts with the distinct impression that America intended to take a hard line toward Syria as the Soviet Union's chief client state in the region. By the time the secretary left Israel, there was no doubt in many minds that with a man of Haig's bent running the State Department, Israel could definitely allow itself to adopt a militant posture vis-à-vis Damascus. Begin held one closed session with the secretary at which no minutes were taken, but in sharing his impressions of this talk with his colleagues he dropped a telling remark: "Ben-Gurion used to say that if you're pursuing a policy that may lead to war, it's vital to have a great power behind you."

While these words still hung in the air in Menachem Begin's office, a bloody incident was brewing in the Lebanese city of Zahle, where the Phalange and the Syrian garrison were priming their weapons for battle.

More was at stake than control of a single city. Damascus was drawing up the so-called Program of National Reconciliation—a thinly disguised bid to install a puppet government in Beirut and undermine the position of the Christian factions in league with Israel—and word was out that, as the 1982 Lebanese presidential election approached, the Syrians would intervene to ensure the victory of their long-time ally—and the Gemayels' long-time rival—Sleiman Frangieh. Gauging the situation from this standpoint, Bashir Gemayel decided that he had to act quickly. The problem was that he did not have a free hand to do so. For the better part of a year, the Israelis had been rebuffing any suggestion of mounting a strike against the Syrians and the Palestinians with the aim of driving both out of Lebanon once and for all. The Phalange had received a stream of mollifying visits from senior Israeli officers who promised increased aid for the Lebanese Forces and Israeli support in some always-vaguely-construed "hour of need." But these placebos had lost their effect; Bashir wanted action, not hand-holding. He had to devise some way of drawing the Israelis into a clash with the Syrians—even if it meant resorting to naked provocation.

The most promising arena for pursuing such a strategy was Zahle, the third-largest city in Lebanon with a population of 200,000 (mostly Greek Orthodox) and, more to the point, the capital of the Bekaa Valley—an area that the Syrians regarded as vital to the defense of Damascus and for which they would be prepared to take up arms even against Israel. Bashir told the Israelis that the city was a Phalange stronghold in danger of being surrounded and captured by Syrian commandos, then went about baiting the enemy into enacting his scenario by smuggling some eighty Phalange fighters into the city via the slopes of nearby Mount Senin, cutting dirt roads from Zahle to the Christian heartland in the west, and finally shelling the Syrian army's main headquarters in Lebanon in the nearby town of Shtura. On April 1 Bashir's provocations came to a head when a detail of Phalangists attacked Syrian sentries guarding the bridge over the Bardouni River, one of the most sensitive points on the Beirut-Damascus highway. Even if Assad were not itching for a fight, with two of his tanks in flames and a number of soldiers dead he had to respond vigorously.

Companies of Syrian commandos were rushed to Zahle to place the city under siege while a second force, some of it transported by helicopter, began the rugged climb up Mount Senin to block off the dirt paths that linked the city with the Christian enclave in its rear. The Syrians behaved with their usual extravagant brutality, burning crops and bringing life in Zahle to a halt with incessant barrages of artillery. Their thrust up toward the "French Room," a fortified position at the peak of Mount Senin, threatened to gain them domination over all the Christian-held territory from Zahle to the outskirts of Junieh.

The Syrians' tactics smacked of anger, as if they were out to teach the pesky Phalange a lesson. Yet Assad was keenly aware that he could not act quite as freely as he might have liked, for he also had to take Israel into account. To avoid any misunderstandings, he decided to send the Israelis a carefully calibrated signal that although he was quite determined to win the battle for Zahle he had and wanted no quarrel with them. South of the city, in the Bekaa Valley, Syrian teams began to dig four emplacements for stationing SAM-6 antiaircraft missiles. They left these dugouts empty, as if to say that they could install and launch their missiles on short notice whenever they pleased; it all depended on what moves Israel would make. The message was unmistakable, especially since an enemy is not in the habit of revealing where he intends to set up a weapons system whose chief advantage lies in its relative mobility. Israeli intelligence duly discovered these dugouts weeks before they were fitted with missiles.

Soon after the siege of Zahle began, Bashir Gemayel and Camille Chamoun asked for a meeting with Begin. They brought yet another of their grim warnings: if Mount Senin fell to the Syrians, the road to Junieh would be wide open and the entire Maronite mountain "fortress" would fall to the Syrians. What they failed to tell the Israelis was that Assad had offered a compromise on Zahle: the siege would be lifted if the Phalangists left the city. But Bashir had promptly spurned the proposal and spurred his men on.

One Israeli who suspected that the flare-up in Zahle was essentially a Phalange plot to draw Israel into a clash with Syria was the army's chief of intelligence, Maj. Gen. Yehoshua Saguy. Saguy had long been of the opinion that no good would come of the arrangements with the Phalange, but when he voiced his fears to Begin, the prime minister's response bespoke a flinty resistance to any suggestion that the motives of the Phalange were less than pure: rather than accept Saguy's reading for whatever it might be worth, Begin asked to see the raw data on which it was based. The prime minister's other intelligence adviser, Yitzhak Hofi, head of the Mossad, was not at first convinced that the Zahle affair could be summed up as a sly Phalange maneuver, but before long suspicions similar to Saguy's began to stir in his mind. Hofi also had an inkling that the Phalangists must have received assurances from some high-ranking Israeli that Israel would bail them out if they got in over their heads in Zahle. His chief suspect was Israel's chief of staff, Rafael Eitan, who promptly denied anything of the sort.

When the Cabinet convened to discuss the issue on April 28, the only proposal set before it was Eitan's recommendation to launch an air strike against the Syrian helicopters attacking the Phalange forces on Mount Senin. Saguy argued against the idea, explaining that a move to break the siege of Zahle would effectively be an Israeli attack on the Syrian army in Lebanon, and that the Syrians would immediately respond by bringing surface-to-air missiles into Lebanon. Furthermore, he argued, "the upshot will be that our freedom of action in Lebanese airspace, which is also important for intelligence gathering, will be severely prejudiced." Both deputy prime ministers, Yigael Yadin, and Simcha Ehrlich, added their demurs, and Deputy Defense Minister Mordechai Zippori expressed his objections most forcefully of all by sounding an alarm that Israel was being dragged into a war and that the Cabinet was being fed misleading information. Still, Begin appeared to be undaunted by the perils involved in the plan. He did not want a war—at least not at that juncture—but he was prepared to take the risks entailed in a limited operation. "We won't let them perpetrate genocide in Lebanon" was his practiced reply to all objections. He wanted to prove to the Christians that he was as good as his word and to caution the Syrians against acting rashly. It is doubtful whether he appreciated the military implications of attacking the helicopters; his thoughts ran in a different direction altogether: above all else, he had to save the beset Christians of Lebanon from a holocaust.

When it came to a vote the Cabinet sanctioned a limited air strike, and Eitan left the room to have the air force prepare for action. In his absence the debate continued, and at one point it appeared that Saguy's reasoned qualms were beginning to sway a number of ministers not usually considered doves. The discussion was still going strong when Eitan returned to the conference room and announced that the pilots had successfully completed their mission: two Syrian assault helicopter gunships had been shot down south of Zahle. The ensuing silence and astonished expressions suggested that the air force had worked much faster than the ministers had expected, and now they were faced with a fait accompli. It later transpired that the downed choppers were not assault helicopters at all but troop transports.

President Assad came through with his reply within twenty-four hours, as if he too wanted to prove he was a man of his word. SAM-6 missiles were installed in the prepared dugouts not far from Zahle, additional batteries (some of them joined by Soviet advisers) were drawn up to the Syrian side of the border with Lebanon, and Scud surface-to-surface missiles were positioned outside Damascus, whence their range took in Israeli territory. Not to be outdone, Begin raised the tension another notch with a resounding pledge to destroy the missiles if the Syrians did not remove them from Lebanon. Assad adamantly refused and turned to nursing his own indignation over what he regarded as Israel's violation of a tacit understanding between the two countries on Syria's prerogatives in Lebanon. As the saber rattling grew louder, the siege of Zahle become secondary. Having achieved his aim in precipitating a crisis, Bashir Gemayel quietly capitulated and pulled his men out of the city.

Menachem Begin fully intended to make good on his threat. His air force was scheduled to attack the missiles in the Bekaa Valley on the afternoon of April 30. But about an hour before takeoff the air force meteorologist warned of inclement weather and the mission was scrubbed. That evening American Ambassador Samuel Lewis came to see Begin with the message that Washington still saw a chance to dispose of the missiles peacefully and that President Reagan was sending Special Ambassador Philip Habib to discuss the matter with Damascus. Begin jumped at the diplomatic out. He was sure the mediation would not prove too difficult and that Habib could wrap it up in a matter of days.

Ten days passed, and another ten days, and the Syrian missiles stayed put. Meanwhile, the crest of Mount Senin was captured by Syrian commandos, but no tragedy befell Junieh; neither was there any sign of a panicked flight of Maronites from the Mount Lebanon "fortress." The one certain consequence of Bashir Gemayel's ploy was that SAM missiles were now firmly ensconced on Lebanese soil, making the whole affair a giant step backward for Israel—just as Saguy had warned.

Four weeks later, on May 28, Menachem Begin and Rafael Eitan took another step that would bring their country appreciably closer to a war in Lebanon with an action that was essentially calculated toward that end—though that was not its immediate effect. With his election campaign running at a frenzied pitch, the missile crisis lingering in the background, and the bombing of Iraq's nuclear reactor a mere eleven days away, Begin approved the chief of staff's request to renew the bombing of PLO concentrations in South Lebanon. The immediate purpose of the attacks was political; the long-range goal was to effect a controlled escalation of tension and ultimately trigger the war that Eitan believed was destined to be fought within half a year, at most.

Israel continued its attacks from the air and the sea until June 3; the Palestinians responded gingerly for fear that a vigorous reaction would only provoke a crushing Israeli ground operation. Those fears were well founded, if somewhat premature.

After a six-week respite, on July 10, Israel suddenly renewed its air strikes on PLO strongholds in South Lebanon. This time, however, the action touched off a fierce reaction. After the fifth day of bombings the PLO abandoned its restraint and fought back by shelling the Israeli resort town of Nahariya on the Mediterranean coast. Stung by the potency of the response, Jerusalem weighed various counterstrategies. Yehoshua Saguy suggested hitting a series of military targets, but Rafael Eitan wanted to go for the headquarters of two prominent terrorist factions, Fatah and the Democratic Front for the Liberation of Palestine, both located in the heavily populated area of West Beirut known as the "Palestinian triangle"— the Fakahani, Sabra, and Shatilla quarters. Maj. Gen. David Ivri, commander of the Israeli air force, evinced no enthusiasm for the idea, but the Cabinet went along with Eitan, and he was obliged to discharge its decision.

The results were predictable: despite the great pains taken to pinpoint the targets and achieve direct hits, over 100 people were killed and some 600 wounded; estimates in Israel were that only thirty of the dead were terrorists.

Unequipped to respond in kind, the PLO was nonetheless determined to achieve as close an approximation as it could. Firing off twenty field guns and a number of advanced Katyusha rockets, it placed the settlements in the Galilee under intolerable fire. Even though the number of Israeli casualties bore no relation to the toll in West Beirut—six dead and fifty-nine wounded—the steady pounding all but paralyzed the entire sector of northern Israel from the coastal town of Nahariya to Kiryat Shmonah at the tip of the Upper Galilean "finger." For ten days the IDF tried and failed to provide a military solution to the PLO's artillery challenge. Though only a fraction of the 1,230 shells and rockets fired over the frontier actually hit any of the towns and settlements, the few that did were enough to leave life in the area a shambles. Day camps were closed and industrial plants idled; the army had to take over such elementary services as the distribution of bread; shelters in Kiryat Shmonah proved sorely inadequate for extended stays. Despite all the IDF's advanced equipment, fire continued to rain down on the north. Day by day more PLO guns were put out of action, but in the meantime some 40 percent of the population of Kiryat Shmonah fled the town. That, too, was appalling; never had Israel witnessed such a mass exodus from a settlement under attack.

By the end of the twelfth day of artillery exchanges, the terrorists were on the brink of collapse, but on the other side of the border, and of the ledger, morale in Kiryat Shmonah had been ravaged. The PLO did not emerge from the fray triumphant; still, it had scored an impressive military achievement by maintaining a war of attrition against dozens of Israeli settlements for close to two weeks. That was undoubtedly why Philip Habib found Menachem Begin greatly sobered and ripe for a truce when he arrived at the prime minister's office on Friday, July 24.

Habib and his aides, expecting the give and take with Begin to be tough, were surprised by his accommodating attitude. Earlier, when Eitan and

Saguy had argued before the Cabinet that anything short of a conclusive victory over the PLO would set an unwanted precedent, and that a negotiated ceasefire would deprive Israel of the option to take punitive action should terror squads steal or fire across any of the country's other borders, they found that the mood among the ministers had been different. The spirit of assertiveness that had carried the Cabinet through the days of the Syrian missile crisis and the bombing of the Iraqi reactor seemed to have been shattered by the shells and rockets pummeling the Galilee, and contrary to their advice the ministers voted to call the artillery duel to a halt. By the time Habib met with Begin, the Israeli negotiating team was not even insisting on a freeze of the status quo in South Lebanon to bar the PLO from replenishing its arsenal and otherwise repairing its military infrastructure under the protection of a truce. In short, the ceasefire agreement was a patently harmful one, for it contained the seeds of war. Since the terrorists were not constrained by its terms, they could be expected to beef up their frontline batteries, while every cannon and rocket launcher brought into South Lebanon would only exacerbate Israel's war jitters, even if those weapons remained silent. This shaky accord fostered the grim feeling within Israel that, more than ever before, the sixty-eight settlements of the Galilee were at the mercy of vengeful and capricious terrorists over the border.

Perhaps Begin agreed to such unpromising terms precisely because he was convinced that, whatever the accord, a war against the PLO was fated to break out. He was eager for it. If three months earlier he was prepared to exercise the "long arm" of the IDF to chastise the Syrians besieging Zahle, after the shellings of July 1981 Begin was convinced that Israel had no alternative but to mount a formidable military operation and drive the Palestinian terrorists out of South Lebanon once and for all. He did not speak of Beirut as an objective, but he did envision the necessary action as a war against the PLO in its entirety—all its leaders, advisers, and associates.

Begin's views were not unknown to Ariel (Arik) Sharon, who would soon succeed him as Israel's defense minister (Begin had doubled as defense minister following Ezer Weizman's resignation in May 1980) in the second Begin government. Behind closed doors Sharon, believing that it was only a matter of time before he would take over the helm of defense affairs, explained to trusted aides that a war in Lebanon would be far too complex an affair to entrust to the likes of Menachem Begin and Rafael Eitan; he counseled deferring a major military operation in Lebanon until he himself could plan and prepare for it properly.

Begin's decision to appoint Sharon as his defense minister signaled yet another shift in his political thinking. The energetic and ambitious agriculture minister had had his eye on a defense-related post ever since Begin formed his first government in the summer of 1977. Initially he pressed to be appointed special coordinator of the various security services, but the prime minister's associates were so appalled by the idea of concentrating such sensitive powers in Sharon's hands that it was promptly dropped. When Ezer Weizman resigned as defense minister, Sharon made no secret of the fact that he wanted and believed he deserved the open post, placing Begin in a quandary: he had no more professionally qualified candidate in his Cabinet, but he also knew that he could never get Sharon's candidacy past his coalition partners or even the Liberal faction of his Likud party. Beyond that, Begin was reported to have his own misgivings, and soon snide remarks were circulating—ostensibly in jest—that given half a chance Arik would surround the Knesset with tanks and carry off a putsch. All things considered, the IDF's redoubtable might could not be entrusted to so truculent a type as Sharon. Begin kept the defense portfolio for himself.

By the summer of 1981, however, the prime minister was in a different frame of mind. Within the past three months he had taken on not only the Syrians, the Iraqis, and the PLO but the Israeli Labor party, and although the results of two out of those four bouts were equivocal, Begin was still riding the crest of a generally belligerent mood. From that perspective the irrepressible if somewhat pugnacious Sharon did not appear to be so menacing a figure as in earlier days. In any case, after the 1981 election Menachem Begin set aside his qualms and took the step that he had scoffed at months earlier: he invited Ariel Sharon to become his minister of defense.

Begin's decision epitomized the fundamental and far-reaching difference between his first government, which negotiated and signed the peace treaty with Egypt, and his second, which decided on the war in Lebanon. Whereas the three men with rich military experience in the first government—Dayan, Weizman, and Yadin—consistently restrained the Cabinet from plunging into any imprudent ventures, prodding Begin into the concessions that made peace with Egypt possible, Ariel Sharon played exactly the opposite role in the new Cabinet, constantly chivying the prime minister into taking radical steps. From the day he entered the Defense Ministry in early August 1981, Sharon strove to eliminate the traditional mechanisms that mitigated or blocked the government's natural propensity toward extremism. The delicately crafted system of checks and balances that had obtained to one degree or another in all of Israel's previous governments—largely because of the presence of ministers with military experience—was conspicuously absent in this one. Other Cabinets had always comprised ministers espousing a variety of views on defense questions, thereby providing a sense of equilibrium in the decision-making process. But in Begin's new government, for the first time in the state's history, the group of leading figures who monopolized defense and foreign affairs was monolithic in its hawkish views and its readiness to employ Israel's military power for objectives that went well beyond the country's security needs. Sharon wooed Begin into taking steps that he probably would not have contemplated in his first term. The war in Lebanon, built on Sharon's strategic design, was a natural outlet for a government now looking for opportunities to make war—opportunities that would have been ignored or played down by Menachem Begin's first Cabinet and summarily rejected by all its predecessors.

The lead team that dealt with defense and foreign affairs in the second Likud government was composed of four figures, later joined by a fifth. At the head of this ideologically high-pitched quintet was Menachem Begin, who regarded the PLO and its leadership as no less than the successors of Hitler and his Nazi hordes and used imagery drawn from another, far darker era in his references to the Palestinian leaders. At the end of 1981, during a visit to the United States, Begin told a high-ranking Israeli general who came to see him at the Waldorf-Astoria, "I want Arafat in his bunker!"—as if the historical coincidence of the setting were as important as the man.

Ariel Sharon, the number-two man of the group, was a cynical, headstrong executor who regarded the IDF as his personal tool for obtaining sweeping achievements—and not necessarily defensive ones—and a minister prepared to stake the national interest on his struggle for power.

Yitzhak Shamir, Israel's foreign minister, was a zealous nationalist in striped pants who was turning out to be the most belligerent and uncompromising foreign minister in the country's history. In contrast to all his predecessors, who strove to temper the proposals forwarded by other members of the senior defense and foreign-policy establishment, Shamir always aligned himself with the most ardent of the extremists, supported every proposal for radical military moves, and never brought diplomatic alternatives before the Cabinet or presented the political risks and consequences involved.

Lt. Gen. Rafael Eitan, a hardened soldier who sincerely believed that Israel was still fighting an extension of its war of independence, was convinced that the Arabs were bent on continuing the bloodshed until they had wiped out every last Jew, regarding that relentless enmity as justification for his own merciless attitude toward Arabs everywhere.

The fifth member of this clique, joining it somewhat later and at a distance, was Moshe Arens, who was appointed Israel's ambassador to the United States at a critical stage in the preparations for war. Arens believed his immediate task was to convince the American administration that a war in Lebanon was unavoidable. Traditionally Israel's envoys in Washington had served as channels through which a moderating or at least monitory influence was exerted on Jerusalem; but this was emphatically not the case with Arens, who wholeheartedly adopted Sharon's outlook on the war and backed the military option long before the fighting broke out.

These five senior officials operated within the bounds of a closed ideological system that enabled each one to reinforce the others with well-worn articles of faith that could close their minds to the counsel of most, if not all, of the experts serving under them. Moreover, with Sharon becoming defense minister, one of the last counterweights to this five-man juggernaut was conveniently neutralized.

Mordechai Zippori, a retired brigadier general and the only ex-military man in the Cabinet other than Sharon, had been Weizman's (and subsequently Begin's) deputy in the first Likud government. For a long while, Zippori had been admonishing the Cabinet that it had lost control over events in the north and would find itself blundering into a war with the Syrians, not least because Eitan and his subordinates in the field were making operational decisions without authorization. A bluff, no-nonsense type who prided himself on his "bulldog" image, Zippori was also one of the few watchdogs in the Cabinet. Not easily put off or intimidated, he hammered away during Cabinet meetings and was fast becoming a nuisance to Sharon. Begin, it seems, was persuaded to promote Zippori to a full-fledged minister in his second government, but then readily succumbed to Sharon's insistence that he not be appointed to the Ministerial Committee for Security Affairs. Later, when Zippori spoke out against going to war, Begin resorted to the blunt insinuation that there were ulterior motives behind his opposition, namely, sour grapes at not getting the defense portfolio himself.

In addition to changing the balance in the Cabinet, Sharon's arrival at the Defense Ministry affected certain conventions regarding the role and status of the General Staff. Even after he saw to the retirement or strategic displacement of a number of senior officers, the new defense minister was not prepared to place his confidence in the General Staff. Instead, he cultivated the National Security Unit, turning it into his personal General Staff with its own situation room and special computer. Sharon's bureau in the Defense Ministry took on the air of a Byzantine court deliberately isolated from most of the top brass of the IDF and of the ministry itself. As part of his campaign to remove matters of any political import and even certain military subjects from the General Staff's dominion, Sharon once accused the entire senior officer corps of responsibility for leaks, inveighing particularly against contacts with American officials. Like the Cabinet, the General Staff was not kept abreast of exactly what the minister was planning. A few generals close to him were let in on secrets, but such relationships suffered from periodic shake-ups and mood swings. Most of the men surrounding Sharon gradually accommodated themselves to his demands and style rather than suffer the stigma of exclusion. In matters of loyalty and discipline, the man ran a very tight ship.

To conceal the business of his bureau from inquisitive eyes and minds, Sharon wanted to make sure that the press did not poke around too much, and from his first day in office he tried to keep military correspondents at bay. His standing orders to stonewall the press were among the most stringent in the ministry's history. Yet the more Sharon tried to seal off his bureau and the entire defense establishment, the more he aroused the curiosity of journalists—local and foreign—until a confrontation became inevitable. Twice Sharon tried to bar the press from covering major stories: first in February 1982, when he imposed a literal blockade on the defiant Druse villages of the Golan Heights, and again in April during the forced evacuation of the Sinai town of Yamit (when indignation reached such heights that the editors of the country's major dailies took to the field to demonstrate against Sharon's edicts). In effect, with Sharon having managed to circumvent or overwhelm all the other safeguards built into the Israeli political system, the press remained the last defense against his heavy-handed challenge to Israel's democratic ground rules.

Ariel Sharon did not reveal his grand design for a war in Lebanon all at once. On the contrary, he began his term as defense minister by making numerous public statements to the effect that "war is not good for Israel" and piously vowing that Israel would not initiate hostilities. Within the privacy of the defense establishment, however, he sang a very different tune.

If at first Sharon gave off only abstruse signals, within a short time he was speaking in unequivocal terms of transforming the political scene in Lebanon. No longer was he concerned only with South Lebanon and the security of the Galilean settlements, or even with a solution to the problem of Palestinian terrorism over the border. In September 1981, when Philip Habib put forward a plan to have the PLO withdraw its heavy weapons from South Lebanon in return for Israel's commitment to halt the low-flying sorties over the area and remove IDF personnel from the security belt ruled by Maj. Saad Haddad, Sharon countered with a plan of his own, one of whose clauses called for the evacuation of Syrian and Palestinian forces from Beirut and northern Lebanon! In briefings for activists of the Herut faction of the Likud party—remarks that were otherwise kept secret, or at least never published—Sharon spoke of Lebanon being at the top of the list of Israel's national-security concerns. "Israel's objective is to see to it that Lebanon becomes an independent state that will live with us in peace and be an integral part of the free world, as well as to solve the problem of the Syrian presence in that country." The long and the short of his thesis was that unless Lebanon had a government that would sign a peace treaty with Israel, "everything can revert to its former state. And a government of that kind cannot come into being as long as the terrorists control southern Lebanon and two-thirds of the city of Beirut and as long as the Syrians control whole sections of Lebanon. In other words, it is impossible to deal with this subject without taking care of the Syrians." This was a far cry from breaking up terrorist concentrations that threatened the peace of the Galilee.

If he spoke to the party hacks along such general lines, in lectures before military personnel Sharon was even less circumspect and entered into the finer details of his grand design, details that had to have originated with an understanding, however simplistic, of the convenant between Menachem Begin and Bashir Gemayel. Here again he expressed ideas that had yet to be shared with the Cabinet, that were indeed not conveyed to his ministerial colleagues even after the war broke out. In one of these professional sessions, Sharon revealed his thinking as follows:

I am talking about an action that will mean destroying the terrorist organizations in Lebanon in such a way that they will not be able to rebuild their military and political base. It is impossible to do this without running into the Syrians. The question is how to preserve [the advantage of] such a new situation, for there's nothing worse than a military operation on our part one day and having them renew the shelling of Kiryat Shmonah the next. It is possible to achieve [a long-lasting change] on condition that a legitimate regime emerges in Lebanon, not a puppet government; that it signs a peace treaty with Israel; and that it becomes part of the free world. In order to establish a government of that kind, you need sixty-six out of the ninety deputies to the Lebanese Parliament, and a list of deputies will be prepared. All this demands extreme caution and waiting for just the right moment. . . .

As far back as October 1981, Sharon told the General Staff, "When I speak of destroying the terrorists, it means a priori that [the operation] includes Beirut." After one of these military briefings an appalled partici-

pant phoned one of Begin's aides to warn that "Sharon is talking about a
house-to-house mop-up in Beirut!"

Clearly, Ariel Sharon envisioned a war whose prime purpose was the
establishment of a "new political order" in Lebanon, and to achieve that
end he would not shrink from ordering the IDF to meddle in the Lebanese
elections. The essentials of his grand design were never deliberated by the
Cabinet—or the General Staff, for that matter—either before the war or
once it was in progress. Basically, they determined that the PLO must be
driven entirely out of Lebanon, and to prevent the Palestinian organizations from making a comeback Bashir Gemayel must be sworn in as the
country's next president. Meanwhile, to prevent any interference from the
Syrians, their army too must be evicted from Lebanon. Support for such a
double-barreled campaign would surely be forthcoming from Israel's
staunchest ally, the United States, now under the Reagan administration,
whose secretaty of state had made it so clear during his April visit that the
two country's interests in Lebanon virtually coincided. Then, following
the wholesale expulsion of the PLO—particularly from Beirut, where its
constituent organizations had their headquarters—Israel would be able to
manage its conflict with the Palestinians to its own liking. The PLO leadership, Sharon presumed, would be forced into a "gilded cage" in Damascus and lose any vestige of independence, whereupon its influence over
the West Bank would promptly wither, allowing moderate local Palestinians to step forward and conduct negotiations with Israel on a constitution
of autonomy for the inhabitants of the occupied territories—by Israel's
rules, of course. Under these circumstances, the Palestinians would find
themselves with no alternative but to seek an outlet for their political
aspirations in Jordan. Sharon explained to his aides that, in his estimation,
a successful operation in Lebanon would ensure unchallenged Israeli superiority for thirty years to come, during which time Israel would be free
to establish faits accomplis in its best interests.

This, in a nutshell, was Ariel Sharon's grand strategy, and to implement
it the new defense minister was prepared to effect a radical deviation from
a security doctrine on which there had been national consensus since the
founding of the state—that the Israel Defense Forces were mandated only
to defend Israel and were not to be used for the sake of installing or
toppling governments in neighboring countries. Sharon and the few others
he privately convinced of his plan—including Begin, Shamir, and Eitan—
behaved as if they existed in a vacuum, untouched by any political constraints and oblivious to the danger of causing a rift in the nation—an
attitude far more pernicious than any threat posed by the PLO. And never
did they consider that such an offensive pursuit for strategic gain could

also cause a breach with Jews in the Diaspora. The immense, raw power commended to their hands—a force that had been built with such great effort over so many years—intoxicated their senses and addled their thinking. The result would be an excruciating blunder.

Almost ten months passed between the day Ariel Sharon took over the Defense Ministry and the day on which tens of thousands of Israeli troops streamed over the border into Lebanon. During that time Sharon steered his country steadily down a course to war, waiting for just the right moment to enact his grand design, ever confident that his opportunity would come.

3

Slackening Weak Knees

THE MOST STRIKING POINT about Israel's march toward war from August 1981 until June 1982 was that while it forged ahead implacably, month after month, there were repeated signs that Ariel Sharon's clockwork fantasy of reconstituting the Middle East along new political lines was riddled with flaws. Each of these indications, either reported by senior members of the military or paraded directly before Sharon and Rafael Eitan, was consistently ignored by the defense minister and the chief of staff. It cannot be said that they were disregarded by the Cabinet because they were never brought to the Cabinet's attention.

Among the first high-ranking officers to perceive the direction in which Sharon was moving was Maj. Gen. Amir Drori, who took over as head of the IDF's Northern Command in September 1981. The taciturn, diligent Drori was not particularly eager for war, but promptly upon taking up his new post he ordered his staff to pull out the plan code-named "Little Pines," which charted the conquest of South Lebanon up to the vicinity of Sidon, and simultaneously to review the more ambitious "Big Pines" plan, which covered the conquest of a larger chunk of Lebanon extending beyond the Beirut-Damascus highway. As if anticipating problems on a political level, Drori asked his men to take into account two possible contingencies: first, that most of the forces participating in the operation would be massed at the jumping-off point from the start; second, that only a portion of the force would be waiting to move out at H-hour, on the assumption that the operation would develop in successive stages, as approval came through to advance farther and farther into Lebanon along the lines of an "open-ended" venture.

Meanwhile, in November, a seemingly modest and unconnected political development took place in Lebanon: Bashir Gemayel declared his candidacy for the presidency of Lebanon. The elections were slated to be held the following summer, and Bashir knew that he stood no chance of being chosen over Frangieh, Chamoun, or Sarkis without direct Israeli intervention. None of that was new. What had changed was that after years of imploring the Israeli leaders to send troops into Lebanon, always in vain, Bashir was now informed by Ariel Sharon that he must quickly prepare for a full-scale war in which Israeli troops would take part. No date was mentioned, but the implication was that it would break out very soon. Curiously enough, this message made Bashir privy to information that the Israeli Cabinet did not even suspect!

Among that select group of Israelis who did know that plans were being made for war, a recurrent question was how long the IDF would have to remain in Lebanon before Bashir could firmly establish his regime.

"Six weeks," Sharon ventured confidently in a talk with his aides.

"Not a day less than three months," countered Intelligence Chief Saguy.

Both men proved pathetically wide of the mark, typical of so many of their judgments related to the Lebanese venture. Other Israelis who had been to Lebanon repeatedly observed that Bashir Gemayel might be lavish with his promises to participate as a full partner with the IDF, but the actual situation in the country made such pledges highly unrealistic. Besides, he probably did not mean to keep them anyway. These skeptics were often answered by talk of the new "maturity" that Bashir displayed —and it had to be admitted that ever since declaring his candidacy for president, Gemayel had been showing a new statesmanlike demeanor. Nevertheless, the question remained whether he could and would deliver on his commitments.

One man who pointed out the disparity between hard facts and wishful thinking on a purely military level was Amir Drori. A thorough professional known for his sharp eye and solid sense of judgment, Drori on his visits to Lebanon was not one to be taken in (as were many of his colleagues) by manicured lawns, smart salutes, and an endless flow of charm and embraces. Neither was he a stranger to the ties that had grown up between Israel and the Phalange, for he had supervised the transfer of weapons and equipment to Lebanon as head of the operations department of the General Staff in the late seventies. At about the time Sharon was putting Bashir on notice to prepare for war, Drori was telling his aides— and later repeated to the chief of staff—that it was "out of the question to depend on the Christians. From a military standpoint, they're in very poor shape. Their capability is limited solely to the defensive, and they cannot be expected to participate in a mobile war. Our only course," Drori concluded, "is to depend exclusively on ourselves." But even this professional assessment was shrugged off. Eitan did not report it to the government, and preparations continued as before.

A month later, in December 1981, a shift of gears occurred when the IDF was ordered to concentrate forces along the Syrian and Lebanese borders. The ostensible reason for this move was to create a deterrent to any Syrian response to Israel's annexation of the Golan Heights, but the reinforcement could likewise be viewed as a maneuver to lull the enemy by conditioning him to a substantial troop presence in the north of the country. This beefed-up force was large enough, in itself, to initiate a military operation into Lebanon, so that from December onward the IDF was in a position to launch what Drori's staff had considered under the alternative of an open-ended operation.

As matters turned out, the sudden and spectacular move to annex the Golan Heights at that time caused enough of a stir to divert attention from the troop buildup. Washington held back for a few days, preoccupied by events in Poland, and then responded by putting a freeze on the shipment of various military items and suspending the much-touted Memorandum of Strategic Understanding recently signed by Sharon and Defense Secretary Caspar Weinberger. Rather than chasten the Israelis, however, the American sanctions only heightened Begin's belligerency. The prime minister was still recuperating from a fall that had shattered his hip when he decided to disclose the broader of the two plans for an operation in Lebanon—Big Pines—to his Cabinet. For that purpose, he asked the ministers to convene in his home on Sunday, December 20. First, however, he summoned the American ambassador, Samuel Lewis, and subjected him to an unprecedented tongue-lashing in which he ordered Lewis to inform the American government that the State of Israel was not some "banana republic" that could be treated in the cavalier manner the United States had shown in relation to the annexation of the Golan Heights.

After that warm-up, the still-flushed Begin met with his ministers, told them about his session with Lewis, and went on to remind them that an alert was in effect on the Golan Heights. But then he immediately reassured them that the army had a plan all ready to be executed in the event that anything untoward happened. "And something might well happen suddenly," he cautioned. That was why he had called the ministers together now, to establish a standing initiative that could be actuated in an hour of need.

Sharon took the floor to present the plan for Operation Big Pines. "Our objective is Lebanon, not Syria," he explained. "If the Syrians start anything, we'll respond in Lebanon and solve the problem there."

Most of the ministers sat stunned. They had not suspected that they were being called together to approve a war plan, least of all an invasion of Lebanon. Only a week earlier they had been startled by the prime minister's sudden request to approve the annexation of the Golan Heights, and now Begin had jolted them again by revealing a war plan they had never imagined existed.

The map that Sharon exhibited before the Cabinet showed a black arrow leading up to the Beirut-Damascus highway, the main artery between the two Arab capitals. Sharon tried to reassure his colleagues that, in speaking of Beirut, the plan was referring to the Beirut-Damascus highway, not the Lebanese capital itself. If the Christians wanted to liberate Beirut, he said, they could do so on their own. However, the IDF would retain the option of landing troops in Junieh, north of Beirut.

The explanation was meant to soothe the alarmists, but the ministers were only further astonished, and their consternation grew, when the prime minister asked for their prompt approval of the plan.

"Must we decide today, right now?" asked Interior and Religious Affairs Minister Yosef Burg in a tone combining disbelief with anger.

"Yes," Begin insisted. "It may be necessary to put the plan into action at any moment."

But Burg, who was satisfied with neither the plan nor the way it was being foisted on the Cabinet, protested adamantly—particularly over the latter. Two of the Liberal party ministers followed suit, and quickly Begin realized that he had acted too hastily and that the chances of the plan's being approved were almost nil. Suddenly he retreated. "I see how feelings are running," he said, "and I understand that it is pointless to continue," whereupon he abruptly adjourned the meeting.

From Sharon's previously self-assured point of view, the opposition to Big Pines came as a bitter disappointment, and henceforth his approach to the Cabinet changed drastically. Suppression of reports about contacts with the Phalange became the norm; instead of trying to thrash out differences around a conference table and listening to the views of others, Sharon began to feed the Cabinet the objectives of the war in measured doses, disclosing only what was absolutely necessary to secure approval. Begin received a variation of the same treatment, although he was furnished with somewhat fuller reports about developments in the field. Yet even with these, Sharon was always careful to plane down the jagged edges.

Meanwhile, as debate was deliberately stifled in the halls of government, the military planning proceeded full speed. During the second week of January, Sharon himself made a secret visit to Beirut with a large entourage of military and civilian aides. Escorting him throughout the tour was Bashir Gemayel, who showered his distinguished guest with every token of respect. At one point the defense minister and his retinue surveyed the city from the roof of a seventeen-story building while Sharon lectured that there was no point in an action in Lebanon unless it was a thorough one, and no action against the PLO would be thorough unless it drove the terrorists out of Beirut. He was quite unequivocal on that point, and thereby placed the full weight of his influence behind the broader version of Operation Pines. This was the first time Sharon had spelled out his intentions regarding Beirut, and the only one of his associates who balked at the idea of taking the Lebanese capital was, predictably perhaps, Yehoshua Saguy.

"We mustn't go as far as Beirut. We'll only get bogged down here," he argued softly but urgently. "This is a capital in the heart of the Arab world, and we have never entered an Arab capital before. It's a city filled with embassies. We might find ourselves in confrontation with the United States!"

Saguy's strong reservations about Lebanon were well known in the military establishment, but now there was such a sharp note of alarm in the voice of this intelligence chief that Sharon decided to beat a tactical retreat. "Perhaps you're right," he conceded. "We should let the Phalange take Beirut. We won't have to enter the city at all; they'll capture it instead."

"They're not capable of taking Beirut, it's way beyond their competence!" Saguy protested, and then launched into the familiar litany of the Phalange's shortcomings as a military force.

As if to corroborate his point, it became clear later on in the tour that the Phalange commanders were far from eager to send their troops into action. For the sake of politeness, Bashir asked Sharon what his men were expected to do when the IDF invaded Lebanon. He listened closely to Sharon's brief on the need to defend the thirty-six-kilometer stretch of coast from Junieh to Beirut, but when he was asked to comment on the possibility of a combined maneuver with the IDF, Bashir's replies became increasingly evasive. His uneasiness about the prospect of direct and overt cooperation with the IDF during the "liberation" of Lebanon was plain to see. In the past there had been talk of landing Israeli forces at Junieh and sending them down to surround Beirut on the east and south. At times Bashir appeared to be enchanted by the stratagem, but in the end he always came up with a battery of reasons for dropping it. Without a doubt he preferred to have the Israelis move up from the south rather than come through the port and territory in Christian hands. Standing on that rooftop overlooking Beirut, when the subject was raised again, Gemayel's reply to Sharon was masterly: "By all means, come through Junieh. But then you must remain here in Lebanon to protect us from the Syrians and the rest of the Arab world."

Such swift jockeying was a mere taste of things to come, but a real warning light should have flashed in Sharon's mind during the luncheon that Pierre Gemayel and Camille Chamoun laid out for him and his aides in Bekfaya. The setting was comfortable, the reception gracious, and the repartee brisk, hurtling along in four languages and switching from one to the other with dizzying speed, so that few present were able to follow it all or catch the delicate nuances dropped along the way by the two elderly Maronites, each of whom had acquired a lifetime's experience dealing with enemies who had become friends and self-styled friends who were in fact implacable enemies. Even between the two of them, disputes had been known to end in bloodshed.

"Will you really come to Beirut, as you have said? Or is all this just talk?" Chamoun asked with the uncharacteristic bluntness that Israelis esteem.

"We'll get there!" Sharon declared. "Don't you worry."

"We're prepared to start it, create the necessary backdrop. That's no problem," said Chamoun, who had already invited the U.S. Marines to his country on one occasion and the Syrian army on another. He had extended the same invitation to Begin, and to Rabin before him, but both had firmly declined, so that Sharon's tack came as a pleasant surprise to Chamoun.

Less pleasant was the performance rendered by Saguy, who badgered his hosts with questions that could not be casually parried.

"Let's say that the Israeli army has already reached Beirut and we have driven the Palestinian terrorists out. What will be your position toward Israel and the Arab world then?" he asked.

"We shall have to discuss the terms of peace that will obtain between Israel and Lebanon in the future," Chamoun hedged smoothly. But Gemayel's expression clouded and he pulled himself up straight in his armchair, practically barking, "We are part of the Arab world. We are not like Haddad. We are not traitors!"

"Then what will you do?" one of the Israelis pressed.

"We must remain on good terms with the Arab world. We are a part of it," Sheikh Pierre repeated.

The tense silence that flooded the room was broken only when Saguy muttered to Sharon, "You see, I was right! No matter what we do for them, in the end they'll turn right back to the Arab world."

He was speaking in Hebrew and barely above a whisper, but his tone alerted Bashir that the Israelis were dismayed by the old man's rebuff. "Papa, what do you mean talking to them that way?" Bashir gently chided, addressing his father in Arabic. "Are we going to sit around singing lullabies while they do all the work?"

A few of the Israelis quietly translated this remark for the benefit of their colleagues as Pierre Gemayel began to backpedal in an effort to soften the impact of his words. But they had been too harsh to gloss with thin qualifications. Suddenly Sharon flashed an incongruous smile and wrenched the conversation into an entirely different mode. "Look at you two youngsters!" he teased the Maronite patriarchs. "Why, I remember hearing about you when I was still a boy," whereupon Gemayel obligingly retired into memories of a visit he made to Haifa during the period of the British Mandate.

The next day, as he summed up the visit with his aides, Sharon tried to gloss over the damage. "We'll make Bashir president!" he exclaimed, as if to prove that he was not disheartened by the previous day's talk. Once again, however, Saguy began to remonstrate with him in front of others.

"Even if you make him president, they'll still maintain their allegiance to the Arab world. You heard what the old man said. As far as they're concerned, we're just a tool for purging Lebanon of an evil. They won't make peace with Israel!"

By this point Sharon was exasperated with Saguy and his relentless gloom. "They're a bunch of old has-beens," he snapped at his intelligence chief. "They'll be pushed aside!"

In February, Chief of Staff Eitan was the one to pay a visit to Bashir Gemayel and his commanders, and he received a lavish reception in the barracks near Junieh: a full-dress parade with all the attendant regalia, the Israeli flag fluttering alongside its Lebanese counterpart, the band playing "Hatikvah," Israel's national anthem. The stolid Eitan was visibly moved. Bashir also allowed himself to be more candid than ever, telling Eitan that he was interested in the most extensive Israeli action possible and that he expected the IDF's columns to reach as far north as Tripoli. Yet even as he lobbied for this martial extravaganza, he gave Eitan to understand that he did not want to be directly and patently involved with any Israeli operation.

Bashir also spoke about the future regime in Lebanon and left no doubt about the fact that he intended to take over rule of the country with or without parliamentary approval. "Leave Beirut to us," he told the Israelis, meaning not that the Phalange would capture the western half of the city from the PLO and the Syrian regulars but that the political aftermath of the war should be left to him; in Bashir's scenario, the Israelis were to be purely a military instrument in the rehabilitation of Lebanon.

The fact that Eitan had been to Beirut was reported to the Cabinet in February and sparked one of that forum's most thorough discussions on a possible operation in Lebanon. The ministers spoke in terms of an action that was somewhat more ambitious than the 1978 Operation Litani but nonetheless stopped well short of Beirut. They did not get into a detailed operational analysis, but Sharon did comment that a proper job would have to include the vicinity of Beirut, so as to help the Lebanese rid themselves of the terrorists in their midst. He was careful not to breathe a word about entering the capital proper, but the mere mention of the Beirut area roused Simcha Erhlich and Yosef Burg to assail the notion of a large-scale action. Energy Minister Yitzhak Berman took a different tack by arguing that no military action would solve the problem of terrorism. "Even if we go into Beirut, we can't eradicate terrorism," he contended. "It can keep going on here without any connection to what we do in Lebanon, and those among us with experience in this field know it."

No vote was taken at the close of the meeting, for no war plan had been tabled for approval. The session was more of an airing of views and prospects—and again it changed nothing.

In March Eitan made a return visit to Beirut, accompanied this time by the commander of the air force, army specialists, and the commanders of a number of units slated to play key roles in the combat activity centering on the capital. They were treated to a special *tour d'horizon* by one of Bashir Gemayel's senior advisers, followed by a talk that began with the chief of staff's question: "What do you expect of us?" Bashir's adviser did not mince words; neither did he try to prettify how the Phalange would behave, politically speaking, once the IDF entered Lebanon. "We expect you to invade Lebanon, and when you do we will denounce you," he said without so much as blinking. "We expect you to remain here for three months. That will be enough time for us to form a new government and create a national consensus behind Bashir Gemayel's election as president."

Despite that unalluring but quite unequivocal projection, Eitan and his people continued their tour, and plans moved ahead for a major ground war. Bashir and his aides had clearly indicated that they did not want the IDF to land at Junieh, but a plan was being refined for just that strategy. The likely behavior of the Syrian force stationed in the capital was also discussed while the chief of staff and his men surveyed the positions of the Syrian Eighty-fifth Brigade from one of the tall buildings in East Beirut. Most of the officers believed that the Syrians would withdraw from Beirut as soon as they realized the IDF was closing in on the city, but one of them took the contrary position and reminded his colleagues that the Syrians had been stationed in Beirut for years and had their stores and equipment there. What's more, the Eighty-fifth Brigade was an infantry regiment, and the natural tendency of the infantry is to dig in, not to run. Even if they were threatened with encirclement, the Israeli officer did not think the Syrians would be quick to abandon Beirut. (Three months later, that clearly reasoned if somewhat unorthodox forecast proved to be exactly accurate.)

With all these comings and goings between Beirut and Tel Aviv, by March 1982 the operational plans for a war in Lebanon were well advanced and detailed. Eitan had evidently been won over to an elaborate view of the war, for by March he was saying that "the difference between a small operation and a large one is only in the way it starts . . . because [either way] the operation will develop into a broad one." Few if any dissonant voices were heard outside of Sharon's closed military circle until April, when Menachem Begin heard the first explicit warnings against backing Bashir Gemayel as the next president of Lebanon. The dissent came out of the intelligence community. Skepticism had long been the position of Saguy and military intelligence, but not of the Mossad, which was responsible for the ongoing liaison with the Phalange. Now, however, Yitzhak Hofi joined Saguy in expressing severe qualms about the wisdom and benefits of supporting Bashir Gemayel. Begin heard their misgivings expressed unequivocally during a long discussion of Bashir's dependability as a political and military ally. At the same time, both intelligence men cautioned against assuming that it would be possible to engineer Bashir's election through the "good offices" of the IDF and then blithely turn around and withdraw from Lebanon a few weeks later.

At a critical stage of Sharon's countdown, then, the heads of the Mossad and military intelligence were in full agreement on this ticklish issue and in diametric opposition to the views held by the defense minister and the chief of staff. Begin could not ignore their opinions, for it was quite uncommon for the Mossad and military intelligence to agree on anything related to the Phalange. In strongly implying that Israel should not go to war for the sake of making Bashir Gemayel president of Lebanon, and that the IDF could not rely on the military capability of the Phalange, Saguy and Hofi were demolishing two of the cornerstones of Sharon's strategic design. Apparently the prime minister appreciated this contradiction in all its gravity, for a few months earlier he had inclined toward a broad operation to utterly wipe out the PLO, while after this conversation in April—which came in the wake of assessments that the United States would at best support only a limited action—he reverted to talking in terms of the Little Pines plan.

Despite this shift in Begin's thinking, plans and preparations proceeded as before, as witnessed by the fact that in April a few high-ranking IDF officers were dispatched to Beirut to coordinate operational details with the Phalange. After the Israelis had met with their operational counterparts and the commander of the Lebanese Forces, Fadi Frem, Bashir turned up to participate in the summation session. He chatted with the guests briefly, then got straight to the point: "What are Israel's final objectives in the forthcoming war?" From his tone, the Israelis had the impression that he was interested primarily in driving the Syrians out of Lebanon and far less in overcoming the Palestinian terrorists. If so, there was a huge disparity between the Israeli and the Phalangist perception of fundamental war aims. When one of the Israeli officers remarked that Israel had no interest in picking a fight with Syria, Bashir shot back, "If you don't intend to take on the Syrians, don't come!" The Israelis were astonished by both the point of the message and its force, while the Phalangists fairly glowed over their leader's firmness. Bashir never spoke to Sharon in that tone, but it was just as well that such things come out into the open now. The Israeli generals returned to let it be known that what Bashir had in mind was fundamentally different from the expectations of Israel's political leadership.

None of these officers had any sentimental ties to the Phalange chiefs; like Amir Drori before them, their viewpoint was purely military, and they considered the acute contrast in objectives a serious pitfall. They reported their impressions to the chief of staff, the chief of Northern Command, and a senior figure in the Mossad responsible for liaison with the Phalange. Still, their alarm did not bring about any change in plans or even a clarification with the Phalange—and, of course, it was not brought to the attention of the Cabinet.

The planning went forward—and the training, as well—to the point where Amir Drori observed that this was the most thoroughly planned war the IDF had ever embarked upon. Not only was it plotted out in detail, the army held precombat surveys of the terrain, reconnaissance patrols checked the passability of the narrow roads and the bridges over the Litani River, and combat units practiced maneuvers on a variety of models. The curious conscripts were told that they were engaging in preparations to aid the Lebanese Christians; reservists were less likely to be let in on the secret for fear of leaks.

By April, therefore, it was impossible to conceal the signs of an impending war from the higher ranks of the army itself. At a routine meeting between the defense minister and divisional and brigade commanders in the north to discuss operational plans, Col. Eli Geva, the commander of an armored brigade and at thirty-two the youngest man of his rank in the IDF, was called upon to speak on behalf of the brigade commanders. He began by talking quite matter-of-factly about the need for additional exercises, but then suddenly changed the subject and without any apparent reason launched into an impassioned plea to avoid a war with the Syrians. "This must be a war against the terrorists who threaten our settlements, and we mustn't get involved with the Syrians," he said. "Everything possible must be done to avoid unnecessary wars. We should fight only when there is absolutely no choice!"

Geva's unprovoked outburst should have put Sharon on notice that, if a war in Lebanon exceeded the bounds of purely defensive objectives, a demoralizing debate would probably split the ranks of the IDF itself. But Geva's real point was brushed aside. Sharon did not ignore the remarks, he merely took the wind out of Geva's sails with the curt reply, "I agree that there's no point in clashing with the Syrians," and left it at that.

As April drew to a close, war was in the air—literally as well as figuratively—because on the 21st of that month Israel broke the ceasefire with the PLO by bombing targets in South Lebanon. The pretext for this move was the death of an Israeli soldier whose vehicle hit a mine in the Haddad-controlled enclave. On May 9 the Israeli air force was again sent out to hit targets in Lebanon in response to the discovery of explosive devices near a school in the town of Ashkelon and on a bus in Jerusalem (although there was no tracing either of these attempted bombings directly to Lebanon). The PLO held its fire after the air raid in April, but on May 9 its guns responded with a carefully controlled artillery barrage. More than a hundred shells and Katyusha rockets were fired at Israeli territory; not a single one hit a town or settlement. These misses were not a display of Palestinian incompetence but a clearly framed message that artillery could be aimed where the terrorists chose; it was equally possible to target settlements, and next time the PLO would.

So the winds of war had begun to blow in earnest, so much so that D-day was scheduled for Sunday, May 17. But it was postponed when it became evident that seven ministers—including Begin's two deputies, Simcha Ehrlich and David Levi—still did not support a major ground action. On the other hand, Ariel Sharon had succeeded brilliantly in turning the Israeli Cabinet and the IDF General Staff into two mutually isolated bodies running on very different tracks. One can appreciate the gap in orientation between these two institutions by comparing the Cabinet meeting that discussed the prospective war on May 10 and the special meeting of the General Staff held on May 13, which happened to be the final General Staff session before the outbreak of war. Anyone who took part in the Cabinet meeting and subsequently saw the objectives listed on the blackboard before the General Staff could not help but be struck by the arrant contradictions in assumptions and goals. While the Cabinet meeting ended with a general understanding that any war in Lebanon would be a limited one, the generals focused their deliberations on the Big Pines plan to link up with the Maronite forces around Beirut. The Cabinet talked in terms of an action against the PLO that would steer clear of any contact with the Syrian forces in Lebanon; the General Staff spoke of closing in on Beirut and cutting the highway to Damascus, which (as was explicitly stated at the meeting) would force the IDF to engage the Syrians in battle.

The highlight of the May 13 General Staff meeting was the intelligence assessment presented by Yehoshua Saguy—a forecast which proved to be impeccably accurate. What Saguy had to say was not very encouraging or popular, but whoever heard him could not complain of being uninformed of the dire consequences of a war that could still be avoided.

Saguy told the generals that a clash with the Syrians was unavoidable and that it would occur at the very outset of fighting in Lebanon, for the Syrians would pump fresh forces into the country—at least a division—and certainly throw the full weight of their air force into the fray. In turn, the engagement of Syrian planes would make it imperative for Israel to attack the Syrian missile batteries, thereby escalating the confrontation even further. "Whoever speaks about cleaning out a forty-kilometer zone is going to come to blows with the Syrians," Saguy warned, for there were Syrian troops stationed in that belt, and he did not subscribe to the view that the Syrians would turn tail and run. Saguy also anticipated the response of the Lebanese Christians once the fighting began. "They won't intervene; they won't do a thing. If we bring Bashir here and tell him that the IDF is going into Lebanon tomorrow, he'll bubble over and kiss each one of us, but that won't change anything. When he returns to face the Christian leadership, he'll run into a wall of skepticism. What's more, they'll probably denounce the Israeli attack because they have to show that their [hands are] clean."

Saguy then addressed the question of whether or not the proposed operation could destroy the terrorists' infrastructure. It was an issue on which he had locked horns with Eitan quite a while back, and now he took the opportunity to reiterate that, while the IDF could expect a military victory over the terrorists, that did not mean an end to the PLO or even the destruction of its military infrastructure. Even if the terrorists suffered heavy losses in men and equipment, they could always regroup and reorganize in Syria or even in Tripoli, just seventy kilometers north of the Lebanese capital. Then, once the IDF withdrew from Lebanon—as it inevitably would—the PLO could settle right back into Beirut.

The list of perils went on and on. There would be consequences of acting without an absolutely egregious provocation. Israel and the United States had only one channel of communication on this issue—Alexander Haig— and the secretary was having problems holding his own in the endless rounds of infighting with high-ranking White House officials. And although the Soviets wanted quiet in the area and had strictly forbidden their clients to do anything that might involve them in a war, they had promised Assad that, if his regime were threatened, they would send men to Damascus. If that came to pass, the Americans would surely blame Israel for drawing the Russians into the Middle East, and both powers would demand that the IDF pull out of Lebanon immediately. At the same time, Saguy forced the generals to face up to the lack of national consensus on a war of such far-reaching aims. "One of the worst things a country can do is go to war when it's divided. I fear there's lack of consensus within the army itself, and that's no way to march off to war," he pronounced.

Yet the crux of Saguy's warning had to do with the political aftermath of the war, which he colored in abysmally bleak tones. Once the fighting ended, the issue at hand would not be Israel's security but the swift restoration of sovereign control over all of Lebanon. After all, the Israelis had committed themselves to that principle. "Then we can forget about the support of the Christians in the north and Haddad in the south," Saguy predicted, and while on the subject of restoring sovereignty over territory occupied by the IDF, "I couldn't promise that the issues of the Golan Heights and the West Bank won't be raised for discussion. So from a political standpoint, we're heading into a highly impolitic venture—and that's putting it mildly!"

Saguy's words, harsh in themselves, were voiced with a bitterness born of self-reproach, for he knew that when he addressed the Cabinet, sitting face to face with Begin and Sharon, he never allowed himself to speak as pointedly or forcefully as he did before the General Staff. Yet stinging as his verdict was, within a few days its effect had dissolved, and the rigorous pace of events swept right by the remarkable fact that Israel was going to war against the express advice of its intelligence chief! Gradually Saguy fell silent, withdrew into himself, acquiesced in the self-serving realities of other men. His tragic flaw, the inability to stand before the prime minister and his Cabinet in Sharon's presence and tell them what he told his colleagues in the army with such cogency, turned Saguy, the one man who had fought Ariel Sharon almost every step of the way, into an accomplice in Sharon's effort to divide and rule. For Yehoshua Saguy participated in almost all the Cabinet meetings before and after the outbreak of the war; unlike most of the ministers, he understood precisely what was going on yet held his peace.

Through this hapless conjunction of blind determination on Sharon's part and failure of will on Saguy's, the Israeli Cabinet was reduced to a genteel debating society that received regular but carefully censored reports and was never advised of what was likely to result from the IDF's anticipated moves. It was a body whose decisions were often made after the fact, to rubber-stamp measures in progress or already completed in the field. Its information came from a single, unchallenged source, the minister of defense, who succeeded in building a solid barrier between the Cabinet and the military. Perhaps the most remarkable evidence of this barrier came after the fighting broke out, when in stark contrast to the custom of his predecessors the chief of staff refrained from appearing before the Cabinet, preferring to leave the handling of the ministers—what they should know and how they should be told—to Sharon himself.

And Ariel Sharon filled the role like a natural. He knew that the Cabinet would not approve a war for the purpose of making Bashir Gemayel president of Lebanon and was equally sure that it would shrink from a clash with the Syrians. Yet he was confident of obtaining its endorsement for an action to cripple the terrorists, and within that one area he told the ministers what they wanted to hear. As for the rest, he spoke only in vague generalities, waffled on crucial issues, and sometimes contradicted the evidence before the ministers' very eyes. (With the military he had to maintain a certain degree of ambiguity as well, but while Sharon's obscurantism at the General Staff level necessarily ended when fighting broke out, it continued in the Cabinet throughout most of the war.) By playing on his colleagues' gullibility and ignorance of martial affairs, Sharon herded the Israeli Cabinet into and through a war it did not want and had not approved, treating it "like a kindergarten," in the words of one of its members. This was not a cut-and-dried case of a coup d'état in the classic sense; the army did not impose its will on the Cabinet. Nevertheless, Israel's spirit of democracy was severely abused during the war in Lebanon, for its military machine was operating outside the real control of the country's legitimate government. By manipulating the Cabinet into serving his ends, Sharon achieved through subterfuge and finesse a refined variation of the putsch that Begin had offhandedly hinted Sharon might carry out by force.

Sharon's method was often remarkably simple. At the Cabinet meeting on May 10, for example, maps were again laid out for the ministers' scrutiny. They were the maps of the Big Pines plan, and the arrows on them led north past the Palestinian-dominated area of South Lebanon toward the Christian-held territory around Beirut. Nevertheless, Sharon and Eitan spoke explicitly about a "limited operation." Rather than use the term "war," Sharon went out of his way to stress that he was speaking about a "police action," glossing over his intent to advance along the central axis in the rear of the Syrians and neglecting to explain the military implications of such a move. No mention was made of Beirut or of linking up with the Christians in the north. The ministers were led to understand that if Israel were forced to embark upon a ground action in Lebanon, the scope of such action would be hardly broader than Operation Litani, though this time it would take in Tyre and the refugee camps in the vicinity. Asked how much time an operation of this sort was likely to take, Sharon replied, "Twenty-four hours."

There was a dissenting voice at that meeting, and it belonged to Mordechai Zippori, who spoke out gruffly against using the air force in this presumably limited "police action." Zippori feared that things would get out of hand. "The massing of forces, together with the bombings, will create a snowball effect that will whisk us right into a war," he cautioned. "We're dashing headlong toward an all-out war, and no one can foresee its consequences or the price we will have to pay. A campaign into Lebanon won't be a simple affair, and in the end we'll just have to about-face and come right back again. I suggest we hear situation assessments from the foreign minister, the chief of intelligence, and the head of Mossad."

Begin, everyone could see, was annoyed by Zippori's forebodings, but rather than address the substance of his remarks Begin insinuated, as he had on other occasions, that the minister's objections stemmed from jealousy. Zippori, not easily bullied into silence, vigorously protested the slur. Annoyed all the more, the prime minister continued firing off his barbs at the next speaker, the deputy chief of military intelligence. Brig. Gen. Avi Yaari had been asked to attend the meeting in Saguy's absence from the country, and when the intelligence officer took a cautious line in advising the Cabinet, pointing out, for example, that the UN General Assembly was in session just then, Begin huffed, "You're telling *me* the assembly is in session?" But like Zippori before him, Yaari was not easily rattled. He picked up his recitation in the same soft, even tone as before, issuing another warning. "The Syrians will fight in Lebanon," he said. "So will the Palestinians. It won't be a picnic for the IDF."

This time Sharon cut in. "The Cabinet knows that!" he snapped, whereupon Begin chimed in sententiously: "Never predict anything in an absolute way." When the meeting adjourned, Sharon was overheard grumbling that the only thing the intelligence officer had done was "slacken weak knees!"

A similar method of managing information and controlling impressions through a mixture of omission and suggestion was applied to members of the opposition, who were considerably more experienced in military affairs. At a meeting on May 16 with Shimon Peres, Yitzhak Rabin, and Chaim Bar-Lev of the Labor party—one an ex-prime minister, one an ex-defense minister, and two of them ex-chiefs of staff—Begin reported that if the terrorist provocations continued, Israel would respond with a massive ground action in Lebanon. The figure of forty kilometers was not mentioned, but Sharon did refer vaguely to a line running from Lake Karoun to Sidon as the outside limit of the thrust. Rabin wanted a more precise picture and asked whether Sidon was included in the scope of the operation. Sharon seemed hesitant to commit himself. "I'm not sure," he said, and sensing that this answer was not good enough, he stood up and made for the door. "I'll check it out on the maps." He returned a few minutes later and informed them that Sidon was included in the operation, leaving the impression that if the minister of defense was not sure whether or not Sidon fell within the bounds of the plan, the operation must be limited to South Lebanon.

The question that inevitably arises—and will probably always remain open—is how far Sharon and Eitan took Begin in, and how far the prime minister wittingly lent himself to Sharon's machinations. There is no doubt that Begin was contemplating a war against the PLO well before Sharon entered the Defense Ministry or that he wanted to accomplish more than liberating the Galilee from the dread of terrorist rockets and shells. Well before the war he was heard to vow that the day would come when he would order the IDF to go "as far as Arafat's bunker." A man thinking along these lines would find it difficult to content himself with an action that went only as far as Sidon or the Awali River just north of it.

Yet there is also evidence pointing in another direction. About two weeks before the war broke out, Begin's former military secretary, Efraim Poran, paid the prime minister a visit after having spent some time abroad. Before calling on Begin, Poran stopped by the General Staff and was surprised to find that preparations for a full-scale and far-reaching war had reached an advanced stage. Troubled by the discovery, Poran in his conversation with Begin half-stated, half-questioned whether a war was in the works and whether it was going to extend as far as Beirut.

"Absolutely not!" the prime minister replied instantly.

Perhaps Begin was blissfully unaware of what was going on in the General Staff. Or perhaps his complicity with Sharon had reached the point where he felt obliged to conceal details even from the man who had been one of his closest and most loyal military aides. The truth probably lies somewhere in between, on the assumption that Begin had been assured, or had somehow convinced himself, that the upcoming operation was not really a war at all but a sharply defined and contained ground action. That would explain why he spoke about a limited operation at Cabinet meetings during the month of May and with the leaders of the opposition. Also why he wrote to President Reagan that Israel was undertaking a military offensive to push the PLO's artillery back beyond a forty-kilometer limit. It is highly doubtful that a stickler like Begin would have quoted so specific a distance had he known from the outset that the IDF planned to advance much farther. But Begin was not the man who had planned and would run the war in Lebanon. The man who had and would was in no way constrained by scruples about how Menachem Begin would appear in the eyes of the American president when the Israel Defense Forces surrounded and entered Beirut.

It must be said that there were fundamental differences of approach between Sharon and Eitan, too, though these were for the most part matters of emphasis. Like Begin, the chief of staff viewed the essence of the war as a move against the PLO, but Eitan was not reconciled to a limited operation. From the outset he wanted to send the IDF into the Christian-controlled area of Lebanon to link up with the Phalange and strike at the PLO's headquarters in Beirut. He believed in Bashir Gemayel and considered him a full partner in the war against the terrorists. He even believed that the Phalange would finish the job that the IDF had started, sweeping what remained of the broken terrorist organizations out of Lebanon.

Where he parted ways with Sharon was over the issue of the Syrians, which he considered of low priority whereas Sharon saw a head-on collision with the Syrians as unavoidable. Experience had undoubtedly taught Sharon that any attempt to outflank the Syrians in the Bekaa Valley would force them to fight, and while he did not want a full-blown war with Syria —certainly not one that would include fighting on the Golan Heights or within Syrian territory—he definitely hoped to get the Syrians out of the Bekaa Valley and, if possible, most of the rest of Lebanon. It was a tall order. To mislead Damascus and forestall premature intervention by the powers, Sharon would have to orchestrate two separate moves: first against the PLO in the west, and only afterward against the Syrians in the Bekaa Valley. He would succeed in preventing the war from spreading to the Golan, but in the process he would fail to achieve most of his objectives in Lebanon. And the price that Israel would have to pay for the entire misadventure far exceeded even the grimmest expectations.

4

An Illusion of Collusion

AMONG OTHER PRIMARY CONSIDERATIONS of the Lebanese campaign, its planners realized that one issue of overriding importance had to be resolved before Israel could embark on any formidable military move into a neighboring country: the American reaction. Since the spring of 1981, relations between the Israeli and American governments had become severely strained. Washington's exasperation had reached the point where the shipment of arms had been pointedly suspended after the destruction of the Iraqi reactor in June 1981 and the bombing of the PLO headquarters in Beirut in July. With the reaction to isolated bombing raids so sharp, Israel's concern about the probable response from Washington should have been all the more acute when it came to the matter of a sustained ground action. And there was another, no less weighty consideration that made coordination with Washington imperative—the risk that Israeli troops would tangle with the Syrian forces in Lebanon and that fighting might spread to the Golan Heights. If events were swept up in that widening gyre, the result might well be Soviet involvement and a threat to Israel's very existence. At least such was the likelihood in the absence of a clear indication that the United States countenanced the Israeli operation.

The need for outside backing as a condition for taking military action was hardly a new consideration for the Israeli government. In the past, whenever Israel found itself headed for war, the government strove to secure at least the understanding, if not the outright support, of one of the major powers. The Israelis may have gone to war often, but never rashly. Prior to the Sinai Campaign in 1956, Ben-Gurion entered into a covert military pact with France—and through France with Britain. Had it not been for that alliance it is highly doubtful that he would have succumbed to the urgings of his chief of staff, Moshe Dayan, and agreed to invade the

Sinai Peninsula. In 1967, after Egypt began massing troops on the border and closed the Straits of Tiran to Israelbound shipping, Prime Minister Levi Eshkol stalled for weeks while Israeli emissaries scoured the capitals of the West to solicit understanding for Israel's plight and for a military action to relieve it. Israeli prudence went to even greater lengths in October 1973. When Golda Meir and Moshe Dayan discovered that a joint Egyptian-Syrian attack was only hours away, they ruled out a preemptive air strike just to prove to Washington that Israel could not possibly be held responsible for starting the war; their assumption was that this flaunting of Israel's innocence would earn America's support for the measures they intended to take after absorbing the first blow. Yet in 1982, seemingly contrary to Israel's traditional caution, Menachem Begin's government behaved as though it was not fazed in the least by the possible reaction of its allies. Did this attitude stem from overconfidence, sheer recklessness, or some other less obvious cause? The answer is a combination of all three: a heightened sense of confidence that Israel, as a "Mediterranean power," could afford to pursue a more daring policy, whereas the major powers were limited in the kind of response they could apply to small states; a general readiness to dispense with the precautions that Israeli governments had followed in the past; and the smug feeling that, for all intents and purposes, Washington was "in Israel's pocket" and no unpleasant surprises were to be expected from that quarter.

On the surface it would seem that nothing could have been less justified, for by the time Ariel Sharon became defense minister the Reagan administration was already exasperated by a succession of precipitate Israeli moves. Washington's most bitter and consistent complaint was that the Begin government had the infuriating habit of pulling surprises on its allies no less than on its foes. The effect of these spectacular displays of prowess, such as the bombing of the Iraqi nuclear reactor, was to make America's public position in the Middle East considerably less than comfortable. At the end of 1981, after the sudden annexation of the Golan Heights, official Washington was so irritated that the State Department and the American embassy in Israel were ordered to draw up a list of other surprises that the Begin government might come up with. The possibility that the IDF would invade Lebanon and overrun a hefty chunk of its territory was included in those projections, though not at the top of the list.

In November 1981, a few weeks before the tension between the two governments shot up again over the Golan issue, Ariel Sharon paid his first visit to Washington as Israel's minister of defense. Equipped with a case full of colored maps marked with stark black arrows, he proceeded to initiate the Pentagon's generals into the finer points of the political-military situation in Africa, of all places! Bemoaning the spread of Soviet influence through the Dark Continent, Sharon proposed a program of strategic co-operation to block the expansion of Communism into the Middle East and check its advance through Africa as well. In return, he expected to be granted carte blanche to act against Russia's frontline clients in his own immediate neighborhood—the PLO and Syria—in the belief that such an entente would automatically ease the pressure on Israel to compromise on autonomy for the Arabs of the West Bank and Gaza Strip.

Sharon's thinking and implicit offer of a trade-off were understood perfectly in the Pentagon, but Defense Secretary Weinberger was not buying. On the contrary, he came out strongly against any new commitments to Israel that might nettle the Saudis or any of America's other friends in the Arab world. Nevertheless, the White House directed him to placate Israel by signing a Memorandum of Strategic Understanding with Sharon—though not before the secretary's aides had thoroughly purged the document of the slightest hint that it gave Israel a free hand to act against its Arab neighbors. Weinberger even took pains to play down the signing ceremony as much as protocol would allow.

What he could not control was the way in which Sharon would hawk his dubious achievement to the Israeli public. The defense minister returned home with a classic anti-Soviet document in hand—or so he portrayed it. The other Cabinet ministers, who were not given an opportunity to study the draft of the agreement before it was signed, were forced to swallow whatever Sharon had cooked up and was now serving them. But although the Memorandum of Strategic Understanding was described to the Israeli public in superlatives, Sharon and his aides were the first to admit that it would not do as a fig leaf for a military venture into Lebanon—especially with Weinberger so unlikely a confederate for such an operation. The man who impressed Sharon as a far more promising candidate for a partnership in the Lebanon venture, silent though he might be, was Secretary of State Alexander Haig.

It is not difficult to appreciate Sharon's affinity for Haig. Both men were ex-generals endowed with abundant reserves of self-confidence; both had made their way into political life late in their careers; both espoused a fervently anti-Soviet line and deemed military might a cardinal tool for pursuing political policy; both believed that, reduced to its essence, all international terrorism was a Russian plot. Haig, long a friend of Israel, had a healthy respect for the political clout of the American Jewish community and perceived the Middle East in a way that was consonant with the philosophies of Begin and Sharon. During his first visit to the region, he had tried to convince his hosts that the primary American objective must be to forge a regional strategic alignment to stop Communism from overrunning the area like a rampant weed. If such an alignment were realized, the pro-Western states in the Middle East would automatically find a common language, making it possible for the Israel-Arab conflict practically to solve itself. (Haig had little difficulty persuading Begin and Sharon of the merits of this view, but the Arab states, and particularly Saudi Arabia, demanded that the order of priorities be reversed: first the Israel-Arab conflict must be solved, and only then could a pro-Western strategic alignment be formed.)

For all these reasons, the consensus among Israel's senior policymakers was that Haig could be made to see the benefits of annihilating the PLO— if for no other reason than PLO support of local terrorist organizations around the world—by means of an Israeli military action in Lebanon. To date, Israel's experience with Haig had been generally gratifying, even though he could not always be counted upon to defend the Israelis against the prickly Weinberger in times of crisis.

After the bombing of the reactor, Haig had shown understanding for Israel's motives and tried to mitigate the punitive measures taken by the Reagan government. A quarter of an hour after Israeli Ambassador Efraim Evron was informed that the bombers had returned safely to their bases, Haig phoned him at home sounding quite unperturbed, his tone almost soothing. Above all, he was curious about technical questions: Had a radioactive cloud mushroomed over the destroyed facility? When did Israel believe the reactor was slated to become "hot"? Yet this quietly supportive attitude did Israel little good when Weinberger urged the president to suspend the shipment of planes to Israel and publish a sharp statement deploring the drastic Israeli action. From the outset, then, Alexander Haig's efficacy as a champion of Israel's cause had its limits.

Sharon's way of revealing Israel's intentions in Lebanon was subtle. Essentially, he used the "drip method" to furnish the Americans with selected details of his military antidote to the PLO presence in Lebanon, stopping well short of revealing the whole plan or its timing. In other words, Sharon kept the Americans in the picture, so to speak, but disclosed only what was convenient for them to know; that way he could claim that Israel certainly hadn't sprung any surprises on Washington. Having chosen his method, he concentrated on bringing the Americans round to seeing that the PLO was making a mockery of the July 1981 ceasefire and that sooner or later Israel would have to react with a resounding blow. His aim was to establish in principle Israel's right to respond through a military offensive without having to specify its scope.

Sharon launched his gambit in December 1981—without consulting

Begin or Shamir—and it was the kind of maverick maneuver that caused the striped-pants types in the Israeli Foreign Ministry to shudder. The man he chose to carry his first signal to Washington was none other than the president's special ambassador, Philip Habib. On December 5, Sharon met with Habib and the American chargé d'affaires in Israel, William Brown, and in a lightning move calculated for its effect left his guests reeling by telling them that "if the terrorists continue to violate the ceasefire, we will have no choice but to wipe them out completely in Lebanon, destroy the PLO's infrastructure there. . . . We will eradicate the PLO in Lebanon."

The affable Habib, a diplomat through and through, was appalled by the brutality of Sharon's demarche. "General Sharon, this is the twentieth century and times have changed," he blurted out. "You can't go around invading countries just like that, spreading destruction and killing civilians. In the end, your invasion will grow into a war with Syria, and the entire region will be engulfed in flames!"

"It won't necessarily draw the Syrians into a war," Sharon countered. "We can free Israel and Lebanon of the PLO without fighting the Syrians. Assad won't intervene."

To illustrate his point, Sharon asked an aide to unroll a map of Lebanon and pointed to where the PLO concentrations were located in the western sector. His finger moved in broad circles around Sidon and the area of Damour. But nothing was said about Beirut, nor was there any hint that the IDF would be sent into the Bekaa Valley in the east, along the Syrian-Lebanese border. And no mention was made of the Syrian missile batteries stationed in Lebanon.

"I must emphasize again that this is my personal opinion, but it *is* the way to destroy the center of international terrorism," he assured them.

The two diplomats seemed stunned by the sheer force of Sharon's remarks, but that was fine: the defense minister knew that Habib hadn't missed a single word and would report it all to his principals. In time, he believed, the Americans would grow used to the idea that nothing could stop Israel from mounting a military strike into Lebanon, so they had best reconcile themselves to the idea and prepare to cash in on the benefits.

Habib and Brown were indeed quick to report on the meeting. It was the first time Washington had tangible evidence that Sharon was bent on moving into Lebanon. Yet even before the minister's point-blank revelations in Jerusalem, American intelligence had its own reasons to keep its antennae well tuned to developments in Israel. Military alerts and the concentration of Israeli forces on the Lebanese and Syrian borders had become almost commonplace, and the intelligence people had a strong suspicion that these events were not merely an expression of Israeli skittishness about Syria's possible response to the annexation of the Golan. At this stage, however—January 1982—their assessment was that, the troop buildup notwithstanding, Sharon would fail to drum up a majority in the Cabinet for a full-scale war. The State Department went a step further and credited his ferocious threats to a quirk of style—Sharon's inimitable way of trying to cow his opponents with massive doses of bluster. On an earlier occasion, the American diplomat Richard Fairbanks had heard Sharon threaten that, the day after American AWACS intelligence-gathering planes were supplied to Saudi Arabia, Israel would be forced to shoot them down. Such swagger, therefore, need not be taken all that seriously.

In February 1982, however, Israel moved to show Washington that what Habib had heard should not be dismissed as bluff. This time the messenger was the IDF's chief of military intelligence, Maj. Gen. Yehoshua Saguy, who was charged with trying to obtain at least tacit American approval for a ground operation in Lebanon. In contrast to Sharon's move in December, Saguy's mission was made in coordination with Prime Minister Begin and Foreign Minister Shamir, attesting that Begin had indeed decided in favor of war but knew he could not send the IDF into action unless the United States acknowledged that the PLO was acting in violation of the agreement negotiated through its own good offices. The rub was that while the ceasefire was being scrupulously observed on the Lebanese border, anti-Israel terrorism was continuing on other fronts. On January 29, for example, a squad of terrorists had been caught stealing across the frontier from Jordan, and the Israeli government regarded this, too, as a violation of the ceasefire agreement. Only when and if the Americans accepted this broad interpretation of the accord could Israel throw the full weight of its army against the PLO. Hence Yehoshua Saguy's secret mission to Secretary of State Haig.

Saguy was not Sharon's choice for the job. The two did not see eye to eye on many points related to action in Lebanon, and Sharon feared that, wittingly or otherwise, the general might transmit his qualms to Haig. But Begin ruled that Saguy would be his messenger. Curiously enough, once that decision was made, neither Begin nor any other minister instructed Saguy on what to tell the secretary. The intelligence chief prepared his own brief: if the terrorists continued to violate the ceasefire on any front, Israel would retaliate with a limited military operation in Lebanon while making every effort to avoid a skirmish with the Syrians.

It is relatively rare for an American secretary of state to confer at length with the intelligence chief of a foreign army, and in point of fact the meeting with Saguy was not registered in the State Department log. Once inside the secretary's sanctum, Saguy spread out the maps he had brought and got straight down to business. As the conversation developed, he sensed that the secretary understood his message perfectly. Haig, for his part, made it equally clear that only a flagrant violation of the ceasefire could be accepted as grounds for an Israeli reprisal. He was also concerned that a war might break out before Israel had completed its withdrawal from the Sinai on April 25, thereby wrecking the Camp David accords and perhaps even the Israeli-Egyptian peace treaty. Some very respected professionals in the State Department, Haig implied, were willing to wager that Sharon had exactly that object in mind.

But this was a meeting with Saguy, not Sharon, and a rather pleasant one at that. The only hitch occurred as it drew to a close when Haig's *chef de bureau* entered the room and whispered something in his ear. The secretary broke into a grin and informed Saguy that he would have to leave the office by the back door, through an exit that bypassed the main waiting room. The Soviet ambassador, Anatoly Dobrinin, happened to be sitting out front, and it would be best if he didn't set eyes on Saguy, lest he recognize the general from his press photos.

That pitfall avoided, Saguy's trip to Washington attracted a minimum of attention. The State Department said nothing about it, and when queried about a meeting in Foggy Bottom the Israeli ambassador went so far as to deny that it had taken place. A week after Saguy left Washington, a solitary newspaper noted in passing that Israel had sent the administration a warning letter about terrorist activity and that the bearer of the missive, which had been passed on to Saudi Arabia, was Major General Saguy.

Saguy achieved what he had set out to do when Haig conceded that the infiltration of terrorists over any of Israel's borders qualified as a violation of the ceasefire, assuming the terrorists were sent by headquarters in Beirut. On the other hand, the secretary was not prepared to include in this category terrorist actions against Israel or Jewish targets outside the Middle East. Finally, and most important perhaps, although Haig stressed that only a "significant violation" of the agreement could justify an Israeli response, both sides managed to avoid defining what would constitute a significant violation.

If the Israeli intelligence chief returned home pleased with the results of his mission, U.S. intelligence had equally good reason to savor a sense of satisfaction: through sheer diligence it had pieced together almost all the details of the IDF's operational plan for a war in Lebanon. Very little was still concealed from the Americans. Their men had systematically collected scraps and fragments of data until they knew the size of the force Israel intended to field in Lebanon (according to each of its alternative plans) and the exact axes of advance. And what their operatives failed to turn up in Israel they discovered with ease in Lebanon at Phalange head-quarters, where many of the IDF's presumed secrets were common knowl-edge. They learned, for example, of Sharon's visit to Beirut, the points that caught his interest there, and the gist of his conversations with Bashir Gemayel and other Maronite leaders.

Between tips that the Israelis themselves offered gratis and the yield of their own intelligence networks, the Americans knew more about the prob-able course of events in Lebanon than about any previous war in the Middle East. At one point, the National Security Council assessed that Sharon would choose one of three possibilities: a contained military action combining the bombing of Palestinian targets with commando raids throughout South Lebanon; a limited ground operation to smash the PLO's military infrastructure and occupy South Lebanon until receiving guaran-tees that the guerrillas would not be allowed to return to their positions; or a major ground operation to create a land link between Israel and the territory controlled by the Phalange and to sweep the PLO out of a larger section of Lebanon. These projections were based exclusively on the gleanings from Sharon's conversations with American diplomats!

With the wealth of information circulating among American sources, leaks became inevitable. Sure enough, on April 8, 1982, NBC's John Chan-cellor shared many details of Israel's combat plan with the audience of the evening news. Chancellor, who was known for his Washington connec-tions, told his viewers that the Israeli campaign in Lebanon would not be a modest affair and quoted the figure of 1,200 tanks to convey a sense of its magnitude. His presentation included a map showing where an Israeli column would penetrate the Bekaa Valley and drive northward to block the Syrian armor while a second column made for the refugee camps outside Tyre and Sidon and a third moved farther up the coast to Damour. He saved his biggest scoop for last, however, when he disclosed that some of the Israeli planners were pressing to move on to Beirut, where about 2,000 PLO guerrillas were concentrated. As subsequent events proved, these revelations were an amazingly accurate précis of the Israeli war plan. And what John Chancellor knew and saw fit to tell all America was surely known in far greater detail within the Pentagon and the State Department.

Even so, in April 1982 many top officials in the State Department still believed that war could be averted, and Washington was not above sending messages to that effect to the PLO. If it was impossible to restrain Israel, perhaps the United States could keep the Palestinians in line by letting them know that Israel meant business. Washington's direct channels to the PLO remained open at all times, and on at least one occasion func-tioned like a hotline. On April 21, when Israeli jets bombed targets north of the Zaharani River in Lebanon, the State Department worked quickly to clarify whether this was a softening-up raid in preparation for a ground strike. When word came through that it was not, the Americans sped the tip along to the PLO. This clarification may have been the reason why the Palestinians held their fire on that occasion.

Clearly, however, these were first-aid tactics, not a serious approach to treating the cause of the problem. The Americans knew they couldn't control all the factors involved in the Lebanese conflict, despite the fact that Philip Habib was aiming for a comprehensive settlement in Lebanon —including the removal of the Syrian missiles—rather than a reinforcement of the ceasefire in the south. Toward that end, on March 2, Habib met with Syrian President Hafez Assad in Damascus as some 10,000 people indulged in a clamorous anti-American demonstration well within earshot. Mainly because the Americans had exercised their veto in the Security Council vote to condemn the Israeli annexation of the Golan Heights, relations between Damascus and Washington had been at a nadir since the previous December. But now, despite that affront, Assad was prepared to renew a dialogue with Washington, knowing that the only party capable of exerting any effective pressure on Israel and forestalling an Israeli invasion of Lebanon was the United States.

Habib traveled to Damascus armed with the knowledge that Assad did not want a war at this juncture. Even though, just days before his departure, the Syrian army had completed a General Staff exercise in which two divisions simulated a replay of the battle plan used in the Yom Kippur War, Habib knew that the Syrians were doing everything in their power to prevent the outbreak of hostilities by keeping the Palestinians in Lebanon on a tight rein. Syrian Foreign Minister Abdel Halim Khaddam had just held a secret meeting with the leaders of the PLO and prominent figures in the Lebanese left to speak of Israel's war footing and impress upon them the imperative of acting with utmost restraint lest they furnish the Israelis with a pretext for war. In Damascus, Habib played on Syrian anxieties to the hilt. Peppering his approach with dark intimations about an Israel chafing to unleash its army in Lebanon if the terrorist actions continued, he wielded Israel like the proverbial big stick to make the Syrians wince. Yet even though keenly aware of Syria's fatigue from its prolonged occupation of Lebanon, Habib avoided the subject of removing the surface-to-air missiles from the Bekaa Valley—which would imply abject surrender to Israel—and dwelled instead on the more positive prospect of an overall troop withdrawal after arranging for orderly elections for the Lebanese presidency. Hope sprang in Foggy Bottom that Assad would settle for the election of a pro-Syrian president, perhaps Frangieh.

While trying to put a damper on Syria and the PLO, the Americans still had to contend with a restive Israeli defense minister who took every opportunity to flaunt his impatience and temper. Sharon fumed over Defense Secretary Weinberger's plans to supply sophisticated weaponry to Jordan. When he discovered that King Hussein had asked the Saudis to station their combat planes on Jordanian soil, he curtly informed Washington that Israel would destroy those planes, considering the stationing of foreign forces on Jordanian soil a casus belli even if those forces came from a pro-American country. Sharon's relations with American officials in both Tel Aviv and Washington steadily deteriorated as his style became increasingly abrasive. Now, it seemed, he was determined to close the Israeli defense establishment to the American attachés, and repeatedly he admonished ministry officials and senior army officers to keep their distance from the diplomatic community. All the while he hammered away at the message that the ceasefire with the PLO was a dead issue.

Without being privy to his grand design, the Americans suspected that Sharon was hoping to gain unchallenged control of the West Bank and paralyze the local Palestinian leadership by means of a war in Lebanon. Challenging the logic of that plan, Ambassador Samuel Lewis warned a number of Israeli ministers and senior officials that Sharon was fooling himself, and others, if he thought that by disabling the PLO in Lebanon he could magically transform Jordan into the homeland of the Palestinians and dictate his terms in negotiations over the future of the occupied territories. "It cannot possibly be a brief war," Lewis reasoned about an expedition into Lebanon, "and ultimately it will lead to a clash with the Syrians, which runs counter to American interests." Meanwhile, American intelligence sources were strongly refuting rather ominous Israeli assessments that Syria was likely to provoke Israel with a hostile military move in the summer of 1982.

Given this strong undercurrent of friction, Washington evinced little enthusiasm when Sharon announced his intention to visit the capital again in May. Prior to his arrival, the State Department prepared an assessment paper predicting that the response of international public opinion to an Israeli attack on Lebanon would probably be emphatically negative, especially if the war were to spread to other countries. Nevertheless, reports were reaching Israel that certain quarters in the American capital supported a limited Israeli action, and their support was expected to hold as long as the operation was brief and neat—meaning that few civilians were affected. Foreign Minister Shamir even received word that some senior American officials favored a military action to drive the Syrian army out of Lebanon! These tidings sparked a debate among several ministers in which Sharon contended that here was proof that an Israeli operation, if carried out quickly and cleanly, would meet with understanding from the United States.

It was against this background that Sharon prepared to visit Washington. But before his arrival, the Americans were honored by a secret visit from the man who was to become the next president of Lebanon—though no one dreamed it at the time—Amin Gemayel. The almost anonymous Lebanese guest seemed to spend much of his time talking about an imminent war, and he was particularly interested in grilling the Americans about Israel's war aims in Lebanon. His most persistent questions: What did his hosts know about Israel's intentions regarding Syria? While going for the PLO in Lebanon, were the Israelis planning to attack the Syrians too? Gemayel had come to Washington on behalf of his family—which effectively meant the Phalange party—to determine how deeply the Americans were implicated in Israel's war plans. On the American side, Gemayel's avid interest in Israel's designs on the Syrians aroused tantalizing notions that he might also be moonlighting for Damascus.

Be that as it may, as much as Amin Gemayel's visit to Washington was shrouded by a cloak of secrecy, Sharon's was attended by an astounding barrage of publicity. The defense minister could not have known—and certainly would not have expected from all the hoopla—that the Americans had resolved to drain his visit of any real significance. They were intent on preventing him from meeting with the president and had decided not to relent on the short-lived Memorandum of Strategic Understanding. Even the announcement that the government would accede to various Israeli financial requests was to be postponed until Prime Minister Begin's planned visit, scheduled for the following month. But Sharon had not come to Washington in quest of funds, or even to resuscitate the much-ballyhooed Memorandum of Strategic Understanding. His objective on this trip was something quite different, and he was not at all disappointed that he was not to see the president.

Ariel Sharon had traveled a long way to see the one man whom he believed he could talk business with. Accompanied by his aides, he met with Secretary of State Haig and his advisers for almost two and a half hours, and from the substance of this meeting one can glean an understanding of how Sharon—and through him Begin and the rest of the Israeli Cabinet—concluded that Washington would not interfere with an Israeli action in Lebanon. The two men did not speak about the Lebanon issue alone, but for much of the meeting it hung in the air like a brooding cloud. Systematically, Sharon worked his way toward the subject, until finally he went straight for it.

"We can't hold back anymore," he told Haig. "No self-respecting country would put up with attacks of this kind from terrorists. A response is unavoidable. War could break out any minute, even as we sit here talking!"

At first Haig expressed concern at Sharon's dramatic warning, commenting that he was losing sleep at night, plagued by the thought of an imbroglio whose outcome could not be foreseen. He would therefore expect Israel to exercise appropriate restraint. But Sharon showed little sympathy for the secretary's concern. He replied curtly, "No country has the right to tell another how best to protect its citizens."

Haig nodded his head, even though one might well understand from Sharon's statement that Israel would no longer heed Washington's counsel on this issue. Then the secretary returned to the subject he had discussed with Saguy, namely, that Israel must not act unless the PLO perpetrated a grave violation of the ceasefire agreement; otherwise, any Israeli move would be roundly condemned by international opinion. Still making no mention of the forthcoming action or its date, Sharon kept discussing matters in general terms, but his remarks were studded with innuendos about two objectives that the Israeli Cabinet had not approved for the war: the Syrian garrison in Lebanon and the city of Beirut.

"We do not intend to attack Syria, but it is almost impossible to act without hitting the Syrians," he confided, drawing a clear distinction between Syria and Syrians to imply that he was referring to the garrison stationed in Lebanon. "The question is whether the Syrians will grasp that we are engaged in a limited action, not a move against them; that it is an action designed to rid Lebanon of the PLO's military and political infrastructure." Yet he went on to suggest that far more might result. "Our aim is not to see to the constitution of a free Lebanon or to drive the Syrians out, but these may be by-products of the action." It was his way of conveying that the war might exceed the bounds of an action against the PLO. Sharon's next hint, about his intention to send the IDF as far as Beirut, was far more subtle. "We cannot live under the threat of Palestinian terrorism from Beirut," he complained, raising his voice. "It's a dilemma for us, but we don't see any way of handling it other than going in and cleaning them out."

"How far will you go?" one of the Americans asked Sharon.

"As far as we have to," he replied.

Beyond this one question, Haig and his aides did not press Sharon on operational matters, although one of the secretary's comments caught the Israelis' attention. In speaking of a possible Israeli response to a violation of the ceasefire, Haig said that he would expect the reaction to be swift, and to illustrate his point he used the metaphor of a lobotomy—a quick, clean, neutralizing operation in the event that there was no other choice. Sharon was apparently unsure of what the term meant, for he leaned over toward Ambassador Moshe Arens to check out its connotation. Then his face realigned into a broad smile of satisfaction.

Sharon was clearly pleased with the results of his meeting with Haig: the secretary had confirmed Israel's right, in principle, to respond to acts of terrorism as long as they were indisputable provocations on the part of the PLO. Once again, as in Saguy's visit, Haig had spoken of a "significant violation" of the ceasefire without stopping to define what he meant by that concept. His remarks could be—and were—taken to mean that he expected Israel's response to take the form of an action that, while moderate in scope, would be marked by the éclat that the Israelis had displayed on the battlefield so often in the past. To Sharon's way of thinking, Haig's response added up to American recognition that Israel would not turn the other cheek if sorely provoked and, more important, that such recognition could be construed as tacit agreement to a limited military operation. From Israel's standpoint, this was sufficient. Neither in the Yom Kippur War nor the Six-Day War before it had Israel enjoyed such heartening understanding from Washington.

Sharon was not in the least concerned about verifying whether the position reflected in his talk with Haig should be taken as the official policy of the Reagan administration, whether it tallied with the stand of the secretary of defense and faithfully reflected the views of the president. The Israeli government had grown accustomed to hearing clashing voices from Washington. Alexander Haig was the secretary of state, and that was authority enough for Sharon. He returned to Israel with the tidings that Washington was not averse to an Israeli advance into Lebanon.

It was precisely what Haig's aides had feared. Hardly had the Israelis departed when they began to fret that the secretary had not been discreet enough in discussing a possible war and that his words might be misunderstood, especially since Sharon could mislead Begin by applying a distinctly broad interpretation to what he had heard in the secretary's office. Those of Haig's advisers who had served in Israel were quick to point out that the Israelis had a penchant for reading the studied silence with which the Americans noted their demands and complaints as a sign of consent. Consequently they believed an outspoken approach was now in order; they advised Haig to inform Sharon unequivocally that it would be a mistake to conclude from their talk in Washington that America would condone a war.

The substance of Haig's session with Sharon was also reported to the

White House, where it aroused a considerable measure of concern. It was decided to effect clarification not by a communication to Sharon but by going over his head directly to Prime Minister Begin. According to this plan, Haig would dispatch a letter to Begin elucidating the spirit of his remarks to Sharon at their last meeting.

The letter that Alexander Haig wrote to Menachem Begin is a highly significant document because it reveals the mild tone of the official American admonitions and the indulgent language employed in conveying them at even this late stage in the progress toward war. Despite White House concern, this crucial communication contained no hint of a threat or ultimatum to Israel—a favored technique when Washington wished to head off an undesirable move on Israel's part. The unconventional step of Haig reporting directly to Begin, contrasted with the curiously bland style of the missive itself, encouraged reading between the lines, and the Israelis came away with the impression that the letter represented a cautious diplomatic maneuver—the formal expression of a reservation by which the Americans intended to cover themselves against liability in case Israel got into deeper trouble than it could handle.

Haig's letter is dated May 28, 1982, and extends over five paragraphs. The first refers to the talk held with Sharon at the beginning of the previous week and notes that Haig had already conveyed the essence of Sharon's thinking to the president. The secretary took the opportunity to mention the president's name a second time in those opening lines by confirming that in the interim he had received a letter from Begin brought by Ambassador Arens and had passed it on to Mr. Reagan.

Having established the fact that he was acting on the highest authority, Haig used the second paragraph to address the question of a military action, writing that he wanted there to be "no ambiguity" about the administration's concern over a possible Israeli military action in Lebanon. He told the Israelis that Washington appreciated Israel's self-control but nonetheless wished "to impress upon you that absolute restraint is necessary." Further on he reiterated his fear that any Israeli action, regardless of its scope, might lead to unforeseeable results.

In the next paragraph Haig continued in a similar vein by quoting Sharon's remarks that "no one has the right to tell Israel what decision she must make in order to defend her people," but expressing his faith that nations faced by threats, including the United States and Israel, would carefully weigh the consequences of their actions and "will be able to stand up to challenges of this kind."

The fourth paragraph focused on Washington's latest attempt to mediate the Middle Eastern conflict and noted that Philip Habib would be dispatched to the area in the near future to try to deal with the problem of terrorism against civilians. The American envoy was scheduled to talk with leaders in Beirut and would want to visit Israel before going on to other countries. In the fifth and final paragraph, the secretary added a personal note in saying that he had heard of Mrs. Begin's hospitalization and hoped that she was in better health.

So went the letter that was supposed to assert Washington's views in a way that could not be distorted or denied. In a strictly formal sense, it did represent an attempt to retreat from what had been intimated at the meeting with Sharon a week earlier, but from the standpoint of its practical effect the letter did not change the impression Sharon had brought back from Washington. Indeed, it may well have helped to vindicate his reading of the mood there. After studying Haig's letter, Begin had good reason to accept Sharon's view. He did not bring the communication to the attention of the Cabinet.

The sanguine atmosphere in Jerusalem in May was further reinforced by a report about another meeting with Haig—this one with the Israeli ambassador—at which the need for a security belt in South Lebanon was discussed in a supportive atmosphere. Arens was even able to report his belief that Haig would be prepared to consider the participation of an American force in guarding this buffer zone.

To say that the American government was prepared to wink at an Israeli move in Lebanon is far from accusing the two governments of the brand of collusion that Israel practiced with France on the eve of the Suez Campaign. Yet it is clear that the Israeli government had grounds for believing that Washington had indeed bestowed its tacit approval on a limited military action in Lebanon. It was all part of a cagey dynamic prompted by Sharon in which ears strained to hear what was not said rather than what was; in which style was deemed more meaningful than substance; in which one side spoke in veiled language and allusive gestures that made it possible for the other to understand exactly what it wanted to.

Sharon did not communicate with Haig again until June 27, three weeks after the war broke out and after Haig had been forced to resign. He sent the departing secretary a private and confidential letter. "I vividly recall our last meeting, a few weeks ago in Washington," he wrote.

> Expanding on the serious situation in Lebanon, I insisted on the grave danger the PLO terrorism presented to peace in the area. I also frankly explained to you that we would no longer accept to live under the constant threat of terrorist activity against us in Israel and abroad.
>   In the circumstances which evolved, the Government was left with

no other choice but to instruct the IDF to remove the terrorist artillery threat from our northern border and to restore peace for the Galilee. I have just now returned from one of my visits to our troops in Lebanon. I want to tell you that in the "Peace for Galilee" operation the IDF has brilliantly achieved all its missions, as instructed by the Government. We have succeeded to eliminate the huge PLO terrorist military infrastructure in Southern Lebanon and we are now encircling the bases of terrorism and its headquarters in Beirut itself. In the course of the operation, faced with a Syrian decision to interfere in the air and on the ground, we also succeeded to break the strategic hold of the Syrian Army in Lebanon, which had provided a massive support to PLO terrorism.

On that background, I wish to express to you my deep appreciation for your understanding and your determined stand in the struggle against international terrorism . . . . You are entitled, Mr. Secretary, to be proud of your achievements.

5

The Snare

FOR THE BETTER PART OF A YEAR, Yasser Arafat had been suffering from an acute case of war nerves—and with ample reason. Through his intelligence channels—which were far superior to those of the Israeli ministers —the chairman of the PLO was able to piece together many details of the offensive being planned in Israel. Warning lights seemed to flash all around him as information about Ariel Sharon's broad scheme flowed in from highly disparate quarters. Egyptian intelligence sent him summaries of the IDF's preparations for a major ground operation, certain discreet parties in the United States signaled him obliquely to beware of a trap, and there were countless leaks from the Maronite camp—some deliberate, others the result of simple carelessness. Above all, however, it was the massing of troops on Israel's northern border in December 1981 that put the PLO into an unusually skittish state that sometimes verged on panic.

On a number of occasions Arafat had expressed alarm that the Israelis were going to invade Lebanon "any minute now" and followed up with frantic letters to the capitals of the Arab world begging for help. He could clearly see the war approaching, though it was taking an erratic course, tarrying again and again until the warnings that piled up on his desk melded into the routine paperwork. Arafat had a fairly firm idea of Sharon's thinking early on; it was the exact timing of the operation that eluded him. And when the crunch came, on the day when the warning bells and sirens should have been sounding full blast, Yasser Arafat was far away from his headquarters, where a calm and eerie silence prevailed. Repeated delays and false starts had muddled the sensitive receivers of the PLO's early-warning device. Like the Israelis a decade earlier, Arafat had deluded himself into disaster despite the precise intelligence data right under his nose.

Frazzled nerves were not exactly typical of Arafat. The man was a survivor, schooled in the pain of defeat yet possessed of a resilience that enabled him to spring back time and again to build an ever larger and stronger version of the PLO. It was Arafat, almost single-handedly, who set out to create an underground in the heart of the territories occupied by Israel in 1967. Darting from town to town on a motorbike, he established cells all over the West Bank before he was forced to flee just one step ahead of the Israeli security forces. Then came the 1970 debacle in Jordan, remembered sullenly as "Black September," when Palestinian forces were badly mauled in an attempt to topple King Hussein and subjugate Jordan to their will. After their ouster from both the west and east banks of the Jordan, the PLO slowly began to infiltrate the refugee camps in Lebanon and build a new power base and infrastructure in their midst. More and more, as its other options narrowed, the PLO's attention and efforts centered on Lebanon. In 1977 the organization was expelled from Egypt, and it had always been subject to rigorous controls and limitations in Syria. In effect, then, Lebanon became the last refuge for Arafat and his men.

Paradoxically, the more the PLO prospered through the 1970s, the more vulnerable it became, if only because it had more to lose than ever before from any threat to its new stability in Lebanon. In the decade between Black September and 1980, and especially since the end of the Lebanese civil war, the PLO had essentially created a state-within-a-state in much of South Lebanon (excluding the eastern sector occupied by Syrian troops in 1975–76). Its dominion in the south was recognized in an agreement that followed from a series of battles in which Palestinian irregulars roundly defeated the Lebanese army. Depicting itself as an ally of both Amal, the leftist movement then making inroads among the Shiite Moslems in the countryside, and of the Sunni Moslems chafing under Maronite hegemony in the cities, the PLO had become by 1976 the sole instrument of rule in the western sector of Lebanon stretching from Beirut south to the Israeli border.

In practice these "alliances" proved considerably less benevolent than their original promise suggested. Ruling by means of its military police, the PLO enforced its will with an iron hand. "Revolutionary courts" were established to mete out justice in accordance with the organization's tastes and needs. The municipal governments in Tyre and Sidon, as well as branch offices of the national administration, were taken over by local commanders. Armed Palestinians manned roadblocks to supervise vehicular traffic, collected customs in the ports of Tyre and Sidon, and virtually ran Beirut's international airport. All across the countryside the PLO billeted its men in the homes of intimidated villagers, and in the cities it expropriated whole buildings for use as headquarters, extorting hefty sums from the wealthier residents of Sidon and West Beirut. The flow of fighters into these areas, together with the abundance of funds at their disposal, played havoc with the local economy and sent the cost of building land in Sidon, for example, soaring from $8 to $80 per square meter (which didn't keep the Palestinians from buying up lots at a dizzying pace). But the most infuriating aspect of the PLO takeover was the arbitrary and often brutal behavior of the new rulers. Major Muin, commander of the Fatah battalion in Nabatiye, collected his own tax from every truck that drove into the town's open-air market. His counterpart in Tyre, Azmi Zerayer, murdered a local soccer player for refusing to join the "Palestinian team." And among the lower ranks, rape and robbery reached epidemic proportions.

The inevitable result of this exercise of naked power was a burgeoning antagonism on the part of the same population that had originally welcomed the Palestinian fighters with open arms. Many Shiites chose to express their sentiments by leaving the area, and their emigration northward only strengthened the Palestinian hold over the enclave and made life more difficult for those left behind. Arafat was not blind to the consequences of tyranny, and in his desire to avoid adding both wings of the Moslem camp to his list of enemies, he made great efforts to control his men—sometimes dealing out severe punishments for their excesses. But his attempts were to little avail. Within the area under their control, the local PLO commanders continued to terrorize their opponents into submission.

Perhaps it was only natural that, with the establishment of control over large chunks of territory, the PLO would try to reshape its forces from a collection of ad hoc guerrilla bands into something closer to a standing army. By the late 1970s Arafat was operating exclusively out of Lebanon, though not easily. Given Israel's increasingly effective security measures, he was finding the once-porous Israeli border ever more tightly sealed against terrorist infiltration. If he intended to maintain any kind of credible military threat to Israel, as well as be in a position to defend the territory under his control, Arafat realized he would have to revamp his guerrilla-warfare strategy and begin building a more established military machine. By 1981 he had put together three infantry brigades—Karameh, Yarmuk, and Kastel—several artillery and support units, the workshops necessary to service them, and a fledgling tank battalion. This metamorphosis from a guerrilla movement to a semiregular army with permanent bases and all the rest of a logistic infrastructure (along with its inevitable ponderousness and bureaucratic delays) meant that his irregulars had to undergo a radical psychological shift as well. But so alluring was the vision of solid military power that the PLO even began to found the nucleus of a navy at the Syrian port of Latakia and a combat air wing in Algeria.

Yet paradoxically, while Arafat threw himself into building a standing force in Lebanon, he was curiously ambivalent about using it. For public consumption he gamely portrayed the "Two-Week War" of July 1981 as an unqualified victory for the PLO—or at least a major achievement— though he was actually somewhat appalled at having been drawn into such a direct confrontation with Israeli planes and artillery. After the artillery duel broke out he waited three whole days before allowing the Fatah battalions to join in the shelling—which was being sustained solely by the smaller and more radical elements of the PLO—and then desperately hoped for a quick truce. By the time the ceasefire was hammered out, the PLO had only two cannons still in operation; the rest of its artillery had either been hit or pulled back out of range of Israeli ground fire.

After that sobering episode Arafat was determined to move more deliberately in his preparations for the inevitable "next round," so as to deprive the Israelis of even the flimsiest excuse to strike at his forces. His strategy was to maintain the ceasefire to the letter while acquiring long-range artillery for a more durable threat to Galilean settlements if Israel should launch an offensive. Obviously, he failed to appreciate how this slippery course would deliver him right into the hands of his enemies on both flanks: first by providing Sharon with the evidence (the heavy artillery) to convince Begin—and Israeli public opinion in general—that the PLO posed a grave military threat to Israel's security; second by giving Syria and its proxies in the PLO an opening (Arafat's observation of the ceasefire) to lambast him as too weak and diffident to stand up to Israel.

For all that, Arafat had no illusions about the durability of the ceasefire on Israel's side. As early as August 1981, a mere two weeks after the truce went into effect and while both sides were still licking their wounds, he convened the PLO's Supreme Military Council in a emergency session and told his comrades, "We must prepare for another war." Not only did he plan to beef up the artillery battalions, he also sent his purchasing agents out in search of more mobile artillery that could fire off its rounds and dash away before the Israelis could zero in on its position. Since the middle of 1980, Fatah's standing orders were that, in the event of an assault on PLO positions, artillery would be activated immediately "with the aim of causing maximum casualties" in the Israeli rear. The units in South Lebanon were assigned defined targets and received exact range cards. Each of the major settlements in northern Israel, particularly the large towns of Kiryat Shmonah, Safed, and Nahariya, was covered by a force appropriate to its size and importance. Thus the men of the Grad missile company—dubbed the "Clouds of Hell"—were slated to fire twenty rounds at Safed; the Katyusha unit was responsible for loosing its rockets on Nahariya; and the 1st Artillery Battalion of Fatah was to target the agricultural settlements in the Huleh Valley and the mountains to the west. To prevent the possibility of again blundering prematurely into a clash, the firing orders were to be given in the form of coded signals that changed every few weeks.

Since the most Yasser Arafat could hope to wage against the IDF, even with his new "standing army," was a sporadic war of hit-and-run, the ten-page mimeographed leaflet distributed among his field units as a general briefing on artillery fire focused on the same considerations that had always directed the PLO's actions as a terrorist organization. "The strikes should be directed against the enemy's weak spot: its dwindling population. Thus operations should be undertaken with an eye to choking off all immigration to Israel. This objective can be achieved by hitting the absorption centers housing new immigrants . . . by sabotaging water and electricity lines, by using especially fearsome weapons, and by setting fires wherever possible."

Whatever the soundness of that strategy, there remained the problem of obtaining heavy arms—particularly as the most likely address for such requests was the Soviet Union, and the Russians were less than munificently inclined toward the PLO. In closed meetings with his staff, Arafat liked to tell an anecdote about one of his visits to Moscow to illustrate how the Soviets had a way of tendering camaraderie and precious little else. From the airport he was whisked off to a luxurious villa in the Lenin Hills and treated to a virtual banquet by Vasily Kudriasev, chairman of the Soviet Peace Council. At one point when the conversation flagged, Kudriasev resorted to small talk to pick up the slack.

"How's the weather in Beirut?" he asked quite innocently.

"Hot," Arafat replied, lunging at the opportunity to press his real point home. "The political climate even more so."

"Don't worry, my friend, when the Palestinian state comes into being—very soon now—we'll send you a gift of a few icebergs to cool things down." Kudriasev said this with a superfluous wink, Arafat knowing that the allusion was to the piles of arms the Soviets had promised to provide only when the Palestinians had established themselves in their own national framework.

"You'd better send us at least the tip of an iceberg now," Arafat riposted, "because if the present situation continues, you won't be able to send us any gift at all. There won't be any address to send it to!"

Yet the best the Soviets would offer now was advice: "Take shelter under the wing of the Syrian garrison in Lebanon." Patiently, Arafat tried to show why this was not very constructive counsel: the Syrian forces in Lebanon were situated to the rear of the PLO positions and, besides, the Israelis would have no problem dealing the Syrians a stunning blow if only because they were deployed for policing operations, not for combat. But his logic and entreaties did no good. Andrei Gromyko and Boris Ponomarev (the party's equivalent of foreign minister) went on to add insult to penury by chiding Arafat for the subtle feelers he had sent out toward Washington, and even for his highly publicized meeting with Austrian Chancellor Bruno Kreisky.

"The truth is, the Soviets have refused to commit themselves to new arms shipments," Arafat reported to his comrades upon his return to Beirut.

Some of the PLO command balked at taking the rebuff passively. "We must respond to that kind of evasion by turning to Communist China!" cried Farouk Kadoumi, head of the PLO's Political Department and until then an outspoken advocate of cultivating the Russians.

"Why don't we just come out and denounce them for refusing to help?" said Abu Zohari, another of Arafat's associates peeved by the short shrift the chairman had received in Moscow.

Still, the situation was not entirely bleak. After the July 1981 artillery duels, a solution was found by arranging for arms deals in Eastern Europe and North Korea. Arafat's deputy, Halil el-Wazir (Abu Jihad), signed contracts for artillery and light arms with East Germany, Bulgaria, and Czechoslovakia; North Korea agreed to supply Katyushas with thirty launching tubes or barrels; and Hungary got the go-ahead to transfer a few dozen antiquated T-34 tanks to the PLO.

Before long those tanks turned up in Kafr Yanta, in the Bekaa Valley, as part of the only large-scale exercise to be conducted by the PLO "regular" forces. It was their first brigade-level maneuvers, featuring four battalions of Fatah's Karameh Brigade, and they practiced the conquest of an Israeli settlement on a mock-up constructed specially for the occasion and christened "Begingrad." The exercise included a softening-up barrage from 130-mm guns and a mechanized breakthrough into the objective. Needless to say, the IDF followed the exercise closely and took it as a sign that the PLO was structuring its units for offensive operations. Instead of trying to smuggle small terrorist squads over the border, the strategy would change to attacks by regular units. There might seem to be more bravado than menace in this new message, yet the Israeli officers were surprised (if not exactly alarmed) to discover that the archaic T-34s were still capable of turning their turrets and firing, even if they could barely move on their treads.

For all its obvious limitations, the PLO was buoyed by the "Begingrad" exercise—to the point where it secretly began to seek out night-vision and other sophisticated equipment in the West. Ahmed Jebril's radical Popular Front-General Command instituted negotiations with arms manufacturers in Switzerland, while other envoys reached as far as Brazil in their search for heavy artillery with a range of over forty kilometers. Meanwhile, in the PLO's own workshops, four-barreled antiaircraft cannons were fitted on small trucks, and Unimog trucks were transformed into light armored vehicles. In less than a year, the PLO more than tripled its artillery capacity, from eighty cannons and rocket launchers in July 1981 to 250 in June 1982. They were divided among seven newly formed artillery battalions, four within Fatah, two in Naif Hawatmeh's Democratic Front for the Liberation of Palestine, and the last in George Habash's Popular Front for the Liberation of Palestine. For the time being, this climaxed the process of weaning the PLO's forces away from the traditional pattern of guerrilla warfare and shaping them into an incipient army. Although the artillery was still scattered and concealed in the field and the tanks huddled in small groups, the stress in thinking had clearly switched to building up firepower at the expense of raising the quality of the infantry.

The irony was that this transition made it easier for both the IDF and the Phalange to strike at the more visibly fixed Palestinian forces. PLO troops in the field howled that Arafat was making a bad mistake, but he stuck by the development of regular brigades—his real motive being not so much to take on the IDF in serious combat as to impose order in the ranks during the ceasefire and prepare for battle with the far less redoubtable Christian forces. His senior commanders, including Abu Jihad and the PLO's chief of staff, Saad Sa'il (Abu Walid), understood that Arafat's purpose was not to ready the PLO for a confrontation with the Israelis but precisely to avoid it.

Factionalism might be tolerable in a political movement, but it was anathema to an assortment of military units aspiring to function as an army. It was the military leader of one of the PLO's smaller factions, Mamdouch Nofal of the Democratic Front, who was the first to suggest the new approach to coordination. Nofal had a reputation as a daring officer and had in fact planned some of the more audacious terrorist attacks on targets in Israel. Now he was prepared to surrender a good measure of his organization's independence for the sake of military expedience. "It is out of the question," he wrote in a memorandum to Arafat, "to have one organization's artillery initiate shelling without the neighboring antiaircraft position—which belongs to another organization—being given prior notice. It is deplorable that when a base faces an Israeli helicopter attack, there is no communications equipment available so that reinforcements can be called in from another organization whose fighters are stationed nearby.''

In short, Nofal proposed that the PLO's constituent factions bury the hatchet over ideological disputes so that the overall organization could field its forces effectively. The PLO would require thoroughgoing operational improvements, such as creating a unified communications network, dividing up territory into firing sectors, and deploying units on the basis of need rather than political rivalries. But most of all, the new strategy demanded the concentration of command in a single body, meaning that the men in the field would have to answer to a regional command rather than the political bureaus of the competing factions to which they had pledged their loyalty.

A second feature of the Nofal plan was an attempt to ensure greater flexibility and mobility for the battalions stationed in the south by upgrading the militias operating in the refugee camps of Tyre, Sidon, Nabatiye, and Beirut. His point was that, in an emergency, the inhabitants of the camps should be able to defend themselves so the standing units would be free to man the front line. He therefore recommended providing the militias with antiaircraft guns and training them to hold a defensive line.

Finally, Nofal foresaw how great a burden the civilian population would be during any future battle. The experience of July 1981 had taught him that the public is quickly panicked and that it takes considerable resourcefulness to overcome the traffic jams created by fleeing civilians and to avert shortages of food and fuel. Shelters and adequate stores of basic necessities were therefore a primary requisite of any successful attempt at self-defense.

Arafat readily adopted these three intelligent recommendations and gave priority to the acquisition of communications equipment (including instruments produced by the Israeli company Tadiran) and to the creation of a network of emergency stores in tunnels carved out of hillsides. Most striking of all, however, was the announcement of a mandatory mobilization of Palestinian males from sixteen to thirty-nine. About a week before the war broke out, another order was issued to mobilize boys aged twelve and up whose fathers were serving in Fatah units. The youngsters were promised a salary of 400 Lebanese pounds ($80) a month and were to be attached to the organization's regular battalions, each child serving in his father's company.

These drastic measures were a last-ditch attempt to cope with the severe shortage of military personnel. At one of the deliberations of the Supreme Military Council, Arafat fretted about the fact that ''we can call upon only

3,000 fighters, and we can't move the militias from place to place.'' One solution was to mobilize the Palestinians living in Syria, but Assad wouldn't hear of it. Meanwhile, the mobilization campaign in Lebanon was proving to be an arrant failure. Not only was revolutionary fervor scarce among the younger generation of Palestinians raised in Lebanon, but much of the glory and romance of the underground's early years had faded. The declining ranks of Fatah and the smaller factions, their drawing power considerably weakened, became so sharp a matter of concern that even officials in the PLO's civilian offices were ordered to undergo military training (which included such exotic preparations for facing hardship in the field as dissecting rabbits and dining on snake meat). Arafat had to admit that, given the circumstances, the PLO was nearing the limit of its capacity to grow. When the fourteen-year-old son of Shafiq el-Hut, one of the organization's veteran officials in Beirut, refused to take up arms, his shamed and angry father asked Arafat to have a talk with the boy. "Let him be," Arafat answered with an audible sigh. "He's not the only one. And besides," he added, "we may be needing diplomats, too."

The difficulties in recruiting only seemed to highlight the need for military coordination. Following the new scheme, this was effected by the Supreme Military Council in Beirut and joint area commands, including special artillery commands. Heading them all were Fatah officers loyal to Arafat who were not in the least queasy about imposing their authority by force, if necessary. In a number of instances Fatah commanders entered positions being held by members of George Habash's Popular Front and Ahmed Jebril's Popular Front-General Command and confiscated shells, threatening to shoot any men who refused to yield them. On at least one occasion a short battle broke out, with resultant casualties.

In light of the strains within and the pressures from without, the question of whether or not Yasser Arafat could keep a firm hold on the entire enterprise became more and more pertinent. In many ways the man is an enigma. The embodiment of the PLO and archterrorist to millions of newspaper readers and television viewers around the world, the diminutive, middle-aged Arafat is far from being the physical stereotype of a military hero, or even a revolutionary leader, notwithstanding his attempt to effect the latter role in the Che Guevara mold. Yet he possesses great charisma in the eyes of the PLO rank and file. Known for taking a paternalistic attitude toward his men, including his closest associates, he is referred to fondly as "the Old Man" and is still remembered kindly for his personal courage in laying the foundations for an underground in the occupied territories during the late 1960s. Over the years a thick shell of aides and bodyguards distanced Arafat from regular, firsthand contact with his fighters, and his reputation among them suffered accordingly. Yet his leadership was never seriously challenged until after the 1982 debacle in South Lebanon, when Col. Abu Moussa—a one-time regional commander of that sector—orchestrated a Syrian-backed rebellion in Fatah. Until then Arafat's control of the PLO never seemed to slip, undoubtedly because Abu Jihad held the reins for him—held them short and in an unfailingly tight grip.

As Arafat's deputy—and reputedly his éminence grise—Abu Jihad was (and remains) the real strongman of the PLO, and another matter entirely: steely, exacting, unflappable. His reputation comes replete with an apocryphal and chilling footnote: when in 1966 Syrian soldiers pushed his toddler son off a balcony to his death while conducting a search in his Damascus apartment, Abu Jihad remained frozen, not so much as uttering a gasp. As the equivalent of the PLO's minister of defense, he personally briefed the terror squads that perpetrated some of the organization's most shocking operations, such as the attack on Israeli athletes at the 1972 Munich Olympics. Like Arafat he was popular among the men in the field, but the regard for him was tempered with a healthy sense of fear.

While Abu Jihad kept a close watch on the troops to maintain discipline —and thereby the ceasefire with Israel—the head of the PLO's Unified Security Apparatus, Salah Halaf (Abu Iyyad), was providing a steady stream of intelligence auguring that the hard-won restraint would probably be in vain. Short, thickset, and balding, Abu Iyyad was generally considered the enfant terrible of the PLO top leadership, a man of original views that tended to be both radical and vague. He was the PLO's intelligence czar, responsible for coordinating all its networks, yet was notorious for being an incorrigible chatterbox and publicity hound—in addition to having a highly ambivalent relationship with Arafat.

It was Abu Iyyad's men who first learned of Sharon's secret visit to Beirut and obtained a summary of the understanding he had reached with the Phalangists. Another particularly intriguing piece of information that Abu Iyyad passed on to Arafat was the plan for a joint IDF-Phalangist action in the area of Damour, on the coast south of Beirut. Once a thriving Maronite center, Damour had fallen to the Palestinians during the civil war and was the site of one of the many tit-for-tat massacres of that savage conflict. Now the PLO maintained a training base, radar installations, and ammunition dumps in the deserted Christian town, and as an extra precaution Arafat reinforced the garrison with an armored unit of the Palestine Liberation Army.

To Abu Iyyad's credit it must be said that as early as February 1982 he tended to be skeptical of Bashir Gemayel's intention to honor his promise to the Israelis and send his men into action in Beirut. "Bashir can field only 3,000 men," he reasoned, "and I believe the balance of forces will deter him from taking any independent action. At best, his men will follow in the wake of the Israelis." Still, as an experienced intelligence man, he did not discount the possibility that, elated by the approach of Israeli troops, Bashir might misjudge his own weakness and impulsively take to the field. Since it was imperative to know how the Phalangist leaders were likely to act, whether the PLO should expect a knife in the back from the Maronites while it was busy staving off the Israelis, Abu Iyyad decided to take a bold step and institute direct contacts with the Phalange.

"Are you meeting with the Israelis too?" he came right out one day and asked Amin Gemayel, with whom he was associated in various business ventures.

"Absolutely not!" Amin huffed, as if mortified by the very idea that he was capable of such underhanded behavior.

Stymied on that front, Abu Iyyad tried to open a direct channel to Bashir, for he believed that by addressing the younger Gemayel's sharpened political instincts he could dampen his enthusiasm for cooperation with Israel and thereby thwart Sharon's plan to mount an attack. His bait was a major strategic concession designed to lure Bashir away from Israel, and even if that failed Abu Iyyad hoped that the negotiations would at least buy the PLO more time. His proposition to thin out the armed presence along the front line between the Christian and Moslem camps in Beirut was coupled with a grab bag of other gestures to the Maronites. Its real point was to make Bashir believe that a thaw in his relations with the PLO would boost his chances of clinching the presidency in the upcoming elections.

Beginning in February, Bashir Gemayel met in absolute secrecy with Atalla Atalla (Abu Zaim), head of the PLO's military intelligence, on three occasions, each at night in Gemayel's home in the posh Ashrafiya quarter of East Beirut. At the first meeting, almost as soon as they settled into armchairs, Bashir seized the opportunity to flaunt his position of strength by opening on a threatening note.

"You are undoubtedly acquainted with the scenario of the infant from Acre," he lectured the Palestinian condescendingly, "the one in which an Israeli baby is killed by a bomb in Acre and Begin, after paying a condolence call on the parents, orders Sharon to invade Lebanon the next day. This is a highly realistic prospect, and you know it as well as I do."

"Yes, I know we are up against three terrorists," Abu Zaim said, referring to Begin, Sharon, and Eitan, and fully intending the irony. "You can't know what they're capable of doing next."

"We want to return to Damour and all the other towns we left," Bashir said, dispensing with further preliminaries. "I don't have to tell you that Israel is planning an invasion; their leaders announce it on television at every opportunity. Let us work toward an agreement that will prevent it and forestall a holocaust!"

Abu Zaim understood the warning and its import, but he seemed to hunch down in his chair, wrapped in silence. Bashir had set a very high price on salvation. Worse yet, surrendering Damour to the Phalange would only make it easier for them to link up with the Israeli army south of Beirut if Bashir should betray the PLO as easily as he seemed prepared to two-time the Israelis. Since his superiors already had information about Damour's role in a mooted joint military venture, Abu Zaim became all the more suspicious at mention of the place.

Bashir continued: "Let's assume that an Israeli officer reaches Damour and says to the town's refugees, 'See here, we've liberated your homes. Come on back to the town.' What should I do in a case like that? How do you expect me to react?"

"We're holding talks with the French and building bridges to the Americans," Abu Zaim replied somewhat feebly. "I hope that within no more than three years we'll be able to establish an independent state in Palestine."

But Bashir was not willing to wait three years or three weeks. Damour now—or no deal.

Abu Zaim asked for time to pass the message on to his principals, but when the PLO leadership convened to hear his report it was clear that Arafat had already made up his mind, for he opened the proceedings with a volley of sarcasm. "Let's hear what wondrous proposals Bashir is sending us!" The chairman had a blind spot where the younger Gemayel was concerned, having never regarded him as a serious adversary. Now, however, Arafat feared that Gemayel was setting a crude trap for him. If the Palestinians entered into negotiations with him, not only would he probably sell them out in the end, the talks themselves would make a mockery of the ban that Arafat had tried to impose on any traffic with the Phalange. Moreover, Bashir would earn implicit Palestinian recognition for his candidacy without making a single concession in return. When Abu Zaim tried to persuade the forum to give the proposal a fair hearing, Arafat intervened. "Do us a favor, will you?" he jeered. "Drop the subject." Reconciliation was a pipe dream. If he had harbored any hope of averting the Israeli invasion, Yasser Arafat had just muffed it.

The deep-seated antagonism between the PLO and the Phalange is perhaps best understood in terms of the broader political implications of the

Palestinian presence in Lebanon. In proclaiming that the PLO would never leave Lebanon except to return to Palestine, Arafat had essentially decided to subordinate the Lebanese crisis to the Palestinian problem, making a Palestinian state the sine qua non of a rehabilitated Lebanese one. The Maronites were naturally infuriated by this approach, for it required them to pick up the tab for the Palestinian struggle—and its mistakes. Perhaps if Arafat had undertaken a sincere political initiative to solve the Palestinian-Israeli dispute, leading figures in the Maronite camp might have turned sympathetic. But as it was, Bashir and his associates had no reason to believe that the PLO intended to make any change in policy or basic principles. In private conversations Arafat led foreign visitors to understand that he would be prepared to recognize Israel in return for the establishment of a Palestinian state in the West Bank and Gaza, but he scrupulously avoided any step that would reflect a softening in the PLO's position on initiating a dialogue—at least with the United States, if not yet with Israel. The Reagan administration respected him for keeping the ceasefire, viewing the PLO's self-control as a sign of ''maturity.'' At one point Arafat signaled Special Ambassador Philip Habib that he would be prepared, under certain conditions, to consider extending the ceasefire to other fronts. But he was not prepared to state publicly what he intimated behind closed doors. And as long as he held back on announcing his agreement to UN Resolution 242—which implied recognition of Israel—Habib had strict orders not to enter into any direct contact with Arafat or his aides.

Despite the collapse of the talks with Gemayel, Abu Iyyad still hoped to prevent or delay the Israeli invasion, and with the help of Farouk Kadoumi he worked out an alternative strategy: rather than surrender territory to the Phalange in the Beirut area, he wanted to reach a new understanding with the Americans about pulling back from territory in the south. The two men pressed Arafat to offer Habib and his assistant, Morris Draper, terms for broadening the security belt occupied by the United Nations Interim Force in Lebanon and raising the profile of the Lebanese army there. Kadoumi even offered to relinquish the Beaufort, a ruined Crusader castle from which the PLO had a commanding view of Upper Galilee. The approach was compatible with Arafat's view that the only effective answer to the Israeli threat was a formula bolstering the ceasefire and backed by American guarantees. As Abu Iyyad reasoned, an expanded accord on the ceasefire would tie Sharon's hands. But Kadoumi came up empty-handed. The clarifications progressed at a snail's pace, with the Americans in particular dragging their feet, while Israel categorically refused to give an inch on Major Haddad's status in the south. Equally problematic was Arafat's inability to part with the so-called Iron Triangle, two sectors south of the Litani River held by Fatah brigades. In the end, the proposal was simply dropped, and instead of evacuating the Beaufort castle, the PLO increased its importance in their defense scheme by allowing the Syrians to station artillery spotters there.

If the ceasefire was therefore doomed, and the PLO knew it, it did not necessarily follow that all was lost: if only the PLO's military arm could stretch the fighting out long enough, the Syrians would be forced to join in, and any serious confrontation between Syrian and Israeli forces on Lebanese soil would surely prompt the major powers to intervene and halt the Israeli offensive before the battle had been decided. On this point— Syrian involvement in the fighting—the two poles in Lebanon came together. Though they could agree on little else, Yasser Arafat and Bashir Gemayel were both interested in seeing a head-on clash between Israeli and Syrian troops—albeit for diametrically opposite reasons. It was one of the chief ironies of the war that, despite the ongoing quarrel between the Maronites and Palestinians, their interests converged on this one objective: the planned Israeli action should somehow be translated into a full-scale war against Syria.

After Arafat had sounded his strident false alarm in February, the level of concern within the PLO began to decline somewhat. The Americans kept passing on the soothing advice that as long as Arafat kept the ceasefire he could keep the peace. On one occasion, following Yehoshua Saguy's mission to Washington, Khaled el-Hassan, one of Arafat's close associates, received a private message that the danger of an attack from the south had subsided. But on April 21, after an Israeli soldier was killed by an antivehicle mine in the Haddad enclave, Israel broke the ceasefire to bomb targets in South Lebanon and the American advice was quickly reclassified as wishful thinking. At first Arafat managed to keep his people from responding to the attack, but on May 9, in the wake of another Israeli air raid, PLO forces loosed eight volleys of artillery fire at settlements in the Galilee. These were warning rounds, following Arafat's orders. The fire was deliberately off the mark in an attempt to deliver his message forcefully, though it nevertheless escalated the tension.

Now Arafat was plunged into a two-front struggle, for although the Israelis got the message, members of the smaller, more radical groups within the PLO were harder to get through to. While the high command strained desperately to maintain the ceasefire, the radicals were bent on undermining it. Arafat was forced to hold a thorough clarification of the issue in the Supreme Military Council, resulting in a minor victory for the radicals and an escalation at least in PLO rhetoric. Arafat received a commitment from Ahmed Jebril and the other radical leaders not to initiate firing on their own, but it came at the price of an explicit promise to allow retaliatory shelling in the future. The understanding reached between Arafat and his more restive comrades posited, on the one hand, an automatic response to any Israeli artillery force in the sector from which it emanated; on the other hand there would be no response to an aerial bombardment without the express approval of the highest echelon.

This change in ground rules inspired some further imaginative thinking. The PLO's chief financial wizard, Mahmoud Abbas (Abu Mazen), a man who also dabbled in contacts with the Israeli left, approached Arafat with the suggestion that retaliatory fire be concentrated on the coastal town of Nahariya. His reasoning was that Nahariya was populated mostly by Israelis of Western origin (Ashkenazi Jews), whose plight would more likely impress the Israeli government than had the panicked flight of Jews of largely Middle Eastern and North African origin from Kiryat Shmonah the previous summer. However simplistic these new, more aggressive strategies of response, their effect was to turn what had at first appeared to be an equitable deal between the dissident parties in the PLO into a generally disadvantageous position, for once the Israelis discovered that an appropriate provocation would elicit a shelling of the Galilee, they could dictate the plays that would lead to war.

Whether or not Arafat thoroughly appreciated the bind he had maneuvered himself into, he probably understood the inevitability of an Israeli invasion as soon as Israel broke the ceasefire on April 21, for he issued directives to raise the level of alert and especially to achieve coordination with the Syrian forces in the Bekaa Valley. Based on his intelligence, he assumed that the Israelis would press as far north as the Zaharani River, between Tyre and Sidon, and probably bomb Palestinian positions in Beirut and even Tripoli, but that they would not extend their ground thrust to Beirut proper—even if the Phalangist forces went into action there. On the other hand, he warned the Syrians that Israel's offensive strategy could well include an assault on their forces in the Bekaa Valley, and in May a memorandum of defensive coordination was drawn up between the PLO and Damascus. Col. Abu Moussa, formerly the Fatah regional commander in the south—who had been transferred to a staff job in the rear after sustaining an injury—was dispatched to Damascus to warn of the approaching attack and to request aid. Meanwhile, two of the three Fatah brigades deployed in the south, Karameh and Yarmuk, pulled back and huddled up against the "security belt" provided by the Syrian 1st Division in the Bekaa Valley. Arafat canceled leaves and made the necessary arrangements for a swift mobilization of the camp militias. He also ordered the evacuation of all PLO tanks from the south. They may not have been worth much in real combat, but it would be a pity to lose them.

There was always the possibility—as a French intelligence assessment leaked from the Lebanese Foreign Ministry suggested—that Israel would eschew a ground operation, to avoid casualties among its own men, and throw the full weight of its air force against the PLO headquarters and bases in Lebanon. To deal with the prospect that such bombardments would damage roads and bridges and disrupt the movement of armed personnel, the PLO command instituted a number of changes in logistics and deployment. Mobil ZSV antiaircraft guns were purchased from the Communist bloc in bulk. The contents of centralized ammunition stores were divided among smaller dumps in the vicinity of the presumed areas of combat, and the commands throughout the south received infusions of weapons, equipment, and specialists ranging from Strela (SAM-7) surface-to-air missiles to spare parts for vehicles and medical teams. The main fortification effort centered on the Beaufort ridge and along the axes leading up to Nabatiye in the central sector. Fatah in particular devoted itself to building a new system of fortifications based on a chain of platoon-size, reinforced-concrete dugouts supplemented by forward observation posts. The fighters not assigned to these newly built outposts took up positions in isolated structures on the outskirts of towns and villages rather than in the hearts of these populated areas. Yet this new consideration for the safety of noncombatants had its limits: when areas were mined, for example, they were not fenced off or even marked for the benefit of the civilian population, and "silent sentry" illumination mines activated by trip wires were scattered all over the main roads.

On April 28 the PLO's defensive strategy was finally laid down in what may well have been the decisive discussion on the subject in the Supreme Military Council. The meeting opened on a sullen note as Arafat gave vent to some of his resentments. "I want you to know that we are up against America even before we begin to face Israel," he said bitterly, for he had ample evidence that the United States knew and approved of the planned Israeli action. "What's more, we'll have to go it alone this time; everyone will abandon us," referring to the Shiites and the Druse, allies during the civil war, and perhaps the Syrians too—given half a chance. Still, the PLO's basic premise was that they would not have that chance. The IDF would most probably strike at the Syrians along with the Palestinian centers in South Lebanon. But all of Arafat's intelligence still showed that the Israelis would draw to a halt on the outskirts of Beirut. He anticipated a sharp blow, but he never imagined that Sharon was aiming to drive the

PLO out of Lebanon altogether. The time had passed, he believed, when Israel would seriously consider trying to eradicate the PLO.

Consequently, the Supreme Military Council issued Operational Order 1 putting its forces on notice to be prepared for an Israeli assault that would reach up to the "outskirts of Beirut and include marine and para-troop landings, especially at Damour." At the very least, the IDF was expected to halt at the Zaharani River and overwhelm the Tyre pocket. Yet the author of the order seemed especially troubled by the possibility of marine landings farther in the rear, for he wrote: "Sharon is a man of adventurous leanings, and he has a tendency to take risks behind the lines." By the same token, the 420th Battalion, with its sixty T-54 and T-55 tanks brought from Syria, was ordered to redeploy along the section of coast between Beirut and the Awali River, north of Sidon, and to prac-tice repulsing marine landings. (The heavy emphasis placed on this point shows once again that the PLO had far more accurate information about Sharon's military plan than did the Israeli Cabinet, Beirut notwithstand-ing.)

The front line was to be held by the units that had illegally but thoroughly established themselves in the zone occupied by UNIFIL. (The presence of PLO fighters in this zone had inspired a good deal of resentment in Israel and indeed led to some very curious anomalies. Within the sector held by the Norwegian battalion in the east, for example, the local UN commander and an officer of the Karameh Brigade signed a detailed agree-ment setting down rules for the activities of the armed Palestinians despite the fact that they were not supposed to be there in the first place. One of its clauses even stated that the Palestinians were allowed to confiscate film from any UNIFIL soldier who photographed them, though they were ob-ligated to return the camera itself.) The PLO officers in this southernmost belt received clear instructions on how to proceed once the war broke out —that is, how far to withdraw, if necessary. By May 15, some twenty days before the outbreak of fighting, preparations were in high gear. Haj Ismail, commander of the Kastel Brigade, convened an emergency meeting to inform his officers of the latest intelligence on the expected Israeli moves. "We know from the Jordanians that the Americans have given Israel the green light to mount a short, limited operation," he reported (evidently the results of the Sharon-Haig meeting had found their way to the wrong address). On the spot he put standard high-alert measures into effect: all communications channels and military codes were to be changed, and a war room for intelligence (common to all the organizations) was quickly improvised. In Beirut, meanwhile, work continued on fortifying positions as mines were laid around the city and sectors of responsibility were assigned to various units. PLO lookouts reported that the Phalangists were also digging trenches.

At about the same time, Yasser Arafat sent Menachem Begin a message through the good offices of Brian Urquhart, assistant under-secretary-general of the United Nations, who had come to the area to discuss the reinforcement of UNIFIL as a way of halting a deterioration in the situation. "I have learned more from you as a resistance leader than from anyone else about how to combine politics and military tactics," the message went. "You of all people must understand that it is not necessary to face me only on the battlefield. Do not send a military force against me. Do not try to break me in Lebanon. You will not succeed." A frozen-faced Begin heard Urquhart out and was not impressed; at least he did not respond. This is the only known direct appeal from Arafat to Begin.

As the PLO's units moved into place and waited for history to take them where it would, internal assessments of the Palestinians' chances in a showdown with Israel were not very optimistic. Abu Walid, the chief of staff and only member of the senior echelon with advanced military training, was painfully aware of the gaping holes in his defensive line and knew that if and when the IDF got the order to advance, his forces would be routed with ease. So he hedged that his men should strive to hold back the Israelis but not at the cost of sacrificing units. In the event of a frontal clash, it would be preferable to withdraw—even to take flight—than to sacrifice men in a futile attempt to hold the line. Mamdouch Nofal, whose thinking had been behind the improvements in coordination, estimated that the advanced equipment in the PLO's hands would make it possible to carry on the fighting for longer than ever before. "We have the ability to slow down the enemy's advance," he ventured, "and prevent him from establishing a line." But he also warned that "we must not delude ourselves into thinking that we can stop the enemy in his tracks." He therefore recommended organizing terror squads to infiltrate the occupied territories and strike at the Israelis in the rear while they were advancing to the north; perhaps this would divert some of their forces from the main thrust, or at least make their march into Lebanon more costly.

The one man who had genuine hopes of turning the Israeli venture into another victory of sorts for his scraggly army was Yasser Arafat. Two weeks before the fighting began, he turned up in person in the south. Climbing up to the heights of the Beaufort, which afforded a breathtaking view of the Litani Valley and Upper Galilee, he gathered the castle's fifteen defenders in a circle on the stone floor and, as they shared a meager meal of battle rations, exhorted them to hold out for "just thirty-six hours. By then we'll have a ceasefire." Even the most innocent of them stared at him in disbelief. Without substantial reinforcements, which did not appear to be forthcoming, they wouldn't stand a chance against an onslaught by Israeli troops.

"Impossible!" the sector commander finally protested. "They'll cut us off and swamp us."

But Arafat kept trying to bolster their resolve. He truly believed that these fifteen men could hold back an Israeli drive long enough for the powers to impose a ceasefire, or for the Syrians to come to their aid. That, after all, was what the restructuring of the PLO's armed forces was all about.

Arafat's sanguine scenario lacked one crucial element: the date. And on this vital point the PLO was stricken with incredible blindness. For months on end Arafat and his comrades had been preparing for an attack. They knew the details of the Israeli operation and had guessed its scope. But now, on the threshold of H-hour, their senses misled them all. Information continued to pour in from all the tried and proven sources, yet on June 3, when Arafat met with the Soviet ambassador to Lebanon, Alexander Soldatov, there was no worry in his voice. Even after hearing that day about the attempt on the life of the Israeli ambassador in London, Arafat still did not see what was practically upon him. He published a firm denial of the PLO's responsibility for the deed, and the next morning, June 4, two days prior to the Israeli attack, boarded a plane for Saudi Arabia. While Israel's military machine was moving into gear, Yasser Arafat was wholly immersed in an attempt to mediate an end to the war between Iran and Iraq!

6

The Fuse

LATE THURSDAY NIGHT, JUNE 3, 1982, word came to Jerusalem that Ambassador Shlomo Argov had been attacked in London. At precisely 9:30 the next morning, Menachem Begin entered the Cabinet's conference room and hobbled slowly toward the table, his eyes glued to the floor, his expression and movements conveying a mood of suppressed anger. As he approached the conference table the murmur of conversation fell silent. All the other participants in the hastily called meeting—members of the Cabinet, senior army officers, intelligence men from the Mossad and the General Security Services, and advisers on the war against terrorism— were seated and waiting. Conspicuous by his absence was Defense Minister Ariel Sharon, then on a secret visit to Rumania. But although his chair was empty, Sharon's spirit permeated the room. For months he had planned, labored, and maneuvered to bring the Cabinet to just such a moment. By now the metaphorical bullet lay waiting in the chamber and the safety catch was off in readiness to fire the first shot in the Lebanese war; Menachem Begin did not need Ariel Sharon to pull the trigger.

Begin opened the meeting without any preliminaries, as if the matter at hand had already been discussed and decided elsewhere. "We will not stand for them attacking an Israeli ambassador! An assault on an ambassador is tantamount to an attack on the State of Israel, and we will respond to it!" The prime minister's declaration had effectively become a Cabinet decision as soon as it was articulated. For the fact of the matter was that, by the time the Cabinet convened, the decision not only to react but how to react was a foregone conclusion. Begin had called his chief of staff immediately after the message from London and reached an understanding with Eitan that the air force would be sent into action against the PLO in

Lebanon. Now he made no effort to conceal that he had already discussed, had indeed settled, the matter of Israel's response with Eitan.

A grim-faced Eitan, his thick eyebrows fairly bristling with anger and impatience, waited to brief the Cabinet on the chosen targets. But before he received the floor, the head of the General Security Services, who was responsible for security arrangements in all Israeli embassies and other national institutions abroad, was asked to report on just what had actually happened in London and how the Israeli envoy had fallen victim to the assassination attempt. He explained that Argov's assailants had laid an ambush for him outside the Dorchester Hotel close to midnight and made their move as he left the building. Since receiving word of the attack, he added, Israeli intelligence organs had checked out the identity of the organization responsible for it. Scotland Yard had yet to issue a formal statement on the episode, but the attack was most probably the work of the terrorist group headed by Abu Nidal. He therefore suggested that Gideon Machanaimi, the prime minister's adviser on the war against terrorism, elaborate on the nature of that organization.

Machanaimi hardly had a chance to shift his glance toward Begin when the prime minister blocked him with the retort that there was no need to elaborate on anything. "They're all PLO," he pronounced, putting an end to the subject. Eitan also belittled the importance of this detail. Before entering the conference room, he had been informed by one of his intelligence men that Abu Nidal's men were evidently responsible for the assault. "Abu Nidal, Abu Shmidal," he had sneered. "We have to strike at the PLO!"

The intelligence people were puzzled by this attitude, especially since they had spent much of the night working to discover which organization was behind the operation, a point they believed to be highly relevant. One of the assailants had been caught after being wounded by the British security man guarding Argov. But Scotland Yard was in no hurry to reveal his identity, making it impossible to check his name against any of the intelligence lists in Israel. One way or another, however, it was plain that the hit had been well planned. The assassins knew that Argov was scheduled to participate in a banquet held at the Dorchester for eighty-four ambassadors, and they were able to recognize him and his car on sight. At the end of the meal, when most of the guests moved into a nearby hall, Argov took leave of a few of his ambassadorial colleagues. On the way to his car, a bullet struck him in the head some twenty meters from the hotel.

The news from London was still sketchy at dawn the next day in Israel, but one detail that did filter through kindled a light of recognition in intelligence circles: Argov had been shot by an unusual weapon of Polish manufacture known as a WZ 63, a small, easily concealed submachine gun comparable in size to a medium revolver and therefore an ideal weapon for "special operations." Israeli intelligence knew that this late-model weapon had been supplied to Abu Nidal's organization but not yet to other terrorist groups. The initial assessment of the Israeli intelligence people was in fact confirmed four days later, when Scotland Yard arrested three of the assailant's colleagues and their interrogation revealed that the head of the assassination squad, Merwan Hassan al-Bana, the bearer of a Jordanian passport, was a second cousin of none other than Abu Nidal. The three detainees also disclosed that an envoy from Baghdad had brought them orders to carry out the assassination, and that they had received their weapons from the military attaché's office of the Iraqi embassy in London.

The key point that the intelligence officers wanted to convey to the Cabinet was that Abu Nidal's organization was an exception among the Palestinian terror groups. Once among Yasser Arafat's closest friends, Abu Nidal had over the years turned into the chairman's most vicious enemy. After breaking with Arafat, he kept the name and symbols of Fatah for his own organization, claiming that his Revolutionary Council in Baghdad held to the movement's true historical line, while Arafat and his followers had defected to a course of treason. Abu Nidal referred to Arafat contemptuously as "the Jewess's son" and had made repeated attempts on his life. Arafat, in return, had pronounced a death sentence on Abu Nidal. Needless to say, the renegade terrorist was never again allowed into the precincts of the PLO.

It was at a secret camp near Baghdad that Abu Nidal, with the aid of Iraqi intelligence agents, trained his hit squads to ambush PLO activists and cut them down at short range. Graduates of this special course had been responsible for the murder of the PLO representative in London, Said Hamami—chosen because of his ties with the Israelis—and for the same reason later gunned down Issam Sartawi at a convention of the Socialist International in Lisbon. About a month before attacking Argov, they had planted a bomb in the PLO's offices in Sidon. Abu Nidal's men did not operate within Israel or against Israelis abroad; instead, they specialized in attacks on PLO figures. The British interrogators ventured that, had the assailants at the Dorchester succeeded in escaping their dragnet, they would have gone on to strike another target in London, Nabil Ramalawi, who had succeeded Hamami as the PLO's representative in Britain. The assault on Argov was therefore a major departure from their usual modus operandi.

Abu Nidal's patrons, the Iraqis, had their own reasons for instigating an attack on an Israeli ambassador, aside from vengeance for Israel's destruction of Iraq's nuclear reactor in June 1981. Baghdad, like all the other Arab capitals, was aware of Israel's determination to send its army against the PLO in Lebanon and knew that such an action would place Iraq's rival to the west, Syria, under heavy pressure: if President Assad failed to aid the beleaguered Palestinians in Lebanon, he would be shown up as a man of empty promises; if he did intervene to cushion the blow to the Palestinians, his army would probably be routed by the IDF. Either way, Assad's chagrin would be a source of great satisfaction to the Iraqis.

Abu Nidal had scores of his own to settle. It can be taken for granted that he too calculated the effect of murdering an Israeli diplomat as the fuse that would propel Begin and Sharon into carrying out their threats against the PLO in Lebanon. A few days after the assassination attempt, as the IDF's armor was overrunning South Lebanon, Abu Nidal issued a mimeographed leaflet justifying the shooting as "armed propaganda." The assault on Argov was not an act of terrorism, he argued, because the assassins had refrained from harming anyone in the ambassador's vicinity. Argov was chosen as a target because he was associated, in Abu Nidal's mind, with attempts to bring PLO functionaries in Britain together with internationally known Jewish figures. The leaflet also aimed a poison dart at Arafat in asking, "Where are the $200 million you collected in the Persian Gulf? Why aren't there any barricades and roadblocks in Lebanon, antiaircraft guns and fortifications? Have the funds been squandered on building brothels and trading in drugs?"

It was Abu Nidal's role as agent provocateur that the Israeli intelligence people wanted to bring to the Cabinet's attention, but with the prime minister's adviser on terrorism effectively silenced by Begin, the point was reduced to an ironic footnote to the upcoming war. Having bypassed the intelligence group, Begin turned the floor over to Eitan, who proceeded to recommend that the air force be sent into action against the terrorists and that the target of the raid be Beirut—or, more precisely, selected objectives in West Beirut highly sensitive from the PLO's standpoint. With a little luck, Eitan suggested, it might be possible to zero in on and eliminate the PLO's leadership. No other suggestions were raised before the Cabinet at that meeting. The chief of staff proposed only the option of bombing Beirut, and none of the ministers tabled an alternative motion.

The last time PLO headquarters in the heart of Beirut had been bombed, in July 1981, hundreds of civilians—tenants of the high-rise buildings containing the targeted offices and casual passersby—had proved the main victims of the operation. The deaths of so many innocent civilians and the resultant international wave of outrage had prompted Washington to chasten Israel by suspending the shipment of F-16 fighter planes. Yet the effect on Jerusalem of the previous year's indignation seemed to have been wiped out by the attack on the Israeli ambassador. The mood now was different, inflamed. Word that Argov's condition was critical created a grim determination to exact a bloody price for the life of an Israeli ambassador.

After spelling out the targets, Eitan surprised the ministers by suggesting that the bombing be postponed for a day. He assumed that following the attack in London the PLO would be on high alert in Lebanon awaiting an Israeli reprisal of some sort. As a rule in such circumstances, many of the organization's commanders, and anyone else concerned with saving his skin, went into hiding until the coast was clear. The point, though logical, was nevertheless instantly rejected by Begin, who insisted on reacting immediately so there would be no question that the air strike was in response to the assault on Argov. Begin would have liked the bombing to take place that very morning while the Cabinet was still in session, but aerial visibility was impaired by heavy cloud cover over Beirut and was not expected to clear until the afternoon. The raid was therefore postponed till later that day, before the onset of the Sabbath.

Eitan's remarks made brief mention of the most likely corollary to the bombing: the Palestinians might react, in which case the IDF could embark upon a massive retaliation. He did not elaborate on the latter point, but that was hardly necessary. Everyone in the room understood that if the Palestinians opened fire on the Galilee in response to the bombing raid, their fire would serve as a pretext for carrying out the military action that had long been on the drawing boards. None of the ministers asked to deliberate the question of how Israel would conduct itself if the PLO did indeed react as the chief of staff assessed it would. Silence prevailed even when Chief of Intelligence Saguy seconded Eitan's reading that the PLO could be expected to open fire.

It is highly possible that many of the ministers seated around the table on June 4 were unaware of what the military men knew as a fact—namely, that after the last Israeli bombing the PLO had decided to respond automatically to any further air strike by shelling Israeli settlements in the Galilee, and that orders to this effect had even been issued in writing by the PLO joint military command in South Lebanon. The prime minister must have known it, as did the chief of staff, the chief of intelligence, and the head of Mossad. Yet even if they did not appreciate the automatic nature of the PLO's response, the rest of the ministers had Eitan's and Saguy's word for it: this time the PLO would react in force. And still no one moved to pause and ask where the nation was going. It was as if the limbs of the Israeli ministers had turned to lead; not a single man raised his hand to urge an alternative course.

Menachem Begin understood exactly what was about to ensue, as evidenced by the fact of his announcing that the Cabinet would reconvene within a matter of hours. "We'll react and see what happens," he said. "Let us convene again on Saturday night at my home."

With that the meeting adjourned and one of the ministers proceeded to the Journalists' House in Tel Aviv for a luncheon with a number of correspondents, a gathering that had been scheduled long before the Argov crisis. At one point during the meal, the drone of planes overhead heading north punctuated the conversation. Exchanging speculative glances, the newsmen drew identical conclusions about the destination of the aircraft as the minister muttered abstractedly, "The country is being led by two maniacs." At first the journalists maintained a polite silence; then one of them could contain himself no longer. "Are you referring to Begin?" he asked incredulously. "Not Begin!" the minister shot back, angered at the suggestion that he would commit such an indiscretion and annoyed with himself for failing to control his tongue. His companions understood that he had referred to Sharon and Eitan.

On the other side of the Middle East, in Saudi Arabia on that fateful Friday, Yasser Arafat understood that any artillery response to the Israeli bombing raid would mean the instigation of a war in which his troops would be roundly beaten. Yet there he was, helpless to prevent the self-defeating scenario from playing itself out. His only move was to approve the publication of a statement by Nabil Ramalawi in London deploring the attempt on Argov's life. He also issued a circular explaining that he had reliable information about Israel's intentions in Lebanon from a tantalizingly anonymous "American friend."

At 3:15 P.M. the first Israeli planes swooped down on their targets in West Beirut to release their deadly payloads. Two hours later, at 5:20, the PLO field guns and Katyusha rocket launchers began to fire on Israeli settlements in the Galilee. For all intents and purposes, the line was crossed: the war between Israel and the PLO had begun.

All that was lacking now was official approval for the IDF incursion into Lebanon, and that emerged from the Cabinet meeting held on Saturday night at Menachem Begin's official residence in Jerusalem. The ministers began to gather at Begin's home as soon as the Sabbath ended, and this time Ariel Sharon took his place among them, having been summoned back from Rumania. Every man was keenly aware that the stakes had soared in the past twenty-four hours. Now they would be asked to vote not on an isolated air raid but on a full-scale operation designed to silence the guns of the Palestinian organizations operating out of South Lebanon. Since the Israeli air force had struck the targets in West Beirut on the previous afternoon, twenty-nine settlements in the Galilee had come under shell and rocket fire, including the towns of Kiryat Shmonah and Nahariya. By Saturday evening the Palestinians in South Lebanon had fired some 500 shells and Katyusha rockets. Consequently, well before a vote was taken, it was thoroughly clear that, given the total breakdown of the ceasefire, Ariel Sharon's proposal to invade Lebanon and destroy the PLO's military infrastructure would receive the backing of most if not all the ministers. The only questions remaining concerned the extent of the war: What were its objectives, how far would the Israeli columns penetrate, and how long would the operation take? The minutes of this crucial Saturday night Cabinet session enable us to ascertain what the Cabinet was led to understand about the limits of the operation, and whether the ministers intended for the IDF's columns to go as far as Beirut. They also shed light on the question of whether the Cabinet, wittingly or otherwise, approved moves that made a clash with the Syrian army inevitable.

At first there was explicit mention of forty kilometers (twenty-five miles) as the distance the IDF must cover in order to ensure that the Galilean settlements were out of the range of PLO artillery fire. This was the distance for which the minister of defense and chief of staff asked the government's approval. Nothing was said or even intimated about the IDF advancing beyond this forty-kilometer limit. No one suggested that the ground forces would strive to link up with the Phalange troops in the Christian enclave around Beirut. Nothing resembling the more ambitious version of Operation Pines was approved by the Cabinet. *The only issue discussed at that Saturday night conclave was the need to push back the terrorist artillery.*

There was one exception to the ministers' silence at that meeting, one man who rose to question the plan—Communications Minister Mordechai Zippori. For a number of months, Zippori had suspected that Sharon was cooking up a full-scale war in Lebanon and that the IDF might be drawn into a bruising clash with the Syrians. Like his colleagues in the Cabinet, he was in favor of an operation directed against the PLO's artillery and infrastructure in South Lebanon, but unlike the rest he was uneasy about the odds of becoming entangled in areas farther to the north, such as the Bekaa Valley and even Beirut. Long before Sharon was appointed defense minister Zippori had been opposed to what he considered excessively familiar relations with the Phalange, appreciating how they might obligate Israel to act beyond its own military interests. Throughout his tenure as deputy minister of defense in Begin's first government, he had hammered away at an alliance with the Phalange. He had also warned against permitting the development of a situation in which Chief of Staff Eitan and his

senior officers, and eventually Sharon, might steer Israel into an unnecessary war.

Except for Sharon, Zippori was the only minister with extensive operational experience in military affairs, and his questions on June 5 reflected
his suspicion that the unduly vague war plan being laid out before the
Cabinet concealed a far more ambitious scheme.

"I have a number of questions," Zippori gave notice as soon as he
received the floor. "First, the notion of pushing the terrorists back forty
kilometers is too abstract. I would like to know where the lines our forces
must reach are actually situated. That way we'll be able to follow their
advance from the media reports as well as from what we hear in the
Cabinet. Secondly, since the subject of the terrorists located in the Syrian
sector has come up, in simple Hebrew that means we are going to attack
the Syrians. And I think that that's a mistake!" And then he pointed out,
raising his voice, "Even if terrorists remain in the Syrian sector after we
complete the operation, the Syrians know how to control them and can
stop them from opening fire. . . ."

"May I have your attention," Begin cut in like a stern schoolmaster. "I
said that we will not attack the Syrians!"

"It doesn't matter what we decide," Zippori insisted. "The moves described here will bring us into contact with the Syrians."

A dialogue developed between the two men, with Begin rejecting every
one of Zippori's admonitions. He argued, for example, that it all depended
on who initiated the action; if the Syrians attacked Israeli troops, they
would have no choice but to fight back.

"But if a situation develops whereby we land up in the rear of the
Syrians, they will surely make their own assessments," Zippori countered,
"and these will differ from ours. From my experience with the Syrians
over a period of thirty-four years, I assume—and past events indicate—
that when we strike at them, they hit back. On the other hand, if they have
the choice of becoming involved in a war on their own initiative or of
controlling the terrorists in their territory, they'll opt to control the terrorists. We should take that into consideration and not allow ourselves to be
drawn into a situation in which the Syrians will be forced to fight."

Then, as if adding an afterthought, Zippori introduced an entirely new
subject. "I want to suggest to the prime minister and the Cabinet that we
refrain from thinking in terms of destroying the terrorists' operational capability for the future."

"I never suggested that," Begin retorted.

Yet Zippori, perhaps realizing he had struck a nerve, was determined to
have his say. "I hope we deliver a blow to the terrorists. No doubt we will

capture territory and return it afterward. But in the future we will definitely be faced by a similar problem . . . albeit not of the same magnitude. So we are better off not speaking in terms of eradicating the terrorists' operational capability. As long as Lebanon lacks a government like that of Hussein in Jordan, we'll have a problem. That is how we should approach our moves."

Sharon, like all the other ministers, followed this exchange between Zippori and Begin in silence. After all, the prime minister was doing his work for him, very nicely. Eitan also was keeping his own counsel. But just when it seemed that the debate was about to end, Begin suggested that it would be worthwhile hearing the chief of staff's replies to the questions raised by Zippori regarding the Syrians and the range of operation. Eitan did not respond to the first point at all, but in addressing the second he did determine the forty-kilometer line quite clearly. "Forty kilometers from Metulla is almost Lake Karoun," he began. (Metulla is the northernmost point in the Galilee.) "From Metulla northwest [the line] reaches almost to the Zaharani River," he continued. "Northward it's three kilometers from Lake Karoun, along the coast it reaches the line between Sidon and the Zaharani River."

At that point Sharon intervened to clarify: "Along the coastline, it's twenty-four kilometers up to Sidon. In the east it's up to Lake Karoun."

These lines were a clear-cut commitment. Nevertheless, one of the ministers asked, "And Beirut . . . ?"

"Beirut is outside the picture," Sharon replied unequivocally. " 'Operation Peace for Galilee' is designed not to capture Beirut but to drive the PLO's rockets and artillery out of the range of our settlements. We're talking about a range of forty kilometers. That is what the Cabinet has approved."

Zippori, determined not to be denied, moved on to another issue: the timetable for the operation. How long was it estimated that the operation would take? Sharon replied, "The stage I have spoken about is an operation that will take about twelve hours. I don't know how matters will develop, so I suggest we view it in terms of twenty-four hours. Up to the forty-kilometer point, however, things will be over before that."

With the lines of the operation clearly drawn, the time for the vote had arrived. But now that the issue was war, now that they faced the critical moment where lives hung in the balance, a number of ministers began to waver in their resolve. Yosef Burg tried to defer the inevitable by suggesting that the invasion be postponed while the bombing continued, giving the Cabinet an opportunity to see how matters developed. His proposal was voted down, and the invasion brought up for a vote. Zippori, having articulated his fears and criticism cogently, now joined the majority in voting in favor. Deputy Prime Minister Simcha Erhlich and Energy Minister Yitzhak Berman, both of the Liberal party, abstained.

Berman later recalled that he had been strongly influenced by the fact that the chief of military intelligence and the head of the Mossad had not been invited to speak on the predicted results of the war. When Sharon said that the Syrians would not interfere, Berman had glanced at the two intelligence men and sensed from their expressions a dissenting view. He also thought he heard Saguy murmur to his neighbor that the Syrians would almost certainly be drawn into the fighting. He recalled the old saying that you may know how to get into a war, but you never know how you'll come out of it.

The fact that the plan called for capturing forty kilometers of Lebanese territory was no consolation to Berman, not only because the terrorists could acquire longer-range artillery in the future, but because he feared that American forces would eventually be stationed in the forty-kilometer zone. This possibility had been mentioned at an earlier Cabinet meeting devoted to a military operation in Lebanon. As Berman now thought to himself: What's the point of going to war just to exchange American troops for the UNIFIL, and thereby giving the GIs an opportunity to develop relations with and sympathies toward the PLO, just as many of the UNIFIL soldiers had?

As the Cabinet ministers filed out of Begin's house, most of them were under the impression that they had just approved a short-range operation that would be over within a day. "Twenty-four hours," Sharon had stated. The official communiqué on Operation Peace for Galilee was drafted by the prime minister himself without mention of the forty-kilometer cutoff point. (Begin cited the figure in writing to President Reagan. It was also the figure specified in the operational order issued by the chief of staff after the Cabinet's decision—though it is worth noting that this operational order also put the IDF on notice that it might be called upon to link up with the Christians and destroy the Syrian garrison in Lebanon.) Sharon believed his own prediction—albeit with far broader aims for the operation than those he presented to the Cabinet: He was confident that the IDF would intuitively grasp what he wanted to accomplish in Lebanon and would simply gallop forward to appease his will. He would worry about having Cabinet approval keep pace with the facts established on the ground when the time came.

In one sense, the process of establishing those facts ahead of the Cabinet had already begun earlier that day when Bashir Gemayel finally received the news he had almost despaired of ever hearing: the Israeli ground action would begin at any moment. To aid in advancing that operation, Bashir was asked to perform a few services, first and foremost, to have his men open fire along the Green Line dividing Beirut between Moslem- and Christian-controlled areas—so as to distract and pin down the terrorists in the city—and second to permit Israeli combat teams to land at Junieh. A hastily called meeting at the Phalange headquarters made it possible to relay Bashir's answer even before the lead Israeli companies had crossed the border. He refused both requests, and the next morning he would compound the insult by informing the Israelis that he had nonetheless opened fire in Beirut (though the IDF liaison officers who went out to check on the situation found the city perfectly quiet).

On the brink of realizing his long-standing dream and reaping the fruits of his long alliance with Israel, Bashir Gemayel chose to pull back from the edge and act with extreme caution. Rather than take a definitive stand during the opening stage of the war, he preferred to wait. After all, the Israelis had more than once assured him they would reach the outskirts of Beirut within a mere forty-eight hours, perhaps less. If so, Bashir reasoned, there was no need to rush into action. Above all, he must beware of prejudicing his chances of attaining the presidency. Still unsure of the exact objectives of the Israeli offensive or how far the IDF would actually go, he knew he must calculate his moves prudently lest he appear to have become a tool of the Israelis. For years Bashir Gemayel had been preparing himself for this moment, and now he was determined not to be swept away by the thrust of events. He would keep the reins of history firmly in his hands.

Quiet confidence and a sense of control were far from the mood in the PLO camp on that long, tense weekend. When the PLO Supreme Military Council met in Beirut after the first of two Israeli bombings of the city, Abu Jihad occupied Arafat's chair and presided over the unanimous approval of a heavy artillery barrage aimed at the settlements over the Israeli border. Considering the toll of casualties from the air strike, the PLO leaders felt they had no other choice. Israeli planes had hit a soccer stadium under which the PLO had stored weapons and ammunition, causing havoc in the area. (Arafat, alert to the strong possibility of an Israeli response, had ordered the ordnance transferred, but for some reason the order was never carried out.) Now, as the first of a series of volleys was launched on Friday afternoon, Arafat, still in Saudi Arabia, phoned the PLO office in New York to demand a meeting of the Security Council and confirm his support for the shelling of the Galilee. "We'll teach the Israelis a lesson, as we have in the past," he was quoted saying with his practiced bravado.

By the next day, however, the PLO leadership thought better of its move and tried to halt the deterioration of the ceasefire. Abu Iyyad suggested calling for an immediate truce, but this time, it was clear, the Israeli firing would continue unabated; in effect, it had already become a softening-up barrage that concentrated on weapons stores, antiaircraft guns, and tank positions. The Israeli navy was even firing at PLO vehicles on the coastal road to block a retreat northward.

In the early morning hours on Sunday, Arafat phoned his headquarters in Beirut to order an unconditional halt to the shelling at 6:00 A.M., and a message to that effect was also passed on to the United States. The Palestinian artillery units had actually ceased their fire in most sectors by 3:00 A.M., and despite a rising sense of panic at headquarters the PLO radio remained curiously calm. In contrast to previous episodes, there were no signs of an imminent invasion across the border, no eve-of-war atmosphere. Arafat even decided to stay put in Saudi Arabia.

But at least one man in the PLO's Beirut headquarters knew what was coming. Abu Iyyad stood off to the side observing the frenzy and feeling particularly grim. He had wanted to prevent war. He had done what he could to reach an accommodation with Bashir, and just hours before he had tried at least to restore the ceasefire. But it was all over now, and he felt engulfed by a wave of despair. Suddenly his musing was interrupted by two harried-looking officers who began chattering at him while still at a half-run—they had just been released from prison and were desperately looking for a way to get to their units in Sidon and fight the Israelis.

"Don't bother," Abu Iyyad said softly, but so distinctly that they both swung around and stared at him in bewilderment. "The Jews are coming here."

7

The Lame Blitz

WHEN ARIEL SHARON SPOKE of reaching the forty-kilometer line within twenty-four hours, he had in mind a blitzkrieg-type dash through South Lebanon on two main axes: the coastal road leading through Tyre and Sidon to Beirut, and the central axis heading through the Nabatiye plateau and the Shouf Mountains to the Beirut-Damascus highway. For a number of reasons, however, things didn't turn out quite that way. First, from a purely operational standpoint, the IDF was well behind schedule before it ever got started. And on top of the delay came a number of constraints imposed by the fact that the minister of defense had been less than candid with his Cabinet colleagues. Military logic dictated, for instance, that the commander of the northern front be briefed about the final objectives of the war from the outset. But because the Cabinet had approved an operation extending only forty kilometers into Lebanon, Amir Drori's mission had to be defined vaguely.

The designation of final objectives is of cardinal importance in a military venture, for to no small degree the ends determine the means. If the destination of Northern Command's forces was indeed Beirut, then the best and most efficient course would be to land contingents in the enemy's rear along the Beirut-Damascus highway, at key points along the north-south axes, and perhaps also at a number of spots along the coast. Northern Command's original battle plan had been built around this very kind of creative strategy. But the problem now was that such a course would immediately expose the gap between Sharon's far-reaching aims and the considerably more modest objectives approved by the Cabinet. The General Staff therefore had to opt for the more ponderous and conventional— and predictable—method of a mechanized breakthrough moving directly up from the south and forfeit the advantages of a "leapfrog" tactic that would sow confusion in the enemy camp and undoubtedly save time and lives.

By the same token, it would have been possible to land forces by helicopter at selected points along the eastern front to block the Syrians from sending reinforcements into the Bekaa Valley. Here again, however, Sharon vetoed the more expedient course because he wanted to lull Damascus (not to mention Jerusalem) into believing that the war was directed solely against the PLO and that Israel had no designs on the Syrian garrison troops. He had decided to put off Israel's move against the Syrians until the second stage of the fighting, a deferral that may have robbed the IDF of the advantage of surprise but also delayed the anticipated intervention of the major powers.

For whatever satisfaction it afforded him, Amir Drori discovered that his earlier assessment about the difficulties involved in massing his forces for war was right on the mark. With the outbreak of fighting not prefaced by any period of alert that would have enabled him to organize and call up all his units in a methodical fashion, the war, as he had foreseen, had to unfold stage by stage, as an open-ended operation. What he could not have foreseen, however, was that the fuse would be lit on a Thursday night, placing him at an additional disadvantage. As the Cabinet was meeting in Jerusalem to decide on the bombing of Beirut, units in the north were beginning to send many of their men off on standard weekend leaves. By the time the General Staff declared an alert, most of the men with passes were well on their way home. Besides, gone were the days when an alert in the north inspired genuine agitation. The alarms had become so frequent that some of the commanders in the area had grown quite blasé. And the alert called on June 4 had a distinct quality of déjà vu about it. Two months earlier, after another Israeli diplomat had been gunned down abroad, in Paris, an alert had been called in the IDF, even stating the hour on which the operation into Lebanon was to begin, only to fizzle out like all its predecessors. Little wonder, then, that many officers in the north viewed the latest change in status as just another false alarm.

At Drori's front command, however, the atmosphere was different this time. As soon as word arrived that the Cabinet had approved the bombing of targets in Beirut, no one doubted that they were heading for war. And that meant working fast. All standing plans proceeded from the premise that, once an operation in Lebanon was decided upon, the command would have ample time to mass its forces. Now, however, H-hour for crossing the frontier was set for noon on Sunday, drastically slashing the staging period. And the revision in timing led to another highly significant change: the war would now begin during daylight hours, whereas it had originally been planned to start at night. Consequently the IDF would have to forgo a number of preliminary measures it had planned to carry out under cover of darkness, such as the capture of key areas in Lebanon to help speed up the advance in the opening phase and throw the Palestinians into confusion.

In contrast to these disadvantageous adjustments, there was one tactical change for the better: on Saturday the IDF received permission to discount the presence of the UNIFIL forces in South Lebanon and pass through the zone under their supervision. Originally the General Staff had been told to skirt this area, depriving its troops of the option of crossing the Akiye Bridge over the Litani River in the central sector. Instead, the IDF was to be restricted to the route over the Hardele Bridge near the bend in the river farther east. The Palestinians were keenly aware that the Hardele crossing posed the greatest risk to their own deployment, for it was along the shortest route to the Nabatiye plateau. They therefore had the vicinity of the bridge heavily mined and dotted with outposts. The PLO had even pressured the French to station their UNIFIL contingent by the Hardele Bridge as another way of keeping the Israelis out of the area.

As the Israelis threw their preparations into high gear on Saturday, the force slated to make an amphibious landing somewhere on the Lebanese coast—the one exception to the rule of a straightforward ground thrust northward—began to load onto its landing craft so that at least this aspect of the operation would be in an advanced stage. On Saturday night, as the Cabinet gathered in Begin's home, the tanks, artillery, and paratroops who would hit the beach in the first wave of landings were packed onto their craft and sent out to sea even before the landing zone was determined. The outstanding question was whether to bring them ashore near the estuary of the Zaharani River, south of Sidon, or farther north, beyond the forty-kilometer limit, by the estuary of the Awali River. "As I see it, we'll get approval to land farther north, by the Awali," Drori told Amos Yaron, commander of the seaborne force and the paratroop officer who would later play a focal role in the siege of Beirut. "Then you'll probably get the order to move up toward Damour." Once again Drori's prediction, based on the assumption that the Lebanon operation would burgeon from one stage to the next, was accurate. On Sunday afternoon Yaron received word that the landing was to take place at the site farther north, between Sidon and Damour.

Establishing the landing zone north of Sidon was of major political significance, for it extended the operation beyond the forty-kilometer limit. It was also a fateful operational decision, given the question of how long it would take before the armored forces driving up the coast—and bringing

Yaron's paratroops their armored personnel carriers (APCs)—could link up with the force that had landed from the sea. Some armored officers were brightly confident that their column would reach Yaron within a few hours if he landed at the Zaharani, south of Sidon. But the paratroop officers, who would be sweating it out alone in the interim, were far less sanguine about the timetable. They had visions of the armored forces sustaining heavy casualties along the way, recalling the intelligence assessment that fighting in Sidon, which is difficult to bypass on the east, could retard or even halt the flow of forces northward. At the risk of being mocked as gloom-mongers, the paratroops stuck to the conservative assessment that it would take well over a day for their armor to reach them. As matters turned out, even this cautious estimate was overly optimistic.

While the issue of the landing zone was being weighed, a far more momentous decision was made that Sunday, June 6—a decision regarding another sector and, effectively, another war. It called for a division to make its way up the central axis through the Shouf Mountains to the Beirut-Damascus highway and then turn east to secure the strategic Dahr el-Baidar pass. The corollary of this decision was incontestable: it meant war with the Syrians, for it implied outflanking a large portion of the Syrian troops stationed in Lebanon, closing in on them from the rear, encircling some of them, and in the process taking the main highway to their capital. Whoever arrived at this decision must have seen that it would force the Syrians to make a clear-cut choice: either fight or withdraw from Lebanon in a humiliating rout. Anyone with the least understanding of the stakes involved in Lebanon must have realized that President Assad could not possibly order his forces to flee the advancing Israelis and still remain in power. Long before June 6, Yehoshua Saguy's military intelligence had warned that the Syrians would respond to a drive up the central axis by digging in and fighting. Mordechai Zippori had said much the same at the last Cabinet meeting, even though, when the chips were down, he had voted in favor of the strategy, like everyone else around the table. Exactly what their expectations of this move were remains hauntingly unclear.

By the time of Sunday's Cabinet meeting, however, Prime Minister Begin was clearly enchanted by the idea of a deep flanking movement. Over and over again, he made a circular movement with his hand, happily depicting how his army would steal up on the Syrians from behind. "A tactic worthy of Hannibal!" he exclaimed to the Cabinet in unabashed delight. Naive about military matters, Begin evidently believed that the Syrians would be so daunted by this maneuver that they would abandon their entire logistical investment in Lebanon and scurry back to Damascus. How anyone, let alone the Israeli prime minister, could assume that the

Syrians, a formidable enemy in the past, would meekly take whatever Israel dished out defies reason. But that is precisely what Begin must have assumed; otherwise it is impossible to understand the Cabinet communiqué, which he worded personally, stating categorically that "the Syrian army will not be attacked."

The Cabinet's approval of the lunge northward in the central sector also contradicted Begin's message to President Reagan stating that the purpose of the Israeli operation in Lebanon was to push the PLO's artillery back beyond a range of forty kilometers. From the outset, the division climbing up the Shouf Mountains was aiming farther than forty kilometers. And it had orders to take on the Syrians as well as any Palestinian forces it might encounter on the way! But questions of hypocrisy aside, this decision attested to the Cabinet's total ignorance of even the simplest realities of military strategy, and to Sharon's blatant exploitation of that fact in neglecting to explain the true import of the moves he proposed. For as we shall see, Sharon knew perfectly well that this maneuver in the central sector would lead to fighting with the Syrian forces in Lebanon and thereby make a mockery of the Cabinet's intentions. Long since resolved to drive the Syrians out of Lebanon by force, he had chosen the expedient of encirclement as simply the best tactical course open to him.

The tactic did have an operative logic of its own—assuming, of course, that it was effected quickly and included moving forces in by helicopter before the Syrians could capture various key positions. It was predicated on a broad pincer movement. One arm was to traverse the Shouf Mountains and, upon reaching the main east-west highway, turn, as noted earlier, eastward to Dahr el-Baidar. The other arm was to advance northward at a certain point into the Bekaa Valley and likewise head for the Beirut-Damascus highway (east of the Dahr el-Baidar saddle), cross it, then move on toward the Rayak airfield and the towns of Shtura and Zahle. It consisted of a massive force—larger, in fact, than the one slated to operate in the western sector: a multidivision body commanded by Maj. Gen. Avigdor Ben-Gal, Drori's predecessor at Northern Command. The most striking point about this plan was not its extravagance but the fact that the Israeli Cabinet ministers did not approve it! They were indeed quite unaware of it when they agreed to send a division up the central axis in a bid to emulate Hannibal.

The advance through the Shouf's central axis was therefore conceived as the pivot around which the entire Lebanese campaign would revolve. It was not designed—as would later be claimed in some disingenuous explanations—to protect the flank of Ben-Gal's forces in the Bekaa Valley, for it preceded their advance by two whole days. More to the point, if it succeeded in reaching and establishing itself on the main highway to Damascus, this central-axis division would both complete its half of the pincer movement to surround the Syrian garrison in the Bekaa and isolate the Syrian force stationed in and around Beirut; and this would, in turn, open up other alluring possibilities, such as a thrust farther north into the Bekaa Valley, or a detour to link up with the Maronites without having to pass through Beirut, or even a plunge east from Dahr el-Baidar toward the Syrian border and Damascus!

Sharon might be able to conduct a war without the Cabinet being "unduly" informed of his moves—as when he conveniently neglected to inform the ministers of his plans to send Ben-Gal into the Bekaa Valley and to attack the Syrian missile batteries at the first opportunity—but he could not continue to operate without the knowledge and cooperation of the IDF's senior commanders. Sharon might have avoided discussing the subject in explicit terms, simply dropping broad hints, had it not been for a number of comments that made him lose control of his tongue—and of his temper. As the plans for the central and eastern fronts came under scrutiny that Sunday during a situation assessment with his commanders, one of the participants remarked matter-of-factly that a Syrian brigade was stationed in the area of Dahr el-Baidar and that the surface-to-air missiles were deployed to the south of it, making a clash with both garrisons inevitable. Sharon pounced on him. "You don't imagine that we'll bring this operation to a close with those missiles still in place! Everyone knows exactly what we are about to do. Why are you playing the innocent? Everybody knows!"

Excluded from the category of "everyone," of course, was the prime minister, his Cabinet, and the heads of the opposition, who heard a quite different version of their country's war aims and strategy later that day. First there was the Cabinet meeting, and then, just as the first Israeli forces were crossing the border at 11:00 A.M., Begin invited the leaders of the opposition to his office in Jerusalem to inform them that the Cabinet had decided to mount an action against the PLO in Lebanon. When the Labor delegates arrived, they found Sharon awaiting them too. Since Begin refrained from telling them that the operation had begun, Chaim Bar-Lev was unaware of the fact that Israel was already at war when he responded to Begin's statement by criticizing the bombing of Beirut on the previous Friday and warning against allowing a major ground operation to spill over and beyond the scope just outlined by Begin. "It will get us entangled with the Syrians," he stressed.

"There are special instructions about that," Begin soothed his guests, "orders not to open fire and not to get too close to the Syrians." For details he deferred to Sharon, who began to sidetrack by elaborating on the operation's timetable. "We'll reach the Sidon-Karoun line within twelve hours," he predicted, but then he returned to Bar-Lev's misgivings and assured him, "As for the Syrians, there's an explicit order to keep a minimum of four kilometers away from them."

There was still another opportunity that day to discuss the question of involvement with the Syrians when Begin made a visit to the northern-front headquarters in the afternoon. But an odd conspiracy of silence occurred. Despite their discussion with Sharon that morning, none of the officers at Northern Command made mention of any deliberately instigated war with Syria. Neither did Begin display real anxiety about, or even special interest in, the subject of the Syrians. His sole reference to them was the arbitrary question, addressed to Chief of Staff Rafael Eitan, whether the Israeli forces were getting close to their lines—and even then he didn't wait for a reply but immediately continued with another, more pressing question: had the IDF advanced past the Beaufort castle? The redoubtable fortress looming on the skyline seemed to preoccupy his attention.

"We haven't reached it yet," Eitan replied laconically.

"The Beaufort looks so close," Begin mused abstractedly, "as if you could touch it with your hand."

It is not clear whether he thought the fortress would come under attack or be bypassed by the Israelis and left deep in the rear while they continued on their swift advance northward. One thing is certain, however: Begin was told nothing about the intent to attack the Syrian missiles. The issues aired during the earlier military session had been mysteriously censored when the situation assessment was repeated for the prime minister's benefit. Evidently it was still too early to bring him in on the real picture. Sharon's preferred method of dealing with Begin was to approach him at the veritable eleventh hour, convince him—almost breathlessly—that the men in the field were in mortal danger, and elicit his support for whatever move would presumably counteract the threat hovering over them.

Begin was in a buoyant mood that afternoon at Northern Command headquarters. He was tickled by the news that Arafat still had no idea of what was going on at the front and that the commander of the PLO in South Lebanon, Haj Ismail, was desperately calling Beirut for help but getting no reply. And he seemed to glow in the company of the officers and enlisted men buzzing around him. With characteristic exuberance, he told them of his own role in the struggle—the challenge he withstood that very morning when the American ambassador called upon him at the ungodly hour of 6:30 with a letter from the president.

"It was a polite letter, but the president asked us to refrain from any action. I answered him by explaining the situation and wrote that we will uphold our sacred obligation, so help me God! That was how the letter closed, so the president will understand that there is nothing more to discuss. That's it."

"What did Lewis [the American ambassador] want?" Eitan asked off-handedly.

"He wanted us to agree to a ceasefire at nine in the morning and said that the PLO had already consented to it. I told him: 'Mr. Ambassador, I am very angry with you. You must never draw any kind of parallel between us and the PLO.' He had the nerve to tell me that they had turned to the Saudis, and the Saudis to the Syrians, and the Syrians to the PLO and the PLO had agreed to a ceasefire! In the end Lewis apologized, and I told him that I would convene a Cabinet meeting."

If Begin seemed pleased with himself, it was because he believed that he had a short, neat war ahead of him. After all, that was what his defense minister had promised, and who was in a better position to know? Before leaving for his office in the building adjacent to the front headquarters, he phoned his wife, Aliza, to ask how she was feeling, and was overheard telling her, "It will all be over the day after tomorrow, and then we'll see each other."

Before leaving Northern Command the next morning, Begin himself readjusted that timetable, for when Eitan commented to him that "if the politicians give us another twenty-four hours, the whole picture will change completely and we'll be standing on different ground," the prime minister replied impulsively, "You have thirty-six hours!"

In either case, the magnitude of Begin's misjudgment would not be manifest for many days, but even that Sunday the indications that the war would be a quick, "effortless" one were not wholly encouraging. The division charged with breaking through on the central axis had not even been deployed in the north when the tension began to rise on Friday, June 4. About a week earlier it had been sent south for maneuvers, and its commander, Brig. Gen. Menachem Einan, was informed that in the event of war the division would probably fight on the Golan Heights or in the Bekaa Valley, but it should also prepare for the possibility of an arduous drive through the Shouf Mountains to cover the flank of the forces in the Bekaa or to turn westward and aid the divisions advancing up the coast, should either prove necessary. It was not until Friday, after the bombing of Beirut, that Einan learned that his force would be aiming for the Beirut-Damascus highway.

Despite the fact that the dash up the central axis was the focal maneuver of the overall battle plan, the front command did not seem to be in any hurry to send Einan's force into action. At 5:30 on Sunday morning, when Sharon met with the division commanders, the discussion centered first on the matter of moving H-hour up from noon to 11:00 A.M. The commanders were interested in gaining an extra hour of daylight and air support and readily agreed to the idea, although many of them had not yet completed their preparations and some of their units were still in transit northward. But even with eleven o'clock set as the hour for moving out, Einan was told to sit tight until it was possible to assess how the Syrians were reacting on the Golan. Thus it was not until 3:30 P.M. that Einan got permission to cross the border and proceed northward, four and a half hours behind all the other divisions.

The next delay in Einan's progress was an even graver one. Less than half an hour after his division set out, when its point company was still in the Haddad enclave, Einan received an order to change course and cross the Litani—not over the Hardele Bridge in the east, where fighting was in progress, but via the Akiye Bridge farther west in the UNIFIL zone. That meant turning his force around and taking a long, circuitous route to the same central axis northeast of Nabatiye. As a result of the rerouting, Einan's division now found itself moving in the wake of another force— Avigdor Kahalani's division—and instead of racing northward it was bunched up behind the fuel and ammunition trucks of the force headed for Nabatiye and the coast. So it was that, together with the earlier delay, an entire night was lost. When the lead brigade of Einan's division finally broke free of the traffic jam and pulled up near Nabatiye, it found that it had to refuel, given its tortuous and frustrating trek to what was essentially its starting line. Only then did it begin its journey up the central axis toward the Beirut-Damascus highway. Twelve precious hours had been squandered—a critical loss for the force whose lightning advance was suppose to preclude the movement of Syrian forces and rattle the Syrian high command.

On the first day of fighting, the front facing the still unsuspecting Syrians in the eastern sector (the Bekaa Valley) remained dormant not only because of the political considerations but also because the IDF had not finished massing its forces. Avigdor Ben-Gal, commander of the eastern front, had had to be summoned back from the United States and did not arrive at his command until Sunday afternoon. When the Syrians did learn of the invasion, they made every effort to demonstrate that they wanted no part in a war. Though they took certain precautionary measures, the Syrian General Staff conspicuously abstained from sending reinforcements into Lebanon or changing its deployment on the Golan Heights, while the forward units in the Bekaa Valley were given strict orders not to open fire on the invading Israeli forces. The commander of the forwardmost company in the Bekaa, Capt. Mohammed Hussein Saker (who was later taken prisoner by the Israelis), was perturbed by this constraint and contacted his brigade commander to protest that an Israeli unit had already penetrated the hilly area north of the border known as Fatahland. But even when shells began to rain down on the vicinity of his outpost, Saker was sent explicit orders not to open fire unless he found himself under direct attack.

The Syrians' self-restraint became all the more pronounced when frantic cries for help came from the Palestinians. No sooner had the war begun than the PLO turned to Assad to implement the aid agreement reached by the two parties. Their understanding stipulated that, if Israel initiated a ground action, the Syrian air force would intervene in the fighting and soldiers (disguised as Palestinian guerrillas) would be sent to the aid of the PLO. Damascus was also committed to allow squads of Palestinian terrorists to infiltrate Israel via Jordan. Yet not a single one of these promises was honored—not even the pledge to send ammunition! Damascus chose to keep a very low profile and was quite prepared to let Ariel Sharon maul the PLO in the hope of sparing its own troops in Lebanon.

Two battles that occurred in the western and central sectors that first day of the war are worthy of special attention because they highlight both the valor and the failings of the Palestinian fighters in Lebanon. The first was a clash in the vicinity of the refugee camps around Tyre; the other was the resolute but utterly superfluous battle for the Beaufort.

The Israeli assault on the six battalions of Fatah's Kastel Brigade began with a softening-up action by air and artillery forces well before the armored columns rolled over the frontier. All day Saturday the artillery had zeroed in on its targets at relatively close range, while throughout Sunday morning Israeli planes searched out select targets, such as bunkers and subterranean weapons stores carved into the mountainsides. Since it was difficult to penetrate these strongholds by bombardment, the planes tried to block access to them by dropping delayed-action bombs that would explode from time to time in no calculable order; anyone trying to remove the weapons and ammunition did so at the risk of his life. Together with the panic that gripped the Palestinian organizations with the outbreak of war, these bombs were the main reason why most of the PLO's weapons stores were found still chock full of arms, ammunition, and especially thousands of mines that were supposed to have been laid on the IDF's routes of advance.

The armored brigade that led the attack on the western axis, up the coastal road, was commanded by Col. Eli Geva, who a few weeks earlier had astounded his comrades and superiors by lecturing the minister of defense on the need to steer clear of the Syrians in Lebanon. Only two of Geva's company commanders had seen combat; for all the others, this campaign was to be a baptism by fire. The men of Geva's unit were eighteen-to-twenty-year-old conscripts and included a good proportion of religious soldiers serving in the special *hesder* program, which enabled them to combine their military service with advanced studies in Jewish subjects. Many of them had been called back from weekend leaves and had not returned to their base until some time on Saturday (the religious boys received special dispensation to travel on the Sabbath). Others, delayed even longer, did not rejoin their units until Sunday morning. Geva's mission was to race up the coast, skirting the foci of Palestinian resistance, and deliver the APCs to Amos Yaron's paratroops waiting north of Sidon. The level of motivation among his men was assessed as high, for the extended and repeated alerts in the north had been hard on them, and feeling was strong that the time had come for Israel to put an end to the PLO's threat to the Galilee—at least for the present, if not once and for all.

The commander of the force that was to quell any resistance in the refugee camps in the western sector was Brig. Gen. Yitzhak Mordechai, a battle-hardened paratrooper who belonged to the "second generation" of Israeli officers—meaning that he had begun his service in the IDF rather than in the prestate underground. Born in Iraq, he had come to Israel at the age of six and grown up on a moshav farming cooperative. Mordechai had impressive battle credentials. In the Yom Kippur War he commanded a company of paratroops at the fierce battle of the Chinese Farm, and in 1978 he headed a brigade that took part in Operation Litani. Now he commanded the division that was to take on the Palestinians in earnest.

Geva's brigade massed within the Haddad enclave, which was actually Lebanese territory, and at precisely 11:00 A.M. moved out into the UNIFIL zone. The UN peacekeeping troops appeared to be stunned by the number of tanks rumbling toward them in two columns. They made no attempt to stop the armor; on the contrary, after regaining their wits some of the UN soldiers began to wave amiably, and one soldier even flashed a V with his fingers. The tank crews assumed that such goodwill was motivated more by an instinct for self-preservation than true support for their cause. The UNIFIL troops had no sane choice but to stand aside. Their commanders had ordered them not to oppose the Israeli forces, and although some dutifully tried to keep tally of the number of vehicles passing by their positions, they soon grew tired of counting. Yet despite their studied neutrality, not all of the peacekeepers emerged unscathed. Soon after the Israelis had crossed the frontier, a UN jeep was caught in the crossfire between Israelis and Palestinians, and all four of its passengers were injured.

Half an hour after starting out, the lead company of Geva's brigade had its first encounter with Palestinian fighters when a hail of rocket-propelled-grenade (RPG) fire was loosed at the lead tanks from a fortified position along the road to Tyre. After a brief battle, the position was destroyed. Then, at a nearby crossroads, the same tanks suffered a stroke of bad luck when Israeli planes mistakenly bombed the junction just as they were pulling into it. The force of the blast knocked one of the tanks off the road, and its crew was fortunate to suffer only bruises. Since the standing order was to brook no delays and reach the Kasmiye Bridge over the Litani as quickly as possible, Geva's brigade left the job of mopping up the areas through which it passed to the units that would follow. The result was that the Palestinians were able to fire from the same positions at later sections of the same column (such as the artillery units moving up behind the tanks) and to close the road a second, then a third time. Learning of this, and fearing that his support units would be vulnerable to enemy fire, Geva ordered his fuel and ammunition trucks to stay behind until the road was clear. He chose to risk a shortage of gas and shells rather than expose the drivers and their vehicles to danger.

The Israelis knew that the real battle in this sector would not be for Tyre itself but primarily for the refugee camps that hemmed the city and lined the road running inland to the east. There were six camps of varying size in this vicinity: el-Bas, Beni Maushouk, Burj Shemali, Rashidiye, el-Hanina, and Shabrikha. Since Geva's orders were to bypass the camps anyway, he asked the chief of staff if he could revise the original plan and avoid driving through the crossroads by the el-Bas camp, where he was sure he would meet with stiff resistance. His tanks were allowed instead to move off the road and make a detour past three of the camps before picking up the main route northward. Yet ironically, despite Geva's concern and care, his brigade still suffered a bad mishap at the el-Bas crossroads.

Lt. Col. Uri Geiger, the commander of a paratroop battalion farther back in Geva's column, had taken over his unit a short time before and was unfamiliar with the area through which the brigade was now driving. The course northward passed through citrus groves that swallowed up sections of the column from time to time, making visual contact difficult. On top of that, just as his battalion was crossing the border, Geiger reported that the communications set in his APC was inoperative. He was told to move into another APC, but for some reason failed to do so.

As Geiger's battalion was passing through one of the orchards, a squad of Palestinians suddenly emerged out of nowhere and began firing RPGs at it. One of the tanks sustained a hit, and then an APC was brought to a standstill. Farther ahead, near the Shabrikha camp, Eli Geva looked back and saw a column of black smoke billowing upward in the distance. He tried to raise Geiger on the network but got no reply. From other reports, however, he understood that part of Geiger's battalion had taken a wrong turn and driven smack into the crossroads that Geva had managed to avoid. Geva kept his column speeding northward but told his second-in-command to assist the men pinned down in the el-Bas crossroads, if possible without pumping any additional forces into the area under fire.

Actually, the commander of the tank company escorting Geiger's paratroops suspected they had taken the wrong road. He contacted Geiger over the network and asked whether he had meant to make that last turn. Geiger replied yes, he had done so deliberately, but almost as soon as he confirmed that ill-fated course, the lead tank entered the crossroads and took a direct hit from RPG fire. It slammed through the wall of a nearby building, and contact with it was lost. A second tank strayed off the road and was immobilized. Then an APC was hit and began to burn as men leaped frantically in every direction and joined the crews of the disabled tanks in looking for cover.

Geiger ordered the rest of his force to halt just as the deputy brigade commander pulled up in a tank that was itself promptly knocked out by RPG fire. He managed to climb out of the vehicle and join Geiger in his APC, but they didn't get very far before that vehicle, too, was hit. Most of its men jumped out and scurried for cover, and the deputy commander ran back toward the remainder of Geiger's force. Only later did he discover that in the confusion of battle, caught in the maelstrom of rocket fire and smoke, Geiger had run in the opposite direction and been taken prisoner, along with two of his men. A few days later, Geiger and one other Israeli were murdered by their captors. The second missing soldier, Efraim Talbi, was rescued when his guards ran into an IDF patrol while fleeing northward.

Extricating the remaining men of Geiger's battalion proved to be a difficult task. After Geiger disappeared it was evident that without massive air support there was little hope of breaking the Palestinians' grip over the junction. This was the first time the Israeli senior command had had to deal with the question of how to use the air force in a heavily populated area. At the Sunday early-morning meeting in Northern Command headquarters, Sharon had admonished his generals not to use the air force casually or liberally. "We mustn't come down hard on the population if we want to build a new relationship with it in the future," he explained. But now that Uri Geiger's battalion was caught in the crossroads, this declaration was put to its first test. Would it really be possible to stick by such good intentions when the men in the field were in dire straits and the command was under heavy pressure to save them? Sharon happened to be at Drori's headquarters when the news of el-Bas came in, and it was he who decided what to do next.

The pilots did as they were ordered, and their heavy bombing helped ferret the Palestinians out of their positions. But stubborn resistance continued in other places, though in a different way. Obviously the Palestinians were not functioning in the large frameworks expected of a quasi-regular army. There were no signs of organization as battalions or companies, and it is doubtful whether even platoons were operating in concert. They seemed to be limited to groups even smaller than squads. And although these groups were armed with abundant quantities of RPGs, their chances of halting armored columns were nil. At best they could cause losses, exact a certain toll from the formally organized Israelis, and prove for posterity that they were not afraid to take on enemy tanks. No one disputed that they showed inordinate courage. To a large degree, however, it was reckless bravura, and their triumphs proved short-lived and Pyrrhic.

Well after the battle of el-Bas, Eli Geva analyzed the Palestinians' conduct from a purely professional standpoint. "They were brave," he conceded, "but they acted illogically. A squad would suddenly pop up under a tree to fire on our tanks. We blasted its men from a distance—for the most part before they managed to fire off their weapons. Then, a few meters away, another squad would pop up and attempt to fire on us—even though its men had seen what happened to their comrades—and they, too, were cut down by heavy fire. Israeli soldiers would never behave that way. They wouldn't stand up and expose themselves after witnessing the fate of their predecessors. It was foolish but uncommonly brave. To stand up in front of a tank after seeing what happened a moment before—that's almost irrational. But that's what happened all along the road."

Another tactic used elsewhere to catch the Israelis off guard was to send a civilian vehicle out against tanks. A car would innocently draw up to the first tank in a column, and suddenly its passengers would scramble out and open fire on the nearest, most open targets. The chances of surprising the first tank were usually good, but as soon as the tactic was exposed it became a suicide mission.

By the time darkness fell Sunday night, Eli Geva's brigade had reached the town of Sarafend, about halfway between Tyre and Sidon. It bivouacked for the night in a soccer field, arranging its tanks in a circle with their guns pointing outward in classic laager fashion. The gunners were told to open fire every so often, shooting at random into the darkness, to deter the enemy from trying to sneak up on the camp. Even so, occasional fire was directed at the laager, though there were no casualties.

While Geva's men settled down for the night, an action was just beginning farther north on the coast. At 11:00 P.M. the amphibious landing commenced near the Awali estuary above Sidon. First a marine-commando unit secured the beach while another squad came ashore farther north to prevent reinforcements from that direction. The first round of landings brought ashore a mixed force of tanks, APCs, self-propelled artillery, even a tractor. With the help of a full moon, the landing went off without a hitch. A second round of landings was scheduled for the next day. In the meanwhile, as the landing craft returned to Israel to take on more troops and equipment, gunboats anchored offshore to cover the men on the beach. Brig. Gen. Amos Yaron spent the night pitching and bobbing on one of those boats, close to the radio that would bring him instructions on how to proceed. He had still not received the order to advance up to Beirut, but he assumed that as soon as the APCs arrived from the south he would be told to speed northward and reinforce Bashir Gemayel's men.

It was quite a while before the Palestinians at Sidon sensed that something peculiar was happening to the north. Yaron's troops received isolated shots from nearby orchards, and an occasional Katyusha rocket fell in their vicinity, but they suffered no damage or casualties and certainly could not claim to be under attack. In his Sidon headquarters, Col. Haj Ismail, commander of Fatah's Kastel Brigade and the officer responsible for the entire sector, finally got word that an Israeli raiding party had set down near the Awali River. He immediately sent a reconnaissance patrol to observe the small bay and report back to him, but when the men returned with news that the alleged raiding party was actually a mass landing of Israeli forces, he accused them of exaggerating and announced that he was going out to see for himself. That was the last anyone in his headquarters saw of Haj Ismail. Stopping just long enough to load the command's safe into an ambulance, he made a clean getaway, driving right through the Israeli lines. The next morning he turned up in one of the command posts near Shtura, in the Bekaa Valley, reporting that with his own eyes he had seen the U.S. Sixth Fleet landing Israeli troops north of Sidon and had beat a tactical retreat so that he could continue to exercise command over his men, who had likewise withdrawn from the city. His incredible news did not save him from infamy: Yasser Arafat relieved him of his command and established a commission of inquiry to investigate his conduct under fire.

The other major clash that took place on the first day of the fighting in South Lebanon was the battle for the Beaufort. Perched 717 meters above sea level, the fortress commands Upper Galilee and much of south-central Lebanon—the heart of the Haddad enclave. More than any other position in the area, it had become a symbol and constant reminder of the PLO's power over the lives of Israelis and Lebanese alike. The Beaufort was a formidable structure whose battlements afforded a view for miles in every direction and enabled spotters to direct mortar and artillery fire at towns and settlements on both sides of the border. The Palestinians could not have asked for a better observation point, and even the Syrians had sent a team of artillery spotters there. Time and again the Israelis had bombed and shelled the fortress, blasting gaping holes in its roof. The IDF had also sent a number of raiding parties into its vicinity. But Israeli soldiers were never able to enter the fortress proper.

To the Palestinians, the ruined fortress was a massive memento of Saladin's great victory over the imperialist Crusaders after a two-year siege, and in more contemporary terms it was an emblem of their own endurance in the face of the terrifying power of Israel's air force and artillery. So closely was the Beaufort associated with Palestinian prowess that a pose of its defenders standing defiantly on the ramparts served as the colophon on leaflets printed by the PLO.

The capture of this scourge of the Galilee had been planned in detail by Northern Command long before the war broke out, and the mission had been entrusted to one of the army's elite units, the Golani commandos. The Beaufort became something of a sideline if not exactly an obsession for Golani's prized unit. Its men studied the castle's fortified positions and connecting trenches, sat through films shot by intelligence drones, and practiced various assault tactics until they had them down pat. Thus when the war came it was only natural that the conquest of the fortress should be assigned to the unit that had been preparing for it for years.

On the other hand, actual developments in the field dictated that an assault on the Beaufort should be avoided altogether—or at least postponed—because it might well prove unnecessary. The Israeli divisions sweeping into Lebanon would quickly put the fortress behind them. The campaign was envisioned as a full-fledged war to conquer the whole of South Lebanon up to Beirut and the highway to Damascus, not as a localized punitive action or a replay of Operation Litani. Within a day, the mighty Beaufort would at any rate be reduced to a small pocket of futile resistance far to the rear of the Israeli juggernaut. And its Palestinian defenders could not help but realize that they were best off fleeing for their lives, their courage and perseverance having become pointless.

Under only one circumstance would it have been necessary to take the Beaufort during the opening stage of the war: if the IDF's main thrust north and west had been over the Hardele Bridge, just below the fortress and firmly in the sights of the weapons positioned there. But the IDF's main drive in this area was channeled farther west, via the Akiye Bridge —the main artery for Einan's division headed up the central axis and for Kahalani's division on its way to take Nabatiye and then continue on to Sidon. The Beaufort could have no effect on this flow of men and equipment. The fifteen Palestinians stationed on that lone and lofty height did not even fire at Israeli settlements when the war broke out.

On the Israeli side, as soon as the IDF's operational plan was adjusted and the main thrust was redirected to the Akiye Bridge, there was no special urgency to neutralizing the Beaufort. Amir Drori's staff grasped this fact only after the invasion started and tried to postpone the Golani attack. The chief of staff happened to be in the command's war room when the subject came up, and he personally confirmed the postponement. Drori issued an order not to go through with the Beaufort operation that night, but for some reason it never reached the Golani commando. The order was simply swallowed up, misplaced or forgotten somewhere down the line. At midnight, therefore, when urgent requests for helicopters to evacuate the wounded from the Beaufort resounded through his war room, Amir Drori was thoroughly bewildered. It was his first clue that the action had gone ahead despite his order to postpone it. After the war an investigation was held to find out why the order failed to reach its destination but the results were inconclusive.

The original strategy for capturing the Beaufort called for a night attack with the assault force silently approaching the objective from the east. Since the war was to begin in the morning, Drori had approved a request that the attack take place instead in daylight, with the commandos approaching from the west on APCs and mounting their assault with the aid of tanks after a massive softening-up action by air and artillery units. The assault was scheduled to begin between 3:00 and 4:00 P.M., but when H-hour was set for 11:00 A.M. the plan put the Golani commando an hour behind schedule. The commander of the Golani Brigade did suggest to his division commander that the commandos be placed at the head of the column, and in fact if they had reached the Beaufort just one hour earlier than planned, at 2:00 P.M., their assault might well have begun that afternoon. As it was, they had to creep along at the end of a long, sluggish column that came to a halt countless times along the way, and they did not reach the Nabatiye plateau until late in the afternoon. A daytime assault with massive support was out of the question now; the action would have to begin after dark.

At 4:00 P.M., when the column finally wound its way up to the Nabatiye highlands, the deputy commander of the Golani Brigade asked the division command if there were any new instructions. He noted that the assault on the Beaufort was supposed to be carried out in daylight but that it would inevitably turn into a night attack now. Not that he had any particular misgivings about an assault under cover of darkness. After all, that was how the operation was originally conceived and how his men had trained for it. But it did occur to him that the front command might want to postpone the attack till dawn the next day. He was told that there was no such change.

The men of the commando unit had spent hours on the road just reaching their objective and had begun to doze off in the APCs as they grew bored with eyeing the fortress from afar. The only worrisome problem faced by the men that afternoon was the tanks that had been attached to their unit. The Golani commando had been honored with a platoon of tanks that the men snidely referred to as "whores" because they were passed from hand to hand and were not cared for and regularly serviced by any one unit. Little wonder that they were in poor mechanical condition and ground to a halt every few hundred meters, further exacerbating the delay. In the end they never even made it to the Beaufort; all they accomplished was to hold up the column. The remaining fire support would come from artillery and mortars. Yet the closer the men drew to the fortress, the more this fire abated.

Seated in an APC, as a stowaway of sorts, was Guni Harnik, the one-time commander of the Golani commando. Just the night before, the unit had thrown a party for Guni to mark his discharge from the IDF, and it was during this celebration that he got wind of the latest alert and heard that the commando had been summoned back north. A brand new civilian who had spent all his adult years in the army, the twenty-six-year-old Guni was looking forward to realizing an old dream of traveling coast to coast across the United States. His final months in the army had been marked by the polarization that seemed to be straining the fabric of Israeli society at large; repeatedly, he found himself involved in heated arguments about the future of the Israeli-Palestinian conflict. Guni was known for un-abashedly dovish views, and his remarks often elicited strong reactions from other officers. His political foil in the unit was Motti Goldman, who prided himself on being an adherent of the Greater Land of Israel movement and supported the annexation of all the occupied territories. On more than one occasion, the debates wandered onto the subject of the anticipated war in Lebanon, and Guni made no secret of the fact that he opposed a deliberately instigated war.

Yet now the soldier in Guni Harnik came to the fore. His comrades were going out to battle, and he just couldn't bear to be left behind. His first instinct was to contact the brigade's deputy commander at home, but he had already left for his headquarters in the north. So Guni rushed north on his own and asked to receive his old command back. For lack of any official response, he climbed into an APC and waited to see how the battle would develop.

When the commander of the Golani commando was reported wounded —he had taken a bullet in the chest while still on the road—nothing could have been more apt than to send Guni in to replace him. The problem was to get him to the unit in time to lead the assault. In a flash, he commandeered an APC and had it barreling forward so quickly that it flipped over as it careened around a curve. Guni and the other occupants spilled out, but except for some bad bruises they were uninjured. After dusting himself off, Guni continued his journey on the run, with two men from the APC in tow.

He was greeted by about twenty APCs brimming with men from his old unit and from an engineering company assigned to take the outpost adjoining the Beaufort. The APCs were scattered in the darkness that had fallen minutes before Guni's arrival, and his first step was surprising from a tactical viewpoint, though it proved a great boost to morale: announcing himself over the network with his old code name, Guni told the APC drivers to turn on their headlights. This would give them away to the enemy, but at least it would allow them to close in quickly, get a sense of their own strength, and feel that they had a leader again.

Guni's second order surprised his troops even more. He told them to jump off the APCs and prepare for an assault on foot. The members of the engineering company, sixty-five in all, were supposed to take the southern outpost and its bunkers, while the Golani commandos would attack the northern outpost and clean out its trenches and other fortified positions at the foot of the fortress.

Some of the Palestinians stationed in the Beaufort may have escaped, but those who remained fought like tigers to the end, even though their cause was hopeless. For many of the Israelis, the capture of the fortress was also a battle of prestige. "We fought to take the flag away from them," was how Motti Goldman explained it in retrospect.

Twenty-one men began the assault behind Guni Harnik and Motti Goldman, dashing up the asphalt road that seemed to gleam in the moonlight. They had to cover 150 meters with enemy positions all along their left flank. All Motti could see were the flashes of fire coming from three or four positions on his left. He did not know what was happening behind him, and when he dove down beside Guni and turned back to glance at his men, he was dismayed to see that only ten of them remained, less than half. The clatter of machine-gun fire must have drowned out the cries of the boys who were hit and sent the others to cover. Guni ordered Motti to renew the assault on the main trench and promised to send in a second wave after him. Neither of them knew that, of the group that remained behind, two men were already dead and four others were wounded.

For a moment Motti hesitated to pick himself up and keep going. A heavy machine gun was spewing fire from one of the positions opposite, and long bursts were being returned by an Israeli fire-support unit farther down the hillside. From time to time an illumination flare exploded in the sky and bathed the fortress and its surroundings in a pale, ghostly light. In the space between the dimming of one flare and the launching of the next, Motti and seven other men got to their feet and began the second assault.

Along with two other men, Avikam and Razi, Motti reached the main trench just as a Palestinian bobbed up and began to rush them. The three Israelis fired simultaneously and the figure collapsed. Avikam was the first to jump into the trench, followed by Razi. Motti was still standing over them when a long burst of fire exploded in the trench and he saw both of his comrades cut down. From his position above the two men, Motti could hear their groans. A fourth man to reach the spot tried to drag Razi out of the trench, but suddenly the click of a grenade pin was heard and instinctively the man jumped back for cover. The grenade's fragments were Razi's coup de grace.

Motti moved still farther up the line, reluctant to jump into the narrow trench. For a moment he felt frozen, alone with his fears, but then he leaped blindly toward the position that had fired on Avikam and Razi. After tossing a grenade, he jumped down into the trench only to find himself standing opposite a man who seemed stunned by the blast, or perhaps wounded. Either way, Motti shot him dead before he could recover his wits and mow him down instead. Since the magazine of Motti's Galil assault rifle was almost empty by now, he decided to take the dead Palestinian's Kalashnikov. Only then did he notice how thick were the cement walls of the castle's defenses.

Climbing out of the trench again, Motti continued to shoot at the positions from above. He was sure that he wouldn't get very far, that any second now a burst of gunfire would put an abrupt end to the whole grotesque scene. The battle struck him as a surrealistic dream played out in a deafening racket. As he ran along the edge of the trench, he could see his silhouette flickering on the fortress wall like the dance of a crazed giant. He shot a Palestinian who was scurrying through the trench firing and shouting incomprehensibly. Then two Israeli soldiers came up from behind and offered Motti additional grenades. Right afterward Guni arrived.

Together Motti Goldman and Guni Harnik stood facing a long concrete position that contained a single Palestinian fighter spraying the area with occasional fire. The Israelis did not call on him to surrender, and he showed no signs of giving himself up in order to save his life. Two Israeli fighters—Motti Goldman, a self-proclaimed hawk, and Guni Harnik, a man who called for compromise with the Palestinians—stood side by side in a trench at a ruined Crusader castle in Lebanon opposite a lone, trapped Palestinian, sharing a single choice: kill or be killed. As one man lobbed grenades at the concrete position, the other pumped out bursts of gunfire. Some twenty grenades had been futilely expended on the position when Guni suddenly jerked backward and let out a short moan as his head fell limply forward. A few moments later he was dead, a bullet embedded in his chest. The Palestinian continued to fire until Motti, in a mixture of terror and anger, hurled a huge explosive charge at the concrete position and blew it to bits.

The battle was over. The Beaufort and its defenders had been defeated by the Golani commandos. But now the enormous cost became apparent: five members of the unit had been killed in the main assault, and a sixth fell when the support force went into action. The next day, troubling thoughts began to gnaw at the Golani fighters, the doubts of victors who would neither deny nor belittle the noble stand of their vanquished adversaries but who had to question the point of it all. The heroes of the Beaufort on both sides had fought each other to the end. "In retrospect, though, I would have left the Beaufort alone, not attacked it," confessed the commander of the Golani Brigade. "I mean I would have kept it under fire, but not assaulted the positions."

The pain and doubt might have been mastered more easily had not political pettiness entered the scene. On Monday Menachem Begin, dressed formally as usual in a dark-colored suit, was brought to the fortress that had monopolized his attention the previous afternoon. He was preceded by Chief of Staff Eitan, who was astounded to learn of the cost of the victory. But Begin and Sharon, who came accompanied by newsmen and photographers, knew nothing of the losses, and Sharon failed to inquire before impulsively declaring that no men had been killed on the Israeli side. A junior lieutenant from the commando unit who had been left

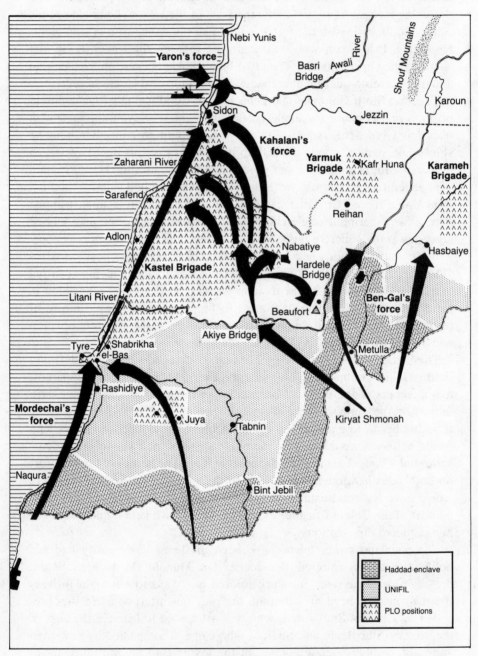

SWEEP INTO SOUTH LEBANON

to man the fortress was so rattled by the carefree mood of the visit that he suddenly blurted out, "What are you talking about? Six of my friends were killed here. Six boys from my unit!" Sharon seemed dazed by the statement.

Still, the news did not change plans for the curious event that followed. Saad Haddad had been transported to join Begin and Sharon at the Beaufort, and in a short ceremony the prime minister announced that he was officially turning the fortress over to the Lebanese major. The Palestinian guns there had harassed the population of Haddad's Christian enclave even more than the Israeli settlements over the frontier, and it seemed only just to include Haddad in the celebration of its defeat. But the real reason behind the pause for ceremony in wartime was an attempt to smooth ruffled feathers. Haddad, it seemed, deserved some compensation for the indignity he had suffered on the previous evening, when he had been summoned to a meeting with Bashir Gemayel at Northern Front headquarters. At first Bashir had tried to wangle his way out of the meeting by sending an aide in his stead, but Haddad had refused to receive the surrogate. So Bashir came in person, but still in a truculent mood: when Haddad entered the room, he turned to his aide and said disdainfully, "Shake his hand for me, will you." Cut to the quick, Haddad turned on his heels and stalked out of the room. He had come prepared for a reconciliation with Bashir, but Gemayel could see him only as an irritating rival for Israel's patronage and a tool who might yet be used against him. Now Begin was trying to placate the spurned Haddad by lavishing an attractive gift on him.

Then the helicopters whisked the self-congratulatory and slightly ludicrous figures away. Begin did not proceed to the front command. Instead, he continued south to Jerusalem and never set foot on Lebanese soil again. From then on, reports from afar were good enough for him. He had partaken of the glory of war; other men had paid the price.

8

The Snag at Sidon

NO ONE ON EITHER SIDE OF THE BORDER believed for a moment that the Palestinian forces had any chance of repulsing the IDF brigades thundering toward them in South Lebanon. The only questions on that bright June morning were how long the newly organized semiregular forces would be able to stave off the Israelis and whether the IDF would succeed in completing its mission with a minimum of losses.

From H-hour, three Israeli divisions relentlessly closed in on the Palestinians from all sides. Yitzhak Mordechai's brigades drove up the western axis over the coastal road, while farther north, between Sidon and Damour, Amos Yaron's forces landed from the sea. At the same time, the Israeli navy placed a blockade on the coast and shelled the ports of Sidon and Tyre to prevent the transfer of reinforcements from Beirut, or even from outside the country. In the central sector, Avigdor Kahalani's division climbed up to the Nabatiye highlands in a classic pincer movement, then headed northwest toward Sidon. The routes taken by these armored and mechanized forces were chosen to achieve the encirclement of South Lebanon while isolating the various Fatah battalions in the field. The prospects of the PLO's escaping this snare or receiving assistance from the Syrians stationed in the Bekaa Valley to the east were further reduced by the drive of Menachem Einan's division up the central axis toward the Shouf Mountains, which effectively cut South Lebanon off from the Bekaa Valley. And to cap this highly lopsided strategic advantage, the skies were exclusively in Israel's control, with its ground forces receiving generous support from helicopters and fighter planes. In fact, though this option was not exploited, there was nothing to prevent the IDF from landing airborne troops at selected points behind the Palestinian lines.

From the moment the war broke out, it was also obvious that the Palestinians were facing the Israeli war machine completely alone. The lavish promises of their Arab brothers turned out to be empty bombast; their efforts on behalf of the trapped Palestinians boiled down to anemic formal protests. The Syrians, who boasted the largest and closest military force available, made a mockery of every one of their commitments to the PLO. Except for sending out some MiG fighters on a few random and rather aimless sorties, they essentially abandoned the Palestinians in South Lebanon—and would do precious little more during the battle for Beirut. Algeria, another outspoken friend of the PLO, contented itself with sending three Antonov transport planes filled with arms. The aircraft landed in Damascus on the second day of the war, but the weapons were delayed in reaching the Palestinians. The Saudis did their part by dispatching a number of trucks loaded with medical equipment, but they got only as far as Syria. Libya, on the other hand, announced that it was sending a contingent of its forces by sea, yet the plan was never implemented. The Libyans claimed that the troops were to have landed at a Syrian port and continued on to Lebanon but that President Assad refused to allow this.

The only Arab state that actually sent military support in the form of personnel was Jordan, of all countries. Despite the fact that his government was traditionally hostile to the PLO, King Hussein allowed a battalion of Palestinians serving in his army to set out for Beirut as soon as the fighting broke out. Called "Force Bader," the battalion included a number of Palestinian criminals who were given the option of a release from prison if they were prepared to fight. Part of Force Bader actually did make it to Beirut before the IDF surrounded the city, but much of it got caught in the Bekaa Valley and never saw action.

Outside the Arab world, the PLO's patrons in the Kremlin, who were also its main arms suppliers, limited themselves to mouthing vacant declarations of support throughout the war—even during the siege of Beirut.

The Palestinians, then, were virtually cut loose and left to fend for themselves. Not that they were the only armed camp in South Lebanon. The Shiite and Druse communities were also capable of taking up arms against the Israelis—at least no less than the Palestinian militias in the camps—and for years the senior echelon in the PLO had gone out of its way to cultivate a sense of common cause in South Lebanon toward precisely this end. Arafat believed that it would be fairly easy to draw the Lebanese Druse and Moslems, especially the Shiites, to his side in a war if only he could prevent a deterioration in communal relations.

To improve the PLO's image and standing among the rural and largely indigent Shiites, Arafat had ordered his forces to stay clear of their villages and deploy instead in the nearby countryside. Nevertheless, friction to the point of armed clashes between the Shiite militia and the Palestinian cadres seemed almost unavoidable. Every so often a *sulkha,* a traditional reconciliation ceremony, was held to shore up the crumbling foundations of Arab solidarity, at which the leaders of the PLO did everything they could to placate and compensate the Shiite villagers. But it was to no avail. On the day the IDF invaded Lebanon, the Shiites decided to sit out the war. Mahmoud Ghadar, the military commander of the Amal movement in the south, ordered his men not to resist the entry of the Israeli army, and even to surrender their weapons if necessary. His order was obeyed by all but a small group of Amal members, who joined in the fighting in the Burj Shemali refugee camp near Tyre. And so the Israeli armored columns advancing on Sidon from the southeast rolled through the heavily populated Shiite district without meeting resistance. The villagers received them with complete equanimity.

Farther north in the Shouf Mountains, the PLO suffered a similar slap in the face from the Druses when the leader of the community's leftist faction, Walid Jumblatt, ordered his men not to fire on the Israelis and to limit Druse opposition to "passive resistance." If they had wanted to disrupt the IDF's advance through their mountain stronghold, all they had to do was lay mines and ambushes on the narrow, serpentine roads, and their well-armed militias could easily have played havoc with the Israeli supply convoys. But appreciating through bitter experience that the stakes in Lebanon were always high, they feared Israeli reprisals against their villages. Rather than make any show of armed resistance, therefore, Jumblatt's men were ordered to conceal their weapons and the rest of their abundant military supplies in special caches. The decision to abstain from battle came as an enormous disappointment to Arafat, especially because Walid's father, the late Kamal Jumblatt, had been a strong and respected ally of the Palestinians during the Lebanese civil war. Now, it seemed, the Druses—like the Shiites—were looking out for their own interests first and were in no mood to indulge in any heroics for the sake of someone else's patently lost cause.

Thus foresaken by all their erstwhile allies and backers, the best the PLO could hope for was a quick ceasefire that would prevent Israel's tanks and infantry from overrunning all of South Lebanon.

The PLO's deployment was based on a chain of platoon-size outposts built on the high ground and replete with trenches and bunkers protected by fences and mine fields. Other Palestinian troops were scattered in tent camps throughout the region in open areas, groves, and narrow wadis. Israeli intelligence estimates put the number of PLO fighters in South Lebanon at 6,000 divided into three concentrations: about 1,500 south of the Litani River in the so-called Iron Triangle (between the villages of Kana, Dir Amas, and Juya), Tyre, and its surrounding refugee camps; another 2,500 of the Kastel Brigade in three districts between the Litani and a line running from Sidon to northeast of Nabatiye; and a third large concentration of about 1,500–2,000 men of the Karameh Brigade in the east, on the slopes of Mount Hermon (popularly known as "Fatahland"). This last group was essentially integrated within the Syrian disposition in the Bekaa Valley and under the protection of its missile umbrella. The central sector also contained most of the rear headquarters and ammunition dumps.

The overwhelming majority of men under arms were Palestinians, joined by volunteers from other Arab and Moslem countries, including hundreds from Pakistan and Bangladesh and a smattering from India and Ceylon. The foreigners were for the most part employed in professional and staff jobs in the commands, though some could be found in the field units. Pride of place among the Arab countries for supplying volunteers went to Egypt, Yemen, and Jordan, followed by Iraq.

Beyond their large reserves of personal weapons, the Palestinians had a few dozen T-34 tanks and field guns; dozens of Katyusha rocket launchers, antiaircraft guns, and shoulder-born Strela (SAM-7) antiaircraft missiles; and many RPGs and other antitank weapons. The arms depots and bunkers in South Lebanon contained mostly ammunition and rifles (5,000 of them of Western manufacture alone), also a plethora of machine and submachine guns (some 3,500 of them) and other automatic weapons (1,400). From a purely statistical standpoint, this quantity of men and matériel represented the power of about one infantry division with enough weapons in its stores to equip another force of approximately the same size. From an administrative standpoint, it was a force still in transition between a rough collection of guerrilla cadres and a regular army.

The greatest problem plaguing the Palestinian units in South Lebanon was related not to armaments, however, but to the officers who were supposed to supervise and coordinate the fighting. Put bluntly, at the command level the PLO's military force proved to be an unmitigated disaster. The most striking evidence of this was the fact that the field units used only a fraction of the thousands of mines at their disposal. Thus when the Israeli forces crossed into South Lebanon, they found the roads wide open and utterly free of obstacles. Even the bridges over the Litani and Zaharani rivers were intact; no attempt had been made to sabotage them. Eli Geva's men did not reach the Kasmiye Bridge on the coastal route until 2:00 P.M. on Sunday, but to their amazement they found it in perfect condition and crossed it without incident. The same was true of the Akiye Bridge in the central sector. It was as if the order to blow up these key strategic points simply had not been issued, evidently because there was no one capable of issuing it. Almost immediately, the local Palestinian command lost control over developments in the field and failed to coordinate between one sector and the next, while the high command in Beirut was completely out of touch with the south—though not because of anything for which the Israelis could take credit. Israel's air force had tried to cripple the PLO's operations room on Friday afternoon but had missed the mark and hit a nearby building. Nonetheless, Arafat and his commanders in Beirut remained unaware of what was happening at the front for a full forty-eight hours!

The reason for the breakdown in communications was that the first to flee South Lebanon were the most senior PLO officers. Haj Ismail, overall commander of the area, disappeared on Sunday night, leaving Abu Walid, the PLO's chief of staff in Beirut, with no contact at the front. The commander of the Jarmak Battalion in Nabatiye, Major Muin, ran out on his men when he heard that advance companies of the Israeli force were closing on the town. Col. Abu Haldon of the Yarmuk Brigade, who ordered his men to beat a retreat and scatter as soon as the Israelis reached the central axis, was the first to carry out his own order, though many of his subordinates fought on. Farther to the east, Col. Abu Hajem, commander of the Karameh Brigade, vanished behind the Syrian lines, later claiming that he had gone to consult with his military superiors.

In all of South Lebanon, only one high-ranking officer stood fast, and oddly enough it was Azmi Zerayer, the dreaded head of the Fatah battalion in Tyre. Zerayer was an improbable hero: feared and detested by the native Lebanese as a murderer, rapist, and a generally ruthless character, he was also suspected by his comrades of being a double agent ever since Moshe Dayan had released him from an Israeli prison in the early 1970s. Yet Zerayer remained at his post and directed the fighting in his sector for about a day before losing control over his forces and slipping away into the nearby orchards. He took refuge in a deserted villa, but then one of his fighters was captured and told his interrogators where Zerayer was hiding. When the Israelis attacked the house, Zerayer fought back and met his end, at least, with honor.

The corollary of this complete failure of nerve on the command level was that the plan for a holding action, based on a determined stand at the Hardele Bridge and on the Nabatiye plateau, fell victim to chaos. The minute the Palestinian troops saw that their commanders were gone, countless members of the semiregular units stripped off their uniforms and tried to melt into the local population or hide out in the wadis. Others moved carefully but steadily north toward Beirut or into the Syrian-occupied Bekaa Valley. From his operations room in Beirut, Abu Walid kept broadcasting calls to stem the Israeli onslaught because a ceasefire was on the way. But when forty-eight hours passed without any signs of a truce, or even credible support from the Syrians, he finally issued orders to withdraw to the north or the east. The Syrians, for their part, were quick to sneer at the Fatah brigades for turning tail and running before even attempting a defense. "We thought the fighting in South Lebanon would last longer," noted Ahmed Iskander, the Syrian propaganda minister.

Iskander's scorn may have been appropriate where the Fatah's semiregular forces were concerned, but it certainly was not a just assessment of the resistance in South Lebanon as a whole, where many of the Palestinian fighters showed inordinate courage and determination. Throughout the western sector, Palestinian irregulars stood up to armored forces that came at them in daunting quantities and with unstinting air support. Indeed, their resistance absolutely shattered the Israeli timetable. It took the cream of the IDF's men—the Golani Infantry Brigade, vetern paratroops, and an armored force—two whole days to overcome the PLO stronghold in Sidon. The link-up with Amos Yaron's paratroops at the Awali River was not accomplished until Wednesday, June 9—days, rather than the predicted hours, after the invasion began. And although the distance from the Israeli border to Beirut is less than ninety kilometers, the Israelis did not reach their Maronite allies until June 13, a full week into the war. In the event, erratically armed and barely trained militiamen detained the vastly superior Israel Defense Forces for much longer than their deskbound planners or field commanders had thought possible.

The real war in South Lebanon was not fought by the Fatah's semiregular forces but by the homeguards in the refugee camps. It was a static, tenacious battle fought in built-up areas cut through by narrow alleyways that barely accommodated a vehicle but afforded the Palestinian irregulars excellent conditions to fight back and defy the Israelis to the end.

Then again, the Israeli forces should have expected it. Two days before the war broke out, a meeting of senior Israeli commanders had taken place at which Amos Yaron raised the question of how hard the Palestinians were likely to fight. Since his forces would be deprived of all but air and naval support until they were joined by the men pushing up the coast, his concern was legitimate. The most detailed reply came from Intelligence Chief Yehoshua Saguy, who warned his colleagues that "we tend to forget the conclusions from six years ago and the problems others faced. The Syrians," he pointedly reminded them, "stood at the gates of Sidon for no less than seven days, losing men, tanks, and APCs. I suggest that we assume there will be strong Palestinian resistance in these places. You can flee from an outpost, but it's not so easy to get up and run when you're in a city, and especially not in a refugee camp, where there are families—old people and children. They'll fight in these places; these are the vital centers of their lives. They'll lay mines, fire off RPGs from every nook and cranny. Wherever we advance, when night falls we'll find ourselves cut off from behind. And we should take this into consideration from the start."

Saguy's prediction was borne out repeatedly. The conquest of Nabatiye, for example, where the semiregular forces had six T-34 tanks and were supposed to be prepared for a long holding action, took all of three hours without costing the Israelis a single casualty. But the fighting in the refugee camps around Tyre went on for days, and the defenders of the Ein Hilweh camp, adjoining Sidon, held out for an entire week. Even the armored force on the coastal route took some punishing blows when it passed through built-up areas.

The thrust northward on that axis was renewed by Eli Geva's brigade at dawn on Monday. The brigade had to pass through the town of Sarafend, whose houses hug the main road. Geva knew that he was heading into a problematic area, for the Palestinian organizations had a long-standing foothold in Sarafend. He was therefore surprised to see civilians pouring out of their houses and energetically waving their greetings at his tanks and APCs. Some of the women even threw handfuls of rice at the Israeli vehicles as their token of homage to a victorious army. Others made victory signs. It all seemed strange to Geva, not at all what he had expected after hearing the intelligence assessments.

Indeed, the idyll didn't last long. When the head of the column reached the center of town, a group of armed men suddenly sprang up behind the civilians and opened fire on the Israelis with machine guns and RPGs. The commander of the lead tank was killed in the first burst of fire. He had been sitting in his turret waving back at the crowd when the bullets cut him down. Immediately afterward a company commander was shot in the head and crumpled into his turret. Suddenly the street dissolved into bedlam as the shrieking civilians began to run for cover. Geva's tanks were shooting back now, and civilians were caught in the crossfire. The column lurched to a halt when one of the APCs took a hit from RPG fire, and then the vehicle carrying the brigade medical team was knocked out. From that point on the advance was slow, almost deliberate. The brigade's machine guns sprayed the houses on both sides of the road, and whenever fire erupted from one of the buildings, a tank would volley back with its cannon.

As it drove out of Sarafend, Geva's force bore two dead men and three wounded, one of them in serious condition. The clash had been the brigade's first experience with fighting in a built-up area, and it showed that the Palestinians had no qualms about involving and endangering innocent civilians. Still pondering the lessons of the battle, Geva moved on to the second river in South Lebanon, the Zaharani, and again found no obstacles in his path. The bridge was fully intact, not even mined, and his tanks made the crossing with no problems and began to close in on Sidon.

Behind Geva, fighting continued in the refugee camps around Tyre. That it received relatively little attention in Israel and abroad was due to the fact that it went on in the rear, as it were, while all eyes were focused on the constant push of the armored columns farther and farther northward. Yet the clashes in these camps were by no means inconsequential. The battle for Rashidiye, south of Tyre, went on for four days before Palestinian resistance was quelled. The fighting in Burj Shemali, in the same sector, continued for three and a half days, during which repeated attempts to penetrate the camp were firmly repulsed. Since there was no urgency about subduing these camps, the Israeli troops were ordered to avoid frontal attacks and do whatever was necessary to hold down their losses. The camps were to be overcome by a strategy of steadily lopping off chunks of their territory. The ground action was accompanied by announcements over loudspeakers combining intimidation and the assurance that no harm would befall anyone who surrendered. But for all that, the IDF still sustained many casualties in its clashes with the camp militias. The battles in the Tyre area alone cost the Israelis twenty-one dead and ninety-five wounded.

Each refugee camp was independently organized into neighborhoods and sections that were assigned different defensive tasks. While the fighting raged, there was no contact between one camp and the next, just as there was none between various civilian sectors and Palestinian units in the countryside. But unlike those more exposed areas, the camps were ideal battlegrounds for fighters under attack. Their buildings huddled up against each other, making it easy to block the narrow roads and alleyways, use antitank weapons at short range, and toss hand grenades into the Israeli APCs. The invading troops found themselves fired upon from windows and rooftops, as well as at ground level. From the resistance rising out of this network of shelters and bunkers, many of which doubled as arms stores, it was obvious that the Israelis had long been expected. And such fortified hideouts were in ample supply: in Rashidiye alone the Israelis uncovered seventy-four bunkers plus another eighty in Burj Shemali and no less than 213 subterranean shelters and arms stores in el-Bas.

What made the fighting particularly difficult for the Israeli troops was the fact that these camps were essentially residential neighborhoods and were therefore crowded with civilians, especially swarms of children. The Palestinian fighters blended in easily among the population; the only thing distinguishing them from the noncombatants was the weapons they bore. Efforts were made to persuade the civilians to abandon the camps for their own safety, but to mixed results. The PLO fighters were of two minds on this issue: they fully appreciated that the civilians could not only serve them as excellent cover but would probably stir pressure for Israel to accept a quick ceasefire; yet the longer the ceasefire was delayed, the more the PLO softened at the sight of their wounded and suffering compatriots, and permitted them to seek their salvation outside the camps. The Israeli officers, for their part, halted the shelling at irregular intervals to give the unarmed residents a chance to escape.

When, after two days of fighting, the Israelis managed to cut Rashidiye in two, the Palestinians tried another tack to gain more time. They sent a representative of the Red Cross out of the camp bearing a message that if the attacks were suspended they would release an Israeli prisoner of war. The troops were promptly ordered to hold their fire, and a little while later an ambulance bearing the markings of the Red Crescent slowly approached their lines and came to a halt. With suspicion high that this was all a ruse just to get close enough to the Israelis to unleash a deadly attack or explosion, tension was visible on many faces watching the long white vehicle standing among the battered buildings. But then an Israeli soldier emerged holding a plastic infusion bag attached to one arm. Accompanied by a group of Palestinians, he began to walk haltingly toward the Israeli tanks, shouting all the while, "I am an Israeli. Don't shoot!"

The man was Gideon Shmueli, a crew member of a tank that had been hit on the outskirts of Tyre and had smashed into a building. At first he had tried to hide out with another member of his crew, but Shmueli had been wounded and a day later both men turned themselves over to the Palestinians. Shmueli was separated from his comrade and taken to a crowded subterranean infirmary run by the PLO in Rashidiye. As he took in the scene around him, the Israeli soldier didn't know what to fear more: retaliation by the sullen-faced patients or the bombs and shells that his countrymen were showering down on the camp. During one of the air raids, a bomb fell so close to the infirmary that the entire structure shook violently. Shmueli must have gone particularly pale, because one of the Palestinian nurses tried to soothe him. "We don't kill prisoners," she said in an odd mixture of compassion and acrimony. Without questioning the woman's sincerity, Shmueli may have just been lucky. Other Israeli POWs, including his own battalion commander, Uri Geiger, were executed as soon as their captors ran into trouble. In Shmueli's case, his captors were almost as distraught as he was. Sensing consternation in their every gesture, he played on the situation by advising them that their only hope of emerging from the mayhem unscathed was to let him save them along with himself. He told his captors to have the Red Cross approach the Israelis on their behalf and ask for an ambulance. A Red Cross envoy was dispatched, but when no such vehicle could be found, a doctor from the infirmary mobilized a PLO ambulance instead. Shmueli, a number of wounded refugees, and the doctor who had been instrumental in obtaining the vehicle, plus the doctor's wife, were all loaded into the ambulance, which then gingerly approached the Israeli lines, with Shmueli announcing himself over a loudspeaker in properly accented Hebrew.

Shmueli's plan worked—he and the others in the ambulance were transferred without incident—and shortly thereafter the same Red Cross envoy appeared among the Israelis a second time and made the same offer to produce a prisoner of war if the assault stopped. Again the Israeli troops were told to hold their fire, and again they waited. But this time neither the PLO ambulance nor any Israeli prisoner showed up.

The battle was even fiercer in the el-Bas camp—which the Israeli forces tried to penetrate on foot. When the assault was rebuffed, planes were called in. This kind of quick and general call for air support became something of a habit among the field commanders, even though the air force made clear its reluctance to be used as an extravagant display of power. On more than one occasion, the air-support officer attached to Yitzhak Mordechai's division loudly protested the system of arbitrarily citing targets spread over a wide area and demanded an exact citing of the places where enemy fighters were concentrated. Nevertheless, air power became an important part of the psychological war waged against the camps. At one point, for example, the Israelis announced over loudspeakers that any resistance to the entry of their troops would bring in its wake a heavy bombing of Tyre and the surrounding camps. To illustrate their determination, they told the camp residents that planes would shortly be coming in to demonstrate their "skills" in the port area. Two pairs of jets came shrieking in low over Tyre and released their loads in quick succession, causing great clouds of dust and smoke to billow up from the port.

Yet still the fighting went on. Most of the camps in the south did not fall until the third day of the war, Burj Shemali and Rashidiye being the last to surrender.

None of these refugee camps gave up easily, but the battle for Ein Hilweh made the difficulties in subduing the others pale by comparison. What happened at Ein Hilweh can only be described as a suicidal battle, a senseless and costly outpouring of rage. It was the Palestinians' last stand in South Lebanon—their Masada, as it were. There, rather than surrender to the Israeli army, they preferred to die to the last man—deliberately taking many civilians with them. The fighters in Ein Hilweh succeeded in holding up the Israeli advance past Sidon for two days, wrecking the timetable of what was supposed to be a lightning drive up the coast to the Awali River. And again, despite the intelligence warnings about the bitter fighting to be expected in the camps, the Israeli victors were astounded by the extraordinary valor of their adversaries. "Our big surprise in Sidon was the terrorists' determination to fight," said the commander of the Golani Brigade. "They made no attempt to escape and, in fact, did everything in their power to cause us as much harm as possible."

Two parallel battles took place in the Sidon-Ein Hilweh struggle: first, an attempt to thrust open the main north-south road that traverses the city, and second, a simultaneous effort to penetrate and capture the refugee camp, essentially an immediate suburb of Sidon spreading out to the southeast. The first force to try its hand at breaking through this combined barrier was Brig. Gen. Avigdor Kahalani's division, which had come up through the Nabatiye plateau. Initially the battle was carried on from a distance, through exchanges of fire. Shortly after midnight on Monday, however, Kahalani received an order to move in and capture Sidon—or at least its main thoroughfare—so the force that arrived from the south (Eli Geva's brigade) could continue up the coast. Kahalani was then to proceed northward too; Mordechai's division would take over the battle for the city and the adjoining camp as soon as he was able to move on.

Earlier that day, one of the battalions of the Golani Brigade and the armored brigade accompanying it had begun to apply pressure on Ein Hilweh from the south. Their aim was to open a route through the camp, not capture it in toto. But it soon became evident that there would be no passing through Ein Hilweh without subduing it altogether. After the Israeli force had advanced a short way into the camp, the road closed again behind it. Those who came in after the lead unit found that they had to fight the same battle all over again on the same spot. PLO militiamen waiting for the tanks and APCs attacked them at short range. On the hills around the camp, no fewer than five artillery battalions had been placed at the disposal of the penetrating force. But their shelling did little good, and when darkness fell the Israelis pulled out of the camp to seize a commanding hill nearby.

The two-pronged attack was renewed at 8:00 A.M. on Tuesday, and now the air force was called in—on top of the artillery fire—to execute dozens of sorties against the main positions in Ein Hilweh and the center of Sidon, where the northward breakthrough was planned. Before long the men of the Golani Brigade realized that the Palestinians were fighting out of well-camouflaged fortified positions, some of them built underground with a network of special embrasures and subterranean passages connecting the bunkers. The instinctive reaction was to try to increase the firepower being used against these positions, but first the civilians would have to be given a fair chance to get away. So the air force was again called in and a flurry of printed handbills came wafting down on Ein Hilweh like a freak snowstorm at the height of summer. The notices called upon the residents to abandon the camp, and some began to do so. But the Israelis had to pay a price. From their lookout posts, the soldiers of the Golani Brigade could see that occasionally the camp's defenders blended in with the fleeing civilians, only to dash back to their bunkers and continue the fight after getting a close look at the IDF positions.

The Golani Brigade's dogged advance into Ein Hilweh was finally halted in front of a well-organized tank position in the heart of the camp, and the Israelis shifted into reverse. First the tanks were pulled out in the afternoon, then came the infantry withdrawal at nightfall. It was necessary to refuel the vehicles and replenish the men's ammunition, but the move was also directed by a wise decision not to fight at night on the unfamiliar territory of the enemy's home ground. Once again the way through Ein Hilweh, which had been penetrated merely to a distance of a few hundred meters, had snapped shut like a steel trap. The next day, the Israelis would have to start all over again.

On Tuesday afternoon, as the Golani units were preparing to withdraw from Ein Hilweh, attention shifted to Sidon proper, where the first attempt to break through on the main road had ended in failure. A new attempt was undertaken by a crack paratroop brigade. They managed to advance a bit with generous air support, but then met very stiff resistance and withdrew from the city at nightfall. As they did so, with another day gone and no breakthrough in sight, the leading commanders on the scene debated the wisdom of searching for an alternative route over the steep slopes skirting the city on the east. The point was to send at least Eli Geva's brigade northward as quickly as possible. Geva himself argued that, rather than sit around idly waiting for the Sidon barrier to be broken, it was worthwhile taking a stab at the eastern route. Earlier another armored force had tried its luck on the rocky bluffs and got nowhere, but Geva believed that his Israeli-manufactured Merkava tanks could handle the route under consideration, a steep, narrow, mountain path with a sheer drop to its left, and toward evening he received permission to move out.

Geva's tanks began to pick their way over the slopes in a slow, agonizing drive that continued all night. They drove without benefit of headlights, so as not to alert any irregulars who might be in the area. Two tanks broke their treads and were disabled, and another two suffered damage to their mine-clearing equipment. But all in all the experiment was a triumph: by dawn on Wednesday Geva's brigade reached the Awali River and received a rousing welcome from Amos Yaron's men.

At about the same hour, the paratroops under Kahalani's command were renewing their attack on Sidon's main thoroughfare. The plan was to concentrate on the route that passed through the newer section of Sidon and brushed against the edge of Ein Hilweh. The paratroops began to press forward on two axes: the main thoroughfare itself and a street running parallel to it on the east in the shadow of Sidon's high-rise buildings. The lead unit was preceded by a merciless artillery bombardment that created a rolling screen of fire, and occasionally planes came shrieking out of the sky to bomb sources of small-arms and RPG fire. Terrified civilians came rushing blindly out of their houses to try to escape the onslaught, and in one instance a narrow alley became choked with panic-stricken people just as a new wave of planes was about to descend on the city. The screaming crowd was surging toward the street targeted for bombardment, and it wasn't until virtually the last minute that the pilots received orders to abort the attack.

That afternoon, through a combination of steady advance by the paratroops and infantry and a dazzling and relentless display of firepower, the way through Sidon was finally opened. There was no time to savor the victory. The moment the road was clear, Kahalani's men began to speed north toward Damour and Beirut. Ein Hilweh and the casbah of Sidon still had not fallen, and responsibility for resuming the battle passed into the hands of Brig. Gen. Yitzhak Mordechai, whose men were veterans of the battle for the camps around Tyre.

Beginning on Wednesday afternoon, the battle for Ein Hilweh entered a new phase as Mordechai's men embarked on a strategy to systematically shatter the camp section by section. With the road north having been opened, and Israeli troops flowing through the city, there seemed no logic whatever to continued PLO resistance.

The fighters in Ein Hilweh must have known that they were doomed in their contest with the Israelis and that no one was going to intervene to save them, yet many of them fought like men possessed. Indeed, it later came out that the leader of the diehards in Ein Hilweh was not a military commander at all but a man of the cloth by the name of Haj Ibrahim, a mullah who had assumed control of the front in Ein Hilweh after Haj Ismail had bolted. Dressed in traditional black turban and robes, Haj Ibrahim was a zealous Moslem fundamentalist in the Khomeini tradition, and he fired the men of his Soldiers of Allah group with an unshakable dedication to the motto "Victory or death!" These same words rang out in reply to every one of the Israelis' calls to surrender.

On Wednesday afternoon, Mordechai's force—paratroops, infantry, and armor—began its campaign by capturing the hills above the camp and the villages south of Sidon. At dawn the next morning, the two pronged attack was renewed, with the paratroops moving into the casbah while the infantry units, supported by tanks, took on Ein Hilweh. One of the community leaders of Sidon warned the Israelis that they would do well to avoid being drawn into bitter fighting in the crowded alleys of Sidon's old quarter. "Don't move in on the casbah," he counseled, "destroy it!" Like so many residents of the city, he recalled how the Syrians had stood seething with frustration at the gates of Sidon in 1976, stopped in their tracks when their armor and commando units tried to enter the city against the will of the PLO. Israeli intelligence also recalled that same Syrian experience in warning the division's officers that this time the fighting would be much fiercer.

Yitzhak Mordechai did not rescind the order to move into the casbah, but he did warn his paratroops to steer clear of protracted battles and always to advance slowly behind the bulldozers that were being used to smash the barricades and widen the streets to accommodate tanks. He also ordered the artillery units to fire on a flat trajectory at buildings that were harboring armed men. Mordechai's strictures more than proved themselves in combat. The capture of the densely built casbah took three days, but it was achieved without Israeli casualties.

The remainder of the battle for Ein Hilweh proved to be far more complex and trying. Early Thursday, the troops overcame two mosques north of the camp, both sources of heavy fire. Then the method of penetration was changed. Rather than the tanks, the infantry was placed in front. That choice was made by the soldiers themselves, who preferred to enter the camp on foot rather than in the armored vehicles that had proved such easy targets for RPG fire and antitank missiles. But whenever the infantry met with stiff resistance, they called on either the tanks or the artillery to move up front and blast the enemy's positions.

Once the two mosques were taken, the forces proceeded to the next major position held by the defenders: the camp hospital. Heavy fire issued from the four-story building, but to engage its defenders in battle would have meant endangering the noncombatants inside. In addition to the militiamen and the hospital staff, the building was filled with civilians—some wounded, others simply seeking refuge in a place they assumed would be treated as inviolable. From that standpoint they were quite right. Rather than attack the hospital outright, the command decided to send an emissary into the building with a proposition designed to save the innocent people inside and neutralize the others—at least temporarily.

The mission was conferred upon a doctor who had been found in the PLO infirmary in Sidon. He spoke fluent English in addition to Arabic and identified himself as a Canadian, though it was later discovered that he had been born in Egypt. Even though the man was in the pay of the PLO, Mordechai decided to use him for the humanitarian mission. The proposal was that everyone—fighters included—would be permitted to leave the hospital unmolested and go down to the shore on condition that they go unarmed. If the fighters refused to leave the building, the doctor was told to suggest that they at least permit the civilians and medical staff to go. Accompanied to the door by five ambulances, the emissary remained in the building for a long while. When he finally returned, only six civilians were with him, all patients. "The evacuation will continue tomorrow," he pronounced. The Israelis suspected a ploy to give the Palestinian fighters time to get away, but nevertheless agreed to continue the next day. And so, Friday morning, the doctor reentered the hospital, only to return with the predictable news that the place was deserted.

It was on Friday afternoon that the ceasefire agreed upon by Israel and Syria went into effect in Beirut, but in Ein Hilweh the fighting continued full force. Special Ambassador Philip Habib, knowing of the bloodletting in Sidon, had made a point of proposing that the ceasefire be applied to all of Lebanon, not just to the forward lines. For the Israelis, that would have meant backing out of Ein Hilweh again and leaving it as a beleaguered pocket of Palestinian resistance. Sharon, appalled by the very thought, summarily rejected the proposal, and for Habib's reassurance depicted the clashes in Sidon as mere mopping-up operations—the swan song of the PLO in South Lebanon. In any event, the fighting in Ein Hilweh continued for another four days.

As has been pointed out, the greatest problem the Israelis faced was to get the civilians out of the most dangerous areas of the camp and evacuate them to the seashore or shelter them in buildings that had already been checked or cleaned out. Again and again, the half-pleading refrain was announced over loudspeakers: "Whoever does not bear arms will not be harmed." The effect was minimal.

Friday morning began with an air raid on positions at the edge of Ein Hilweh, but at 10:45, after fire continued to pour from a variety of positions and concentrations farther inside, the planes returned to bomb the heart of the area. It was also on Friday that efforts were resumed to talk some sense into the fighters holed up in the camp.

On the previous day, three separate delegations had been tried, each comprising leading personalities from Sidon. After being briefed on the situation, they were asked to explain to the defenders of Ein Hilweh that the area was surrounded, their cause was hopeless, and whoever was willing to lay down his arms would be allowed to leave the camp unharmed. Those who did not heed this warning and continued to fight would be responsible for the consequences. The first delegation never got to speak with the besieged fighters; it had barely approached the fortified positions when angry cries were heard: "Traitors! Tell the Jews that no one is leaving this camp, civilians included!" As evidence that they meant business, Haj Ibrahim's men sent a spray of bullets into the dust around the feet of the intermediaries who had come to save them. The second delegation managed to hold a brief exchange with the defenders by shouting at them from a distance, but it too was rebuffed. The third delegation returned with the most harrowing tale of all. Residents of Ein Hilweh had told its members that the militiamen were shooting civilians who tried to escape. In one particularly grisly incident, three children had been riddled with bullets before their parents' eyes because their father had dared to suggest calling an end to the fighting so at least the children of Ein Hilweh could be saved.

Where the local notables had failed, the Israelis believed that Arab comrades-in-arms might succeed, and they decided to organize a delegation of Palestinian fighters who had fallen prisoner to the IDF. The hand-picked group was headed by a PLO officer who was prepared to give the defenders his professional assessment of Ein Hilweh's grave military situation and ask them to spare the lives of the innocent civilians. This time Mordechai added an offer to meet personally with the commander of the forces in the camp—no small concession for an Israeli officer. But the POWs also returned empty handed, except for some more discouraging details about their meeting with the religious leader Haj Ibrahim. They described how he had whipped his men into a frenzy again and again, and had, in fact, coined the suicidal motto "Victory or death!"

Mordechai decided to try yet another approach. A team of psychologists, including a professor from one of Israel's universities mobilized as a reservist, was flown to Sidon to advise the command on how to deal with such irrational behavior. They were told about the failure of the four delegations and heard that Mordechai had also resorted to some menacing muscle-flexing executed with the aid of the air force. In a repeat performance of the ploy used in Tyre, the residents of Ein Hilweh had been informed over loudspeakers that planes were going to level a certain building on the outskirts of the camp, and if they did not leave Ein Hilweh forthwith their homes would suffer the same fate. The planes dropped their payloads and even followed up with napalm bombs for special effect. But for all that, only a handful of people escaped the grip of the militia and came scurrying out of the camp.

Upon hearing that sorry summary of events, the best advice the psychologists could offer was to organize yet another but considerably larger delegation comprising some forty or so people and including women and children as well as dignitaries and POWs. Perhaps the supplications of a group of this kind would soften the hearts of Haj Ibrahim and his men. The new delegation was briefed, with the aid of the experts, and sent on its way. Haj Ibrahim agreed to receive it, but his reply remained exactly the same three words.

"But there's no hope of achieving a victory!" one of the dignitaries wailed in anguish.

Haj Ibrahim merely glowered at him, pursed his lips, and waved the delegation to return whence it had come. The forlorn envoys crossed back over the lines bearing the same message as their predecessors, plus the news that many of the civilians in the camp had been persuaded to believe that anyone who surrendered to the Israelis would be promptly shot. As evidence for this vicious claim, the resisters had cited the shooting that could be heard in the distance and said they were executions. "The Jews are killing everyone," Haj Ibrahim warned his people sternly. "Better to die in the camp, at home, bearing arms, than on your knees in front of a firing squad!"

This fifth, expanded delegation was also the last. When it failed to move Haj Ibrahim and his men, Mordechai disbanded the group, dismissed the psychologists, and got back to doing a soldier's work. He had come to the conclusion that his only option was to continue gnawing away at Ein Hilweh, house by house, block by block, until it was vanquished—even if that meant reducing the entire camp to rubble. For days a thick, black cloud of dust and smoke hung over Ein Hilweh as the artillery and planes pounded away. Time and again there was a bright flash of flame, then the roar of a blast resounding like summer thunder. The air was suffused with a sickening stench of gunpowder, sewage, and rotting corpses, and whenever the planes swooped in to bomb Ein Hilweh, the ground virtually shuddered. On and on it went for days, without letup. One of the authors was there, throughout the battle. The Israeli soldiers watching the devastation seemed to become inured to the din and the smoke and the smell of death. Sensibilities became dulled; the destruction engendered a chilling tedium.

These troops represented a new brand of Israeli soldier, young men who had not fought in Israel's desperate wars for survival. Their commanders were older, more professional than the previous generation of officers, but what had their military expertise bought them? Did they regard the pulverization of Ein Hilweh as just a grim necessity to be carried out as best they could? Or was this relentless battering a dose of retribution for all the acts of terrorism perpetrated against innocent Israelis? And was it perhaps fueled by an even deeper sense of vengeance for all the harm and hatred that the Jews had suffered at the hands of others over the centuries? The author found no hint of an answer to these questions in the blank expressions and vacant, tired eyes of the young Israeli soldiers. And looking at them, he could not help thinking: How would the grandparents of these boys have reacted to the scene of mayhem that was visible from Yitzhak Mordechai's rooftop headquarters? What memories would have flooded their minds? What collective fears would have gripped their hearts?

Israeli artillery spewed flat-trajectory fire into buildings where the militiamen took cover. When penetration by the infantry and paratroops was able to resume, their first objective was the school, but the advance was halted when the lead tank was hit by RPG fire. First it was attacked from the flank, then a Palestinian rushed forward and hit it directly from behind. Meanwhile, other Palestinians filtered in behind the Israeli assault force and laid antitank mines, making it necessary to reclear the road.

The school was taken at twilight Friday, and as darkness fell the fighting stopped. Another patch of Ein Hilweh had fallen. The noose around the stubborn defenders was growing tighter. No one knew exactly how many armed Palestinians were still left in the camp and how many civilians were hiding in cellars and bunkers. Though estimates put the number of PLO fighters at 300 to 100 or less, they sometimes seemed to be doing the job of a division.

On Saturday, June 12, the fighting centered on the main bunker in the western part of Ein Hilweh, where the Israelis prepared to mount their final assault. Fire issued from the bunker without respite; evidently the men inside had stocked an enormous store of arms and ammunition and could go on shooting for hours, if not days. The advance on the position began at twilight, and the battle ended just after 7:00 P.M. with a deafening explosion: a massive charge laid alongside the bunker had reduced it to chunks of concrete and a lingering spray of dust.

The fall of the central bunker was the turning point. Although fighting continued for another two days, the local defenders were by now splintered into small groups without any real organization, so that for the Israelis the fighting became a genuine mopping-up operation. The last stand in the camp took place in one of the mosques. Whether or not Haj Ibrahim was still alive and directing the battle, the men in the mosque refused to surrender, continuing to resist even when explosives were hurled into the building. Unintelligible shouts and cries could be heard echoing inside until the mosque collapsed on its defenders. A sudden eerie silence descended on Ein Hilweh.

On Monday, June 14, Ein Hilweh was finally conquered. Bereft of any hope of victory, the camp's defenders had remained true to their motto and fought to the last. Their defeat marked the end of the battle for South Lebanon, but not of the fighting between Palestinians and Israelis. For even as the firing subsided in Ein Hilweh, a new drama of grim defiance was taking place in Beirut.

9

The Second Front

DURING THE FIRST THREE DAYS of the fighting in Lebanon, before it was obvious that the IDF was going all the way to Beirut, Israel could not have asked for a better spokesman for its cause than Secretary of State Alexander Haig. Washington—unsolicited, it seemed—was going to do its part by protecting Israel's political flank, giving Menachem Begin good reason to feel that he was standing on solid ground. President Reagan was in Paris when the war broke out, on the first European tour of his presidency, and some of his aides feared that the Israeli action would upstage or disrupt the visit by making demands on the president's attention and perhaps even arousing Russian pressure. But Gen. Alexander Haig commanded the breach. By some uncanny stroke of luck, Defense Secretary Weinberger had remained behind in Washington, and Haig was able to prevent any criticism of Israel from leaking out of the president's entourage. His daily briefings for the American reporters traveling with the president were unmistakable testimony that the secretary, at least, stood squarely behind the Israeli action.

On Friday, June 4, after the Israeli air force had bombed PLO positions in Beirut, Haig told the press corps that the air raid had to be seen in light of the previous night's attempt on the life of the Israeli ambassador in London. Pointedly he reminded the journalists that Jerusalem had long been warning the PLO that it would respond vigorously to attacks of that sort. Two days later, when the air strikes had developed into a full-fledged ground action on Lebanese soil, Haig read out to the reporters all of Israel's communiqué's about the aims of Operation Peace for Galilee. And he added some news of his own: the president, who was concerned about the escalation of the hostilities, had spoken with Prime Minister Menachem Begin; he had also summoned Philip Habib (who happened to be attending a conference in Oxford) and would be dispatching him the next day on an urgent mission to meet with the Israeli prime minister.

But it was Haig's briefing on Monday, June 7, that proved the most illuminating of all. The secretary told the reporters that Washington had relayed to Damascus the reassuring message that Israel did not intend to attack any Syrian forces unless attacked by them first. Clearly Haig believed that Israel had no intention of locking horns with the Syrians, otherwise he wouldn't have troubled his officials in the State Department and the American embassy in Damascus to serve as Menachem Begin's messenger boys. Then, as if to underscore his categorical belief in the Israeli cause, he added that the Israeli government's sole desire was to clear terrorists and their bases from a forty-kilometer strip of Lebanese territory; Israel was not interested in holding on to any part of Lebanon. Haig estimated that there were about 6,000 well-armed terrorists on the coastal axis alone and that the operation would therefore not be an easy one. At this opportunity, he also revealed some of his own thoughts about future arrangements in South Lebanon. Achieving a ceasefire, he ventured, would not be sufficient. For a ceasefire to work it would be necessary to make certain changes in the political equilibrium in Lebanon. UNIFIL was not adequate to supervise the buffer zone that the Israelis wanted. And as part of the changes to be effected in Lebanon, Haig expressed his hope that the Syrian presence in that country would be reduced substantially.

Evidently Haig was unaware that, even as he was speaking, an Israeli armored column was making its way toward the Beirut-Damascus highway in a bid to reduce the Syrian presence in Lebanon to nothing; that a few hours hence Ariel Sharon would ask (but fail to get) the Israeli Cabinet to approve an overt attack on the Syrian force in Lebanon; and that within two days Ariel Sharon would achieve his goal of bombing the Syrian missile batteries in Lebanon out of existence. But Alexander Haig was not the only senior American diplomat to come out of that week looking, at best, like an Israeli dupe.

Philip Habib reached Israel on Monday morning and whiled away the day in his hotel room until 6:00 P.M., when Begin agreed to see him. When he was finally shown into the prime minister's office, Habib seemed determined above all to find out how long the operation was likely to take. But as the conversation progressed, his resolve seemed to change, and the suggestion was offered that, for the sake of peace, Habib add to his mission for his president another on behalf of the prime minister of Israel. (Habib's agreement led Begin to believe and later tell his Cabinet that "the American reaction is better than we expected.") The next day, Habib would fly to Damascus to meet with President Assad and assure him that Israel was

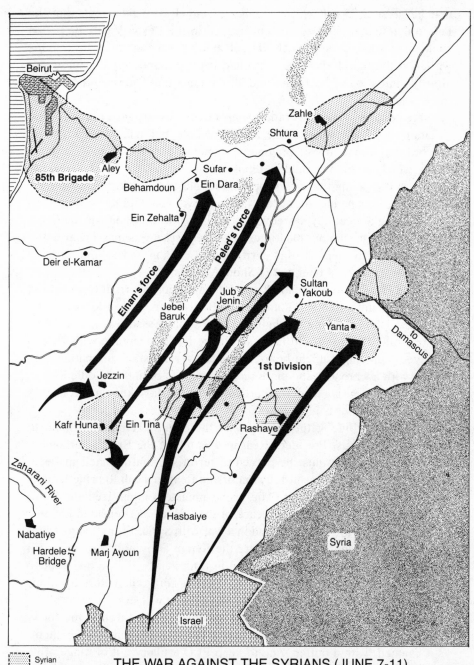

Beirut

Zahle

Shtura

85th Brigade

Aley

Behamdoun

Sufar

Ein Dara

Ein Zehalta

Deir el-Kamar

Einan's force

Peled's force

Jebel
Baruk

Jub
Jenin

Sultan
Yakoub

Yanta

to
Damascus

Jezzin

1st Division

Kafr Huna

Ein Tina

Rashaye

Zaharani River

Nabatiye

Hasbaiye

Syria

Hardele
Bridge

Marj Ayoun

Israel

Syrian
positions

THE WAR AGAINST THE SYRIANS (JUNE 7-11)

not planning to attack his forces. At the same time, however, Begin asked that he present Assad with a number of Israeli demands: first, that the Palestinian fighters and equipment located in the Bekaa Valley be pulled back forty kilometers from the Israeli border; second, that the Syrians withdraw the missile batteries that had been stationed on Lebanese soil after the initiation of hostilities and all the units that had recently entered the Bekaa.

These could be viewed as rather simple demands designed to restore the situation on the front lines to the status quo ante, but in fact they added up to a brazen ultimatum, and anyone who knew Hafez Assad and the terms under which he ruled could not possibly have believed that he would accede to it. Having failed to supply direct aid to the Palestinians in their hour of need, as he had promised, he was now being told to prevent them from fighting altogether. Moreover, Assad was being asked—if that's the proper word—to thin out his forces just when Israel was massing armored divisions directly opposite his garrison in Lebanon and sending a large contingent up its right flank in the Shouf Mountains.

Arming Habib with such an ultimatum was either incorrigibly naive or a calculated gamble that it would be rebuffed. Begin, a man known to be given to wishful thinking, probably believed that Assad was in such desperate straits that he would have no choice but to negotiate with Habib, however degrading it might be to negotiate over an Israeli ultimatum. But Habib, with his broader and more realistic view of both the Middle East in general and the Syrian leader in particular, should have known that he was going off on an impossible mission.

On Tuesday, June 8, the third day of the war, as Habib was about to leave for Damascus, President Reagan was telling the British Parliament that the Middle East must be purged of terrorism, and Menachem Begin was addressing the Knesset, fully endorsing Reagan's call to bring Israel's soldiers back from Lebanon. The prime minister emphasized the bitter price Israel was paying for the peace of the Galilee and repeated his declaration that "we are not interested in a war with Syria. From this rostrum, I call upon President Assad to order the Syrian army not to harm Israeli soldiers, and no harm will befall them in return . . . . We do not want to clash with the Syrian army. If we reach a line forty kilometers from our northern border, our job will be done; the fighting will stop."

The IDF had, in fact, just finished making its way through the forty-kilometer strip in South Lebanon. If the Israeli government were content, as it claimed, with a buffer zone to keep PLO artillery out of range of its population, it would have ordered its army to stop that day. But it did not. That very afternoon, one of the IDF's armored brigades attacked Syrian positions in the town of Jezzin and prepared to continue its drive against other sections of the Syrian disposition in nearby villages. And even before Begin made his statement in the Knesset, the Israeli air force had attacked one of the Syrian units in Lebanon, while at Northern Command headquarters Ariel Sharon was rehearsing the deputy commander of the air force on how to sell the Cabinet on the idea of destroying the Syrian missile batteries in the Bekaa Valley.

Whether Begin knew any of these details is still an open question. It is incontrovertible, however, that the first clashes with the Syrians began on the *second* day of the war, June 7. One of them was a chance encounter, the other was at Israel's instigation. Both were ignored in the IDF communiqués that day. In the first, an Israeli column moving through South Lebanon toward Sidon fired at an APC and was subsequently surprised to find dead and wounded Syrian soldiers in the vehicle; the APC, it turned out, belonged to a Syrian force that had blundered too far south. The other clash was deliberate and constituted the first signal to Damascus that Israel did not intend to limit its military operation to South Lebanon. On Monday the Israeli air force destroyed two Syrian radar stations in Lebanon. One was in the western sector, near Damour; the other was deep within Syrian-controlled territory—near the Rayak airfield north of the Beirut-Damascus highway and well beyond the forty-kilometer line that Begin and the Americans were making so much of. While the Syrians were surprised that the Israelis even knew about the radar at Damour, it was the second bombing that set them wondering about Israel's true intentions in Lebanon.

Still, the Syrians did not act. In fact, so cautious were the members of the Syrian General Staff that they did not even beef up their contingent on the Golan Heights, despite the fact that they could see the IDF doing so. Meanwhile, Assad, troubled by the mixed signals coming out of Israel, decided to send a personal scout to Lebanon to get a feel for what was going on in the field and try to figure out what the IDF's next move would be. His choice for the job was Deputy Chief of Staff Ali Aslan, who had commanded the Syrian forces in Lebanon for two years and was considered one of the best professionals in the Syrian army. For all his sterling credentials, however, it would take Aslan another twenty-four hours to grasp that the IDF was headed for the Beirut-Damascus highway.

As of Monday, then, two wars were going on in Lebanon: one against the PLO, the other against the Syrians. It was possible to keep them separate because Damascus was turning itself inside out to avoid an all-out war with the IDF—a disinclination to fight that grew stronger as the Syrian chief of staff, Hikmat Shihabi, realized that he had indeed been surprised by the Israeli moves against his troops and by the scope of the

Israeli action against the PLO. This left Israel with some real options. If the Israelis wanted to deal a stunning blow to the Syrian air force as a way of deterring Assad from any thoughts of a full-scale war in the future, they could have done so without becoming involved in a costly ground war. The IDF could even have tacked on a raid against the missile batteries in the Bekaa Valley, thereby achieving its aim of deterrence at a relatively low cost and by operating on a level at which it had an unequivocal advantage over the enemy. In other words, despite Monday's actions, Israel could still have avoided a serious confrontation with the Syrian army in Lebanon and spared itself the cost, losses, and grave political consequences of a two-front war.

But Sharon wanted all these wars—against the PLO, against the Syrians both on the ground and in the air, and against the missile batteries—and he wanted them all now. In chivying the Cabinet for permission to send Menachem Einan's division up the central axis, Sharon placed only two choices before the ministers: a frontal attack on the Syrians or a flanking maneuver that meant "placing pressure on them and coming up on them from behind on the assumption that the danger of encirclement will lead them to withdraw." A third possibility—fighting against the Palestinians alone and only in South Lebanon—was not discussed at all. Sharon led his colleagues to understand that he recommended the threat of encirclement over a frontal assault. The prime minister, he said, had given his blessings to this tactic (Begin was at Northern Command headquarters at the time of this meeting), and the ministers did not understand that the flanking movement would not necessarily obviate a fight with the Syrians or that, quite to the contrary, it might well force them into battle. Moreover, the defense minister took pains to emphasize that the force moving up the central axis would come at the Syrians from behind.

Perhaps Begin and his ministers honestly believed that the Syrians would be cowed or at least startled by the move and would quickly withdraw over the border. But anyone listening closely to the situation assessment that Yehoshua Saguy presented to the Cabinet would have heard him say that the advance toward the Beirut-Damascus highway meant "moving under fire." Exactly whose fire if not the Syrians'? Of Sharon's two choices—a frontal assault or a flanking movement leading to encirclement—the ministers chose the second. None of them asked what would happen if the Syrians refused to withdraw from Lebanon, despite the encircling movement, or if they rejected the Israeli ultimatum and did not pull the PLO fighters out of the area under their control. To a man, they voted for the drive up the central axis and thereby, whether they knew it or not, set off a war with Syria.

In the field, the point of no return in that war was reached much earlier than was subsequently claimed during the thick of the fighting. It came with a battle in the town of Jezzin, nestled in the hills west of the Bekaa, twenty-four hours before the Israelis attacked the Syrian missile batteries in the valley. Jezzin's importance stemmed from its location near a critically strategic junction. One road passed through the town and led to the southern Bekaa Valley; the other headed north to Jebel Baruk (the highest peak in the area), passing west of Lake Karoun. The road being taken by Menachem Einan's division ended at a fork just west of Jezzin and required that the division pass through the town, though not the crossroads. If the IDF could gain control of both the town and the junction, it would have access to the southern Bekaa Valley from the west as well as the south. The Syrians, fully appreciating the importance of the junction, had stationed their 424th Infantry Battalion in the town.

Following his orders to reach the main highway as quickly as possible, Menachem Einan steered clear of the sensitive crossroads as his division closed in on Jezzin at 1:00 A.M. on Tuesday, though leaving a blocking force behind as he continued pushing north. From a distance, at the outskirts of the town and on the opposite ridge, the men of that force could see Syrian tanks in their emplacements. The two forces might have continued eyeing each other tensely without engaging in combat had not the Israeli blocking force spilled over the slope above the town and opened fire. No attempt was made to mount an assault on the town, but even at a distance both sides suffered hits, with the Israeli force losing two tanks. The temptation to take on the Syrians—and perhaps capture the junction and the town—had simply been too strong.

Just a few hours earlier, unbeknownst to the commander of the blocking force in Jezzin, Ariel Sharon had discussed that very prospect at his nightly meeting in Northern Command headquarters. "We know today that there will be a direct confrontation with the Syrians," he told the officers. "The best solution I see is to move deeper into Lebanon." And in pressing his commanders to speed up their drive toward the Beirut-Damascus highway, he explained to them, "We have to build a context because we know that tomorrow we will take on the Syrians." The next morning a reason for taking the town was duly supplied when an Israeli intelligence drone discovered a Syrian force moving south through the Shouf Mountains in the direction of Jezzin. (Actually, Jezzin had already been reinforced on the previous night by a reduced battalion of tanks and a commando unit, but they were not discovered until later, during the assault on the town.) At first Israeli planes were sent up to attack the Syrian force moving south, and its strikes were accurate. This was the first Israeli air attack on Syrian troops, and it is highly significant that the Syrian missiles were not activated to hamper it. By 1:30 P.M., the momentum toward a full-blown war with the Syrians had become irresistible.

The brigade that ended up attacking Jezzin had entered Lebanon on Monday afternoon, crossed the Litani over the Hardele Bridge, and was supposed to follow in the wake of the column headed for the Beirut-Damascus highway. But on Tuesday morning, about a quarter of an hour after the intelligence drone discovered the Syrian force moving south, the brigade received a signal to be ready to change course and move east. Its commander, Colonel Hagai, saw that the only way to move east was through Jezzin, and realizing what that implied, he convened his company commanders and told them, "Gentlemen, we're going to fight the Syrians!"

No assessment could have proved more accurate. A few minutes after 1:30, Maj. Gen. Avigdor Ben-Gal, commander of the eastern sector, contacted Hagai and ordered him to prepare to attack Jezzin. The one problem Hagai faced was that his crack brigade, which included units of the armored-officers course and tank-commanders course, still did not have any artillery or infantry attached to it. But while he was still trying to persuade the artillery officer of Menachem Einan's division to spare him an artillery unit, Ben-Gal's voice came over the communications network again. The time was 2:00 P.M. now, and his orders were to attack immediately, with or without artillery!

The attack on Jezzin was therefore mounted in haste. As one company of tanks waited on the outskirts of the town, another began moving up the main street. Jezzin seemed to be wrapped in slumber until the tanks reached the center of town, where they were assaulted by grenades and RPGs fired from a number of buildings. Even so, the company made it through to the other end of the town and managed to destroy three T-62 tanks stationed to block it at the exit from Jezzin. Meanwhile, the second company waiting on the outskirts of the town fell victim to an attack by Syrian commandos wielding Sagger antitank missiles. The commandos immediately knocked out three tanks and forced the company to retreat. That left the Syrians firmly positioned in Jezzin with an Israeli battalion split between the two sides of the town.

Now Hagai's second battalion was sent into action, and one of its companies managed to penetrate the town. But then it made a fatal error that cost it a number of tanks. The company took a wrong turn at a fork in the road and soon found itself at a dead end. It had in fact reached a high commanding area, but it was also exposed to Syrian armor concealed behind the opposite ridge, northeast of Jezzin. Up to that point, the Israelis hadn't a clue about the existence of the Syrian tanks now blasting away at them. Within minutes five of their own tanks had gone up in flames. The entire company was put out of action.

The brigade's other companies kept up the battle with the Syrian tanks, destroying them one after another, until the company that had broken into Jezzin had fought its way to the edge of the nearby village of Huna. By nightfall Jezzin was in Israeli hands: seven men had died in the battle.

The attack on Jezzin, as it turned out, had a secondary military effect in bringing about a more emphatic Syrian response to Israel's moves in Lebanon—though *still* not a blatantly offensive one. On Tuesday afternoon, after Israeli tanks had smashed the Syrian defense line in Jezzin, five new batteries of SAM-6 missiles were brought into Lebanon. Together with the heavier missiles already stationed in Lebanon, this defense system now comprised nineteen batteries. Yet even while reinforcing their missile system in the Bekaa, the Syrians continued to signal that they did not want war. The new batteries were not transferred from the Syrian heartland but came from the Golan Heights—a definite indication that Damascus was not interested in exacerbating the hostilities and running the risk that the fighting would spread to the Golan or, worse yet, points east.

While the battle for Jezzin ended in an Israeli victory, that same night the lead units of Menachem Einan's force suffered a serious setback that firmly blocked them on the central axis and put an end to the plan of trapping the Syrian garrison between the two arms of a broad pincer movement. A requisite of that strategy was for Einan's column to reach the Beirut-Damascus highway before the Syrians could rally enough of a force to stop it. From the start this race against time was punctuated by repeated delays. The first was caused by the need to turn around and cross the Litani River over the Akiye Bridge behind Avigdor Kahalani's division rather than via the Hardele Bridge. Other holdups stemmed from the crush of hundreds of vehicles on the narrow road. On Monday Einan's column —still bunched up behind Kahalani's men on their way to Sidon—waited from early morning until 2:00 P.M. before receiving permission to cross the bridge over the Zaharani River. The column's presumed dash northward became more of a maddening crawl. And there was further frustration ahead.

By the second stage of the advance, the lead forces began to suffer a shortage of gasoline, and because of the clutter of vehicles on the road the tank trucks had to fight their way through to the head of the column. By Wednesday the situation had deteriorated to the point where fuel could be transported to Hagai's force only by helicopter—and then it transpired that there were no pumps for refueling the tanks. Another unit that should have reached the Jezzin junction on Tuesday was caught in a paralyzing traffic jam for hours and hardly moved at all. More than once its harried commander had to fire his sidearm into the air to "cajole" the drivers of supply trucks into letting his tanks and APCs past. The unit did not reach the crossroads until evening.

During the first three days of the war, then, it wasn't the Syrians who delayed the movement of Einan's division up the central axis but the Israelis themselves. Of course the Syrians made every effort to retard the column's movement by fighting a holding action, but these skirmishes were for the most part brief and erratic. On the other hand, as early as 1:00 A.M. on Tuesday, after Einan's force had passed close to the Jezzin junction and reached the Basri River (the eastern extension of the Awali), it received an order to halt. Drori explained to Einan rather apologetically that he still lacked permission to proceed—though it is not clear from the conversation whether the source of the holdup was the Cabinet, on political grounds, or the chief of staff, for reasons unknown. Either way, the rest of the night was spent waiting, and it wasn't until 7:00 A.M. on Tuesday that approval came through to cross the Basri and continue north.

The advance continued smoothly Tuesday morning until the column neared the road leading down to Damour, where it received another order to halt until further notice. This time it waited about four hours before getting the order to resume its advance, but by then it too was suffering from a shortage of gasoline. So an exasperated Einan threw propriety to the winds and told his men to drive into the nearest gas station and fill up there. The IDF would settle the bill later!

That afternoon a new, unfamiliar weapon made its battlefield debut in a bid to halt Einan's column—French-manufactured Gazelle assault helicopters carrying Hot missiles with a range of more than four kilometers (and regarded as one of the best antitank missiles available). It was the first time any Arab army had used helicopter gunships against Israeli forces, and even though their performance was still less than high, they gained a distinct momentary advantage just by flustering the Israeli tank crews. Ground forces have a hard time dealing with helicopter gunships, which can fire off their missiles well beyond the range of a tank's or APC's machine gun. Portable antiaircraft missiles (SAM-7s) can solve the problem, but for the most part the Israeli armored columns were not equipped with them.

The first Syrian helicopter appeared at 3:30, fired two missiles at the tanks in the lead, and scored a hit on the third one in line. As its men, all wounded, were being rescued, the Gazelle popped up again, and launched another missile that set the lame tank ablaze. Since the road was flanked by a sheer drop on one side and a cliff face on the other, it was quite impossible to bypass the tank.

Meanwhile, pressure to move on to Ein Zehalta, a Druse village in the heart of the Shouf region, was mounting by the minute. Drori was by now practically hounding Einan, and Einan passed the pressure on to the commander of his lead brigade. Finally, while most of the brigade was still waiting for the road to be cleared, a platoon of tanks and a battalion of infantry managed to find a way around the obstacle and began hurtling toward Ein Zehalta. By then, however, their surge forward was pointless, for the Syrians had not only won the race to Ein Zehalta but had already set up an ambush by stationing a few dozen tanks in hastily improvised emplacements where the road wound down into a deep wadi. Together with the Syrian commandos who had streamed into the town, these tanks comprised a force of almost brigade size.

It was close to 11:00 P.M. on Tuesday, June 8, when the first Israeli armored unit entered Ein Zehalta. As the tanks and APCs, after passing through the village, began to descend the steep slope that led into the wadi, they were caught in one of the deadliest battles of the war. The bloodletting on that hillside continued until Thursday and crushed all hope that Einan's division could cut the Beirut-Damascus highway before the advent of a ceasefire. A single brigade of Syrian tanks and commandos had thwarted the IDF's pincer strategy by bringing the division to a standstill just four or five kilometers short of its goal. But the Syrians would pay a price for that resolve: the battle of Ein Zehalta became Ariel Sharon's principal argument for mounting a devastating attack on their missiles in the Bekaa Valley.

A bright moon lit up the countryside as the Israeli tanks began to negotiate the serpentine road into the wadi. Had infantrymen been in the lead, they probably would have discerned the Syrian ambush lurking at the sides of the road. But the tank crews had their attention diverted by the silhouettes of a cluster of Syrian tanks on the opposite side of the wadi. One platoon even scored three hits and watched almost hypnotized as the enemy armor burst into flame before itself succumbing to a fiery assault by tanks and RPGs shooting from below. Two Israeli tanks were stopped in their tracks, and the rest quickly pulled back. After two hours of heavy, almost futile fighting and three abortive attempts to get infantry down into the wadi to deal with the Syrian armor, the brigade commander reported that the situation was very serious; it was proving impossible to target the enemy!

Upon receiving this report, Menachem Einan summoned the brigade commander for a consultation at his forward command post. Not only had the advance come to a complete halt, but fire was raining down relentlessly on the APCs and tanks lined up along the road—to the point where one battalion commander ordered the entire column to try moving slowly in reverse. The brigade commander returned at dawn and called a meeting of his officers in the center of town to brief them on a new plan of attack. While they were studying the strategy, however, dozens of Syrian commandos appeared as if out of nowhere and began to fire on the vehicles from a range of about 200 meters. Machine guns clattered away incessantly as RPGs popped and Sagger missiles came shooshing in from the ridge on the opposite side of the wadi. The APCs parked opposite an orchard at the edge of town were hit particularly hard and had to move out quickly. So it was that a disorderly retreat began, with all the vehicles trying to move at top speed in reverse while some were taking direct hits. When a tank was set aflame by RPG fire, all attention focused on getting its crew out to safety. Three men lost their lives in one rescue attempt before an order came down to stop trying to reach the wounded and to concentrate instead on straightening out the line and waiting for the next stage of the battle. Eleven Israelis died on that cool summer dawn, and another seventeen were wounded.

As the battle raged in Ein Zehalta, Ariel Sharon was being helicoptered to Northern Command headquarters, now the nerve center of the war. With all the fighting going on in the north, the General Staff had essentially abandoned its sophisticated war room in Tel Aviv and moved in on Drori's far more modest accommodations in the Galilee, making for some rather cramped conditions. Not to be outdone, the defense minister began flying up to front headquarters after each Cabinet meeting to keep his finger firmly on the pulse of the war. With all this shuttling back and forth between Jerusalem and the front command, the daily briefings with Sharon had to be held late at night—usually starting no earlier than 10:00 P.M., though often much later, and sometimes continuing into the small hours of the morning.

When he turned up at Northern Command late on June 8—the day on which Jezzin was captured and the column moving up the central axis was stopped—Sharon was no longer speaking in vague terms about the need to attack the Syrians on a broad front. Events were moving so quickly that, during a situation assessment that night, Saguy projected that Israel might have to accept a ceasefire the next morning, making it necessary to determine then and there how they wanted the war to end. Sharon was visibly irritated by the fact that the barrier at Sidon had not yet been broken, that Yaron's paratroops had not moved any farther north, and that Einan's division was still considerably short of the Beirut-Damascus highway. This last shortfall seemed to irk him most of all.

The minister was in something of a bind. On the one hand, he was fighting a war against the Syrians even though he still did not have the Cabinet's permission to do so and therefore felt obliged to proceed with caution. "It's not clear how the Cabinet will react to an [all-out] attack on the Syrians," he told the men assembled at Northern Command that Tuesday night, "so we must nibble away at them without creating the impression of a full-scale war." At the same time, his army's advance was being slowed by stiff enemy resistance, so that it would be necessary to throw the full weight of the air force behind the ground action. But that meant crippling the Syrian missiles first, and Sharon knew that it was best to postpone an attack on the missile batteries for as long as possible because a massive air strike was sure to evoke political pressures to halt the war. Without an air strike, Sharon predicted, "the Americans will allow us three more days." With it, who could tell?

Dawn on Wednesday did not bring any better news about the progress of the IDF columns. The force at Ein Zehalta had not broken through the Syrian defense line to cut the highway, and on the coast Kahalani's division was still bogged down by heavy fighting in Sidon. By the time Sharon flew north for an early-morning meeting at the front headquarters, his tone was close to a growl. "Why weren't they aiming for the main highway farther to the west? Why aren't they being leapfrogged by helicopter?" he complained upon hearing that one of Einan's brigades had been stopped dead at Ein Zehalta.

Switching his attention to the Bekaa Valley, Sharon pronounced that Avigdor Ben-Gal's forces would have to get moving northward as soon and as fast as possible. Maj. Gen. Yekutiel Adam, a former deputy chief of staff who had been designated as the next director of the Mossad, seemed startled by that remark. He had not been at the previous night's meeting, when Sharon discussed the need to go full tilt at the Syrian defense line in the Bekaa, and now he blurted out to the man sitting next to him, "That means a war with the Syrians!"

Adam then addressed the meeting and heard himself challenging Sharon: "Doesn't that contradict the objectives set by the Cabinet?" Before the minister had a chance to react, the deputy chief of staff, Maj. Gen. Moshe Levi, issued his own challenge by implying that the IDF was operationally unprepared to send Ben-Gal's force into action.

A spark of anger lit up in Sharon's eyes. Clearly he was straining to control his temper. "That was discussed last night, and you weren't here," he snapped at Levi, then turned on Adam, saying, "We never promised to spare the terrorists beyond the forty-kilometer range. I have said time and again that we don't need a war with the Syrians, but *they're* the ones who are shooting at us. If they don't want a war, they don't have to have one.

And I want you to know," making the point sound more like a threat than a clarification, "that every order, *every one,* is anchored in Cabinet decisions!" Earlier, when other senior officers had voiced similar misgivings, Sharon had responded with derision. "Relax," he had told the doubters and worriers. "Whoever's feeling the heat can pour a pail of water over his head!"

Yekutiel Adam had voiced a doubt shared by many of his colleagues that the Cabinet didn't really know where the war was heading and what its true objectives were. Was the army indeed following the ministers' wishes? Or was it racing ahead of the Cabinet under orders from the defense minister, who was assuming he would get retroactive approval for his faits accomplis? Sharon could play the maligned innocent in front of his generals, but even while he was flying back to Jerusalem Wednesday morning, Eitan and Drori were proceeding to the headquarters of the coastal axis, with Drori bringing Amos Yaron the order to advance toward Beirut. Drori had received the go-ahead from Sharon, though the Cabinet had never discussed the matter! Also at that hour, Deputy Chief of Staff Levi was flying to Ein Zehalta to tell Menachem Einan that the air force would be attacking the Syrian missiles that day, though the Cabinet had not yet approved the action.

It was to present these moves to the ministers that Sharon was flying back to Jerusalem that morning. The Cabinet meeting on Wednesday, June 9, was to prove the defense minister's toughest test, because on the agenda —actually for the first time—would be his true conception of and plan for the war. The campaign against the Syrians had begun in Jezzin and was continuing in Ein Zehalta. Although Damascus was still trying to avoid an all-out clash, the Syrians were finally waking up to Sharon and had already begun to move their second armored division (the Third Division) south. As Sharon saw it, the time had come to push forward into the Bekaa with full force. Waiting any longer could make entry into the Valley a terrible business. From the standpoint of the political timetable, Tuesday had been too early to attack the missiles, but Thursday would be too late to save the ground action. The time to act was now.

As an extra precaution, Sharon took the deputy commander of the air force, Amos Amir, to the Cabinet meeting with him. The chief of staff had decided to remain in the field, for Eitan was still making it a point to stay away from these meetings and leave the work of explaining and persuading to Sharon. In this particular case, however, the chief of staff was himself rather ambivalent about the issue. At that morning's meeting in the north, Eitan had suggested confining the action to an emphatic but still limited signal to the Syrians. Not that he lacked confidence in the air force's ability to deal with the missiles. Being one of the few people familiar with every detail of the attack plan, he knew that the odds of absolutely devastating the system with minimum losses was excellent. His hesitation evidently stemmed from a belief that, as soon as the missiles were destroyed, intervention by the powers would go into high gear, and Israel would find itself under enormous pressure to halt the fighting altogether.

Amir Drori felt even more strongly that an attack on the missiles was superfluous. As Sharon was holding forth before the Cabinet, Drori was commenting sadly to his officers, "We could easily get our forty kilometers quietly—without striking the missiles, without a full-scale war—finish off the PLO, and go home."

Be that as it may, Sharon arrived in Jerusalem to find many of his colleagues less than pleased with developments on the battlefield. The IDF had crossed the forty-kilometer line that Sharon and Eitan had established as its goal when the Cabinet approved the action on Saturday night, and it did not look as though it was about to stop. As if to goad Sharon on this critical point, Mordechai Zippori walked into the meeting carrying a map and a ruler, demonstratively measured the distances, and at the first opportunity commented on the discrepancy. Sharon was flushed as he explained slowly, trying to control his fury, that the measurements could not be taken from anywhere along the border but had to be marked out from the northernmost point, the town of Metulla at the tip of the Upper Galilean "finger." Using a compass—not a ruler—one had to draw an arc that would represent the artillery range. After a dramatic pause, Sharon made a caustic dig at Zippori by musing aloud that, when he was a boy, the children used to come to school with handkerchiefs pinned to their shirts. "Now every minister will come to Cabinet meetings with a ruler!"

Troubled not by the extent of the advance but by its pace, Sharon tried to further defuse Zippori's complaint by diverting the Cabinet's attention to the perils facing the men in the field. He told the ministers that the forces in Ein Zehalta were being exposed to Syrian artillery fire that would certainly be intensified during the coming hours, making it necessary to act quickly and extend all possible assistance if they were to retain hope of extricating the men at Ein Zehalta. In short, it would be criminal to deny the massive air support that the troops were crying for but that was impossible without first destroying the missile batteries in the Bekaa Valley.

Interior Minister Yosef Burg questioned this gloss of the situation and pointed out that, in contrast to what the Cabinet wanted, the incidence of fighting with the Syrians was on the rise. Attacking the missiles would only aggravate matters and perhaps even lead to an all-out war with the Syrians.

But Sharon stood his ground and effectively played on the conscience of each minister by harping on the vulnerability of the soldiers in the field. During one heavy pause, Begin turned to Amos Amir and asked for his projection of the air force's losses in an attack on the missile batteries.

"I cannot promise no losses whatever, but they will be minimal," he replied.

Satisfied by that answer, Begin threw his support behind the proposal to neutralize the missiles. Even Burg came round in the end. "If there's no choice, we must act," he conceded.

That was all Sharon needed. Having received permission to strike at the missiles, he immediately left the conference room to issue the appropriate order over the phone. Most of the ministers he left behind did not understand that they had been speaking not just of an air raid on the missile installations but of a major ground operation as well. For as soon as the batteries were eliminated, Ben-Gal's forces were to begin their drive up the Bekaa Valley. The second arm of the pincer would complete what the first had failed to achieve when it became locked in combat at Ein Zehalta.

When the action against the missile batteries began at 2:00 P.M., nine years of exercises, meticulous planning, and enormous investment in weapons systems were put to the test. Since the Yom Kippur War, a giant question mark had hovered over the air force's ability to cope with the missile network. The debilitating losses suffered by the Israeli air force in 1973 had raised doubts among military experts the world over as to whether it could stand up to the newest and most sophisticated missile systems, even after successive commanders of the Israeli air force had promised that their planes could not only cope with the missiles but could probably wipe them out.

Now the moment of truth had arrived, and the commander of the air force, Maj. Gen. David Ivri, was so keyed up that he had to closet himself alone in his office, leaving his chief operations officer to phone each of the squadron commanders for a last talk. Then the planes were on their way.

Although the war was by now at its height, the Syrians manning the missile system in the Bekaa were caught by surprise. The missile brigade that had most recently entered Lebanese territory was still deploying and never had a chance to act at all. The others did what they could, but to little avail. The result: of the nineteen Syrian missile batteries in the area, fourteen were destroyed and another three were severely damaged.

Ever since that day, the Soviet Union has invested untold sums in a supreme effort to figure out just how its missile system took such an ignominious beating. This is not just a matter of saving face; it is a vital necessity in order to plaster over the cracks in its own defense network and those of its allies. Israel, for its part, has kept its secret absolutely secure, for it believes that the war against Russian weapons is not yet over. The best minds on both sides are engaged in this contest to uncover the other's secrets, on the one hand, and keep its own concealed, on the other. For that reason, one should treat the many details that have been published about the destruction of the Syrian missile system with a healthy measure of skepticism. Nor would there be much point in presenting a partial and therefore deficient description of the method of attack. Suffice it to say that the missiles were destroyed through a combination of air action and long-range artillery fire.

Yet the battle itself can be described. The moment the Syrians apprehended what was happening, they made a desperate bid to save their missile batteries by throwing scores of interceptors into the fray. On the day before, they had already begun sending out planes in large groups in the belief that this would enable them to down at least a few Israeli planes, which usually operated in small formations. The Syrians often sent up packs of as many as twelve planes, which appeared to be coming at the Israelis in an aerial phalanx. This tendency to crowd the skies reached its peak during the attack on the missile system, when dozens of Syrian interceptors were sent up to do battle. The result was one of the biggest air battles in history: some 200 supersonic jet fighters targeting, dodging, and firing at each other over an area of approximately 2,500 square kilometers.

The Syrian losses were staggering. Twenty-nine planes were shot down in dogfights on Wednesday alone, and overall about 30 percent of the Syrian planes that crossed into Lebanese airspace were damaged or destroyed. (The totals would undoubtedly have been even higher had the Israeli pilots not been forbidden to pursue their prey into Syrian airspace.) But the real losses were not so much in sophisticated aircraft as in pilots. Equipment can be replaced—and relatively quickly at that, especially when a great power is prepared to open up its stores and to provide the weapons at half price, even for free—but the same cannot be said of pilots, who require years of training. It is a fair estimate that about half of the Syrian pilots of downed planes either lost their lives or were put out of action indefinitely, so that the Syrian air force lost a total of forty to fifty combat pilots, including many of its most experienced men.

By Wednesday evening, to all intents and purposes, the Syrian air-defense system had ceased to exist. The battle had been between two opposing weapons systems, and the Israeli triumph should be regarded as the victory of an entire system, not of plane over missile or of Israeli pilot over Syrian. It would likewise be a distortion to claim that a Western or American weapons system had won out over a Russian one. It wasn't the

Russian equipment that failed; the failure lay in how the Syrians employed or failed to exploit certain types of Russian weaponry. And the victorious system embraced an outstanding command that planned and conducted the battle, excellent control and communications units (including radar planes), experienced electronic-warfare units, and sophisticated armament. Above all, there was the human element. Even when using the most sophisticated technology, the people who manned the Israeli system—pilots and all the rest—had been painstakingly trained and interminably rehearsed for just this occasion.

It is doubtful that the Syrian General Staff and air force command in Damascus knew what was actually happening on the battlefield that day, and they probably did not realize the magnitude of the debacle until Wednesday evening. Thoroughout Wednesday night the Israeli air force continued to batter the Syrians on the ground and score gains in the rear in an interdiction action to isolate the Bekaa from the Syrian heartland and impede the supply of reinforcements. When the Syrians began to move their Third Armored Division westward, its Forty-seventh Brigade was discovered north of Baalbek, and Israeli planes were sent in at night to devastate its tank transports until only the ragged remains of the brigade were left to join the battle.

The air battles and destruction of the missile system were a spectacular performance that any army could envy, but, as Sharon had expected, they also changed the timetable of the war. Now, for the first time after four days of fighting, the powers entered the scene in earnest. Philip Habib had reached Damascus with Israel's ultimatum on Wednesday morning, but President Assad was in no hurry to receive him. As Habib cooled his heels in his Damascus quarters, the missile batteries were being demolished, making the heavily conditional peace proposal that he had brought from Israel obsolete. With his air-defense system a shambles, Assad's instinctive reaction was to turn to Moscow by sending his defense minister, Mustafa Tlas, on an urgent mission to ask for nothing less than a Soviet air umbrella. The Russians kept their distance. Aid in the form of equipment and personnel—planes, advisers, and the most advanced missiles—fine; but direct intervention in the fighting was another matter. However, the Kremlin, taking nothing for granted, did begin preparing for the possibility that Israel would invade Syrian territory. Massive quantities of equipment began to be stockpiled at airfields in the southern part of the Soviet Union, ready to be rushed to Syria at a moment's notice. It was all alarmingly reminiscent of the prelude to the Russian airlift during the Yom Kippur War—and that was enough to spur Washington into action. Steps had to be taken to prevent a further escalation and spread of the war.

Philip Habib was finally ushered into President Assad's office late Wednesday afternoon and proposed a ceasefire to take effect at 6:00 A.M. on Thursday, June 10. But harking back to the original Israeli ultimatum he had in his pocket, he added the condition that the Syrians see to the removal of the Palestinian forces huddling under their wing in the Bekaa Valley. Assad agreed to the ceasefire but would have no part of any demand that he humble himself before the Israelis by turning his back on the Palestinians.

"Is that so much to ask?" Habib asked.

"Yes," Assad pronounced without the slightest hesitation. "It is both a big demand and an unreasonable one." And then he added somewhat cockily—considering his situation—"We also have a condition for a ceasefire: a full Israeli withdrawal."

With that counterdemand in hand and the shadow of a scowl on his face, Habib took his leave of Assad, drove to the American embassy to pass the condition on to Israel, and then returned to the presidential palace after midnight—this time with a message from President Reagan (sent concurrently with another communication to Begin). The White House was prepared to guarantee an Israeli withdrawal from Lebanon, but then Assad insisted that it begin forthwith. Blocked on that issue, Habib fought back with a new demand from Jerusalem: Israel now wanted satisfactory security arrangements in the forty-kilometer zone.

"That is not within my power to decide," the Syrian leader parried. "If I were the president of Lebanon, and it were up to me, I would refuse to recognize Israel's right to impose security arrangements on the soil of another country. But this is a matter for the Lebanese to decide. I will not decide for them."

Meanwhile, at 2:00 A.M. on Thursday, President Reagan's message to Israel was handed to Prime Minister Begin by the American ambassador, Sam Lewis. The Americans had finally grasped what the Israeli Cabinet was having trouble seeing, namely, that Begin's commitment to confine the Lebanese operation to a forty-kilometer belt had been violated along with the equally solemn pledge not to attack the Syrians. Somehow the war had mushroomed far beyond what had been promised or expected, and now the Russians were starting to show signs of edginess. For Washington that meant the time had come to rein Israel in before the whole affair got out of hand.

So it was that, at the dismal hour of 4:00 A.M. on Thursday, the Israeli Cabinet convened to discuss President Reagan's demand that Israel accede to a ceasefire. Formally, the ministers bowed to the president's will, but they did so in a way that effectively scotched his initiative by appending a string of provocative conditions to their consent: that the Syrians promise not to send additional forces into Lebanon; that the Palestinians in the forty-kilometer strip be withdrawn from the area; and that the Syrian units that had moved into the Bekaa Valley from the north pull back to their previous positions. As the Cabinet's reply was being worded, no one doubted that Assad would reject these terms, just as he had bounced back the ultimatum that Habib had brought him the previous day. And after all, why should he pull his troops back when Israeli divisions were steadily moving up his left flank in a bid to encircle his army, and when the ceasefire did not entail *their* withdrawal?

While Begin was dictating his reply to the president, an aide entered the room to tell him that Secretary of State Haig was on the phone. Haig sounded very perturbed about the sprawl of the war and urged the prime minister to accept Reagan's call for an immediate ceasefire. Begin, in turn, informed him of the Cabinet's decision, with all it conditions, and urged that Haig come to Israel—that very day, if possible. When the secretary replied that this was a good idea and promised to consider it favorably, Begin knew that the IDF had been given a temporary reprieve. "Let's wait for Haig," he told his ministers when the Cabinet reconvened that morning. "It will probably take a day for him to get here."

The secretary of state never made it to Israel because President Reagan vetoed the trip. Haig's phone conversation with Begin played right into the prime minister's hands, for Israel's chief concern right then was to gain time. At the start of the fifth day of fighting, its war aims had not yet been achieved on either the coastal or the central axis. At that Thursday Cabinet meeting, Sharon told the ministers that their forces would be standing on the Beirut-Damascus highway by midnight and that taking the road was absolutely imperative to deny the Syrians any possibility of ruling Lebanon. "They won't have control over Beirut, and without Beirut they won't be able to install a puppet government with a president who's under their thumb," Sharon told the Cabinet. "This is a very sensitive point."

Thus the capture of the Beirut-Damascus highway became a vital objective at this stage of the war, even though it had not been mentioned in the Cabinet's original decision to go to war. This latest change shifted the plan back to Operation Big Pines, which had been rejected by the Cabinet less than a month earlier. Opting for a flanking movement up the central axis had, as expected, inaugurated a struggle over the political future of the Lebanese regime. At stake now was not only the issue of the terrorists and the security of civilians in the Galilee but also who would rule in Beirut.

Sharon had told the Cabinet that the key road would be cut by midnight, but even with the missiles out of the picture Menachem Einan's men remained hopelessly bogged down on the narrow axis in Ein Zehalta. "The Syrians moved their forces before we got to them," Sharon explained to the ministers. Thus the task of cutting the road now fell to Ben-Gal's divisions working their way up through the Bekaa Valley.

Maj. Gen. Avigdor Ben-Gal had come all the way back from America to lead this drive up the Bekaa against the Syrians. A hero of the defense of the Golan during the Yom Kippur War, he had preceded Drori as head of Northern Command and was now waiting out the rest of Rafael Eitan's term as chief of staff to find out whether he would be appointed as his successor. His campaign against the Syrian garrison in Lebanon could therefore be either a feather in his cap or, if something were to go awry, a less than illustrious end to an otherwise distinguished military career.

The force placed in Ben-Gal's hands was larger than either Einan's or the divisions operating on the western axis, and the balance of power vis-à-vis the Syrians was greatly in his favor. In addition to the unlimited air support his men enjoyed now that the Syrian missiles were no longer a factor, the ratio of forces on the ground was sufficient for an attack according to even the most exacting strategical requirements, which suggest that an assault force be three times as large as a defensive one. Rarely had the IDF found itself facing an enemy with that kind of numerical advantage. The only catch was that Ben-Gal would have very little time to meet his goals. While the advance northward in the other two sectors had begun late on Sunday morning, his divisions didn't really get going until Wednesday afternoon, after the missiles had been blown away. As matters turned out, Ben-Gal had less than two days to reach the highway; the ceasefire would go into effect at noon on Friday.

Oddly enough, Ben-Gal's division and brigade commanders did not seem touched by a burning sense of urgency. Their behavior on the battlefield reflected more of a feeling that they had world enough and time to fight each battle twice over. Stress was placed first on firepower and less on pressing relentlessly forward. Whenever the men ran into problems or suffered losses, their commanders preferred to draw to a halt and treat the enemy to a massive dose of fire, both on the ground and from the air. Thus an operation that was conceived as one long push forward turned into a succession of static battles. The night was hardly ever exploited to advance; much to the contrary, every evening this massive war machine ground to a halt, and all momentum ceased.

Ben-Gal's multidivision force was divided into three parts as it moved out against the Syrian First Division in the Bekaa. The main, frontal thrust was up through the center of the valley along and parallel to the main road leading to Jub Jenin. There were two subordinate drives. One was in the east, along the slopes of Mount Hermon, to do double duty protecting the operation's right flank along the Syrian border. The other was designed to protect the operation's western flank, moving along the slopes of the Shouf Mountains and the foot of Jebel Baruk to continue around both sides of Lake Karoun up toward Kafraya and Kafr Huna.

The central drive up the Bekaa Valley was essentially one long, exhausting frontal attack, since the hilly terrain and mountain roads placed endless obstacles in the paths of the two flanking forces and prevented their unwieldy columns from fully expressing their power. Literally hundreds of the tanks sent into Lebanon never fired their guns, while the lead units bore the brunt of the fighting. And although the Israelis exploited the difficult terrain better than their Syrian adversaries, the campaign was plagued by a spate of operational and logistical snafus that often affected the entire front.

Ben-Gal was given the order to advance into the Bekaa on Wednesday afternoon, and the two main battles of that day were in Ein Tina, south of Lake Karoun, and on Jebel Baruk, which the Golani Brigade climbed to capture the Syrian communications and intelligence installations on its peak. The thrust north in the central sector was renewed at dawn on Thursday, which proved a day of hard fighting. On that morning, after negotiating the obstacles that the Syrians had prepared in the sharp turns on the main road, the lead brigade reached the first latitudinal road in the Bekaa, one running between Rashaye in the east and Lake Karoun in the west. The Syrians, fully appreciating the importance of these junctions, had reinforced them with armored units to halt the Israeli advance. At the first junction, a head-on battle broke out with Syrian T-62 tanks. The air force provided occasional support for the Israeli armor, and Syrian helicopter gunships were called in on the other side. More and more Syrian tanks were knocked out until the junction finally fell to the Israelis at 3:00 P.M. following a brigade assault. With the conquest of that first crossroads, the front line of the Syrian First Division was, to all intents and purposes, broken. The problem then was to exploit this success by advancing at night and breaking through to the main highway the next morning.

But the night between Thursday and Friday, June 10–11, was filled with disasters for Ben-Gal's troops. The Israeli advance was essentially halted on most sections of the front, with the exception of the western sector—originally considered a subordinate effort—when a force under Brig. Gen. Yossi Peled broke forward and got as far north as the IDF was ever going to reach in the Bekaa Valley.

Peled's force was moving through the hilly flank of the Syrian-controlled area, where the enemy deployment was thin compared to its emplacements to the east in the Bekaa proper. Before nightfall, his troops captured the villages of Ana and Zanoub el-Jedida, and at night his point unit got as far as five kilometers from the Beirut-Damascus highway. But close to midnight, Drori called Ben-Gal and ordered him to do the unimaginable: to pull Peled's force a few kilometers back! The front commander explained that Operation Peace for Galilee was nearing its conclusion, the ceasefire would go into effect at noon the next day, and there were definite signs that the Syrians had begun to send their second armored division (the Third Division) into Lebanon to mount a counterattack, probably the next morning. "Peled's point force is too far north," Drori said, "and before the counterattack we have to straighten out our lines and deploy differently."

Ben-Gal did not give way easily. Some four hours earlier he had issued an order telling his troops that on the following day they were to forge ahead past the Beirut-Damascus highway to the vicinity of the Rayak airfield. How could he now tell them to turn around and move back south? But after remonstrating with Drori, he finally conceded that he would have Peled pull back a few kilometers to organize for defense and see to it that his flank was not exposed to the enemy. The order was received at Peled's forward command post with clear resentment, but in fact the pullback was only two to three kilometers.

The situation was considerably different along other sectors of the front, where the advance was slowed to a virtual stop. There wasn't much of an enemy presence in the hilly eastern region along the Syrian border, but progress there was hobbled by a snag that was basically logistical. The order to the column moving up the longitudinal road in this sector (known as the "Arafat Trail") was to aim for the town of Rashaye and points north. Rashaye fell at dusk on Thursday, and the lead unit proceeded another few kilometers to a destroyed bridge. While it waited for army engineers to arrive and set up an alternative means of crossing the wadi, the remainder of the brigade's units organized in a laager for the night, postponing their advance till the next morning.

Chaos broke out at 2:30 A.M. when Syrian commandos attacked one of the brigade's laagers and an APC burst into flames. The rest of the vehicles returned fire, but they were unable to pull out and continue north, not because of the commando attack but due to a grave shortage of gasoline. Most of the tanks had only enough fuel left for an hour's drive, and the massive force crammed onto the one narrow mountain road prevented the tank trucks from reaching them. The entire route was clogged with vehicles, to the point where even the engineering unit that had been summoned to improvise a bridge had to fight its way through the traffic jam and didn't arrive until 3:00 A.M. Meanwhile, Ben-Gal's deputy, Maj. Gen. Ehud Barak, kept telling the local commander not to wait until all his vehicles had filled up. "Whoever's refueled should get going!" he shouted. It did him little good.

The advance did not really resume until dawn, and then Syrian helicopter gunships descended on the column and managed to cripple a number of vehicles. Had it not been for the crush and commotion along the road, there was a good chance that the column would have reached as far north as the route to Jedidat Yebus. As matters stood, its mission was only partially accomplished: the column got as far as the vicinity of Yanta, where it came up against advance units of the Syrian Third Division.

Meanwhile, in the central sector, a major operational blunder had led to a grim battle that totally halted the advance through the heart of the Bekaa. The scene of the fighting was a narrow valley hemmed in by high hills near the village of Sultan Yakoub. Just after sunset on Thursday, one of the brigades operating in the sector received an order to proceed north on the Bekaa's eastern axis and capture Sultan Yakoub. The purpose of the move was to establish a line of defense against the expected counterattack by the Syrian Third Division on Friday morning. As the brigade began to move out, none of its officers knew exactly how the Syrians up ahead were deployed. Certainly they had no idea that the enemy was poised on the hills overlooking Sultan Yakoub, or that its positions there were the forward deployment of the First Division's relatively fresh mechanized brigade, which had taken less of a beating than the division's armored units.

Intelligence on this deployment—gathered from aerial photographs and other sources—was available somewhere, but it never reached the brigade in the field. Exactly who was privy to the latest information on the Syrian deployment in Sultan Yakoub and how far down the line that information reached is still subject to dispute. But there is no disputing the result of the communications foul-up: an IDF brigade headed for Sultan Yakoub without the slightest inkling that it was moving right into the forward positions of a Syrian mechanized brigade. These tanks weren't falling into a Syrian ambush; they were driving headlong into the enemy's deployment. (The Syrians, it should be added, were equally shocked by this development and took a while to recover their wits.)

The commander of the lead Israeli battalion in this ill-fated advance, Lt. Col. Ira Efroni, was a reservist, a computer engineer by profession, and by all accounts an experienced and effective officer. His men were mostly religious boys from one of the special *hesder* units, and the mechanized infantry attached to his battalion were all reservists in their thirties. Morale in the battalion was high, though the men were understandably tired after over twenty-four hours of fighting in a mobile battle. As they headed for Sultan Yakoub, they knew only that their mission was to set up a battalion defense line and wait for the Syrians.

As the brigade approached Sultan Yakoub, it could see the houses lined up along both sides of the road. Before its men knew it, fire was coming at them from these buildings and from positions farther east, much of it in the form of Sagger missiles that were released too close to their targets, veered upward, and missed their marks. The Israelis' immediate reaction was to escape by rushing forward, shooting in all directions. Efroni soon discovered, however, that not everyone in the battalion had charged ahead. While three companies of tanks and APCs under his command had sped through Sultan Yakoub and continued into the valley beyond, the rest of the battalion had remained behind at the entrance to the village. That was how a part of Efroni's unit hastily entered the narrow valley by Sultan Yakoub and found itself right in the middle of the Syrian deployment—though even then the men didn't know it.

Although there was some fighting during the night, Efroni decided to stay put and wait until first light before moving any farther. He still believed that the problem was a localized one, and because of the fighting in the village he was keenly aware that the enemy was also behind him. When he finally realized that he was missing part of his battalion, he sent his deputy, Major Micha, back for the remainder of the force. But on the way Micha encountered stiff Syrian resistance and, unable to get through, had to return. Still, neither officer suspected how grave the situation really was.

Efroni's men, up to this point, had not suffered heavy casualties. They were physically exhausted, of course, and during the night they hardly slept a wink, sensing that the hills were crawling with Syrian soldiers closing in on them under cover of darkness. Some of the Syrians did penetrate close to the vehicles, hiding behind the trees of a nearby grove, but they stopped short of mounting an attack. The brigade's machine guns kept sweeping the area with fire, and this undoubtedly kept the enemy at bay.

But shortly after the sky began to pale, the battle took on a different character. It now became painfully obvious that Efroni's battalion, far from setting up a defense line to stop the Syrians, was itself caught in a death trap. Efroni was unaware that a fresh force had been sent up from the south to take responsibility for the entire sector, only to be caught in a bitter battle with the Syrians east of the road to Sultan Yakoub, five kilometers from where Efroni and his men were trapped.

What Efroni did perceive, soon after dawn, was that his battalion would not be able to survive without assistance. His tanks and APCs were scattered through the valley in three concentrations, with his own company approximately in the middle. As long as the vehicles were under some sort of cover, they were reasonably safe. But if they exposed themselves for so much as a moment, they would immediately draw fire from the high ground around Sultan Yakoub—armor-piercing shells from tanks to the north and missiles from the west and southwest. At one point Syrian soldiers with RPGs and antitank missiles began to filter into the nearby grove and the houses of Sultan Yakoub in an attempt to hit the Israelis at close range. And no less serious than the heavy Syrian fire was the battalion's growing shortage of ammunition.

The number of destroyed and disabled tanks mounted by the minute. One tank took a direct hit from an armor-piercing shell that left its commander and gunner mortally wounded. The communications man, also wounded, jumped out of the tank as the driver was steering it over to a neighboring company. When the tank came to a halt, two officers climbed in and found that the commander was already dead, the gunner still breathing. Over and over again, the officers called on the tank's radio for a doctor, only to find that the battalion's medical team had remained with that part of the force outside the valley. When they finally climbed out of the tank to seek other help, the driver was suddenly seized by panic and began speeding around in circles. Then he took off directly southward, back toward the village. Failing to respond to any calls to stop, he kept speeding blindly down the road, the bodies of his two comrades beside him, until he came upon one of the abandoned Israeli tanks at the edge of Sultan Yakoub and abruptly came to a stop. It must have been the sight of another Israeli tank that brought him back to his senses. At any rate, the crew of the disabled tank called to him from the house in which they had taken cover, and he finally climbed out and joined them. In the end, the runaway tank was abandoned with a number of other vehicles in the field. Its wounded gunner, in critical condition when last seen, is still officially missing.

After repeated discussions with his brigade commander got him nowhere, Efroni asked to speak to someone higher up and got the sector commander. As soon as the officer got on the network, he asked Efroni how long he could hold out. Efroni—who was to recall how much that question infuriated him—countered by asking whether there was any plan to deal with his predicament. Without addressing himself to Efroni's point, the sector commander said that a solution would be found within half an hour to an hour.

"You won't be able to do it within half an hour," Efroni grumbled, convinced that the sector commander was merely humoring him. "You can't be serious."

"Considering your pessimism," the officer replied a little too brightly, "I'm willing to grant you an hour to an hour and a half."

But Efroni was not appeased. And after two artillery battalions were dispatched to aid his trapped companies, and failed to break through, the Syrians, emboldened by their success, sent out another squad with anti-tank missiles to tackle the Israelis at close range.

These skirmishes were steadily depleting what was left of the Israelis' ammunition, and the mood didn't improve any when a pair of MiGs suddenly swooped down over the battalion. Efroni had asked for air support much earlier and been promised that the planes would be arriving forthwith. When he now put in a fresh call for air support, he was told that the planes would be there in another ten minutes. But again they failed to show.

While waiting for the planes that would never come, Efroni had a second conversation with the sector commander and was now told that it would take about four hours before the fresh force coming up from the south—and still engaged in battle with the Syrians—could reach the valley.

"I haven't got that kind of time," Efroni replied, his voice edged with anger. "I need a radical solution. By the time you reach us, we probably won't be here anymore!"

"If that's the case," the sector commander told him, "then close your slats and get the hell out of there. Make a dash for it."

"That's practically suicide," Efroni protested. "The company commander behind me says there are about thirty APCs waiting for us. We'll drive right into them!"

"Have you got anything better to do?" the sector commander shot back.

There was silence over the network as Efroni digested what he had just heard. For the first time, he realized he was entirely on his own. The sector commander had offered him a Hobson's choice: if he sat tight, he would lose all his vehicles, one after the other, like sitting ducks; and if he tried to make a dash for it, his remaining tanks and APCs would be immediately exposed to enemy fire. Even if he absolutely flew out of the valley, he still had to cover a distance of four or five kilometers of open fire.

Before making any decision, Efroni climbed out of his tank and began to move among the other vehicles to check the supply of ammunition and try to encourage his men. It was then, while he was away from his tank, that one of his officers grabbed a microphone and began raving at no one in particular, "We can't hold out any more!" Everyone plugged into the network—all the soldiers of the battalion and the officers of units outside the valley—could hear his cry of despair. "Why have we been abandoned?" the young man continued to shout almost hysterically. "You have to airlift us out of here. Our ammunition is almost gone. Do you want us to surrender, or would you prefer to see us wiped out?"

Stunned by what he was hearing, the sector commander was at a loss to respond. He had no idea who was talking, and it took him a while to decide how to react. Finally, he cut in on the network and barked at the anonymous complainant, "You also have the option of fighting!"

It wasn't until later that Efroni heard about this frenzied dialogue between the sector commander and one of his officers. In the meanwhile, he had returned to his tank and heard the sector commander ask him what the situation was. "Time is running out," he replied, venting his anger and gloom. "I can see the end coming from three directions."

At that point Efroni's brigade commander got on the network and seconded the advice about trying to break out. So Efroni summoned his second-in-command and analyzed their condition in all its bleakness. "Considering the situation, we have three choices," he posited coldly, "to break out of here—and the odds of making it are pretty bad—to fight to the last bullet, or to surrender."

"We are not going to surrender!" Micha exclaimed, staring at Efroni in near horror at the very thought.

"Then we'd better get out of here," Efroni pronounced. The matter had been settled. The remains of his battalion would make a dash for it, come what may.

Once his mind was made up, Efroni set to work quickly, gathering the wounded and the crews of disabled vehicles into the available APCs. What would be needed most during the escape was concentrated fire support—heavy artillery barrages and massive aerial bombardments so that the Syrians on the surrounding hills would have to keep their heads down and be unable to aim their missiles and artillery. That was when the air force would be most needed, but still no Israeli planes were available to Efroni and his men. On the other hand, no less than eleven artillery battalions had been sent in to create a fearsome barrage the minute Efroni's vehicles got moving. It was an extraordinary concentration of artillery power, testifying to the fact that the entire front had been paralyzed because of the trapped battalion. The cannons were to create a box of fire around Efroni's vehicles to prevent an armored or infantry assault, but they could not protect the tanks and APCs from being hit by missiles, RPGs, or other forms of antitank fire.

At 8:45 the battalion completed preparations for its perilous journey. The tanks gunned their motors, went into gear, and began to tear out of the valley. It would take sixteen minutes for the column to reach its salvation—sixteen minutes under murderous fire. The drivers floored their gas pedals, Israeli shells were falling just meters away from the speeding column, and the mechanized infantry sprayed the sides of the road with machine-gun fire while the rest of the men hunkered down and prayed silently to be saved. Not all their prayers were answered: four men died and six were wounded in that mad dash for safety, and one tank disappeared somewhere along the way and was never seen or heard from again. (No one could say how it was hit, but one of its crewmen subsequently turned up as a POW in Syrian hands; his three comrades are still listed as missing.)

"I'm out!" Efroni shouted into his mouthpiece at precisely 9:06. Helicopters descended on the battalion to evacuate the dead and wounded, and the search for the missing tank continued for a while, without success. Seven other abandoned tanks remained behind in the valley. They contained a number of innovations and material classified as secret until then —such as the Arrow shells manufactured by the Israeli arms industry and the substance that serves as a protective layer against RPGs and shells with hollow charges. For whatever reason, no special effort was made to evacuate those tanks or at least destroy them, and the next day the Syrians simply towed them off. It was an appropriate coda to the fiasco at Sultan Yakoub.

With the ceasefire between Israel and Syria due to go into effect at noon on Friday, and despite the flight from Sultan Yakoub, the Syrian Third Division did not begin to enter the area until 11:00 A.M. that day. From the western part of the captured town, the Israelis could see the advance units of the division coming toward them—T-72 tanks moving along smartly in a column. But then, in an ironic double twist, the Syrians drove smack into the Israeli deployment—just as Efroni's force had driven unsuspectingly into the Syrian deployment at Sultan Yakoub—and found themselves in a trap. The hapless Syrian unit, vanguard of the Eighty-second Armored Brigade, was the first to lose T-72 tanks in the war. Chief of Staff Eitan happened to be in Ben-Gal's headquarters just at that moment and gave his permission to continue firing until the Syrian brigade was destroyed. At noon, however, Ben-Gal's forces were not allowed to go on fighting. Eitan went as high as the prime minister for special permission to violate the ceasefire in this sector so as to batter the Syrians as much as possible, but Begin turned him down.

All in all, the Syrian force in Lebanon took a thorough drubbing, but it was not utterly destroyed or even driven out of the country. Although they suffered heavy casualties and lost hundreds of tanks, the Syrians withdrew in an orderly fashion, not in a rout. Unquestionably, the Syrians made many tactical errors, but their forces certainly did not collapse. Quite to the contrary, the Syrian army remained firmly entrenched in Lebanon, even after sections of the Beirut-Damascus highway were captured in the second round of fighting, and Beirut remained within range of its artillery. It had succeeded in holding up the Israeli advance in both the central and eastern sectors, and had prevented the IDF from taking the main road all the way from Beirut to the Syrian border. Most important of all, perhaps, as soon as the Syrians' tenacious holding battle began, the sand in the political hourglass began to run swiftly toward the imposition of a cease-fire.

At noon on Friday, the battle with the Syrians was over, with mixed results for Israel. But the war, as it turned out, was barely under way.

10

The Ba'abda Connection

THERE IS NO GETTING AROUND THE FACT that the Israeli Cabinet never ordered or sanctioned the IDF's entry into Beirut. When Israeli troops and vehicles began to sweep through the streets of the Lebanese capital, they did so in express contradiction not only to what their government wanted but to what their defense minister had promised. The events of Sunday, June 13, were among the most critical of the war in Lebanon, for they proved that Ariel Sharon had led Prime Minister Begin and his Cabinet down the garden path. Most important of all, perhaps, the IDF's arrival in Beirut marked the transformation of Operation Peace for Galilee from a limited military action to protect Israeli citizens into a runaway war to conquer an Arab capital, and eventually a kind of Frankenstein monster that would turn on its creators with terrible consequences still to be measured.

All of Israel's governments had lived by the axiom that the capture of an Arab capital—any Arab capital—was to be stringently avoided. Yet now, in what was supposed to be a relatively limited ground operation in South Lebanon, the inconceivable seemed to be happening. Only in retrospect did the ministers realize that the penetration of Beirut, the subsequent siege, and all that followed shattered the hallowed consensus on security, raised disturbing moral issues in Israel, offended international public opinion, and altered the attitudes of formerly sympathetic governments.

More than all else, the IDF's approach and entry into Beirut again demonstrated how well Ariel Sharon had managed to divide and isolate the political and military echelons. For while the Cabinet was lulled by talk of a forty-kilometer limit, throughout most of the first week of the war the commanders in the field strongly suspected, if they did not actually know, that they were headed for the Lebanese capital. As early as Tuesday, before the capture of Sidon, Colonel Yair, the commander of the paratroop brigade that had landed at the Awali River, told his men, "I'm going to lead you into Beirut, to the main highway." It was no empty boast. "From the outset, from the very first stage," Brig. Gen. Amos Yaron later attested, "we prepared ourselves to link up with the Christians. We talked about the Beirut road back on Tuesday, even before reaching Damour." Yair and Yaron knew, from the moment they reached Damour on Wednesday, that the next step would be the capital. That had been the plan when both had toured Beirut and participated in drawing up a campaign for surrounding the city.

Whatever doubts may still have remained among the military leadership were settled on Thursday morning when Maj. Gen. Amir Drori flew to Damour by helicopter and began to speak in explicit terms about the objectives ahead. "Our direction now is Beirut," he told the field commanders. "We must continue northward as quickly as possible." Drori still did not have official sanction to go as far as Beirut proper, but more than any other senior officer he knew the surrounding events. In fact, Beirut had long been included in Drori's plans in the form of a two-division attack—by Amos Yaron's and Avigdor Kahalani's forces—to take the city from the south. So sure was Drori that the IDF was going for Beirut that beginning on Thursday he had the air force drop leaflets over the city calling on the Syrian units to flee while they still could.

Thus from Thursday, June 10, onward, while the Cabinet ministers were groping their way through a smokescreen of blather about "confusing the enemy"—when they seemed to be the most confused parties of all—the commanders in the field knew exactly where their columns were going.

The long march to Beirut began on Monday, June 7, and by evening of that day—the second of the war—Yair's paratroops were already located on the commanding ridge above Damour, having covered the way from the bridgehead by the Awali on foot. The paratroops moved from hill to hill east of the coastal road as the tanks brought in on the landing craft followed slightly behind on the road proper. It was a method of advance chosen to deal with the likelihood that the enemy had laid ambushes on the road. From time to time shots rang out at the advancing force, but it nonetheless continued to move steadily along until it reached Nebi Yunis, where an unpleasant surprise awaited. An ambush—consisting of a jeep mounted with a heavy machine gun—was concealed in one of the shops lining the road through the town. As soon as the paratroops had moved past the shop, the Palestinians hauled up its iron shutter and machine-gunned the Israelis from behind. Three of the paratroops were cut down before the jeep was destroyed and its men killed.

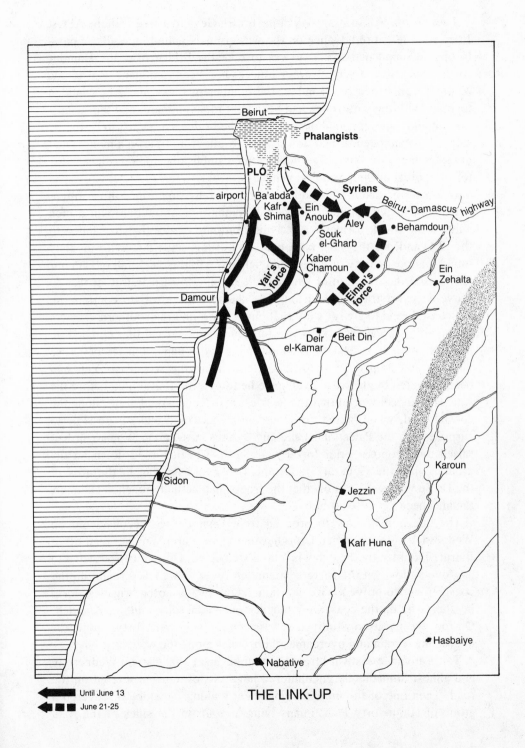

THE LINK-UP

Until June 13
June 21-25

Tuesday, June 8, was spent waiting for Eli Geva to arrive with the APCs. In effect, the entire advance on the western axis halted, and all the para- troops accomplished that day was to take the bridge over the Damour River. Because the senior armor officers had been confident of reaching Amos Yaron's men on Monday, the number of tanks and APCs landed together with the paratroops had been kept to a minimum, and the sugges- tion to hold another round of landings at the bridgehead—just to be on the safe side—had been turned down. As a result, Amos Yaron's men waited until Wednesday—sixty-five hours after establishing their bridgehead— for the arrival of their armored vehicles.

Damour was taken on Wednesday in a two-division attack after soften- ing up by heavy artillery and aerial bombardments. When Yair's men entered the town, formerly a thriving Maronite center that had fallen to the PLO and, for the most part, had lain in ruins since the civil war, they found it almost empty of Palestinian fighters. Yet the quick fall of Damour now raised the question of which route to take toward Beirut. It was to prove a major strategic decision. The shortest route was to continue up the coastal road to Beirut's international airport and the southern quarters of the city. The alternative was a tortuous country road that climbed up into the mountains east of Damour, passed through a cluster of Druse villages, and dipped back down to Beirut from the southeast. Yair had been attracted by this road ever since he toured the Beirut area before the war. He was convinced that the heaviest resistance would come along the coastal road, while taking the mountain route would make it possible to surprise both the Palestinians and any Syrians in the area. When Yair had raised this proposal prior to the war, he had been turned down on the grounds that the General Staff wanted to avoid fighting in the area of the Druse villages. But now that the troops had actually reached Damour, the idea became more attractive.

The question of how to proceed from Damour was reconsidered on Wednesday morning, when Drori flew in to give Yaron's men a send-off to Beirut. Troubled by the delay in Yaron's advance, Drori was persuaded to approve a move on the eastern, mountain route as well as straight up the coast. It was to prove a wise decision, as the two armored brigades work- ing their way up the coast were blocked on Wednesday south of Khaldeh. On foot the paratroops moved surprisingly quickly over forty kilometers of grueling terrain and overcame all obstacles along the way.

Yair's advance eastward from Damour began at 1:00 P.M. on Wednesday and almost immediately encountered hundreds of mines scattered on the road. Then one of the units moving silently along the slope discovered a group of about forty Palestinians lying in wait on the sides of the road below for the Israeli armor. The members of the ambush were astounded to be attacked from behind; twelve were killed in the action and ten taken prisoner.

Maintaining their advance until past midnight, Yair's men came to a halt just before Kafr Mata when they discovered that they lacked illumination flares and therefore could not clear the mines scattered along the road. While they waited, and unbeknownst to the Israelis, a fresh group of Palestinian fighters reached Kafr Mata. They belonged to Force Bader, the battalion that King Hussein had so generously detached from his army to send to the aid of the PLO. Like the Palestinian fighters on the previous day, Force Bader also took up positions along the road, believing that the equipment-rich Israelis would advance in a vehicular column. But because the paratroops were on foot on the slopes rather than on the road, when Force Bader did engage the tanks it was quickly attacked by Israeli infantry. The Palestinians tried to fall back, but their men were hunted down in a battle that lasted about four hours. When it was over, Force Bader had taken a bad beating, losing some fifty men while the Israelis had only three wounded and no damage at all to their armor.

The next day, Friday, when the first ceasefire with the Syrians went into effect, was ironically the day of the first battle with the Syrian Eighty-fifth Brigade, deployed south of Beirut. The fighting took place along two separate axes; the mountain route taken by the paratroops and the coastal road being followed by the Israeli armored columns and the Golani Infantry Brigade. In essence, the confrontation with the Eighty-fifth Brigade was not a single battle but a series of bloody clashes that went on for two days.

Back on Thursday afternoon, the paratroops could see Syrian reinforcements streaming into the area of the Kaber Chamoun junction and the ridge to the north of it. A brief description of the topography around Beirut is in order here. Built on the narrow coastal plain, Beirut is skirted by successive ridges that form the western spurs of the Mount Lebanon range. Kaber Chamoun is the last junction before the Shemlan ridge, which in turn is the final ridge before Beirut and the main highway to Damascus. It stood to reason, therefore, that the Syrians were deployed on Shemlan, especially as the ridge overlooks the coastal road as well. By holding Shemlan and the area to the east, they were able to control the two main axes into Beirut with their fire.

The Israeli assault on the Kaber Chamoun junction began at 11:15 A.M. on Friday, and within three-quarters of an hour the first of the paratroop units had thrust its way into the crossroads. When the ceasefire took effect at noon, the Israelis called upon the Syrian troops to lay down their arms,

but the latter knew exactly what was at stake and kept on fighting. Consequently, the capture of the crossroads became a costly affair, with the
Israelis losing first a platoon commander and then a deputy battalion commander. The paratroops also had many wounded, and at nightfall, though
they had captured the junction, they were still in the vicinity of Kaber
Chamoun. As many of them opened sweets from their battle rations to
mark the start of their first Sabbath in Lebanon, they knew that another
tough battle awaited them in the morning on the Shemlan ridge.

Removing any remaining doubt that they were making for the capital,
the Israelis on Friday morning established the direction of their advance
as northwest, toward Bassaba and the eastern suburbs of Beirut—Kafr
Shima and Ba'abda—rather than northeast, toward Aley. On Thursday
night, Yair had been told that the ceasefire scheduled for noon the next
day would not apply to the fighting against the Palestinians, and early
Friday morning he suggested to Drori that the direction of his assault be
changed from Aley, in the east, to Ba'abda farther west. Yair reasoned
that, since a relatively large Syrian force was concentrated in Aley, an
attack on the town would undoubtedly constitute a flagrant violation of the
ceasefire, whereas approaching the Beirut-Damascus highway in the more
western section of the road would avert a clash with the Syrians. "I like
the idea," Drori pronounced, and went on to clear it with the chief of staff
and minister of defense. Everyone knew, however, that even if the IDF
moved by way of Aley, its aim was to link up with the Phalange on the
way down to the Beirut highway. Even Ariel Sharon later admitted that
this was the point of the move.

For the second time in as many days, however, "everyone" did not
include the members of the Israeli Cabinet, and what Sharon had them
believe was something quite different. On Thursday, for example, he patiently explained to his ministerial colleagues that the capture of the Beirut-
Damascus highway was vital to deny the Syrians control over the capital
and, by extension, over the Lebanese government. Then, without prompting or questions, he added, "I wish to stress that despite the fact that [the
place where the highway was to be cut] is very close to Beirut, the men
have explicit instructions not to enter or in any way operate within Beirut.
We prefer not to have to deal with Beirut, to leave it to the Lebanese army
and the Lebanese government, if they so choose. But for that they need
our help. . . . We've had an unofficial request from the Lebanese government to shell the terrorists' quarters in West Beirut . . . but we still
haven't responded because we consider this too premature. . . . We don't
want to get ourselves involved with that . . . ."

Later in that meeting, in describing the battles that the paratroops had fought on the road moving east from Damour, Sharon said emphatically, "I've spoken with the commanders of the force and have made it clear to them—so that they know exactly where to set up the roadblocks in the direction of the city—that their destination is eastward to link up with the other [Menachem Einan's] division. . . . We will not, on our own initiative, link up with the Christians. If they come toward us, of course, we won't drive them off." On the next day, Friday, during a morning session of the Cabinet, Sharon reiterated, "If we arrive at a situation in which [the Christians] make their way up to us, all fine and well. That's why we didn't want to accept liaison officers from them."

What was actually happening in the field was quite another matter from what Sharon was telling the Cabinet. That a Phalange liaison officer joined the paratroop force moving up toward Beirut on the morning of Friday, June 11, may be a minor detail. Not so minor is the fact that, despite the Cabinet's understanding that the IDF had orders not to reach Beirut and to leave the initiative of a link-up to the Phalange, its forces were continuing to press, in the face of great resistance, straight toward the city.

It is true that some of the ministers had begun to suspect Sharon's real objectives in the war, but even when the IDF advanced beyond the sacrosanct forty-kilometer line they never quite got to the point of asking its ultimate destination. In landing at the Awali estuary, the paratroops had already exceeded the forty-kilometer limit cited by Sharon and Eitan in the meeting at which the Cabinet decided to invade Lebanon, and while the ministers did not know of the move northward on Monday or of the capture of the ridge above Damour, enough had become clear of the Israeli presence beyond the forty-kilometer line to trouble sticklers like Mordechai Zippori and Education Minister Zevulun Hammer. Both men commented on the situation. And then Energy Minister Yitzhak Berman—who more than most ministers was on to Sharon's tactic of creeping from one objective to the next, always asking for a little more leeway to protect the previous day's gains—fired off a cutting barb when Sharon asked the Cabinet to approve yet another of his "protective" moves, this time an attack eastward from Damour to Aley. Recalling that Sharon had told the ministers "We have achieved almost all our objectives!" a mere twenty-four hours after the war broke out, and now having reason to believe that on Sharon's orders the IDF was actually implementing Operation Big Pines—including the conquest of Beirut—even though the Cabinet had approved nothing of the kind, Berman quipped, "Arik, perhaps you'll be good enough to tell us what you're going to ask us to approve the day after tomorrow so that you can secure what you're going to ask us to approve tomorrow morning." The rest of the ministers burst into laughter as the stung Sharon shot back somewhat feebly, "What a sense of humor you have!"

Remarks like Berman's heightened Sharon's fear that some of the military people were taking the trouble to keep certain ministers abreast of what was happening at the front and filling them in on the discussions held at Drori's headquarters. On one occasion he let drop the acid comment that, while his helicopter was still in the air on its way from the front command to the next Cabinet meeting, some people were busy phoning up ministers and leaking their reports. At one point after returning from a Cabinet meeting, Sharon fumed at the officers, "After the little crisis we had at the war room, I thought it would stop. But someone is still making those phone calls. I fly a few kilometers, and when I reach Jerusalem, every schmuck is waiting for me with details and a map and a ruler in hand!"

Yet the ministers did approve the push eastward from Damour into the mountains after being told that it would ease the way for the troops and make it possible to extend aid to the men pinned down in Ein Zehalta on the central axis. Still and all, the entry into Beirut could not possibly be explained away as a means of aiding or easing the lot of the forces on the coastal axis! Sharon, having stressed during the Cabinet meetings on Thursday and Friday that the troops had orders *not* to go as far as Beirut and that any link-up with the Phalange was to be wholly dependent upon the initiative of the Christians, conveniently neglected to tell the ministers on Friday that the decision to go as far as the eastern edge of Beirut—to Kafr Shima and Ba'abda—rather than cut the Beirut-Damascus highway near Aley had already been made that morning. Even the prime minister was kept in the dark. Sharon also failed to mention that, contrary to all his declarations about leaving a hook-up with the Phalange solely up to the Maronites, he was about to depart for a meeting with Bashir Gemayel to pressure him into fielding his troops and to establish the precise spot where the Phalange and the IDF would meet.

That caucus between Sharon and Bashir took place in Junieh on Friday afternoon, a few hours after the ceasefire between Israel and Syria went into effect, when it was already obvious along the battle lines that Israel had no intention of applying the truce to the Beirut sector—not even to the Syrian forces there. When Sharon's helicopter landed outside the city, the defense minister and his aides expected that the meeting with Bashir would be marked by an atmosphere of near jubilation after so many months, even years, of the Phalange exhorting the Israelis to bring their army to Beirut. Instead, Bashir looked depressed, evidently because he knew that now he would be expected to deliver on his promises. Even though he finally agreed to field his troops—and even managed to murmur the sentiment that great days were ahead—Gemayel's response fell far short of Sharon's expectations. For hardly had greetings been exchanged when the Israelis began to sense that Bashir was trying to squirm out of his commitment to fight in Beirut.

When Sharon told him jauntily, "We want the PLO!" Bashir replied with striking reserve, "We'll do our best, but it won't be easy."

Throughout the meeting, Sharon prodded the Phalangists to get moving quickly and join up with the Israeli forces fighting south of the capital. Repeatedly Gemayel tried to steer the conversation away from operational issues, launching at one point into a monologue about his infant son (born after the murder of his daughter, Maya, in an attempt on his life). The tug-of-war continued until Sharon, his patience exhausted, tried to end the charade of pleasantries. "We're here with tanks!" he shouted at Bashir. *"Do something!"*

But it would take more than Sharon's displeasure to get Gemayel moving. Bashir and his men were clearly loath to commit themselves to a military action of any kind, whether against the PLO in Beirut or against the Syrians on the main highway. They even waffled on the question of whether they would now allow Israeli troops to land at Junieh—a request that Bashir had denied at the beginning of the war. Throughout the meal that Bashir had laid out for Sharon and his aides, it was infuriatingly clear that the Phalangists were trying to avoid committing themselves to anything concrete.

One of Sharon's aides took Bashir's friend Jean Nader aside at one point to feel him out on the problem. "Is there something you want from us before going into action?" he asked.

Nader contemplated the question for a moment and saw his opening. "You have to take the Beirut-Damascus road and beat the Syrians back," he said matter-of-factly, as if asking for little enough.

But the Israeli saw the remark for what it was —another excuse to pass the work of the Phalange onto the IDF—and when Nader neglected to say what his forces would be prepared to do if and when the Israelis complied and began to push the Syrians back, the matter was closed.

There was nothing left for Sharon to do except merely to determine the place where the Phalange would be waiting for the IDF on the outskirts of Beirut. Twice burned by Bashir in the space of a week, the formerly trusting Sharon became absolutely fastidious about establishing the exact location of the union and insisted that the understanding be recorded in the minutes of the meeting. Then he and Bashir appended their signatures to the protocol and—after someone remarked rather lamely, "This is an historic agreement!''—the two men also signed the map on which the meeting place was marked. The Phalange were to be waiting outside Ba'abda after cutting a dirt road through to the edge of the city.

By the time Sharon's party climbed back into their helicopter, it was almost dark. Sharon's anger showed on his face. The Phalange had rebuffed every attempt to be integrated into the fighting in Beirut. They expected the IDF to do all the work, and to do it alone.

"They're acting just like Arabs," Sharon grumbled peevishly in the privacy of the helicopter. "I saw the fear in their eyes!"

The Phalange's do-nothing policy stood out all the more starkly against the background of the intense fighting required of the Israelis to make it to Beirut at all. The battle had become particularly difficult on the coastal road south of the capital, as it had been from the outset, with the advance of the two armored brigades halted as far back as Thursday. To break the block on the road, the commander of the Golani Infantry Brigade proposed closing in on Beirut from the east of the main axis, via Dokha and Kafr Sil, which meant capturing the hills above the road. After obtaining approval for this indirect action, the Golani Brigade, reinforced by a battalion of armor, began on Thursday night to push its way from Dokha toward Kafr Sil, using bulldozers to clear a passage under cover of darkness.

The battle for Kafr Sil, which Chief of Staff Eitan later described as the most brutal of the war, began among the plush villas and private swimming pools of Dokha, a playground of the wealthy residents of Beirut. Here the Syrians targeted their antitank missiles at the Israeli column from a nearby rise known as Radar Hill and immediately hit the two lead tanks—one of which exploded, killing all four crewmen. It took massive Israeli artillery barrages and aerial bombardments to break the Syrian defense line. Then the battle for Kafr Sil and the surrounding hills was resumed on Saturday afternoon by a battalion from Golani, another battalion of paratroops from Yair's brigade (which had been detached when Yair moved east of Damour), and a battalion of armor.

The paratroops were charged with taking Radar Hill, while Golani and the armor would fight their way into the town's built-up area. The Syrians, for their part, concentrated no less than twenty-eight T-54 tanks in and around Kafr Sil and brought in a company of commandos for good measure. They understood all too well that if this line broke, the way to Beirut would be wide open.

It was not until late Saturday afternoon, when the armor and men from Golani reached the center of the village, that the fighting in Kafr Sil became earnest, with the Israeli infantry firing RPGs at the Syrian tanks and trying to toss hand grenades into their turrets. One company commander, Lieutenant Zion, decided upon this method to neutralize a Syrian tank that had hit two Israeli vehicles. In his first attempt, just as he climbed on the Syrian tank from behind it was hit by Israeli fire and he had to jump off. A short while later he spotted the same Syrian tank nearby, and when he climbed on it a second time he could hear the crew talking inside. Within seconds Zion had tossed a hand grenade down its turret and leaped off the vehicle to save himself. He got clear of the explosion, but his luck failed him when one of the men from Golani mistook him for a Syrian soldier fleeing the destroyed vehicle and promptly shot and wounded him.

Certainly no one could accuse the Syrians of not fighting back. The battle for the two main streets of Kafr Sil, which were barely a kilometer long, raged for nineteen hours and did not end until Sunday morning, when the men of Golani gained control of the village and the junction beyond it. From there they had an easy command of the runways of Beirut airport just below.

Farther inland, Yair's paratroops proceeded at an agonizing pace toward the final ridge before Beirut. It took them some nine hours to advance about 500 meters over an area sculpted by terraces and covered with thick vegetation. After retreating from Kaber Chamoun junction, the Syrians, determined to halt the Israelis on the Shemlan ridge, had now evened the balance of forces: four companies of Israeli paratroops supported by armor faced a battalion of Syrian commandos reinforced by Palestinian troops and tanks concealed between the houses of the multileveled village.

The terraced terrain made the fighting such a labyrinthine affair that on one occasion a Syrian company came into range between two companies of Israeli paratroops—one on the terrace below the Syrians, the other on a level above them—and Yair had to order the company on the lower level to take cover so as not to be hit by the Israeli fire coming from above. By 4:00 P.M. the Israelis had worked their way fairly close to the outskirts of Kafr Shemlan. If they could get through that village, they would be on the road to Ein Anub, just beyond which was Basaba, the first Maronite village under the control of the Phalange.

Suddenly Chief of Staff Eitan's voice came over the radio calling to Yair, "The Christians are waiting for you!"

"I'm doing the best I can!" Yair shouted over the rattle of gunfire with just a touch of annoyance, as if anyone doubted that he and his men were giving their all. He knew that Eitan meant no offense and had himself hoped to make contact with the Phalange on Saturday night, but after eight hours of combat his paratroops were exhausted. The Syrians were displaying unexpected tenacity, and the paratroops had to advance on them almost meter by meter.

As Eitan was urging the paratroops on, a destroyed Syrian tank stood burning in the middle of the road, belching explosions of ammunition at irregular intervals. There was no way to get past the deadly vehicle without endangering the lives of the paratroops. A young officer volunteered to push the tank out of the way with a bulldozer. When he was killed by RPG fire, another driver took his place at the controls while Yair and his second in command literally led the assault, each commanding a section of soldiers and dashing forward while the bulldozer advanced between them and slowly pushed the burning tank off the road. Once the tank was out of the way, the remains of the Syrian force began to withdraw, and Yair and his deputy continued to lead the two squads up to the edge of the village, securing Shemlan for the Israelis.

Yair's assault was halted at nightfall, but at 1:30 the next morning the paratroops again got the signal to advance toward Ein Anub. It appears that, despite everything, the Syrians still believed the IDF would turn northeast and head for Aley. They were taken wholly by surprise in Ein Anub. As dawn broke, the paratroops discovered a concentration of some thirty Syrian and Palestinian soldiers directly below them. They approached the capture of the village not through firepower but by applying psychological pressure. Instead of daunting the Syrians with the might of their fire, the Israelis addressed them over loudspeakers and encouraged them to run for their lives. At first the Syrians tried to take cover, even though the Israelis made mention of the places where they knew them to be hiding, but eventually they understood that the game was up and began to withdraw in a rout. It wasn't long before the *mukhtar* of the village sent an envoy out to announce that the Syrians and Palestinians had fled. Ein Anub had fallen without a battle. The way to Basaba was open now. Just two kilometers remained between Yair's men and the site of the link-up with the Phalange.

At 1:00 P.M. on Sunday, June 13, the first of Yair's paratroops greeted the men of the Phalange force stationed at the roadblock outside Basaba. Awaiting the Israelis there was Bashir Gemayel's deputy, Fadi Frem, who enthusiastically shook hands with the paratroops as they filed past. One of the Israeli soldiers took a snapshot of the occasion for posterity, a photo that caused Frem to boil with rage when it was published in the IDF weekly magazine.

"I've joined up," Yair hurried to report directly to Drori over his radio.

"Actually physically done it?" Drori asked unbelievingly.

"Yes. They even kissed me on the stubble of my beard!"

"I join in those kisses!" Drori bubbled in an unusual show of feeling.

Shortly thereafter Bashir Gemayel turned up, followed by his father,

Sheikh Pierre Gemayel. They were joined soon afterward on the Israeli side by Chief of Staff Eitan and General Drori, and all were whisked off to Junieh to mark the occasion of the meeting. The paratroops continued to Ba'abda and the vicinity of the Lebanese Ministry of Defense, where the Beirut-Damascus highway was finally cut.

The oddest part of the link-up was that even on Sunday, June 13, Menachem Begin was as astonished as his ministers to discover that Israeli troops were in Beirut. As countless Israelis were driving openly through the streets of East Beirut, taking in the sights and shops, quite unaware that they weren't supposed to be there, Begin was continuing to deny that the IDF was in Beirut at all. In one particularly ironic coincidence, his statement of denial was quoted by the Israeli state radio in its hourly news bulletin only to be immediately followed by a live report from Beirut describing the streets of the city jammed with Israeli vehicles! The prime minister of Israel, it seemed, was either ignorant of what his army was doing or was trying to conceal the truth—and doing a sloppy job of it at that. Either way, Menachem Begin emerged from the incident looking rather like a fool.

The simple fact of the matter is that no one had bothered to inform the prime minister of the IDF's arrival in Beirut. On the previous evening, the military censor had quashed a report scheduled to be broadcast on the television news because it stated that Israeli troops had reached the edge of the Christian sector of Beirut and were already in control of the runways of the city's international airport. "When contact is established in a few hours," the suppressed report stated, "Israel will have achieved territorial continuity with friendly forces from Junieh in the north to its border in the south." But what the TV reporter had learned at a briefing in Sharon's office was not conveyed to the prime minister.

To say that Begin was embarrassed is to stretch understatement to its limit. At no time was his discomfiture more evident than in a meeting that day with Philip Habib. When the prime minister insisted that the IDF was not going to Beirut, Habib fairly sputtered with anger, "Your tanks are already in Ba'abda! Our ambassador in Beirut has already reported the presence of Israeli tanks next to the presidential palace!" As fate would have it, while that very exchange was taking place, Sharon phoned the prime minister's office, asked to speak to Begin, and was told of Habib's complaint. "So we'll move the tanks," he retorted with an insolent shrug.

That is how the IDF came to arrive at and enter Beirut. It was a process whereby vital concerns masqueraded behind innocuous names: Rather than speak of marching into Beirut, the terminology of the hour was "linking up with the Christians." When the location of that link-up was dis-

cussed, instead of using the word "Beirut" everyone spoke of Ba'abda—
as if that quarter were not part of Greater Beirut. The result of all this
clever wordplay is that the minutes of the Cabinet meetings contain no
mention of a decision to send the IDF into Beirut. Afterward, when the
Israeli army was deeply involved in fighting in the city, Mordechai Zippori
picked at this sore point as at a sensitive scab in asking time and again
when, exactly, the Cabinet decided to go into Beirut. Where was the
decision recorded? Sharon would respond angrily, but the other ministers
shrank from joining in Zippori's accusation, and Begin remained mute.

11

The Siege of Beirut

AS THE ISRAELI APCs CARRYING COLONEL YAIR'S PARATROOPS SWEPT INTO BA'ABDA, headlights blazing, a grim-faced PLO officer stood peering at them through binoculars from the room of a high-rise building in an adjacent quarter. Soon the line to the PLO's central operations room was crackling with the somber news.

"Jewish forces just drove by us," the field officer reported directly to Yasser Arafat. "They're moving into the city."

"Are you mad?" the PLO chief exclaimed. "What are you talking about!"

A day earlier, an armored unit of the Palestine Liberation Army had reported stopping the Israeli armored column on the coast at Kafr Sil, by the southern entrance to Beirut, but since the task of blocking the roads that spill down from the mountains had been left to the Syrians, no one had bothered to inform Arafat of the dire results of the fight for the Shemlan ridge. Thus, accurate as the report was from that rooftop lookout, for almost two days Yasser Arafat refused to believe that the IDF had closed a ring of siege around him. He comforted himself with the illusion that either his men were confusing the Israelis with the Phalangists (an understandable mistake considering the similarity in their uniforms and vehicles) or that, shaken by the news from the south, they were imagining their worst fears projected before their eyes.

Sunday, June 13, was therefore a day marked by confusion in the PLO strongholds in West Beirut. On the command level, some officers prepared to quit the city or take asylum in foreign embassies, while men from the ranks began to strip off their uniforms, burn their documents, and blend in with the civilian population. Whole files from the Fatah archive were committed to flames in such a state of panic that the material was not even microfilmed first.

By late Monday, Arafat not only realized that the Israelis had arrived but had become convinced that within a short time the IDF would storm the southern quarters of Beirut—Fakahani, Sabra, Shatilla, Burj el-Barajneh, Uzai—where his fighters were concentrated. In growing alarm, he turned to Brigadier General Hilal, commander of the Syrian Eighty-fifth Brigade, also trapped in Beirut. But Hilal couldn't or wouldn't give a straight answer about his intentions. Through a trusted intermediary, Arafat then contacted the head of Lebanese military intelligence, Col. Jonny Abdu, and asked him to confirm whether the Israelis would allow his men to leave the city and, if so, over which road. In that event, there might never have been a siege at all.

At about the same time, however, Ariel Sharon, replete with combat helmet and flack jacket, was making his triumphant but slow progress to Beirut. In Damour he was told that the trip over the mountain road would take no more than an hour, but it was five hours before his APC managed to negotiate the twists and turns and pulled into Ba'abda. The IDF's tenuous hold over the capital was still dependent on that single problematic road, so vulnerable to enemy fire that no supply convoys had risked driving through—a point not lost on Sharon. From the southern edge of Beirut, a Lebanese car carried him to Junieh for yet another meeting with Bashir Gemayel.

Sharon, still rankling from their last confrontation, began with a prickly rebuke. "On my way here, I thought I would see people digging trenches and filling sandbags. I expected to see long lines outside your recruiting offices. Instead your people are sitting in cafés, and the only lines I see are outside the movie theaters!"

Gemayel blushed and remained silent. Having resolved to stave off all Israeli demands to intervene in the fighting, he knew that he would have to suffer these indignities. But he was prepared to aid the IDF short of actually going into combat, and at this latest meeting he sat obediently copying down Sharon's demands, point by point, in a small notebook: the Phalangists were to reinforce their presence along the so-called Green Line in Beirut, which divided the Moslem and Christian sectors of the city and faced directly on the PLO's positions; it was especially important to ensure that none of the PLO's leaders escaped to Tripoli; and as an added gesture Bashir took it upon himself to see to it that Lebanese President Sarkis would back Sharon's demand that the PLO be unconditionally expelled from the city.

While Sharon was meeting with Bashir, his officers were beginning to take stock of their situation. Like Arafat, they did not at first comprehend that their arrival in Beirut might mark the beginning of a long siege. In

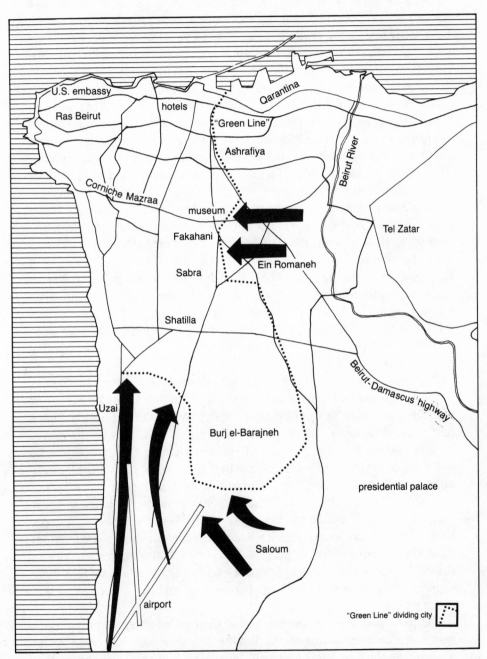

THE SIEGE OF BEIRUT

discussions prior to the war, Israeli intelligence had more than once warned of the likelihood that the PLO would fortify itself within Beirut, but a siege had certainly not been planned. The IDF's view of the link-up with the Phalange on the Beirut-Damascus highway was as the culmination, rather than the start, of its operations around Beirut. But the intelligence predictions proved correct: by the second day of the encirclement, Arafat had reversed himself and clearly signaled that the PLO was not about to give up. He informed Jonny Abdu that his men were no longer interested in securing safe passage out of the city. And that same day, June 14, Dr. George Habash was already talking about "a second Stalingrad." The Israelis, lacking enough of a force in the area to consider an immediate assault on the PLO strongholds in Beirut (though in the course of time some of them would come to the conclusion that they probably would have been better off continuing straight into West Beirut), held their positions. And so, as if on its own, the IDF encirclement turned into a siege. Sharon knew he was in for a tough time. "We're walking a thin, a very thin tightrope," he told the General Staff on July 15. "If we proceed ever so carefully, *really* carefully, we may see to it that there aren't any terrorists left in Lebanon. But that's walking a really thin line." Within a few days it became woefully clear that a protracted battle for Beirut was under way, a struggle that would prove far more difficult and costly than the fighting in South Lebanon.

The same conclusion was beginning to dawn in Jerusalem. In fact, as soon as the dust had settled in Ba'abda, a sharp debate broke out about the IDF's presence in the Lebanese capital. When the opposition Labor party voiced severe criticism of both the logic and efficacy of the move, Sharon told the Knesset Foreign Affairs and Defense Committee that he did not intend to mount an attack on Beirut. "This is neither a blockade nor a siege," he declared, but his explanations came up against a wall of skepticism. In the Cabinet itself, the disgruntled ministers wanted to know why the IDF had entered the Lebanese capital in the first place—indeed, without that objective ever having been presented for their consideration. Sharon's response was to deflect all criticism by hiding behind the men in the field. "Questions that imply doubts about my probity," he told them angrily, "may undermine the trust between me and my soldiers, and that is dangerous!"

The most prominent exception in the Cabinet was Begin, who did not regret the consummation of the link-up but was quite prepared to let Sharon take the heat while having his own aides hint to all and sundry that the prime minister knew nothing about the entry into Beirut. Yet as long as the IDF was there anyway, Begin was prepared to exploit the situation by sending troops into action. The catch was that he did not intend to field his own soldiers in the cause of liberating Beirut; the troops he intended to activate were the Phalangists.

As Begin explained to his ministers, "The concrete proposal to the Phalange is that you can and must, in our opinion, capture the part of Beirut inhabited by the terrorists, and you must get rid of them . . . ." At this point Begin paused briefly for effect before adding a highly significant sentence to the message meant for Bashir Gemayel. " 'If you need help of any kind, we won't turn [you] down, but you must do the job.' Our boys will not shed their blood in this matter," he pronounced, mostly for the benefit of his dovish ministers.

The problem was that Bashir Gemayel had something quite different in mind. On the day before the Cabinet meeting, as he briefed the men of his elite units in their barracks at Qarantina, Gemayel counseled his young admirers to temper their zeal for fighting alongside the IDF. "We have not supported what's happened," he lied shamelessly, "but we must exploit it to save Lebanon. Tomorrow you will return to your villages and find your homes destroyed and looted and memorials to the leftist and Communist dead. But I say to you now: You must honor every memorial to our adversaries and defend their people, property, slogans—even if they are hostile." The Phalange soldiers took in his words in shocked silence. Most of them assumed they had been called together for an eve-of-battle exhortation, and here was Bashir preaching tolerance at them. But he did end his speech with the heartening if enigmatic comment, "We will find a place for the Palestinians outside Lebanon," though he did not elaborate.

For all that, Bashir knew his Israeli partners well enough to appreciate that, unless he at least made some motions approximating combat, he would lose their trust irrevocably. Thus on June 16 he ordered a company of Phalangists to capture the Faculty of Science building in Reihan, one of the quarters in the southern part of Beirut, in order to open up a short and more convenient axis for the Israelis. A few hours later, the Lebanese flag was raised over the building after a battle that claimed the lives of the Christian commander and about fifteen Palestinians. This turned out to be the Phalange's total contribution to the conquest of Beirut—a token gesture that did little to change the resentful consensus growing in the IDF that Bashir expected Israel to do his dirty work for him.

Still, the Israelis were not about to write off the Phalange. About a week later, Bashir and his aides were invited to Jerusalem for a penetrating discussion as to just what the Phalange should do. "If you take the initiative to liberate Beirut," the Israelis told him, "we'll help you with everything we've got." The statement sounded almost like a promise that the

IDF would bear the brunt of the fighting if only the Phalange would be good enough to act as the vanguard and provide political cover. When that carrot failed to lure Bashir, he was reminded of the promises he had made during the months prior to the war and was pointedly scolded for refusing to fight his way to a link-up with the Israeli troops after the ceasefire.

"I'm willing to fight," Bashir protested, however disingenuously, considering his record. "I'm not afraid. But in that case you will find me at the head of a small Christian state within a divided Lebanon under constant threat from its neighbors." The price for his participation in the fighting was nothing less than a formal defense treaty and clear-cut Israeli guarantees of his position in the future. In short, Bashir presented the Israelis with a bill amounting to military support for his political position, while frankly advising them to exempt him from the present bloodletting. "You're better off having me as president of a united Lebanon friendly to Israel than compelling me to make a military contribution—which you don't really need anyway—and then have me be a burden on you."

But the Israeli pressure was beginning to tell on Bashir, and a more doubtful mood was expressed in his later meeting with the Druse leader Walid Jumblatt, of all people. The Lebanese Druse were running neck and neck with the Palestinians as the Maronites' most implacable enemies. Yet when Bashir met privately with Jumblatt as part of an American-sponsored attempt to reconcile internal Lebanese differences and enable the enervated central government to reassume control of the country's affairs, his mood was surprisingly subdued.

The meeting began with a warning from Jumblatt. "I don't deny that you're likely to emerge the big winner from Israel's intervention," the Druse leader told Bashir, "but this is not the time to exploit the new situation for political gain."

"Perhaps I'll come out the winner and perhaps not," Bashir replied far less guardedly than Jumblatt had expected. "I may be able to reap gains now, but in the end I might just take a beating because of the Israeli attack. I still haven't forgotten our experience with the Syrians, you know. Everyone thought that their army's intervention would work in our favor, but in the end fate reversed itself, and you were the ones who came out ahead." Clearly, Bashir Gemayel was leery of his own good fortune.

A few days later, in response to the latest message from Begin urging him to "Arise and lead your warriors out to liberate your occupied capital!" Bashir remarked bitterly to Sharon, "If you wish me to come down on West Beirut, I am willing to go out at the head of my men. If that is your decision, I will follow it. I may die in battle," he continued, indulging his self-pity, "but that's not important. You can invest seven years in someone else, and you'll have a new Bashir."

This mock neutrality became the policy of the Christian leadership throughout the siege, and in time the Israelis would despair of Bashir's collaboration and drop their demand that he step forward as an ally. His old pledge, "Leave Beirut to me," became lost somewhere in a welter of complaints, accusations, and new lame promises to compensate for broken vows.

That left the Israelis with two choices: to let Philip Habib negotiate a withdrawal of the Palestinian forces or to force their way into West Beirut and clean it out themselves. The dialectic between these two options is what spun the siege of Bierut out into a nine-week affair in which almost every one of the debating parties—members of the Israeli Cabinet, ranking officers of the Israeli army, and American negotiators—clashed head on with Ariel Sharon.

On June 14, while Menachem Begin was still entertaining visions of inspiring the Phalange to throw itself into a glorious *guerre à outrance* for Beirut, Philip Habib arrived in the Lebanese capital and began to organize himself for the task at hand. Through the intermediation of Lebanese Prime Minister Shafiq el-Wazzan, a colorless Sunni-Moslem functionary from West Beirut, Habib urged Arafat to bow to the Israeli demand and have his men quit the city. "You'll have to negotiate with me face to face," came Arafat's reply, leaving little doubt of his determination to wring a political victory out of a military defeat.

Somewhere on the edge of their consciousness, many Israelis in positions of authority had to be aware of this hazard, if only because Yehoshua Saguy had warned that "whoever reaches Beirut, like it or not, will be touching upon the basic problem of 1948," and "whoever tries to remove the Palestinians from Lebanon will necessarily be asked what the solution to their problem is." Thus it should have been no surprise when Arafat chose to drag out the siege through the sultry days of June, July, and half of August as a way of keeping the PLO in the headlines and doing precisely what Saguy had feared: bringing the essence of the Palestinian problem to the fore more effectively than dozens of terrorist actions ever could.

The tenacity with which Jerusalem refused to see this simple fact was one of the wonders of the war in Lebanon. Menachem Begin, who had every reason to cancel his scheduled trip to Washington, considering the fact that his country was in the grip of a war, not only went forward with his plans but undoubtedly expected to receive a hero's welcome for laying siege to what he repeatedly referred to as the center of international terror. There was no denying the fact that Beirut was the headquarters of the PLO, but it was hardly some isolated mountain hideaway crawling with terrorists that could be depicted as a fair military target. Beirut was a city of well over half a million people, the capital of a sovereign country, the once (and perhaps future) commercial heart of the Arab world. Nor did Begin command the standing in Washington that he did at home, where he had become something of a cult figure to his many followers; his rhetoric would not go down as readily in the White House and Congress as in open-air rallies in Tel Aviv. Yet there were times when the prime minister of Israel seemed utterly bewildered by, if not unaware of, his misapprehension.

Begin's American trip began during the second week of the war, three days after the IDF entered Beirut, but friction with the Reagan administration was already evident before he reached Washington. In light of Israel's bombing and shelling of the Lebanese capital, Reagan's aides were giving out unmistakable signals that the president might cancel his audience with Begin unless the violence stopped forthwith. During a stopover in New York, Begin had in fact phoned Jerusalem with orders to bring the shelling to a halt pending his return. But it went right on. Apprised of this in Washington, Begin asked to speak to Sharon personally and was told by the defense minister, "I am obliged to protect our men!"—a claim that would become a blanket explanation for every one of Sharon's controversial moves throughout the siege. When the administration began to make threatening noises, rather than try to placate his hosts in Washington Begin truculently phoned home to his stand-in, Deputy Prime Minister Simcha Ehrlich, and told him, "Take whatever decisions are necessary, and I'll back whatever you decide." It was a message of defiance meant for American ears, and evidently it had the desired effect because, through Haig's mediation, a meeting was finally arranged in the Oval Office. "Hold out for what you want!" Haig had advised Begin privately just before the meeting began.

On June 21, Ronald Reagan and Menachem Begin sat in the White House eyeing each other cautiously as the president opened with words of protest from a prepared statement. "The best course today is diplomacy, not employing an army to excess," he chided.

Begin's initial response impressed the Americans as flippant. "The combination of American planes and Israeli pilots is an excellent commercial symbol," he quipped. But he could not sidetrack the conversation once Reagan laid aside his text. "What's done is done," the president was willing to concede, "but now we must move forward." He maintained that the objective of that forward movement should be the withdrawal of all foreign forces from Lebanon and the constitution of a stable government there—though he was quick to add, "We must not impose that." Still, on Habib's recommendation, the administration had reviewed its attitude toward Bashir Gemayel and had begun to lean toward Begin's assessment that the young Maronite would be able to bring a measure of stability to his country.

As the meeting concluded and the various participants stood up to leave, Haig surreptitiously gave Begin the thumbs-up sign. A new Israeli-American formula of understanding had been reached. Both sides were interested in maximizing the results of the war and had managed to avert an open breach over the issue of Beirut. The backdrop to their understanding was an American demand that Israel exercise restraint, though Begin had the impression that this did not constitute an absolute ban on military pressure.

The prime minister's initial reports from Washington encouraged Sharon to secure the siege as a "going concern." This meant, first of all, extending the IDF's access to Beirut beyond the narrow and highly vulnerable corridor opened by the paratroops after the ceasefire of June 10. Essentially, the Syrians remained at the backs of the Israelis looking down on them from the Aley ridge. Sharon wanted to correct that situation by pushing them back and taking the Beirut-Damascus highway. But to order an outright attack on the road would be too flagrant a violation of the ceasefire with Syria and would, moreover, require Cabinet approval. What Sharon did instead was simply urge the officers in the field to "creep" northward, hill by hill, under cover of the catch phrase "improving positions" and in response to alleged Syrian and Palestinian fire. But there was a price for this skulking around in the hills: the army could not concentrate reinforcements or use the air force at full strength to aid the ground forces.

The slow and costly thrust toward the resort town of Behamdoun began on June 19. Trudging over rocky and heavily forested mountain terrain, the paratroops had to contend with Syrian commandos well dug into their positions. Amir Drori asked for an unequivocal order to take the road so that he could mount an orderly attack, but Sharon held back. Within twenty-four hours, the paratroops inching their way toward Behamdoun had lost seven men in an operation that officially wasn't even happening.

This time, however, word of Sharon's ruse quickly reached members of the Cabinet, and three ministers practically stormed into Simcha Ehrlich's office to complain about what was going on without their knowledge or authorization.

"I'm looking for Sharon myself, but I can't seem to find him," Ehrlich told them. "I can't get through."

"What do you mean, you can't get through," Zippori thundered, "when you can call up practically every tank commander!"

Afterward, Sharon would claim in his defense that he had been seeing to a ticklish situation that had arisen in the field and demanded immediate action. But this latest instance of what was already being called "the creeping ceasefire" further eroded Sharon's standing in the Cabinet. Bald mistrust began to attend his every explanation. Having long felt themselves disregarded at best, misled at worst, the ministers were no longer prepared to accept Sharon's word without a full interrogation. And to further aggravate the mood, rumors soon reached Jerusalem that Sharon was deriding his colleagues on his visits to the front. "In the morning I fight the terrorists and every evening I return to Jerusalem to fight the Cabinet," he was reported to have complained in the field.

On June 23, after an Israeli armored force was stopped by an antitank ambush of Syrian commandos, Sharon found that he was fighting his own officers as well. Drori pressured him to send in the Golani Infantry Brigade, and that night the men of one of the Golani battalions reached the trapped armored force on foot. But it wasn't until the next day, after more pressure on Sharon, that Drori received permission to shift over to an orderly division attack rather than continue the deadly stratagem of "creeping forward." Finally the air force was called in to strafe and bomb the Syrian commandos deployed on the hilltops, with artillery battalions contributing support fire.

At 6:00 P.M. on June 24 the assault began toward the Beirut-Damascus highway, some three or four kilometers beyond the lead companies of Brig. Gen. Menachem Einan's division. Parallel to this division attack in the east, Israeli paratroops advanced along the highway from Ba'abda toward Aley. Through huge loudspeakers, they called upon the Syrians entrenched in the hills to flee. This time they found the enemy's resistance weak, and soon Syrian trucks laden with troops were escaping eastward— right past the men from Golani, who had begun to close in on Aley after taking Behamdoun earlier that day. The Israelis had orders to let the Syrians pass safely. It was one of the eeriest scenes of the war: Syrian and Israeli soldiers filing past one another in tense and almost total silence.

Near the close of the operation, Ariel Sharon reached the battlefield by helicopter to congratulate the men on their accomplishment. Menachem Einan embraced him heartily but advised him against visiting the paratroops who had participated in the action. "Go to another battalion," he murmured in embarassment, "Golani, perhaps. They're still fresh."

It fell to the deputy chief of staff, Moshe Levi, to meet with the battalion of paratroop reservists who had suffered the worst losses in the earlier "creep forward" phase, and he was aghast at the sullen mood among the men. "I want to make you aware of a number of things," a company commander addressed Levi aggressively. "We're an assault battalion. Tell us to capture Beirut and we'll capture Beirut. Tell us to take Damascus and we'll take Damascus. But why wasn't there an orderly plan of attack?

In the morning we would get an order to dig in, and two hours later I'm told to charge forward!'' Levi noticed that most of the company's soldiers nodded their heads vigorously in assent at their commander's litany of complaints, and some of these battle-hardened veterans were weeping silently. The battalion had lost ten men in the battles along the Beirut-Damascus road, and another thirty had been wounded. "You can check for yourself whether this reflects the views of the battalion. Just ask the men to raise their hands."

Levi ignored the suggestion, with the likely results of such a vote so obvious. "Don't lose your sense of proportion," he told the shattered company softly but firmly. But the company commander was not about to let him off the hook.

"What does the Beirut-Damascus highway have to do with the peace of the Galilee, anyway?" he pressed. "Why do we find ourselves on the attack and hear the IDF spokesman announce that it was the Syrians who opened fire? What have we got against the Syrians? I want you to know that the consensus has been shattered—around here, at least—and with alarming signs of a breakdown in credibility."

"The army carries out the orders of the civilian echelon," Levi parried. "That's democracy."

"That's not democracy," the officer lashed back in a tone close to insubordination. "That's just taking advantage of Begin's absence!"

Similar flashes of anger and opposition would become a feature of the war among many of the field commanders. For just as the Cabinet's trust in Sharon eroded over the weeks of the siege, a deep crack began to spread through the army's belief and confidence in the minister of defense.

At the close of June 25, with the highway secured as far as Behamdoun, another ceasefire was declared. But then a very different, though equally distressing, development took place on another kind of battlefield, far from the Middle East, to leave its own mark on the course of the war.

For a whole day, Menachem Begin had kept to himself a secret communication from Alexander Haig that he had probably reached the end of his tenure in the Reagan administration. It was no secret that the secretary of state was Israel's chief ally in Washington and that it was to Haig's influence that the successful conclusion of Begin's recent visit should be credited. But Haig's prerogatives in the conduct of American foreign policy were not as exclusive as he would have liked, and after months of bickering with Reagan's White House aides over a variety of issues he now discovered that the president's national security adviser, William Clark, was trying to sabotage his policy in Lebanon. Or so the secretary believed. Clark, it seems, had been using the Saudis as a channel to advise

Arafat that the PLO could afford to take its time in agreeing to the evacuation of Beirut. Livid with anger, Haig stalked into a meeting with the president only to find an even more bitter surprise awaiting him.

"I hear that you've decided to resign," Reagan said curtly, preempting Haig's complaints, "and I have decided to accept your resignation."

A stunned Haig left the White House to consult with some close aides and quickly came to the conclusion that he indeed had no choice but to tender his resignation. George Shultz was appointed in his stead.

Haig's departure came as a blow to Jerusalem, a disappointment compounded by the fact that Shultz was known to be well connected in the Arab world. On June 27 Sharon, fearing an imminent shift in American policy, brought a number of military moves before the Cabinet and recommended that they be implemented before Shultz took over at State. For the first time, the defense minister was proposing that the IDF actually penetrate West Beirut. Patiently Sharon explained that contact had been made with the leader of the Shiite militia in Beirut, Nabih Berri, who was prepared to allow the IDF entry into the Shiite quarters of South Beirut— the so-called poverty belt populated mostly by families who had fled from PLO-dominated South Lebanon. "There are no terrorists in the area," Berri had told the Israeli officer to whom he made his offer. All the Shiites asked in return was that the Israelis not confiscate their weapons. "My men and I will hole up in one building and fly a white flag, so that you know where we are."

Most of the ministers questioned the value of such a commitment from the relatively weak and politically unreliable Amal, in addition to which Saguy confirmed that the PLO had already begun to take up positions in the Shiite quarters. Still, the Cabinet devoted three sessions to the prospect of sending forces into the Moslem half of the city. Sharon's main argument was that Arafat, being comfortably ensconced in West Beirut, was obviously pussyfooting with Habib in order to gain time. The PLO, he said, would never agree to leave Beirut unless it was placed under constant and oppressive military pressure. But the Cabinet feared that sending troops into the southern quarters of West Beirut would only lead to a bloody battle of attrition in a densely populated area, and it was rightly worried about the reaction to such an initiative both at home and in Washington. All things considered, with the siege just two weeks old, the ministers still preferred to allow Habib's mediation efforts to run their course, especially as Habib had promised to come up with the draft of an agreement "within ten days." At the same time, Habib had conveyed a warning to Arafat: "If an agreement is not reached quickly, the Israelis will break into West Beirut."

"Don't threaten me," Arafat shot back through the standard channels. "They wouldn't dare come in here."

Arafat was equally defiant when he received a message from Sharon through a Lebanese go-between. "I'll give you better conditions of surrender than the British gave the Argentinian soldiers in the Falklands," the Israeli defense minister offered on June 27. All Arafat had to do was hoist a white flag atop the tallest building in West Beirut. But the chairman was not about to fly any flag other than the PLO's own colors. "My bodyguards have orders to shoot me if I decide to surrender," he replied.

Begin tried the good offices of an American journalist to send Arafat a communication of his own: if the PLO were to surrender, its men would be permitted to leave Beirut unmolested. "Have you forgotten that we have you surrounded? Or is it that you believe you have Tel Aviv under siege?"

"In being beleaguered within Beirut," the Palestinian leader replied, "I am imposing a moral siege on all capitals."

At that point Arafat still believed that the Arab countries—particularly Saudi Arabia—would find their wait-and-see posture difficult to keep up, relying solely on the results of the pressure being applied by Washington. The PLO assessed that it could hold out under siege conditions for at least three months, perhaps for as long as half a year. It faced no shortage of arms or ammunition; even a generous supply of gasoline had been laid in. Thus there was little reason to collapse in the face of Israeli pressure. Most outspoken of all in their determination to stand and fight were a number of Fatah officers who had earlier been removed from command positions because of their political opposition to Arafat. One of these hard-liners, Col. Abu Moussa, now emerged as the moving spirit behind the defense of the city. His friend Abu Khaled el-Amlah volunteered to take charge of the defense of the airport and Uzai. In less than a year, these two men would be leading the rebellion within Fatah against Arafat.

Yet it wasn't as if Arafat himself showed signs of weakening. In a circular distributed among his men on June 29 he wrote: "We must beware of the psychological warfare being perpetrated against us and the talk of our willingness to surrender our arms and leave by plane or boat . . . . The sole aim of these rumors is to sow confusion in our ranks." In almost every one of such daily circulars, he made a point of urging his men to keep digging in and fortifying their positions. When told that there was a quote from the Bible prophesying Israel's defeat ("The violence done to Lebanon will overwhelm you," Habakkuk 2:17), he insisted that it be published at once (even after the editor of the PLO's newsletter argued against it on the grounds that the Israelis could probably come up with an endless stream of counterquotes justifying their cause). At staff meetings and on tours of the city, the chairman tried to lift the spirits of his fighters by relating what Nasser had told him during the war of attrition along the Suez Canal—that he would be satisfied if the PLO kept just one Israeli brigade occupied. "Now," Arafat crowed with an infectious grin, "we alone are holding down 100,000 Israeli soldiers!" Once he was heard to mutter, "If only the other Arab armies would enter the fray, we could demolish the legend of the invincible IDF."

But the other Arab armies showed no inclination to come to the aid of the Palestinians in Beirut or anywhere else. And three weeks into the siege, with sporadic artillery fire and bombing falling mostly on the Palestinian quarters, Arafat's local allies were showing signs of cracking. Walid Jumblatt, head of the leftist Druse militia in Lebanon, explained to the Palestinian leader that he must bow to Habib's demand and commit himself to leaving Beirut. Then former Lebanese prime minister Saeb Salam and Prime Minister Shafiq el-Wazzan turned up at Arafat's door to pass on messages from Habib and from the Moslem community at large. Arafat adopted the same tactic with them all. "My departure from Lebanon is up to you," he told them with practiced cunning. "If you believe the time has come for me to go, I'll leave tomorrow!"

Arafat's clever turning of the tables placed the Moslem leaders on the defensive, and slowly but surely they not only backed off from pressuring the PLO but, to their cry of "Save Beirut!" they added a call to save the Palestinians. At one point, in a placating show of solidarity, Walid Jumblatt even described how Begin was planning to fly Arafat off to Jerusalem in a cage dangling from a helicopter and then subject him to a show trial. If the PLO had to go—and there was little doubt that it eventually would—the Moslem leaders could at least assure that it would go with dignity and with Arafat's political standing intact, lest it be said that his local allies betrayed him just when he most needed their support. Their conclusion: an unconditional PLO withdrawal was out of the question.

Thus Habib's next formula for solving the Beirut impasse, reached early in July, implied a compromise. It outlined an evacuation in two stages: first the PLO fighters would gather in the refugee camps of South Beirut to turn their heavy weapons over to the Lebanese army, while the IDF pulled back five or ten kilometers from the city—thus lifting the siege; the second stage would be the actual evacuation of the Palestinian forces, though the PLO would be allowed to leave behind a political-cum-propaganda office and two units of 800–1,000 men each, placed under the command of the Lebanese army—a force that would be allowed to remain until all Israeli *and Syrian* forces had withdrawn from Lebanon.

The Israelis actually considered accepting the formula, until Sharon told Bashir about it. The Maronite leader's reaction was vehement. "Under no circumstances should you do it. If you fall back," he warned grimly, "the terrorists will *never* leave the city." Lebanese President Sarkis was equally adamant. Like Bashir, he expected lengthy and complex negotiations over the ethnic makeup of the Lebanese force that would be sent into West Beirut. He also feared that, rather than surrender its arsenals to the army, the PLO would simply pass its arms and equipment over to the leftist militias in the city. Thus the notion of a partial Israeli pullback became a dead issue.

On the night of Saturday, July 3, Ambassador Sam Lewis came to Begin's home with a highly interesting and unexpected piece of news: to expedite the evacuation of the disarmed Palestinians, President Reagan was prepared to send Marines to Beirut; the French were also willing to contribute to a multinational force under the terms outlined in the Habib proposal. The prime minister did not respond immediately, but Sharon and David Kimche, director-general of the Israeli Foreign Ministry, later met with Habib. They minced no words in telling him that Israel had grave reservations about the Reagan formula. In addition to ruling out a pullback, the Israelis had no intention of letting the PLO leave a political or military representation behind in Beirut. Sharon stressed as well that there was no reason to bring Marines into the city before the terrorists began to leave, for he was convinced that a multinational force would be exploited as a screen to protect the Palestinians from Israeli pressure and enable them to violate the agreement with impunity.

Three days after Lewis's confidential message to Begin about U.S. readiness to send Marines to Lebanon, Kol Yisrael, the Israeli state radio, broke the story. Reagan's aides were in such a lather over the leak that they woke the president in the middle of the night to inform him that the Israelis had broadcast his offer over the airwaves before he had had a chance to apprise Congress of the plan. They also made plain their suspicion that the leak was itself calculated to abort the embryonic agreement. Begin was no less enraged over the breach of confidence, though he did not reprimand any of his ministers directly. Instead, he vented his anger at the radio correspondent who had broadcast the item. "Look at what a scoop can do!" he railed at the journalist. "My advisers are pressuring me to find the source of the leak, and although I am against investigating public figures, this time I fear I'll have no choice."

No one cowered at the threat, however, and no investigation ensued. Neither was the plan for a multinational force scrapped. But Habib's efforts had been temporarily sidetracked, and in the meanwhile, of course, the siege went on, with the pressure of the intermittent shelling, bombing, and tank fire augmented by cutting off the water and electricity supply to West Beirut.

The problem of getting the PLO to leave Beirut was now compounded by another question: Where would it go? Algeria had revoked its earlier agreement to take Palestinian fighters, and no one was prepared to have them go to Libya for fear that they would become pawns of the unpredictable Kaddafi. King Hussein of Jordan begged the Americans to guarantee that if the armed Palestinians went to Syria they would be shipped off to bases far from his border. His anxiety on that score quickly proved premature, as Assad's regime adamantly refused to host more than the PLO's senior political leadership.

On July 16 the foreign ministers of Syria and Saudi Arabia, Abdel Halim Khaddam and Prince Saud, met with President Reagan and top American officials to find out what they could get in return for extricating the PLO from Beirut. Khaddam called upon the president to "fulfill the historic role that Eisenhower played during the tripartite attack on Egypt" and, on a more pragmatic note, absolutely insisted that the PLO's withdrawal from the city be paralleled by at least a partial Israeli withdrawal.

Secretary of State Shultz tried to steer the conversation back to the heart of the matter. "The question is where the Palestinian fighters will go. I want to ask Minister Khaddam whether Syria is prepared to receive the Palestinian leaders and some 1,000 to 1,500 fighters, so that the rest can be sent to North Lebanon and thereafter distributed among the Arab states which agree to accept them."

"We have indeed expressed our readiness to take in the PLO leaders and host their offices, if they so request," Khaddam replied. As for the rest of the fighters, he contended that the problem wasn't only the men under arms—whom he exaggeratedly estimated at 30,000 strong—but their families as well. By Khaddam's reckoning, some 150,000 Palestinians would be involved in the exodus from Beirut. Syria, he explained, "cannot sustain that burden."

"I think you have exaggerated what we are proposing," Reagan was quick to respond. "When we speak of a few thousand armed men in West Beirut, it is the leaders and some thousand fighters who will go to Syria. The rest will be disarmed, and the Lebanese government will be responsible for them." The president then revealed that Habib would be sent on a tour of Arab capitals that had expressed a willingness to take in Palestinians, so that Syria would not be the only country asked to do its part. Essentially, however, the meeting ended inconclusively, and Habib was left with the problem of finding a new address for the PLO—assuming he could get them to leave Beirut in the first place.

Meanwhile, perceiving these negotiations as so much foot-dragging, Ariel Sharon had become convinced that a ground assault on West Beirut was unavoidable. On July 11, a date that would become a watershed in the conduct of the siege, a critical discussion of the issues was held in the defense minister's office in Tel Aviv.

"The terrorists are demanding that the multinational force be brought in to protect the Palestinians from the vengeance of the Christians," Sharon began, immediately spotlighting his main concern. "What worries the PLO is who is going to search the camps and bring bulldozers in to uncover weapons caches under the houses . . . . We're not waiting any longer. I want an attack next week!"

Throughout his presentation, the minister of defense was consistent in using the expression "terrorist camps" when speaking of the refugee camps in South Beirut—as if this could obscure the fact that he was talking about residential neighborhoods brimming with civilians. "We could distinguish between the Lebanese part of the city . . . and its more southerly, terrorist part—divide Beirut in two," Sharon suggested, indicating that the ground assault would be limited to the quarters south of Corniche Mazraa, which traversed the city from east to west. "At this stage we won't take any action in Ras Beirut, though eventually we'll go in there too. But the southern part must be cleaned out, utterly destroyed! We don't touch the Lebanese population," he stressed for a second time. "We're dealing with the terrorist camps. These camps must be in our hands so that the terrorists can't build a new infrastructure there, so that they don't start restoring them. . . . You should know that the prime minister has issued a directive not to have anything to do with the reconstruction of the camps in the south, just as we won't have any interest in doing so in Beirut. It's in our interest to have [the Palestinians] move on elsewhere. The Lebanese will take care of that, but we have to lay the groundwork."

The destruction of the refugee camps in Lebanon and the mass deportation of the 200,000 Palestinians from that country was an objective that Bashir had proposed well before the war. Now Sharon was coaxing his senior officers to set their minds to the task.

"The northern part of Beirut should be pampered with electricity, water, food, every possible comfort," Sharon outlined, "but the southern part must be destroyed, razed to the ground. We won't touch the city, just the terrorists." He conceded that a ground assault on the southern quarters would be "complicated as a mopping-up operation, but first we can bomb for a week. To my mind, we mustn't leave a single terrorist neighborhood standing."

(In one of the more uncanny coincidences of the war, on that same day, in a circular distributed among his men—and though unaware of the discussion taking place in Sharon's office—Arafat reflected the spirit if not the letter of Sharon's new approach. "The objective of the hellish plan," he wrote, "is the destruction of Beirut. According to reports that have reached us, the city has been divided into nine squares that will be shelled one after the next to bring about the surrender of Beirut in stages.")

Yet even as Sharon hammered away at his distinction between the "terrorists" and the "city," some of the others at the meeting began to voice their qualms. None emphatically opposed Sharon's approach or its implications, but it was evident that a number of officers felt uncomfortable with the plan.

"You can destroy, the air force can level the whole works," said their representative, Brig. Gen. Giora Forman. "The question is whether we have to, and I'm not at all convinced that we do."

Outright objections followed, especially to a ground assault on any part of West Beirut, together with a familiar warning that had been borne out in the camps of the south. "They'll fight, you know," said Yehoshua Saguy. "It won't be easy."

"How long can we limit ourselves to firing on the city?" Sharon countered. "Ultimately there will be an accommodation with the Palestinians over the refugee camps, and they'll stay put, together with their weapons stores."

"We're talking about heavy fire," Deputy Chief of Staff Moshe Levi pointed out. "Not just the air force, but artillery too. To my mind, we haven't exhausted all the pressure that we can put on them."

Three options came into sharp focus in the course of the discussion: to keep waiting for a negotiated settlement; to subject the city to heavy fire; to mount a ground assault into the southern quarters of West Beirut. Yet before calling the meeting to a close, Sharon delivered himself of a highly significant caveat about the differences that had come out in the session:

"It's not necessary to present the dilemma in all its complexity before the Cabinet, as it has been raised here. The Cabinet has enough problems to deal with. It doesn't have to grapple with the question of whether to opt for massive fire with limited local movements or a single, full-scale assault. I want to raise [the issue] before the prime minister. Whatever we do, he must back it."

The minutes of that meeting support the doubts of Sharon's Cabinet colleagues about the way in which he conducted both the war and his reports to them. By presenting a partial and "polished" picture to the Cabinet, rather than the full background data and alternative considerations, and by winning Begin over to his plans before presenting them to the other ministers, the defense minister was taking a convenient shortcut to Cabinet support for an attack on West Beirut. His final admonition to his officers was not the first time he had warned them about telling the Cabinet more than he wanted it to know. Nor was it the last. After an officer from Northern Command had briefed the Cabinet on the situation in West Beirut, including the PLO's military strength and readiness to stand up to an attack, Sharon passed him a note complaining that it wasn't necessary to alarm the ministers.

Even without being properly apprised of the complexities of the issue, nine ministers expressed their emphatic opposition to a ground assault. Their opposition stood even though the prime minister supported the plan of attack, which called for two divisions to break into the southern portion of the city, one moving north along the coast, the other west along Corniche Mazraa. Sharon and Eitan gave their assurances that, prior to the IDF's entry, an especially daunting rain of fire would blanket the 6,000 buildings in the area.

By then the Cabinet was poised in a delicate balance between two factions. Mordechai Zippori, Sharon's veteran opponent, was now joined by the ministers from the National Religious party (Yosef Burg and Zevulun Hammer) and four others, including two ministers from Begin's own Herut party—Deputy Prime Minister David Levi and Finance Minister Yoram Aridor. Opposition to the ground assault was so strong that the observant Dr. Burg came to Begin's home on the Sabbath to subtly warn him that the NRP might cause the government to fall if Begin attacked West Beirut on the basis of a thin majority in the Cabinet.

"What are you getting at?" Begin asked, intent on forcing Burg's hand.

"This is a Cabinet composed of factions, not just individuals," Burg replied, refusing to make his threat plainer.

But the prime minister stood by his right to take decisions by majority rule, and the next day he had the Cabinet pass a resolution giving a small committee of ministers the power to order a ground assault on West Beirut. Burg counterattacked by enlisting the leader of the coalition, Avraham Shapira of the ultraorthodox Agudat Yisrael party, and having him tell the prime minister that "Burg and Hammer speak for us as well." Begin evidently got the message, for he never put the matter to a vote again.

Nevertheless, the struggle over the storming of West Beirut went on. Clearly, the siege strategy was not bearing fruit. The heavy, concentrated shelling of the city's southern quarters had been halted time and again after frantic appeals from Habib—including, in one case, a threat to halt his mediation and leave Lebanon. These intermissions reduced the effect of the pressure designed to break the PLO's morale, or at least prompt the local civilian population to rebel against the organization and demand that it get out. Cutting off the supply of water and electricity to West Beirut had aroused American anger (though there are artesian wells in West Beirut, and while the local residents were greatly inconvenienced by being forced to store water in jerricans and other available containers, the shortage was not unbearable). Even when the decision came down to block the entry of foodstuffs to the western part of the city, crates of fresh fruit and vegetables continued to make their way over the Green Line with Christian merchants (in league with Phalangist militiamen) racking up fat profits from such smuggling activities. And choking off the supply of gasoline seemed to have little or no effect at all, as vehicular traffic continued within West Beirut.

What astonished the Israeli observation officers most of all was the equanimity with which the Beirutis confronted the siege. Even at the height of the shelling of the southern quarters, the "beautiful people" of Beirut continued to swim and sun themselves on the beaches just a kilometer or two farther north. While the desperate residents of Fakahani, Sabra, and Shatilla huddled in their shelters, bikini-clad young women sauntered along the shore at Ras Beirut, and cafés on fashionable Hamra Street enjoyed a record business. Residents of Beirut continued to cross between the two halves of the city by the thousands. Even the Galilean apples being exported to Lebanon began to turn up in the markets of West Beirut—along with Arabic newspapers from Israel telling of the acrimonious debate racking the country over the issue of the siege.

As General Saguy pointed out, the issue was being underscored by the fact that both sides in this contest of wills were anticipating its outcome in nigh-apocalyptic terms. Arafat saw the exit from Beirut as the "end of the revolution" and of his last chance to maintain an independent base within striking distance of Israel. If he were driven into Syria, he would have to live under close and restrictive supervision, while going to Egypt would require him to accept the Camp David line. Israel was in the opposite bind: from the moment the IDF reached Beirut, Saguy explained, it had committed itself to achieve a decisive victory, for allowing the PLO to remain in Beirut would be a political fiasco.

Even if Sharon did not have the full Cabinet behind him, his word was law in the army, and by mid-July General Drori found himself presenting a plan for the conquest of West Beirut before a group of brigade commanders. He spoke of taking West Beirut in forty-eight hours, and immediately most of the brigade commanders expressed vehement opposition to such a schedule. They said they would need at least ten days to conduct the battle at the proper pace, with the maximum security and minimum casualties for their men. Some hinted resentfully that the politicians were too ready to squander Israeli lives in an unnecessarily rash operation. Others argued that an assault was at any rate premature. "We've hardly maintained a proper siege, and you're already talking about taking the city!" one paratroop officer complained after outlining ways to increase the psychological pressure on the PLO by massing forces, conspicuously moving in reinforcements, and similar measures.

But the most outspoken opponent of an assault at this session was Col. Eli Geva, whose elite armored brigade had been picked to break into the city on one of the most difficult axes. Geva's objections, it must be said, were not solely on operational grounds.

"This is not our fight," he protested directly to Rafael Eitan after the chief of staff joined the meeting. "We mustn't let ourselves be dragged into Lebanon's internal affairs. It's fine if there's a stable regime here that can control the terrorists, but we have no right to impose it at the price it's going to cost us and the civilians here." And while on the subject of the cost to Israel, he added, "Our actions are pushing the Palestinian problem into the spotlight. What we're doing is raising America's consciousness about the Palestinian problem, and we may find ourselves confronted with solutions not at all to our liking."

After the meeting many officers went up to Geva to shake his hand, though most of them had kept their opinions to themselves. For Geva was indeed unique among the dissenting officers. From the moment his brigade had come to a halt outside the city, he had been asking himself, "What am I doing here, anyway?" Now that the conquest of West Beirut was officially on the agenda, he had made up his mind "to sound the alarm" and "break the conspiracy of silence," as he put it.

For a few days after the session with the brigade commanders, Geva struggled with his conscience and decided that he would have to relinquish command of his brigade. It was a radical step absolutely unprecedented in the history of the IDF, and a number of high-ranking officers tried to dissuade him. But Geva's mind was set, and finally he approached Drori and asked to be relieved.

Like those before him, Drori tried to persuade Geva to change his mind. Geva said he would not, although the next day he did return and asked to remain in his brigade as a tank commander. "I couldn't not be there," he later explained, "and I couldn't be there merely as an observer. After all, I was resigning for the sake of my men, in order to avert the decision to go into Beirut." When Sharon overruled his being allowed to stay on as a tank commander, Geva asked to be attached to the brigade's medical team. This request was never answered. Instead, in an extraordinary attempt to get him to change his mind, Geva was sent to a series of sessions with Eitan, Sharon, and finally Begin. "Going into Beirut means killing whole families," Geva told the chief of staff, and implied that it would destroy any hope of reaching an accommodation with the Palestinians in the West Bank. But Eitan refused to discuss the political aspect of the issue and confined himself to the question of Geva's obligation to his men. He strongly urged the colonel to stick by his command and not cause a "rift" in the army. After two fruitless talks with Eitan, Geva was sent to meet with Sharon, who heard him out and relayed him to Begin. The prime minister spent less than half an hour with the young colonel and seemed to take the most interest in the likely scope of casualties in West Beirut—to the point that the issue of Geva's resignation never came up.

"How many casualties do you think we'll have?" Begin asked.

"Dozens, for sure," Geva replied.

The prime minister pointed out that his assessment contradicted the "few losses" forecast made by the chief of staff. "Do you dispute the chief of staff?" Begin challenged.

"I do," Geva said firmly.

Forty-eight hours later, Eli Geva was sent word that he should not return to Beirut and that his service with the IDF was terminated forthwith. In a word, he was fired—as well as refused the opportunity to take leave of his men and denied any position in the reserves.

When it became public in late July, the "Geva affair" was an instant cause célèbre, revealing as it did the depth of misgivings within the IDF. Opponents of "Arik's war" hailed the young colonel as a symbol of the country's moral strength and identified his personal quandary as a function of the intolerable situation in which the army had been placed. Their political opposites cited Geva as a dangerous example of a military officer trying to involve the IDF in political affairs and thereby undermining one of the basic tenets of Israeli democracy. Yet all had to agree that the young officer's resignation indicated how sharply divided were opinions about the conduct of the war even within the army command.

But Israel was facing more than a knotty military problem in Beirut; above all, the predicament was one of basically insoluble moral distress. By the time of Geva's dismissal, the dispute over the pragmatic wisdom of extending the war up to the Lebanese capital had given way to agonizing over the army's position. It seemed to many of the soldiers stationed on the heights around Beirut that the IDF's self-image as a defensive force was being demolished along with whole neighborhoods of Beirut. The line between firing at the enemy in the form of armed terrorists who fired back and shelling innocent civilians seemed to have vanished, and the IDF's sense of moral propriety was being overwhelmed by an unqualified dependence on force. The harrowing sight of civilian casualties in West Beirut, especially in the rubble of high-rise buildings that had collapsed under the bombings, fueled the debates raging in the IDF positions, and it wasn't long before the old issue of the "Palestinian problem" was overshadowed by moral questions and differences over the conduct of the war.

After the violation of the forty-kilometer limit, after the war against the Syrians and the "creeping ceasefire" in the mountains east of Beirut, faith in Ariel Sharon's leadership had become so battered among the ranks of the army that the defense minister was constrained to cut back his heavily publicized visits to front-line units. This man renowned as a "soldiers' general" found himself forced to relinquish the prized affection of his fighting men. Stung by personal setback, Sharon lashed out blindly, accusing the press of distributing "poison." But his volatile reaction only made matters worse. On the heels of his reckless accusation, the defense minister decided to visit one of the elite units stationed near Beirut. As he climbed down from his helicopter with a packet of newspapers in hand, the men jeered at him, "There comes the poison." Sharon even tried to lay the blame for what he called "incitement" at the feet of the Labor party, and his aides—less discriminating in their choice of language—spoke of "knifing the soldiers in the back."

Aware of the grumblings in the IDF ranks, the PLO went out of its way to exacerbate Israel's problem of distinguishing between military and civilian targets by scattering its artillery through the courtyards of the densely built residential quarters and establishing its ammunitions stores in the basements of apartment buildings. Several mobile, fourbarreled ZSU antiaircraft guns that proved bothersome to the Israeli air force were actually located alongside the fences of foreign legations, such as the Czechoslovak embassy.

But even without these deliberate efforts to draw fire to sensitive areas, in a city of half a million people it would have been almost impossible to zero in on purely military targets. The IDF invested great efforts in preparing a gigantic master map on which each and every one of the 25,000 buildings in Bierut was given a number so that it would be possible to issue exact firing orders. Even so, and with the most precise fire, civilians were hardly spared. On one day several artillery battalions were activated simultaneously against targets throughout the city with the foregone conclusion that civilians were doomed to die in the barrage. The same was true of the IDF's attempts to thwart the movement of terrorists and to target fire at buildings from which the PLO was known to be shooting—even though the buildings were inhabited by civilians, as could be seen by laundry on the clothes lines.

As in the camps in South Lebanon, the attempt to promote the flight of residents from the beleaguered city yielded mixed to poor results. Tens of thousands did pack their belongings and leave their homes in response to Israeli leaflets advising them to flee for their lives, but most returned as soon as there was a lull in the fighting, usually for fear that their property would be looted. And the great majority chose to stay put. Even in such heavily and systematically shelled quarters as Burj el-Barajneh or Sabra, tens of thousands of civilians chose to sit tight in their shelters.

Strangely, Israel's political establishment was for a long time oblivious to or at least unmindful of the impact on world opinion of the TV broadcasts from West Beirut. As if to underscore this blindness, the Israelis took to busing delegations of honored guests from abroad to an observation point in East Beirut to watch as planes dropped their bombs from high altitudes and plumes of black smoke billowed up from the city—treating the war like a spectator sport. It was some time before the government realized that such actions were offensive to the sensibilities of others or acknowledged the shift in attitude on the part of the Western public, which was being treated almost nightly to horrific film clips from West Beirut. Even the IDF—accustomed to being the darling of the press in the well-worn David-and-Goliath cliché—was surprised to find itself the object of denunciation and rebuke in the international media. Nor could they take comfort from the fact that certain of the televised reports were exaggerated or slanted, sometimes out of sheer ignorance. The pictures spoke for themselves.

So while Arafat may have been losing the military duel with Israel under its punishing fire, he was winning the public-relations war hands down in his role as plucky underdog. In one interview after another, he spuriously presented himself as the spokesman of the shell-shocked residents of this city being besieged by the wicked Begin. But it must also be said that Begin on his part seemed to go out of his way to alienate Israel's traditional sources of support in the West—with such demagoguery of his own as referring to the Palestinian fighters as "two-legged animals." While Arafat was skillfully reshaping his image from remorseless terrorist to long-suffering leader of a homeless and hounded people, Israel was earning itself the reputation of a country that indulged in overkill to achieve objectives far beyond its legitimate security needs.

Flushed by his success in the arena of world public opinion, Arafat became convinced that the Israelis would now more than ever seek to eliminate him and his senior associates. Abu Iyyad, head of Fatah's security apparatus, claimed to have trapped a number of Arab agents carrying miniature communications sets meant to direct Israeli planes and artillery to the PLO's top officials. As a result, Arafat kept on the move, fleeing from one hiding place to another, sometimes twice a day, and holding staff meetings at night in secret bunkers. There were days on which he believed Israeli planes were chasing him through the streets of Beirut, trying to pinpoint him with their bombs. In one instance, an Israeli pilot just missed the window of the basement room in which Arafat was seated, hitting the adjacent building instead. On another occasion, Abu Iyyad left his head-quarters moments before it was destroyed in an air raid.

Convinced that they were being systematically tracked down, the PLO's leaders responded resourcefully and adopted effective camouflage mea-sures, so that throughout the weeks of siege only one ranking PLO figure was seriously injured. This was when Abu Abas, the head of a pro-Iraqi faction, caught a round of Israeli machine-gun fire in his groin. The only mishap for Arafat was severe back pains after a wooden ceiling beam fell on him during an air raid, an injury that did not prevent him from continu-ing to function as usual.

Yet for all his narrow escapes, Arafat knew his position was ultimately untenable. If, at first, he had conducted his negotiations with the aim of postponing PLO evacuation as long as possible, by the middle of July his illusions about the Palestinians' ability to hold out had decidedly frayed. During his early contacts through the auspices of Saeb Salam and Shafiq el-Wazzan, Arafat would send Habib long questionnaires about the details of his proposals. Once, when asked why he refused to agree to an evacu-ation by ship, he had replied churlishly, "My men are prone to seasick-ness." When Bashir Gemayel, in a private phone conversation, appealed to him, "Let West Beirut be. If it's a Stalingrad you want, do it in your own country!" all Arafat would say was, "The matter is too complicated to be discussed over the phone." (Although Bashir categorically refused to meet with Arafat, Amin Gemayel was known to have visited his old friend Abu Iyyad twice during this period.) But now, as the siege—and the destruction—wore on, Arafat shifted the point of his bargaining to ensur-ing that the exodus from Beirut would not mean the demise of the PLO. He was especially fearful of being forced into what he called a "gilded cage" in Damascus or, worse, in Moscow.

Arafat had recently stopped meeting with the Soviet ambassador to Lebanon, Alexander Soldatov, in protest over the Soviet Union's lack of response to his plight. At the beginning of the siege, Arafat had spoken to the ambassador daily in the expectation that the Kremlin would act to extricate him from Israel's grip. But when Soldatov proposed bringing in a Soviet warship to carry Arafat and his associates to safety, the PLO chairman responded angrily, "Are you planning to do to me what you did to Barazani?" (the Kurdish leader who lived in exile in the Soviet Union for years, unable to conduct any political activity). Within days, Arafat's lieutenants began denouncing the Soviets for their policy of neglect, adding to their disappointment over the absence of any Arab initiative a new resentment against their Soviet patrons. For weeks Arafat had refused to place a phone call to Assad on the grounds that "the Syrians know my number." Now he added Leonid Brezhnev to his long list of "friends who collapsed in the crunch."

Feeling increasingly isolated and desperate, Arafat sent a message to Habib though Saeb Salam in which he dropped his earlier demand for an Israeli pullback as a sine qua non of the evacuation. At the same time he cleverly added a threat: if the Israelis attempted to break into West Beirut, the PLO would simultaneously blow up 300 ammunition dumps and bring holocaust down on the city. This threat of mass suicide was not taken entirely seriously, but just the thought was enough to make the Lebanese mediators shudder.

Not so Sharon. Despite the growing protests at home and abroad, he was determined to keep up the pressure on the PLO. And he had the prime minister firmly behind him, though it was not always clear which war Menachem Begin was fighting. "In a war whose purpose is to annihilate the leader of the terrorists in West Beirut," he wrote to Reagan during that period, "I feel as though I have sent an army to Berlin to wipe out Hitler in the bunker." The president was not won over by the metaphor, and Sharon, in consideration of the constant American pressure on Begin not to penetrate West Beirut, decided at the end of July to try another tack. His aim now was to break the Palestinians' staying power with a double-barreled strategy of nibbling away at the edges of West Beirut while stepping up the bombing from the air. Concurrently, Begin increased the pressure on Habib by warning that it still might be necessary for the IDF to move into West Beirut and clean out the terrorists. "We won't wait weeks or months," he stressed, after Habib had difficulty giving him a clear-cut answer about the PLO's intentions.

A few days later, Begin was at Habib again. "When will I find out about the terrorists' readiness to leave?" the prime minister demanded to know.

"As soon as possible," Habib hedged.

"What does that mean?" Begin pressed.

"I am returning to Beirut to deal with just that."

The chronically suspicious Sharon was sure that Habib was deliberately misleading Israel about the progress of the negotiations while cooking up an accommodation to help the PLO save face. Thus it wasn't long before he began to clash head-on with the American mediator. During one of their meetings in Beirut, Sharon virtually ranted at Habib, ruffling the diplomat to the point where he required medical attention after the session. Every time Habib uttered the word "evacuation," Sharon corrected him, insisting on "expulsion." When Habib outlined the terms of the understanding that was beginning to crystallize—namely, the evacuation of the PLO by plane from Beirut airport—Sharon exploded and vowed that no such plan would be carried out as long as he was minister of defense. "I am the representative of the president of the United States, and this is what I have accomplished," Habib replied icily.

Later, Habib complained bitterly to Begin about Sharon's behavior and, in response to intimations that he was being less than absolutely fair to Israel, protested indignantly, "I was a Zionist as a child in Brooklyn before I even knew what Zionism was!" Habib made his point, but then the Israelis insisted that his assistant, Morris Draper, was being antagonistic toward them. Worse yet was the American ambassador in Beirut, Robert Dillon, an envoy so tactless in his remarks to the Israelis, on every possible occasion, that to a man they began to regard him as an incorrigible anti-Semite—especially when he spoke bluntly about "braking" the Jewish lobby in the United States so the president could have a free hand in dealing with Israel.

In despair of handling the Israelis alone, Habib asked Washington for help in making the elusive ceasefire stick. Reagan complied by sending Begin a special letter demanding that he observe the truce and warning of "grave consequences" if he did not. Stern language became commonplace in the exchanges between Washington and Jerusalem after August 1, the date on which the Israeli air force carried out its heaviest bombing yet— 127 sorties in the course of ten hours. That date also marked the inauguration of a new phase of the siege, as Israeli firepower escalated considerably and ground forces began to press in on the city from the south and west. In addition to the saturation bombing, the Israeli navy joined in the bombardment of PLO positions along the coast with Gabriel missiles. At the same time, ground units captured the runways of Beirut airport to quash any notion of an evacuation by air. Then Sharon gave orders to continue "nibbling away" at the edges of West Beirut. By August 5 the IDF had taken over the half-deserted quarter of Saloum east of the airport, the Uzai quarter north of the airport, and the vicinity of the museum as far as the Hippodrome at the eastern end of Corniche Mazraa. This advance brought the vanguard of the Israeli froces up to the edge of the Palestinian neighborhoods, with Burj el-Barajneh already surrounded.

On the night of August 5, with tempers strained on both sides of the Israeli-American dialogue, Begin flouted the president's demand that the IDF return to the lines of August 1. "Jews do not kneel but to God," was

Begin's answer to the president. He did, however, issue orders to halt any farther advance into West Beirut.

A credibility gap was growing between the two governments. On August 4 the Americans claimed that the IDF was moving troops into the area of the port. Their concentration was based on a report cabled to Washington from the American embassy in Beirut. Miffed by the suggestion that the Israelis were lying, Sharon summoned the American chargé d'affaires in Tel Aviv, William Brown, and subjected him to a tirade on American errors.

"You'd better phone home and tell them that nothing is going on, so that they won't be under the impression we misled them . . . . Yesterday none of the artillery fire was ours until evening. I myself was there under a barrage," Sharon claimed.

"The report we got was that people on the embassy roof saw IDF artillery fire," Brown countered.

"That was a terrorist barrage along the northern edge of the airport, not ours. Our men had strict orders not to fire."

Sharon reiterated that the IDF was not making any attempt to cut Beirut in two. He did, however, indicate that he planned to keep advancing. "If they fire on our forces today, we'll move to capture the positions they're firing from. It's a very simple approach, and that's what's been happening the last few days."

"Then I understand you have given me a declaration of intent," Brown struck back. "If they fire, you'll move to capture the area." He was trying to maneuver Sharon into a corner, and the defense minister sensed that he had gone too far in revealing his hand.

"We won't necessarily act that way from now on," he backpedaled. "We'll review the situation daily."

At this point, as if to regain the offensive, Sharon began to quote the cable from Beirut to Washington that Brown had shown him: " '. . . [The Israelis] are advancing westward in Beirut. The embassy people held the telephone receiver out the window so Charlie Hill [in the State Department] could hear the firing. He personally counted eight shells within thirty seconds from the IDF artillery deployed near the embassy . . . .' Come by helicopter and see for yourself that we don't have any artillery near the embassy," Sharon fumed. "How does [Dillon] know who is shooting? Do Israeli mortars have a special sound? If one of my officers stuck a phone out the window to report to me like that, I'd fire him in thirty seconds for not going out and checking on his own!"

His protestations to Brown notwithstanding, Sharon had already begun massing three divisions around Beirut. His purpose was twofold: to increase the psychological pressure on Arafat and to prepare renewal of the advance into the western half of the city. But during the days of heavy bombing in early August, the defense minister's standing in the Cabinet became severely undermined. On August 7 Begin himself expressed misgivings about Sharon's conduct—albeit obliquely—in a terse but highly significant statement. "I know about all the actions [being taken in West Beirut]," the prime minister said, "sometimes before they are carried out, sometimes afterward." Nevertheless, Begin continued to restrain his ministers from allowing their anger against Sharon to reach the point of a showdown. When President Reagan, in another strongly worded communication, demanded that the Israelis restore the water supply to West Beirut, and IDF officers spent three whole days tracking down the apparatus necessary to activate the pumps, Sharon explained to the disapproving ministers, "There's no such thing as a deluxe siege. There are lines for water and no bubble baths." But when the matter of the bombings came up at the same session, and David Levi asked the simple but pointed question, "Have the bombings been approved?" Begin quickly suggested, "If anyone wants a vote on the bombings, we can have one." Not a minister responded.

And so the bombings continued with ever greater ferocity. On Monday, August 9, the Israeli air force renewed its sorties against West Beirut. Once again, most of the bombings were directed against the southern, Palestinian-inhabited suburbs and refugee camps. There were thirty-six sorties on that day, sixteen on each of the next two days, and finally seventy-two unrelieved sorties on August 12. These blows were conceived as the "softening-up" stage prior to a ground assault as well as a way of forcing Arafat to climb down a few notches in his terms for an evacuation accord—though Sharon still thought it preferable to take the city.

While the pounding from the air continued, Sharon took another step that was to have an important effect on the growing crisis. From his talks with Habib, he inferred that the Americans might attempt to land units of the multinational force in Beirut before the start of the evacuation and without a full understanding with him on the matter. His suspicions were heightened when Draper complained to Sharon that his refusal to allow the deployment of the multinational force would delay the evacuation—to which Sharon replied sarcastically, "The husband comes home, tells his wife that their neighbor's teenage daughter is pregnant, and adds, 'They'll blame *us* yet!' " Then, almost as if to stir up whatever hard feelings had not yet surfaced, he publicly denounced Habib's plan as a "fraud" when the special envoy claimed (and Begin confirmed not long thereafter to the Knesset) that Arafat had agreed to leave Beirut. And finally, on August 8, perhaps trying to prove his intention to still have his way, Sharon ordered paratroops sent to Junieh for the express purpose of preventing American helicopters from landing French troops on the beach. The men were duly deployed on the helicopter landing area, and when an American chopper came in and attempted to set down, Israeli jeeps began to scurry about on the tarmac to prevent it from doing so. At this point Morris Draper came careening onto the scene and literally screeched at the chagrined officer in charge, "You're causing a scandal! That's Habib's helicopter!" The entire force was removed from Junieh a few hours later, but by then other IDF units were deployed along the coastal road as far as the outskirts of Jubayl (Byblos) in the north.

This late movement of Israeli troops north of Beirut was among the pressures that sparked a change in Syria's position. For weeks President Assad had stood firmly by his refusal to accept any of the Palestinian fighters, at the same time ignoring demands to remove his own units from Beirut. But after monitoring the build-up of Israeli forces north of the Lebanese capital with growing alarm, on August 9 he instructed his foreign minister, Abdel Halim Khaddam, to phone Habib in Beirut and express his government's fear of an imminent Israeli attack on the Syrian forces in the northern Bekaa Valley.

"I appreciate your concern and agree with you that Israel is holding back on its true intent," Habib told the Syrian.

"Then what should we do?" Khaddam asked, betraying his own anxiety.

"I don't know," Habib replied. "I have no control over Israel's behavior."

The American diplomat was hoping to play on the jitters in Damascus to soften Assad's stand on the evacuation issue. And his gambit seemed to work, for the next day, after Habib had moved on to Jerusalem, Khaddam contacted him through the American embassy to say that Assad was reconsidering his position and to request that he try to prevail upon Begin to postpone any military move he might have in mind. Soon afterward Khaddam relayed a second message: President Assad was prepared to take in the 4,000 or so Palestinian fighters for whom no other refuge had been found. The deadlock had been broken.

That same day, August 10, the so-called Habib document setting forth the terms for the evacuation of the PLO was presented to the Israelis in Jerusalem. Ambassador Lewis reported that Lebanese President Sarkis had already agreed to its conditions, but Sharon, as belligerent as ever, immediately countered that he didn't believe it. Moreover, he had a long list of objections to the plan: he would not agree to have a French officer command the multinational force; he vehemently opposed the entry of the force before most of the terrorists had left; he demanded a pledge that if the evacuation were halted the multinational force would promptly withdraw; and he wanted guarantees that the pullback would be by sea, not overland. In short, he believed to the last that the Americans, like all the others, had been setting a trap for Israel, and that the Palestinians who quit Beirut would merely relocate in the Bekaa Valley or, alternatively, that Arafat would have a change of heart with the presence of American, French, and Italian troops hobbling Israel's ability to revert to blasting him out of Beirut. Sharon was particularly insistent that the multinational force not remain in Beirut more than thirty days. Behind this insistence was the unvoiced plan that the Phalange and the Lebanese army could then go in and see to the removal of *all* the armed Palestinians in West Beirut.

But the Cabinet saw things differently from Sharon, and on Wednesday, August 11, it approved the Habib document "in principle," subject to "suggestions for a number of amendments"—the most pressing being the submission of at least a numerical breakdown of evacuees by country of destination. Thus by Thursday, August 12, it was clear that an agreement on the evacuation was finally within reach. At this point Ariel Sharon, contrary to any scrutable logic, ordered the air force to mount its fiercest attack on the city to date. "Black Thursday," as it came to be known, was a nightmare in which the saturation bombing came on top of a massive artillery barrage that began at dawn and continued throughout the eleven hours of the air raid. Unofficial statistics counted 300 people dead in West Beirut that day.

The assumption among the Israeli General Staff was that the terrorists, and most of the population, were managing to cope with the artillery fire by going down into cellars, shelters, and even into a network of tunnels that had been dug under the refugee camps years earlier. On the other hand, the PLO was having difficulties coping with the aerial bombardments, since it had already lost most of its antiaircraft guns. What made "Black Thursday" so terrifying was the sense of brute violence run wild, given the sharp contrast between the progress in the negotiations and the savage attack on the city. The wife of Prime Minister Wazzan declared a hunger strike to protest the action, and the Moslem leaders of West Beirut phoned the American embassy with harrowing descriptions of wanton destruction and frantic cries for help.

The Americans were furious over what they deemed to be a brutal and wholly unjustified action. President Reagan tried to phone Prime Minister Begin for over an hour but couldn't get through. When he finally did reach Begin, at his office in the Knesset, the prime minister was napping on his couch. Reagan called the bombings "unfathomable and senseless" and demanded an immediate ceasefire, adding the warning that if the Israelis did not cooperate he would pull Habib out and cancel the American mediation mission. By then the bombing had been called to a halt anyway, for the Cabinet, convened earlier that afternoon at Sharon's request, was equally appalled by the mayhem being perpetrated in its name.

The minister of defense wanted approval to close the noose around the city even tighter by having the army advance into Beirut in a number of sectors, particularly in the area of the Hippodrome on Corniche Mazraa. What he got, instead, was an irate attack by his colleagues, who were peeved beyond sufferance by the bombings.

"This is damaging to the negotiations," Simcha Ehrlich exclaimed.

"What's the point of sabotaging the political settlement?" asked Zevulun Hammer.

"We'll end up withdrawing from Beirut yet without having achieved anything!" David Levi groused.

"What's going on is contrary to the Cabinet's decision," Yosef Burg complained.

"Is your source by any chance a member of the family?" Sharon snapped back in a snide reference to Burg's son, Avraham, a leading activist in the budding antiwar movement.

"What kind of talk is that?" Begin cut in, genuinely indignant. He then turned to Burg and said, "The minister of defense apologizes to you."

Sharon tried to stave off the flood of criticism by arguing, "We mustn't cave in!" But that only seemed to annoy the prime minister, who took the remark as a personal affront.

"*I've* caved in!" he huffed. "Do you know what pressure I've been subjected to, and I haven't even bent. *Three times* I said *nyet* to the Americans!"

It was David Levi who pulled the conversation back to the real matter at hand. "Not only is the nation confused," he told Sharon, "the *Cabinet* is confused!"

"Any decision not to advance is a bad one," Sharon insisted, by now shouting with anger.

"Don't raise your voice!" Begin growled at his defense minister. "I want it to be clear who is running this meeting."

Taking a long look at the faces around that table, Ariel Sharon found himself completely isolated. Even Foreign Minister Shamir criticized him for failing to consult the prime minister before ordering a resumption of the bombing. One minister alone—Yuval Ne'eman of the radically right-wing Hatehiya party—tried, unsuccessfully, to get his colleagues to adopt at least one of Sharon's proposals. At the end, the minister of defense was divested of his authority to activate the air force—a decision quite unprecedented in the history of the state, and an unmistakable declaration of no confidence, even if it did come late in the game.

On the night of August 12–13, after a frenzied search over the phone for Habib, Yasser Arafat finally dropped his last demands and announced his readiness to withdraw from Beirut. During a talk with Moslem civic leaders who had come to plead the cause of their city, one elder politician, a former prime minister, appealed to Arafat in tears. "We'll all die, we'll all die," he wailed. The Palestinian leader realized that if he refused to go now he would be held responsible for the destruction of Beirut. The Moslem politicians refused to continue supporting his terms, since the Americans had arranged a place of refuge for him in Tunisia so he could avoid Assad's "gilded cage." Left with no viable choice, Arafat broke. Abu Moussa, one of the PLO's senior commanders, subsequently confirmed that "we finally understood that the Arab states were not interested in having us hold out any more."

By then seven Arab states, in addition to Syria, had agreed to accept a portion of the PLO's fighters, or at least the organization's leadership. All the Palestinians under arms in Beirut got orders to report to their headquarters, where they were issued new uniforms and told to shave and get their hair cut for their exit from the city. Arafat paid his outstanding debts to the merchants and landlords of Beirut, thereby injecting a massive dose of cash into the city's economy in the hope of leaving the Lebanese with sweet memories of the PLO's stay in West Beirut. Then, after several days of mass mourning and tearful partings, against the background of gunfire from the traditional fantasias celebrating a fantasized victory, at 3:00 P.M. on Saturday, August 21, the first contingent of PLO evacuees left Beirut by ship.

Ariel Sharon and Philip Habib celebrated their achievement with characteristic acerbity.

"Mr. Habib," Sharon remarked, "don't you think that in light of this great accomplishment, our brave soldiers deserve a special decoration: the Expulsion Medal?"

"A yellow ribbon, perhaps?"

"Why yellow?" Sharon asked, his first association being with the yellow star that the Nazis forced the Jews to wear on their outer garments.

"Why, for cowardice," Habib replied with aplomb. "Not *yours,* of course!"

But Sharon had not come to the end of his collision course with the American negotiators, and during the evacuation he clashed with them again. One day the Israeli observers in the port area noticed that the evacuees were about to board their ship with jeeps, in contravention of the agreement. Sharon ordered the local Israeli unit to halt the evacuation until the jeeps were released, but Morris Draper, who happened to be present along with Amir Drori, suggested turning a blind eye, especially as the French troops from the multinational force had already checked the jeeps out and removed the RPG launchers hidden inside them. Sharon stood his ground, in response to which Draper threatened, "Before you know it, Reagan will be on the line to Begin."

The possible consequences of the situation were actually more danger-ous than an unpleasant phone call, for by then the Pentagon had relayed orders to two of the Sixth Fleet's ships anchored outside Beirut harbor to enter the port and escort the Greek ship and its Palestinian passengers out. Their orders were to break out of the harbor by force, if necessary, and if the IDF opened fire to fire right back! Relations between Israel and the United States had reached a potentially disastrous nadir.

It was Sam Lewis who negotiated the incident to a successful conclu-sion. After conferring sternly with David Kimche, the director-general of the Israeli Foreign Ministry, enumerating the American ships anchored off Beirut (an aircraft carrier and two destroyers) for special effect, at 7:30 Lewis appealed directly to Begin to concede on the matter of the jeeps. "They don't compromise your security," he argued before the prime min-ister. Sensing the American determination not to yield on the point, Begin gave in. "This time you've honestly earned your salary," an Israeli official told the slightly shaken American ambassador.

Altogether, over the course of twelve days, 14,398 Palestinian and Syrian fighters, including 664 women and children, were evacuated from Beirut; 8,144 left by sea, and 6,254 Syrian soldiers and members of the Palestine Liberation Army left overland on the Beirut-Damascus highway. Yet even in this hour of triumph, the smoldering anger and hatred of the Christian communities in Lebanon could not be contained. Maj. Saad Had-dad, invited to watch the "expulsion" of the Palestinian fighters, stood gritting his teeth and finally gave them the finger as they embarked on ships in the port. In East Beirut, thousands of Maronites lined the road carrying offensive signs and shouting their hostility as truckloads of Palestinians drove past on their way to Syria. And every day Bashir Gemayel feasted his eyes on the departing convoys from a rooftop alongside the road, joined by senior IDF officers counting the number of vehicles and studying the faces of their Palestinian adversaries.

The PLO had lost its defended foothold in Beirut. But even in the clamor of the evacuation, it was plain to see that the Palestinians had not been crushed in defeat. The exodus from Beirut augured hard times for Arafat and his men, but they showed no signs of despair or dismay. Already they were weaving a myth of valor around the chapter of the siege, laying the basis for their political and psychological recovery. The 60,000 shells and countless bombs that had rained down on Beirut had not buried the PLO.

On the Israeli side, a number of senior officers urged Sharon to commemorate the evacuation with some form of declaration on the Palestinian question that would signal a new approach or at least provide a spark of hope for those who championed a political solution. But Ariel Sharon was in no mood for magnanimity.

12

The Making of a Quagmire

AT FIRST IT LOOKED as if all the pieces had finally fitted into place. The fighting was over in Lebanon, the PLO had been expelled from Beirut, and opposition on the home front was muted by the sheer magnitude of the victory. The time had come for phase two, the constitution of a "new order" in Lebanon. This was, after all, the real point of the war and the keystone of Ariel Sharon's grand design. In the simmering sectarian cauldron of Lebanon, however, the political situation was not quite as neat as the Israelis believed.

Certainly, Bashir Gemayel was aware that Menachem Begin would not cancel his political debts with the same wave of the hand and burst of generosity that had once saved Bashir a million dollars. "Begin and Sharon were not schooled by the Jesuits, as I was, and they are certainly not patrons of charity," was Bashir's oft-repeated way of reminding his associates that there was a price to be paid for Israel's support of his candidacy. The weeks of siege had also been a time of quiet work behind the scenes preparing for the presidential election to be held in the Lebanese parliament. Bashir gauged that it would be difficult to mobilize a two-thirds majority, as required by the Lebanese constitution, without obtaining tacit Israeli backing. At the same time, he consistently assured the Israelis that he was confident of obtaining the necessary votes, though he was actually experiencing considerable difficulty gathering support and remained five or ten votes short until almost the last minute.

The main obstacle in Bashir's path to the presidential palace was the ban declared against him by a united front comprising the Moslem leaders of West Beirut, the parliamentary representatives from Tripoli and the northern Bekaa Valley, and even a few Maronite delegates from the unforgiving Frangieh bloc. Their decision to boycott the vote in parliament—

ostensibly because it was convened in the shadow of Israeli guns—was calculated to prevent the quorum required for the election. To compensate for their absence, Bashir would have to ensure the presence and support of almost all the delegates representing the areas under Israel's control. To make that task even more daunting, some of his closest political allies were doing their best to derail the ambitious Bashir at this late date. The elderly but ever nimble Camille Chamoun, who commanded six votes in parliament, shunned all appeals to proclaim his support for Bashir, while his aides worked feverishly to drum up backing for his own election as president. Even Bashir's close friend and most trusted adviser, Jean Nader, tried to dissuade him from running for the office, reasoning that, by eschewing the presidency in favor of a bland compromise candidate, Bashir could function as the real power in Lebanon while avoiding having to pay up on his promises to Israel.

While all this eleventh-hour jockeying was keeping mischievous minds busy in Beirut, a team of Israeli experts put together by the Ministry of Defense convened in Tel Aviv to present its recommendations regarding the forthcoming election in Lebanon. Ironically, considering the toll taken by the fighting in and around Beirut, some of its members counseled that, rather than back Bashir, Israel should push for extending President Sarkis's term for another two or three years by means of an appropriate constitutional amendment or, failing that, should support the search for a compromise candidate. Yet all the advisers knew that Bashir would not readily withdraw from the race, especially when he had no less than Philip Habib's verbal assurance that the United States favored his election.

The participants at that meeting in the Defense Ministry decided to help Bashir Gemayel pick up the seven or so votes he still lacked. Rafi Etian, the prime minister's adviser on the war against terrorism, met with Chamoun and urged him to come out for Bashir, while Bashir himself promised to appoint Chamoun's people to key posts in his administration. To seal Chamoun's support, as Bashir's aides were eager to tell whoever would listen, a healthy sum changed hands—in cash. Meanwhile, the Israelis busied themselves dropping portentous hints to Shiite parliamentary delegates in the south about showing up for the vote, and the IDF was solicitous enough to provide a helicopter to pluck one elderly delegate out of an isolated village in the Bekaa lest he be intimidated by the Syrians. In other cases votes were bought by Zahi Bustani, the head of Bashir's campaign staff, at a going rate of about two million Lebanese pounds (half a million dollars) apiece.

Where persuasion failed, the Phalangists were not above indulging in blunt threats. At one point Bustani went so far as to suggest that if the necessary quorum were not achieved his party would take steps to wrest control of Lebanon by force.

"We think you're going to lose in the parliament, but you see, we're backing you anyway," an Israeli officer remarked to Bustani, as if to remind him of his loyalties.

"Fear not," the campaign manager assured him, smiling to cover his contempt for the incorrigible Israeli naïveté. "If we lose, we'll go to Ba'abda and get Sarkis to sign on the dotted line," meaning that the Phalange would simply force Sarkis to sign a document appointing Bashir prime minister so that, in line with the procedure dictated by the constitution, he would automatically acquire presidential powers, though not the title of president, when Sarkis's term expired.

This new mood of bluff self-confidence among the Phalangists extended to their relations with Israel as well. Bashir's election may have rested on at least a modicum of Israeli intervention, but in public, at least, he maintained a very cool stance toward Israel that sometimes bordered on hostility. Whenever he was asked about the prospect of peace with Israel, he vowed not to enter into such a far-reaching commitment "without the agreement of *all* the Lebanese"—by which he was of course referring to the Moslems. Questioned about the extent of his prior coordination with Sharon, he replied in mock innocence, "Coordination? How could there be any coordination with *me* when three-fourths of the Cabinet ministers in Israel didn't know about the plan?" It was not an entirely frivolous point. At other times, however, he dropped all pretense of circumspection and boasted publicly about how he got out of fighting alongside the Israelis. "The word around town was that if only the Israelis would reach Damour, I would attack West Beirut in a pincer action. But you saw for yourselves: the Israelis passed Damour and made it all the way to Beirut, and I didn't move an inch."

Bashir's new and liberally advertised positions troubled his Israeli liaisons, not least because they feared a backlash in public opinion back home. Cautioning Bashir that Begin and his Cabinet could not ignore the censorious mood of the press, they encouraged the Maronite leader to court popular support in Israel by appealing directly to the Israeli public. Bashir heard them out but responded with a shrug, turning his palms upward in a gesture of helplessness. "What can I do?" he said hollowly. "None of my people is willing to speak to the Israelis openly. They're all afraid!"

On August 23, two days after the PLO began its exit from Beirut, Bashir Gemayel was elected president of Lebanon by fifty-seven of the sixty-two parliamentary delegates who attended the session. Squads of armed Phalangists equipped with walkie-talkies drove the delegates to the site of the vote at a military barracks in East Beirut. Some of the delegates took the precaution of coming with their own armed bodyguards, and at least one of them asked his Phalangist escort to press a gun into his back so that others would believe that he was being brought there by force. When the results of the vote became known, ecstatic demonstrations—replete with gales of whooping, blasting horns, and wild gunfire—spread through the Maronite quarters of Beirut. Israelis, too, were swept up in the jubilation, and one group of Mossad men emptied a full case of ammunition into the air, convinced that after years of patient and persevering labor they, like Bashir, had finally arrived at their coveted goal.

It took no more than a few hours for them to realize just how mistaken they were. The first signs of backsliding in the Maronite camp came when a senior Israeli official presented himself at the Gemayel home at Bekfaya, where hundreds of people stood waiting to bestow a brief word of blessing on the president-elect. Bashir and his wife, glowing with pleasure and a new aura of stateliness, posed for photographs with their well-wishers as brother Amin stalked around the room, his face pinched in a scowl like a mourner among revelers.

"Personally," Bashir told the Israeli who had come to pay his respects, "I shall always be with you. Politically, however, I shall opt for my father's line." And with that the game was up. Ariel Sharon's confident prediction that Bashir would break with Sheikh Pierre's school of political wisdom fell flat at the very moment it should have come true.

Nevertheless, a week later, on August 30, the Israelis decided that the first installment on Bashir's debt had come due. It was time to firm up the date for signing a peace treaty. Bashir was flown to Nahariya for his first meeting with Prime Minister Begin in his new status as president-elect. He arrived in a buoyant mood, expecting Begin to congratulate him effusively on their shared victory in the election. Instead, he was kept waiting two whole hours before the prime minister turned up. Bashir could not have known, of course, that during that time Begin had been meeting with Sam Lewis, who was delivering a message from President Reagan about a new American initiative to be made public on the following day. Begin perused the new American formula and mumbled dramatically, "The battle for Eretz Yisrael [the biblical Land of Israel whose borders approximate the State of Israel plus the West Bank and Gaza Strip] has begun."

The so-called Reagan Plan descended on Begin like a new bolt in this season of unpleasant surprises. Yet another accommodation to Saudi Arabia and Jordan, it proposed a Palestinian entity that would be linked politically to Jordan. If the prime minister had imagined that the defeat of the

PLO in Lebanon would be the key to securing Israel's hold over the West Bank and Gaza, he now realized that the Reagan administration had had a very different scenario in mind. Worse yet, the prime minister strongly suspected that the Reagan Plan was America's recompense to Saudi Arabia and Jordan for their part in getting the PLO to leave Beirut.

From the session with Lewis, Begin went on to his meeting with Bashir and entered the room bristling with anger. He failed to respond to the young man's warm embrace and returned a perfunctory handshake. Champagne glasses were produced, and Begin delivered a respectably ornate speech of greeting, but it was peppered with veiled references to redeeming old pledges. Bashir replied in equally polite but far more evasive language, after which the ceremonial part of the meeting drew to a close and the two men, with a handful of aides and senior officials, retired to an adjoining room to get down to business.

The prime minister was hardly seated before he launched into his attack.

"Where do we stand with the peace treaty?" he began abruptly in his starchiest manner.

"We are with you on a long haul on a genuine peace, not an artificial one," Bashir replied, building up to the bad news. "I cannot decide on such matters alone. There is a government and political institutions in Lebanon, and they must be involved. We will continue to move in this direction, as I have said again and again. But the hasty signing of a treaty is not justified, either from a political or security standpoint. . . ."

"We believe that the first thing you must do as president is to visit Jerusalem, or at least Tel Aviv," Begin cut in. "Such a visit is of great importance in terms of assuring the people in Israel of your sincerity and desire for normal relations. Isn't that why we went to war and paid the price of hundreds of dead?"

Taking a page from the older man's book, Bashir ignored these remarks and proceeded to resume his own monologue. "You know that together with the Americans we have established an order of priorities for ourselves. Our basic aim now is to get the Palestinians and the Syrians out of the Bekaa and the north so that we can restore our freedom of action on the basis of full sovereignty. . . ."

At that point, as if he hadn't heard a word of what Bashir was saying, Begin demanded that they set a target date for signing a peace treaty and, before Bashir could reply, promptly dictated that it be before December 31, 1982, giving Bashir up to four months to get his administration together and on its feet. Jolted by this line of attack, Bashir settled down to bargaining with his erstwhile patrons. First he aked for more time, as much as a year, though in the meanwhile he guaranteed that "normalization" with

Lebanon across open borders would "yield twenty times your trade with Egypt." "I promise you that I shall be the second president to visit the Knesset," he added, summoning up all his earnestness for the statement. But the prime minister's thoughts seemed to be elsewhere, and instead of responding to these assurances he took Bashir to task for failing to participate in the battle for Beirut. On and on he went, like a schoolmaster scolding a delinquent pupil. Bashir was insulted to the depths of his being.

"I know Israel's priorities are different," he conceded. "Your primary concern is to guarantee the security of the northern border, and we will cooperate with you in that. If you are not satisfied with UNIFIL, I am prepared to send down a few thousand men from the Lebanese Forces to serve as a buffer on the Lebanese side of the border . . . and that [arrangement] will hold until the Lebanese administration . . . signs agreements legally guaranteeing peace."

"And what about Major Haddad?" Begin asked, aware that he was raising a sensitive issue for both sides. "What have you decided?"

Bashir placed his hand over his heart and solemnly intoned, "Saad Haddad is like a brother to me. I will not repudiate him; I will reach an understanding with him on an appropriate solution."

"This affair is taking too long," Begin snapped, returning to his chiding tone. "We will not abandon our allies. Haddad should be given a command position in the new hierarchy. Commander of the southern region, for example, if it proves impossible to appoint him chief of staff or commander of the army."

Bashir qualified that Haddad would have to report to Beirut for trial, as the commander of the army had decided sometime earlier. But he assured the Israelis that this would be a mere formality and that the maverick major was certain to be cleared of the treason charges leveled against him. This pointed reminder of Lebanon's independence seemed to fuel Begin's anger.

"Mr. President," he huffed, "I don't want to interfere in the constitution of your first government. We trust you, of course. But we have reports about some officials in the Phalange party indicating that some of your associates are openly hostile to Israel and maintain unacceptable relations with the Syrians. I am prepared to place these reports at your disposal so that you can use them to deal with whoever should be kept far from Ba'abda and so that you won't be surprised one day about their deficient loyalty."

Bashir nodded mutely as the only way to cope with the indignation welling up inside him. The Israeli prime minister was treating him like a spineless vassal, not the president of a sovereign and allied state. Neither were any of the other Israelis at the meeting disposed to interrupt Begin or steer the conversation onto more cordial lines. Ariel Sharon, Rafael Eitan, and David Kimche of the Foreign Ministry, all well acquainted with the prime minister's belligerent moods, were loath to draw his waspish barbs in their own direction.

Sharon did take Bashir aside afterward, however, and try to soothe his feelings by telling him, "I'm prepared to accept peace in stages: first a security agreement and then a political treaty." Yet in return for the concession Sharon demanded a pledge that the daily contact between Israel and the inhabitants of the Haddad enclave would not be disrupted. Then one of the Israelis expressed concern that the considerable number of Palestinians in Beirut could serve as a hotbed for the revival of the PLO. "The terrorists must be driven out of Tripoli," the president-elect was told, "and you must break up the concentrations of Palestinians." It was agreed that the two sides would speak further on the subject of the Palestinians in Lebanon.

"We'll be in touch with you, sir, before September 22," Begin said as he took leave of Bashir. Since the date was the eve of his inauguration as president, there was an edge of menace to Begin's au revoir. Bashir's parting request was that their meeting be kept secret, and Begin gave his solemn promise.

Upon returning to Beirut, Bashir pouted to his father, "He treated me like a child!" But while nursing his wounded pride, he also began to contemplate what would happen if he lost Begin's trust and Israel reversed itself and set about extending its sphere of influence in South Lebanon rather than help him establish his regime throughout the country.

Such fears were not unfounded, for indeed a spirited debate had been going on for weeks within Israeli security circles over how far to go in support of Bashir. To what degree was it necessary to yield to his demands, and at what point was Israel justified in beginning to cultivate alternative sources of support for its policy toward Lebanon? The Israelis were generally divided into two camps: the skeptics—including senior officers such as Amir Drori—who challenged the wisdom of making Israel's interests wholly dependent upon the unpredictable Bashir Gemayel; and the loyalists—including Sharon, Eitan, and officials of the Mossad—who were convinced that propping up Gemayel's regime was the most effective way to solve Israel's security problems in the north.

A few officers from Northern Command actually proposed a complete turnabout in Israeli policy. Put simply, they believed that Israel was becoming deeply mired in a quixotic effort to install Bashir as master over a basically ungovernable congeries of brawling sects when its energies should be used to create a limited security zone in South Lebanon. That would require two measures: shoring up Saad Haddad and wooing the Shiite population, which was the overwhelming majority in the south. The officers conceded that such a policy implied the de facto partition of Lebanon, leaving Bashir as president of the northern Christian enclave alone. But they believed it possible to reach a tacit understanding with Syria on the division of Lebanon into such spheres of influence, with Israel establishing itself in South Lebanon and the Syrians taking over the Bekaa. And they definitely preferred exercising direct control to entrusting any aspect of Israel's security to a central government in Beirut. Needless to say, their approach was a sharp departure from Sharon's grand design, which envisioned not only close cooperation with Bashir but the expulsion of the Syrians from the Lebanese arena.

On August 5, at the height of the military pressure on West Beirut, Sharon had been presented with a memorandum by two Middle East experts who had analyzed Israel's predicament in Lebanon with new cogency and had arrived at the discouraging conclusion that "there is no hope of installing a strong and stable government in Lebanon." They also found that ejecting the Syrians was possible only "by means of a comprehensive military action and the IDF's presence throughout Lebanon," both of which would be equally undesirable. They suggested that the activities of the Phalange be confined strictly to Christian areas, which would counter the impression that the Phalange was the exclusive beneficiary of Israel's support. For example, they recommended encouraging the establishment of yet another militia in Lebanon—this one by Walid Jumblatt's Druse rivals—and arming the Shiites of South Lebanon, while at the same time intervening to prevent the rehabilitation of the Palestinian refugee camps so that their inhabitants could be redistributed throughout the country. "In the long run," the two men wrote, "one must consider ways to exploit the Palestinians' dependence on Israeli protection against retribution by the local population to score political gains." In conclusion, the memo echoed the position favored by IDF field officers: "To facilitate the defense of our presence in the south, we suggest resigning ourselves—albeit reluctantly—to the Syrian presence in the northern Bekaa and the creating of conditions to achieve a de facto [defensive equilibrium] with the Syrians."

"I don't see how we can accept, even tacitly, the Syrian military presence in the Bekaa and North Lebanon," Sharon pronounced in rejecting the memorandum's conclusions.

In the field, preparations for Gemayel's assumption of authority in Lebanon were considerably less than routine. Bashir planned to extend his rule to South Lebanon at Saad Haddad's expense by opening branches of the Phalange party and setting up bases for his militiamen. Joe Eddé, who had commanded the abortive battle for Zahle, was put in charge of operations in the south. Under his leadership, the Phalange embarked upon a major campaign to enlist new recruits in the villages around Sidon. After securing Israel's permission to carry out searches for terrorists as a cover for penetrating southward and maintaining armed patrols, Eddé's men were soon setting up roadblocks, confiscating vehicles, and detaining suspects and political rivals at will.

In the hills east of Sidon, the Phalangists helped the inhabitants of the Christian village of Mia-Mia in their attempts to drive the Palestinians out of the adjoining refugee camp on the grounds that they needed the land. Their modus operandi was hardly subtle: Women were sent into the camp to throw burning branches into the houses, after which armed Phalangists moved in to "help" the Palestinians pack their belongings and flee. When the fire department in Sidon was summoned to Mia-Mia, its commander ducked out of answering the call on the excuse that his truck had "broken down." Word of this terror campaign reached the IDF in time for local officers to thwart it, and the Christian *mukhtars* were summoned to IDF headquarters in Sidon and admonished for the incident.

On July 8, it came out that not the *mukhtars* but none other than Bashir Gemayel had been behind the orders to drive the Palestinians out of Mia-Mia. For on that day the governor and police chief of the Sidon district reported matter-of-factly to the Israeli commander of the city that they had just returned from a talk with Bashir and wished to begin transferring the Palestinian refugees to northern Lebanon. The fact is that Israel had a similar plan for dealing with the Palestinians of the area. But that did nothing to allay the feeling among the field officers that Bashir was meddling in the affairs of the terrorists under their command—to the point where his intervention necessitated a clear-cut decision on how to proceed. In mid-August Sharon was given a detailed list of the excesses perpetrated by the Phalangists, ranging from arbitrary dismissals and the appointment of new local councils in Christian villages to threats against merchants who purchased Israeli products and the random beating of travelers along the roads. The document was sobering.

By then, having been let down by Bashir during the fighting, the defense minister was more attentive to the advice of the officers in Northern Command who tirelessly preached the buildup of Haddad's forces, through which Israel could maintain a direct presence in the area as long as necessary. Since the beginning of the war, Haddad's soldiers had been absolutely forbidden to foray beyond the narrow strip under their control, but in August they were suddenly allowed to deploy as far north as the Zaharani River. When, at the instigation of officers from Northern Command, Haddad crossed this line, his men were sharply rebuked by the Phalange and ordered to withdraw from the Christian villages around Sidon. However, in the wake of pressure from Drori, the Haddad militia was then permitted to move as far north as the Awali River, and the Phalangists were forced out of the territory south of that line. It was a decision of major political import, implying as it did that Israel had begun to back away from the vision of a "new order" in a united Lebanon ruled by Bashir Gemayel in favor of a pragmatic need to protect its own interests in the south.

Once that shift had taken place, the main question for the Israelis was how to go about winning the support of the majority Shiite community in South Lebanon. Their cooperation was vital to the success of any arrangement Israel might want to institute in the area, if only to ensure that the PLO would not be able to return to the south. The first difficulty was the fact that the Shiites were less than eager to embrace the Greek Catholic Haddad as their leader, and Sharon's pro-Shiite advisers warned that any attempt to force Haddad's authority on them would only arouse their hostility. Instead, these officers recommended building Israel's policy in the south on the Shia Amal movement.

Amal had emerged and flourished in the 1970s as a kind of protest movement challenging the traditional discrimination against the Shiites, the largest but poorest and most backward community in Lebanon. Under the leadership of the imam Moussa Sader, a man as zealous in his beliefs as ambitious for his flock, the Shiites, for the first time in Lebanon's history, began to crystallize as an influential political force that succeeded in blotting out its traditional stigma as a "herd without a shepherd." They set about establishing independent religious institutions and, with the aid of Syria and the PLO, even began to build their own armed militia.

The PLO soon had reason to regret its support in this venture, for despite the initial congeniality relations between the Shiites and Palestinians shortly deteriorated to the point of an open breach due to the PLO's high-handed treatment of the non-Palestinian residents of South Lebanon, including countless acts of robbery, rape, mutilation, and sadistic torture. The rift between the two communities widened beyond repair with the 1979 disappearance of Moussa Sader in Libya (the Shiites suspect to this day that Sader was kidnapped and murdered by order of Yasser Arafat, or at least with his collusion), and by the time of the Israeli invasion in June 1982 Amal had behind it two years of armed strife with the PLO.

To cash in on the existing Shiite organization, experience, and anti-Palestinian sentiment, some Israeli officers suggested integrating the members of Amal into the defense of South Lebanon. This was vigorously rejected by military intelligence on the grounds that Amal could not be trusted as a reliable ally, being riddled with radical elements loyal to the Khomeini line and given the close ties between the Shiites in South Lebanon and their brethren in the Bekaa who were under the sway of the Syrians. These objections essentially scuttled all notions of buttressing Amal as a local ally. In fact, every effort was made to weaken its influence in the area by having Haddad mobilize Shiites directly into his militia and by cultivating rival Shiite clans and political hopefuls in the area.

The third and most painful element that had to be dealt with in South Lebanon was the Palestinians, though here, at least, Ariel Sharon knew what he wanted from the start. A special survey showed that, out of a total population of some 300,000 Palestinians scattered throughout Lebanon, the refugee camps overrun by the IDF contained 65,000, with another 40,000 or so living nearby. Most of these people had remained in their homes during the war, and the minority who left the camps returned when the fighting stopped. One of the original, albeit unpublished, aims of Operation Peace for Galilee was to rid South Lebanon of its Palestinian population so the PLO would not have a base of operation should it ever attempt to infiltrate the area again. As early as June 10, in a session of the Knesset Foreign Affairs and Defense Committee, Menachem Begin had made a passing reference to the "transfer" of the Palestinians out of the south, but in the heat of the debate over the clash with the Syrians his remark slipped by without comment. Later in the war, the prime minister issued a directive to prevent the reconstruction of the ruined refugee camps in South Lebanon. When Maj. Gen. David Maimon was appointed military governor of South Lebanon, he told his men on June 13 that the destruction in the refugee camps should be regarded as an inadvertent but welcome achievement of the war. In retrospect, however, it appears that much of the destruction in the camps was neither inadvertent nor ascribable to the war, having occurred quite deliberately during the period after the fighting. In Rashidiye, for example, the houses whose cellars served as bunkers and arms stores—and there was a considerable number of such buildings—were systematically blown to bits.

Beyond leaving the camps in a state of disrepair, Israel's plans for the Palestinians in South Lebanon remained vague. This lack of clarity was undoubtedly related to the unsettled question of Israel's general strategic approach to the south. As long as the accepted intent of the Lebanese operation was to turn all of Lebanon over to Bashir Gemayel, the fate of the Palestinians in the south was sloughed off as his affair, leaving little point to Israel addressing itself to the problem. Gemayel and his lieutenants—most prominently one Moni Arab, who was appointed head of the so-called Gamma Group to deal with the reconstruction of South Lebanon —made no secret of their intention to rid the area—and the rest of Lebanon—of Palestinians. But as the consensus within the Israeli Defense Ministry edged away from unqualified support for Phalange domination in the south and toward a continued Israeli presence, the realization began to dawn that somehow or other Israel would have to face up to the matter of dealing with the refugee population.

The Israelis' approach was to take a middle road, neither repairing the damage in the existing camps nor expelling the refugee population. At the same time, they provided temporary shelter in the form of tents to some 30,000 homeless Palestinians until they could be resettled. The ultimate aim was to break up the refugee camps and move as many of their residents as possible to areas north of the Awali River.

Toward this end the Israelis tried to locate available lands in the public domain, but they could find nowhere near enough to implement their idea. Economic Minister Yaakov Meridor, who had been appointed to deal with the matter on behalf of the Cabinet, pressed the Lebanese government to start breaking up the camps, while General Maimon came up with a plan for dividing the Palestinians among several new housing projects each containing 400 families at a total estimated cost of some $400 million. Even though this would rehabilitate the refugees outside the framework of the camps, the Lebanese housing minister, Salim el-Jahel, refused to even study the plan. In principle there was no serious disagreement between the Israelis and the Lebanese over the need to change the distribution of the Palestinian population in the south, but in practice every feeler in that direction met with opposition by the Lebanese administration. Bashir and his associates had their hearts set on expelling the Palestinians to the last man, woman, and child, and therefore had no interest whatever in a plan to house them in the heart of the country. And without the Lebanese government's approval, there was no chance of drumming up international support for the resettlement plan. The American government refused to allocate money to any program that lacked the wholehearted approval of the Lebanese government, and the United Nations Relief and Works Agency declined to cooperate with the Israeli minister and his proxies. When Meridor tried to circumvent UNRWA opposition at its offices in Beirut by working through the organization's representatives in Jerusalem, the UN secretariat sent the branch head in Israel on an extended leave.

In place of the unwelcome plan for dispersing the population of the camps came a half-hearted attempt to drive a wedge between the PLO and the residents of the camps by recruiting a small Palestinian militia that was to be armed with Israeli rifles and supervised by Israeli officers. The immediate motive behind this idea was to enable the camp residents to defend themselves against reprisals by the Phalangists, but the Israeli officers in the area gradually came to the conclusion that many of the Palestinians preferred to think of themselves as Lebanese and would rather join whatever local military framework was to be established in the south. Before this realization took root, however, Israeli policy had executed a 180-degree turn—from "transferring" Palestinians out of the area to arming them!

Far more vexing than the muddle of conflicting interests in the south was the political and military bind in which the IDF found itself in the Shouf Mountains, a traditional stronghold of the Lebanese Druse. A sect that broke off from Shia Islam in the eleventh century, the Druse have maintained a high degree of communal cohesion ever since. Ariel Sharon and his aides had been so confident of the viability of Maronite hegemony in Lebanon that they had failed to consider what role would have to be allocated to the Druse in any attempt to establish a "new order." When Druse military prowess became apparent, the Israelis were taken by surprise. The 4,000-strong militia of Jumblatt's Progressive Socialist Party, which had been developing in quasi-underground conditions since 1976 and far surpassed the Phalange in both organization and combat ability, had been discounted by Israeli intelligence. Worse yet, the Israelis greatly underestimated the depth and vehemence of the hatred that obtained between the Druse and the Maronites, two communities that had been at each other's throats for more than two centuries over control of the Mount Lebanon area. The Druse comprise only 6 percent of the population of Lebanon, but in the Shouf and certain parts of the Matn (the southern and central sectors of the Mount Lebanon range) they enjoy undisputed numerical superiority.

Before the outbreak of the war, the Shouf Mountains and the district around Aley were free of any Phalangist forces and contained only isolated pockets of Palestinian fighters. (Jumblatt was regarded as a close ally of the PLO, but in return for his political support he demanded that the Palestinians stay out of the Druse villages.) The Syrian army maintained no more than a light presence in the area, so the Druse enjoyed a large measure of independence. When the war broke out in June, Jumblatt's militia did not oppose the IDF's advance through the Shouf, perhaps in the hope that after the fighting had ended Israel would reciprocate with an appropriate political quid pro quo. If so, that hope was disappointed in August when the Shouf's special status as a Druse bailiwick was violated by Phalange units moving into the area in the wake of the Israeli army.

The swift appearance of the Phalange on Druse territory was no happenstance. Eager as he was to eject the Palestinians from Lebanon, Bashir Gemayel was unwilling to commit his troops to that cause. But he was so determined to capture the Shouf region and shatter Walid Jumblatt's hegemony over that hotly disputed territory that, *with Sharon's blessing,* he was quick to send his forces into the Druse areas conquered by the IDF. "We are not capturing the Shouf," Bashir and his men argued before Sharon, "we are simply returning to the homes we were forced to abandon." At first the Phalangists functioned in the role of a back-up force engaged in searching out and destroying arms stores. But it wasn't long before they began trying to establish their control over the Shouf, using the same terror tactics they adopted in the south. They harassed the Druse at their roadblocks and occasionally kidnapped travelers at random, some of whom were subsequently murdered. When the first complaints about the torture of local residents were passed on to Israeli troops stationed in the Druse villages, the commander of the IDF division based in Behamdoun threatened the commander of the Lebanese Forces with expulsion from the area with tank fire, if necessary. But the threat was never carried out, even as the complaints continued to pile up, for Sharon had committed himself to helping Bashir unite Lebanon under his rule, and above all that meant allowing the Phalange to take over the Shouf by whatever means it chose.

Walid Jumblatt behaved with great restraint when his main weapons store in Mazraat Shouf was confiscated by the IDF. That led the Israelis to assume his spirit had been broken and he was ripe for an understanding. But they couldn't have been more mistaken. Despite rumors about his weak character, addiction to alcohol, and flagrant failure to fill the shoes of his late father, Kamal Jumblatt (the revered founder of the Progressive Socialist party, who was murdered by the Syrians in 1977), the wiry, owl-eyed Walid still enjoyed wide popularity as the scion of a family of feudal lords that had ruled in the area for centuries and had become the vanguard of socialism in Lebanon.

When Israeli emissaries arrived at Walid Jumblatt's doorstep, he received them with icy disdain. Contacts did take place on another level, however. The commander of Jumblatt's militia, Anwar Fatayari, approached the ranking Israeli officer in the Shouf and warned him, "You're turning the majority in Lebanon against you, which is hardly politic if you hope to obtain a peace treaty. You entered Lebanon to solve the Palestinian problem and you succeeded at it. You succeeded, in fact, far more than the Syrians. But now you are acting contrary to your own best interests!" His point was to dissuade Israel from basing its policy on the Mar-

onites alone, but it was a lesson the Israelis would have to learn for themselves—though they could not claim they hadn't been warned.

At first the Druse refrained from challenging the Phalange to open combat and limited themselves to guerrilla warfare in the form of ambushes
and mining roads. Still, the Lebanese Forces failed to establish themselves
in the Shouf. Even when the IDF paved the way by opening Druse roadblocks to the movement of Phalangist reinforcements, the latter failed to
gain control of the roads beyond the main Druse population centers.
Within two months it was apparent that even with the IDF behind him
Bashir was incapable of imposing his authority on his rivals. The situation
in the field had reached an impasse.

Then came the Druse counterblow, delivered in stages, and while the
details of the long battle between the Druse and the Phalangists are not
pertinent here, its outcome was of major import: the Druse managed to
push the Phalangists out of most of the Shouf and to isolate the remaining
pockets of Maronite resistance. To consummate their victory, they set out
on a rampage of slaughter in some villages, massacring Christian residents
and prompting a mass flight by the terrorized survivors. When Fadi Frem,
the commander of the Lebanese Forces, asked for permission to pump
about 1,000 fighters into the Shouf and reverse the balance of forces,
Sharon vetoed the idea for fear of a frenzied bloodbath on territory under
Israeli control.

Like the Syrians before them, the Israelis had become a garrison force
reduced to keeping the peace in a land not their own, policemen wedged
as buffers between the warring Lebanese factions and too often caught in
the cross fire. The hope of achieving a Druse-Maronite rapprochement, or
failing that at least Maronite hegemony, dissolved in the crisp mountain
air of the Shouf. The sectarian strife was now perceived as a bog that was
sucking the IDF in deeper with each passing day, toward no apparently
good end.

From the moment the scales tipped in their favor, the Druse began to
send out feelers about holding direct talks with Israel. Their fear of a defeat
at the hands of the Phalange had been superseded by a desire to anchor
their victory in an understanding with their enemy's presumed benefactor.
While sending out emissaries to Arafat and the Syrians, therefore, Walid
Jumblatt personally held a series of secret talks with a senior Israeli figure.
Their conversations were not limited to the subject of preserving the truce
in the mountains; on Jumblatt's initiative they delved deeper, into the
question of a possible political accommodation. One of Jumblatt's top
priorities was to bring into the Shouf the Druse mortars and cannons that
remained in the sector controlled by the Syrians. His argument was that

Israel should be interested in bolstering his forces because, even though he was not a champion of a formal peace treaty between Lebanon and Israel, the Druse were quite determined to keep the PLO from stealing back into the region under their control.

In extension of these secret talks, Jumblatt also sent envoys to Israel a number of times, and through the mediation of local Druse they put forward some far-reaching proposals about covert Israeli aid for Druse autonomy in Lebanon in return for cooperation in keeping the PLO out of the Shouf, thereby ensuring friendly territorial continuity for Israel from South Lebanon up to Beirut. But the Israeli Cabinet took a dim view of making contradictory commitments to the Druse and the Maronites, and decided to maintain a position of ostensible neutrality. Consequently, Israel brought down on itself both the resentment of the Phalangists, who continued to fret about a deal being cut behind their backs, and the hostility of the Druse, who construed Jerusalem's demurral as a sign of continued support for their enemies.

The irony of it all was that, instead of creating a new order in Lebanon, Israel seemed to be going out of its way to maintain the traditional balance of enmities. The vision of a strong central government that would engineer a reconciliation between the communities under the sway of a Maronite majority was a mirage that drew the Israeli army deep into Lebanon and then vanished in a wink once it was too late to turn back. For despite the steady diet of hyperbole that Bashir fed the Israelis for months prior to the war, even with the cover provided by the IDF's presence on Lebanese soil the Phalangists were unable to extend the area under their control much beyond what it had been during the days of the Lebanese civil war.

Other cruel ironies came out in the aftermath of the fighting, such as the fact that the Phalangist command had held a population census but kept the results from the Israelis because they showed that only 30 percent of the inhabitants of Lebanon were Christian. Not in their worst nightmares did the Israelis imagine such a statistic. Had they bothered to investigate the actual demographic composition of Lebanon themselves before embarking on their military venture, they probably would have been more circumspect about backing the cause of Maronite hegemony.

There were men in Bashir's inner circle who urged him to recognize these harsh facts and take drastic measures to cope with them, such as purging the pathetic remains of the Lebanese army and reconstituting it as a thoroughly Christian force, declaring martial law, dispersing the parliament and suspending the constitution, and again taking up arms against the other sects in Lebanon. But the president-elect shunned such advice as too adventurous even for his tastes. He wanted to establish his rule first by merging the Phalangist Lebanese Forces and the Lebanese regular army into a single force loyal to him alone. Thereafter he could strive toward national reconciliation by bringing representatives of the country's other communities into his government. But since these plans required a continued Israeli presence in Lebanon, prudence dictated, especially after his falling out with Begin, that his first priority be to patch up relations with Israel. In this situation, as in many others, prudence failed the Maronite leader.

Bashir was not one to suffer insult lightly, especially when Jerusalem was so quick to leak word of his meeting with Begin despite his explicit plea for secrecy. In a fit of pique, he declared that he was severing all ties with Israel, and to make the point stick he forbade his underlings to meet with any Israelis, though he finally softened and consented to receive Sharon. The defense minister did his best to mitigate the harsh impression left by Bashir's talk with Begin. He sat with his erstwhile protégé for five hours discussing a detailed plan for the next phase of their joint design, and when they emerged from the tête-à-tête Sharon was invited to dine at a restaurant owned by one of Bashir's good friends. The orchestra played "Hatikvah" as a sign that the rift was healed, and Sharon seemed enormously pleased.

The talk between Bashir and Sharon took place on Sunday night, September 12. It centered on two subjects—the purge of West Beirut and official negotiations with Israel—and understanding was achieved on both. Sharon wanted to be sure that the Lebanese army would move into Beirut's refugee camps quickly and demanded that Phalangist units be sent in alongside. Their mission would be to clean out the terrorists who, he was convinced, remained in the city after the evacuation. But once again, Bashir spoke with relish about destroying all trace of the camps in South Beirut and building "an enormous zoo" in their stead. As to their Palestinian inhabitants, he had a mind to "load them onto air-conditioned buses" and dispatch them over the Syrian border. "By October 15," Bashir promised merrily, "there won't be a single terrorist in Beirut!" Consistent to the end, however, Bashir never made a quotable commitment to use the Phalange in addition to the regular army for this purpose.

Both men knew, of course, that this plan was in stark violation of the evacuation agreement, which guaranteed protection to the "law-abiding noncombatant" Palestinian population of Beirut. Nevertheless, Sharon was careful to summarize in writing the agreement he had reached with Bashir as a collaboration on "destroying the terrorists' infrastructure so as to manifest the Habib agreement to the full."

Two days later the whole elaborately conceived scheme collapsed. At 5:00 P.M. on September 14, Bashir Gemayel was sheduled to hold a talk with a group of Israeli intelligence officers touring Beirut. But first he drove to the Ashrafiya branch of the Phalange party to deliver a lecture before a seminar of young women activists. Exactly two weeks earlier, the three-story building had been purchased by the Ashrafiya branch secretary, Jean Nader, having been rented by the party for a number of years. Bashir lectured in this hall every Tuesday afternoon, but this was probably his last appearance on this particular platform, since his inauguration was about to bring the practice to an end.

Bashir Gemayel's enemies also knew about his regular appearances at the Ashrafiya branch every Tuesday afternoon at four and that time was running out if they hoped to exploit it for their own ends. And so on the previous evening twenty-six-year-old Habib Tanious Shartouni, the nephew of the building's former owner, made his way up to his sister's apartment on the third floor to set up the murder of Bashir Gemayel. None of the guards in the building thought anything of Shartouni's presence. His family was renowned for its loyalty to the Phalange, and one of his cousins, who lost both legs in the civil war, was serving as Sheikh Pierre Gemayel's aide-de-camp. No one would have dreamed that the young Shartouni was a member of the clandestine Syrian National party, a small radical movement that had parted ways with the Phalange, espoused the cause of a Greater Syria, and was now fighting alongside the PLO. Habib Shartouni had the perfect cover.

On the previous day, he had received an order from his control, a Syrian intelligence operative in Rome, to assassinate Bashir according to a long-standing plan whereby he was to place an explosive device on the floor of his sister's apartment directly over the spot where the speaker's rostrum stood on the floor below. On Tuesday afternoon Shartouni sent his sister out of the house, set the bomb in place, then climbed up onto the roof of a neighboring building to await the arrival of the president-elect.

"Let me tell you a story," Bashir said, charming the eager young women of the Ashrafiya branch as he began his address just after four. "When the statue of the late president Bishara el-Khouri was sculpted, his sons protested that its face bore no resemblance to their father's portrait. In time, though, they grew accustomed to the statue and forgot that it actually looked nothing like the photographs in their homes. The same thing will happen now," Bashir assured his young followers, raising his voice for emphasis. "The opposition will grow accustomed to the portrait of the new president, even though it didn't want him. . . ."

The time was 4:10. At that moment, Shartouni activated the explosive device by remote control and, in a shattering blast, reduced the entire building to a pile of debris and a thick cloud of dust.

Soon the street was crowded with people, and rumors spread wildly regarding Bashir's fate. Within minutes one of the ranking members of the Mossad arrived on the scene and was told that "El-Bash has already been rescued." One man insisted that he saw Bashir walk out of the rubble and leave the area; another swore that he was taken off in an ambulance bearing the number 90. Within another few minutes word arrived that Bashir was in one of the city's hospitals being treated for a leg injury. Everyone seemed quite confident that Bashir had survived—even President Sarkis, who phoned the state television station and asked to have a crew sent out to film the meeting he intended to have with Bashir that evening to celebrate his miraculous deliverance. Solange Gemayel, waiting at the headquarters of the Lebanese Forces in Qarantina for her husband's return, received a call from the commander of Lebanese military intelligence, Col. Jonny Abdu, to report that Bashir had been taken by helicopter to a hospital in Haifa.

One after another, all the reports proved to be wishful thinking. A search through the hospitals turned up nothing, another check revealed that there was no ambulance with the number 90. Neither was there any trace of Bashir Gemayel in the ruined building, where dozens were still buried in the rubble. An Israeli engineering unit was brought in to assist in the evacuation, and Israeli paratroops were rushed to the scene to hold back the hysterical crowd so the rescue teams could continue their grim labors. Phalange spokesmen kept up a steady stream of assurances that Bashir was safe, but the more time that went by without any sign of the president-elect, the more suspicions of the worst mounted. And as they mounted, the hardened officers of Bashir Gemayel's militia sat on the curbside and bawled like broken-hearted children.

At one point the Mossad agent picked his way into the destroyed building to watch up close as the rescuers dug by searchlight and extricated the mangled bodies of young women. He was deluged by phone calls from Jerusalem but had no news to report. Finally, despairing of the conflicting reports coming out of the Phalange, he took another Israeli officer in tow and began making the rounds of the hospitals. In the morgue of the Hotel-Dieu Hospital, not far from the scene of the explosion, his eye was caught by what he immediately identified as Bashir's wristwatch on the arm of a corpse whose face was bashed beyond recognition. The final proof of identification was found in the pocket of the blue suit: Bashir's white-gold wedding ring; a letter from a nun; and another letter of congratulations on his election from a village *mukhtar*. Beside him lay the body of his friend Jean Nader. This was at 9:45 at night, five and a half hours after the explosion. Bashir's body had evidently been among the first removed from the scene, but no one had identified it.

The bitter news was relayed to Jerusalem, and Ariel Sharon and Menachem Begin began to consult on Israel's next moves. The Maronite community of Lebanon refused to believe it was true. President Sarkis did comment to one of the American diplomats in Beirut that "Bashir was hasty in everything he did, even in going to his death," but he was the exception to the rule. At three in the morning, Sheikh Pierre Gemayel summoned the official responsible for the rescue operation and grilled him on the results. "Did you see him with your own eyes?" he demanded, still unwilling to accept the fact of his son's death. And the next day, at Bashir's funeral in Bekfaya, thousands of Phalangist militiamen chanted insistently, "Bashir lives! Bashir lives! Bashir lives!" as though trying to deny reality by sheer force of will. Soon word spread through the ranks of the Lebanese Forces that for reasons best known to himself their leader had chosen to stage his disappearance at this time, but the day was near when he would return to their midst and lead them to ever greater glory.

His truth was marching on.

13

Anatomy of a Slaughter

"THERE WILL STILL BE TERRORISTS IN BEIRUT," Maj. Gen. Yehoshua Saguy pronounced during a meeting in the defense minister's office in Jerusalem on August 12. It was the day to be remembered as Black Thursday, and as bombs savaged the western half of Beirut to force the PLO into submission, Saguy already had a thick dossier of reports on a plan to send hundreds of Palestinian fighters underground. Area commanders were being assigned to supervise clandestine cells; all the necessary papers —identity cards, work permits, and the like—were being prepared by the PLO's forgery labs; hiding places were being arranged; and funds were being accumulated to cover salaries for up to six months. The plan called for leaving 2,000 fighters in the city, mostly volunteers who were heads of families.

"There will still be terrorists in Beirut, and the Phalange will find a way to get them and settle old scores," Saguy continued somberly. "One day the murders will start, and they will just go on and on without end. Every paper in the world will be there to cover the extermination. They'll photograph anyone who is so much as scratched! How can we operate without being tainted? They'll lay everything at our doorstep!"

"We must get out of Beirut!" Saguy implored his colleagues. "We should remain there only as long as the multinational force does. That way there won't be any complaint against us. But then we must get out, stand aside. . . ."

There was a pathetic note to Saguy's presentation that day. The war was well into its tenth week, and Israel's intelligence chief was finding himself isolated, shut out by his superior, the one man who seemed to hold all the cards and had long wearied of Saguy's dire predictions. Most sadly and ironically, Yehoshua Saguy was having to beg for information about the plans for his own army.

"I'm in a terrible position," he said, appealing to Sharon in front of all the others. "I'm not being kept in the picture. I am speaking to you as a friend now: I *must* know what's going to happen. It's unthinkable that sensitive things may happen without my knowledge. . . . If you must act, let me know!"

The "sensitive things" that Saguy could not bring himself to express openly were what he suspected would be violations of the Habib agreement. All but certain that evacuation of the PLO would not spell the end of "Arik's war," the question most on his mind was whether the "purge" of Beirut would fall to Bashir Gemayel's forces or be assumed by the Israelis. As far back as July 9, Sharon had let it be known that he had discussed with Philip Habib the prospect of sending Phalangist forces into West Beirut, and that Habib had allowed it was a possibility as long as they operated within the framework of the Lebanese army. Sharon had then taken up the point with Bashir, alluding to Habib's condition by observing, "It may be necessary to change their shirts." But whether it was to be the Phalange or the IDF that would take responsibility for flushing out Palestinian fighters and disarming their leftist Moslem allies, Saguy could see only disaster ahead for Israel.

The agreement that Philip Habib and Morris Draper had hammered out with such difficulty meant different things to different parties. Arafat believed that its fourth clause, worded according to his dictates to ensure the safety of the "law-abiding and noncombatant Palestinians who remain in Beirut," and framed as a matter of honor between Israel and the United States, would protect his now defenseless constituency from the vengeance of his enemies. Sharon, for his part, was more concerned about implementing the clause that committed the multinational force to withdraw promptly after the conclusion of the evacuation, lest the American, French, and Italian soldiers become a shield for the men whom Arafat was presumed to be leaving behind. The Habib agreement also stipulated that the foreign soldiers be replaced within thirty days by the regular Lebanese army—which would come under Bashir's control after his inauguration—and Sharon understood that, either in concert with the Phalange or on its own, the Lebanese army would promptly disarm the members of the leftist Moslem Mourabitoun, the Shiite Amal, and other smaller militias, accounting for a total of about 1,000 men. But the first priority, as far as Ariel Sharon was concerned, was to eradicate every last trace of the PLO in Beirut.

The first attempt to "straighten out" the situation in Beirut took place on August 23, 1982, in the Burj el-Barajneh refugee camp, which was surrounded on three sides by IDF units. On Bashir's orders a battalion of the regular Lebanese army entered the camp, began making mass arrests, and searched for arms caches. Some of the Palestinian fighters in Burj el-Barajneh fled to nearby camps—Sabra, Shatilla, and Fakahani—and the Lebanese troops went on to raze "illegal structures" at the edge of the camp (a detail that would later be exploited with a macabre twist when the Phalangists entered Sabra and Shatilla). Altogether, some 230 men from Burj el-Barajneh were placed under arrest.

Following the operation from a distance, the restless Phalangist officers were outspoken about what they intended to do when, at long last, they too would be allowed to enter West Beirut. Well before the murder of their revered commander, with ghoulish delight they bragged of the slaughter they would visit upon the Palestinians and the havoc they would wreak on their other political foes. For instance, soon after Bashir's election, one of the authors was invited by Jesse Sokar, the Phalangist liaison officer attached to the IDF's paratroop division, to join him, in Phalangist uniform, when his men entered West Beirut. "It's time you learned how to use a knife properly!" he teased, his eyes shining. "But note," he added, suddenly stern, as the subject was now one of Phalangist honor, "no rape of girls under the age of twelve is allowed!" When all he received in response was a reproving look, Soker remarked crisply, "This isn't Switzerland or Denmark, you know."

The fact is that some of the Phalangists had reason to view the Israelis as like-minded allies. Weeks before Bashir's death, for example, their chief intelligence officer Elias (Elie) Hobeika, was already engaged in a low-keyed "liquidation campaign" to "take out" purported Syrian agents and partisans of the PLO in Sidon and the vicinity of Tyre—areas firmly under the IDF's control. The slightly balding, thirty-five-year-old Hobeika had a perpetually disheveled look about his thin but muscular body, befitting his reputation as the Phalange's hatchet man. Known for his cold ruthlessness, physical courage, and keen wit, Hobeika had risen to a position of influence in the Phalangist movement well before the war. During the siege of Beirut, when he coordinated intelligence on the movements and hideouts of the PLO's senior officials, Hobeika was in daily contact with Israeli officers and made no secret of his belief that the only way out of the Lebanese imbroglio was through a cathartic bloodbath.

Bashir's assassination was a heavy blow to Elie Hobeika; not only had he been a close personal friend of the president-elect, he had in fact been responsible for Bashir's safety.

Ariel Sharon and Bashir Gemayel had reached an understanding about sending a Lebanese force into West Beirut—be it the regular army, the Phalange, or a combination of the two. But now that Bashir was gone, so, presumably, was the understanding. Worse yet, with Bashir's death the

Israelis had lost their most effective influence on the Lebanese army proper. On the day of the explosion in Ahsrafiya, in a follow-up to the official raid on Burj el-Barajneh, Maj. Gen. Amir Drori held a talk with Lebanese army officers and commanders of the Lebanese Forces to impress on them the need to continue their own searches of the refugee camps. He particularly urged the army's commander of the Beirut district, Col. Michel Awan, to repeat the Burj el-Barajneh operation in other areas of the city. But then, after Bashir's death, the Lebanese army, despite repeated appeals from Drori to come forth and establish its control over the Palestinian areas of Beirut, would not set foot out of its barracks.

At about 9:00 P.M. on the day Bashir was assassinated, though still before his fate had been ascertained, Ariel Sharon summoned Chief of Staff Eitan to his office and told him to prepare to take the key junctions and commanding areas of West Beirut. Eitan's adjutant, Lt. Col. Zeev Zachrin, would later testify before the Kahan Commission of Inquiry into the Events at the Refugee Camps in Beirut—in contradiction to Sharon's testimony—that during this meeting Sharon indicated for the first time that the Phalangists, not the IDF, would be going into the refugee camps. One way or another, the first order alerting the army to stand by to execute "Operation Iron Mind," the takeover of West Beirut, made no mention whatever of the Phalange. (It later emerged that no operational order detailing the role the Phalangists were to take in the refugee camps was ever issued in writing, an intriguing point in itself.)

Shortly thereafter that same evening, when Prime Minister Begin spoke with the chief of staff and expressed concern about protecting the Moslems from the vengeance of the Phalangists, Eitan made no reference to Phalangist forces going into the camps. And at 10:30 P.M. when confirmation of Bashir's death arrived in Israel, Sharon and Begin held a phone conversation in which the prime minister approved the dispatch of Israeli forces into West Beirut to avert chaos, and again Begin was not informed of any decision to send the Phalange into the camps. Nor was the Cabinet called together to decide on the move into West Beirut, which in itself contravened the terms of the withdrawal agreement. It was not until almost thirty-six hours later, when the Cabinet finally convened on Thursday evening, that the ministers, like Begin, were appraised of the Phalangists' involvement in the action.

Yet the plan to use the Phalangists in the camps was known to at least Eitan and Drori, for after receiving the order to move into West Beirut at first light the two men drove to the Phalange headquarters at Qarantina in the dead of night to present the plan for taking the Moslem half of the city. The Phalangist commanders, still stunned by the day's events, agreed to take the mop-up of the refugee camps upon themselves. First they asked for assistance from Israeli armor and artillery, but Eitan turned them down. Then Fadi Frem, the commander of the Lebanese Forces, asked for and got a twenty-four-hour deferral to organize his men. Drori (who would later testify that he had been skeptical about the Phalangists' keeping their commitment) went on to meet with officers of the Lebanese army to ensure that, if their forces were not going to cooperate by moving into the city and taking over the camps, they would at least remain in their barracks and not oppose the IDF action.

With those two points established, at 5:00 A.M. on Wednesday, September 15, the IDF began to move into West Beirut. First Brig. Gen. Amos Yaron's division penetrated the city from the south along two axes running parallel to the refugee camps. Later that day Brig. Gen. Yitzhak Mordechai's division began to enter the northern sector of the city, moving west from the port into the residential quarters of Ras Beirut. Both forces moved slowly and cautiously along main routes only, their immediate aim being to link up. Simultaneously, Yaron's forward command post was moved to the roof of a deserted six-story building overlooking the Shatilla camp, and it was from there that the chief of staff, in his distinctive Australian hat, watched the battle unfold.

At 9:00 A.M. Sharon arrived at the forward command post together with Saguy. After being told of the Phalange's willingness to enter the camps, he repeated his order to send them in "under the IDF's supervision." Of the fourteen men present on that occasion, three—Sharon, his aide Avi Duda'i, and Eitan—would later testify that the subject was discussed on that roof. Saguy denied that he had heard any such order issued, going so far as to place in evidence a photograph showing him seated off to the side. The subject of cooperation with the Phalange was a particularly sensitive one for Saguy that morning, for on the way to Beirut he had made a last-ditch effort to put distance between Israel and the Phalange by suggesting that, with Bashir gone, the Israelis should sever all ties with his lieutenants. Sharon would not hear of it, and Saguy was probably still smarting from this latest rebuff.

Yet he did accompany the defense minister when Sharon drove off to Qarantina for a meeting with Frem, Hobeika, Zahi Bustani, and four other Phalangist officers. The meeting took on as much a political tone as a military one. Sharon chided the Phalangists to pull themselves together, overcome their shock, and not lose control of their men (who had been confined to their barracks as a precautionary measure after the assassination). He also pressed the obviously wary Phalangists to fill the political vacuum left by Bashir's death as quickly as possible and recommended the old scheme of having Sarkis appoint a Maronite prime minister who would assume presidential powers at the end of Sarkis's term. "You must act immediately," he exhorted them, implying that if they delayed the Moslems would exploit the situation to revise all the ground rules and deprive the Maronites of the presidency. As an essential part of their bid to retain power, Sharon advised them to wrest control of the Lebanese army, "either directly or with our aid." And as additional impetus to inspire the Phalangists to swift action, he warned that the Americans were waiting in the wings and might propose Camille Chamoun—a rival of the Phalangists—for the presidency. Then the whole game would be up.

Steering the conversation onto the subject of West Beirut, Sharon kept up the pressure, assuring the Phalangists that the IDF would take control of the city but that it needed their help. "We'll take over the key points and junctions, but your army must go in too, perhaps behind us."

"We'll try to get legal cover [for the Phalangist entry into West Beirut], but if we fail, will we Phalangists still be useful to your plan?" one of them asked.

Hearing strains of yet another attempt to evade taking action, Sharon replied unequivocally. "You make every effort to obtain legitimacy [by operating within the framework of the Lebanese army]. If you don't succeed, we'll support you anyway."

At one point Sharon began to stress the need to destroy whatever was left of the PLO's infrastructure in West Beirut and to point out the danger of letting terrorists remain free in the city. "I don't want a single one of them left!" is how he was quoted in one of the transcripts of the session.

"How do you single them out?" Hobeika asked.

It was an odd question for a high-ranking officer in a militia known for its talent at ferreting out terrorists, and Sharon decided to evade it. "I'm off to Bekfaya now," was his reply. "We'll discuss that at a more restricted session." And on that obscure, perhaps sinister note, the meeting ended.

Months later, Rafael Eitan learned of the existence of a small notebook containing notes on this conversation taken down by an Israeli colonel and kept in General Saguy's office. The chief of staff demanded a copy immediately, hoping to find evidence that would prove a provocative role for Sharon. But he was disappointed by its contents: nowhere in these notes was there evidence that the minister had incited the Phalangists to violence. Eitan then tried to uncover details of the subsequent talk that Sharon had with Pierre and Amin Gemayel in Bekfaya toward noon on Wednesday, September 15, and for days the corridors of the defense establishment were awash with rumors about the nature of the exchange. The transcript of the talk at the Gemayel home was written by a senior Mossad agent, but it too failed to corroborate the claim, eventually made before the commission's investigators, that revenge against the Palestinians in West Beirut had entered the conversation at Bekfaya.

Neither side, Israeli or Lebanese, has seen fit to dispel the persistent rumor about what was in fact said on that occasion. The Kahan Commission did not publish any details from the partial transcript it received through the Mossad; and the Phalange, far from revealing the contents of the talk, established an inquiry commission to track down the leak that was the source for an inconsequential piece on the subject in the French magazine *Nouvel Observateur*.

Whatever was or was not said in Bekfaya would therefore appear to be either innocuous or explosive. And whether or not Maronite vengeance was on Sharon's mind, the prospect was in the air. For while the defense minister was making his way from one Phalangist stronghold to another, the likely behavior of the Lebanese Forces was being discussed in the prime minister's office with Morris Draper, who had come to see Begin and Shamir for an explanation of the IDF's movements earlier that morning. Begin assured the special ambassador that Israel's sole motive was to prevent bloodshed. "The question is how the people will behave," the prime minister put to Draper. "The Phalangists are handling themselves properly. Their commander, Fadi Frem, has survived, and he is in control of his men. He's a good man, and we trust him not to cause any problems. As for the others, who knows?"

Draper left that meeting with the distinct impression that the Israeli action was a modestly defined operation to take key positions in the city. "If we had been told that the Phalange were also going in, I would have let out a howl!" he later remarked bitterly. Based on this understanding of the situation, Draper told the Lebanese that the United States would press the Israelis to withdraw from Beirut quickly, so there was no need for the the Lebanese army to get involved. The Lebanese followed this advice to the letter, and it would become a crucial issue.

Back in Beirut, as they closed in around the refugee camps, Yaron's forces encountered heavy fire mostly from small arms and machine guns, but also rocket-propelled grenades and bazooka rockets. The unit moving west toward the division's forward command post lost one officer and suffered twenty wounded from what it identified as more than a hundred sources of fire. Fire from the camps was also directed at the command post itself, and the officers gathered on the roof were forced to take cover behind a wall. The chief of staff was reportedly the only one who stood his ground to follow the battle.

The question of how many Palestinians were actually engaged in the fighting within the camps has not been answered satisfactorily to this day, and the Kahan Commission did not choose to address itself to the subject. Military men who were on the scene have estimated that a few dozen Palestinian fighters were probably involved in the exchanges of fire, and that there may have been up to 200 armed men in the camps working out of the countless bunkers built by the PLO over the years and stocked with generous reserves of arms and ammunition. The Palestinian fighters also had a network of subterranean tunnels at their disposal. What they lacked, however, was the public backing for a spectacular last stand. Talks with residents of Shatilla have revealed that there was considerable friction between some of the camp's *mukhtars* and the young men ready to fight. The war-weary elders argued that no good would come of prolonging the resistance; it would only lead to more civilian casualties, so better to raise white flags and save innocent lives. But the younger Palestinians, still exhilarated over Bashir's fortuitous death, kept up the fire, and in so doing they bolstered Sharon's resolve to wipe out every last token of resistance. And if the Lebanese were willing to take on the job, so much the better.

It was to settle the details of that very point that General Drori met with the commanders of the Lebanese Forces at eight o'clock that evening and received their assurances that they would be ready to go into the camps on the following morning. Even then, almost twenty-four hours before the Phalangists actually entered Sabra and Shatilla, Drori admonished them to be sure their men behaved like disciplined soldiers. This was but the first and far from the last in a series of fruitless warnings to the Phalangists to conduct themselves honorably inside the camps. Although the prime minister, defense minister, and chief of staff would contend before the inquiry commission that a massacre could not have been foreseen, such repeated warnings would seem to indicate, especially in light of the Phalange's known record of atrocities, that the senior military men in the field were wary of their intentions from the start.

As if to confirm such unspoken qualms, Drori then drove to West Beirut and again appealed to the Lebanese army to move in and take responsibility for the camps. His contact categorically refused, stiffly informing Drori that he had orders from the prime minister to refrain from any endeavor— except to open fire on Israeli soldiers, if necessary. Despite the bitter snub, however, this would not be Drori's last effort to spur the Lebanese army into action.

Early in the morning of Thursday, September 16, it suddenly seemed as though the whole operation was about to be aborted when Ariel Sharon issued an order to halt the IDF's advance into West Beirut. For almost twenty-four hours, he had been under heavy American pressure to pull his troops out of the Moslem half of the city, and now he appeared to be knuckling under. But then, almost as soon as the order was on the wires, something even more potent than American pressure caused Ariel Sharon to reverse himself, rescind the order, and direct the army to continue.

At 10:00 A.M., when Eitan arrived at Sharon's office, he was able to report that all was quiet in Beirut. The refugee camps were surrounded, and if the Phalangists or the Lebanese army were willing to enter them, they would be welcome to do so.

"I'd send in the Phalangists," Sharon observed.

Eitan's comment on the Phalangists later in that conversation was cautionary. "They're thirsting for revenge," he said, "and there could be torrents of blood."

At one point, Sharon picked up the phone and reported to Begin, "It's all over." In light of subsequent events, it is difficult to say just what he meant by that statement. For while the meeting in Sharon's office was in progress, several seemingly contradictory moves were taking place in Beirut. On the one hand, Israeli officers were trying to avert a bloody confrontation between the rival Lebanese elements by imploring the commanders of the leftist militias not to resist. At the same time, a delegation from the Phalange turned up at Yaron's forward headquarters to coordinate strategy for their forthcoming operations. And in the northern part of Beirut, special IDF squads began to assemble men in front of the deserted Holiday Inn Hotel and to interrogate dozens of residents about the location of hideouts and weapons stores. (Over the next ten days, huge quantities of ordnance—including twelve cannons, eight heavy mortars, Katyusha-mounted vehicles, and 520 tons of ammunition—were indeed removed from dozens of caches in West Beirut.) Thus what was originally portrayed as a move to preserve order and protect lives was evolving into an ambitious bid to "clean out" West Beirut.

At 4:00 P.M. on Thursday, Elie Hobeika turned up at Yaron's forward command post to finalize the details of his operation. He still had not managed to rally the full force that he had hoped to send into the camps, but Yaron pressed him not to delay any longer and to proceed with the 150 fighters he had at hand. Then he echoed Drori's earlier warning not to harm the civilian population, and as an extra precaution he set up observation posts on two rooftops with orders to monitor the Phalange's communications network.

A short while later, at 5:00 P.M., Morris Draper, Sam Lewis, and the American military attaché in Tel Aviv settled into chairs in the defense minister's office for a talk with Sharon, Eitan, Saguy, and two senior members of the Defense Ministry's staff. The minutes of this meeting are an astonishing document considering the fact that at that very hour Hobeika's men—most of whom belonged to an "elite" unit that specialized in fighting Palestinians—were waiting outside Shatilla for the signal to commence their operation.

"I was surprised by the IDF's move," Morris Draper began, trying to keep a mild tone. "The Lebanese want you to withdraw; then their army will go in."

"Who will go in?"

"The Lebanese army and the security forces," Draper repeated.

"And the Phalange," Saguy added in a flat, matter-of-fact voice.

"Not the Phalange!" Draper exclaimed in horror.

"Who's to stop them?" Saguy challenged in the same dry fashion.

"Are you *sure* the Phalange will go in?" Draper asked, his irritation giving way to curiosity as to what Saguy might know that he didn't. But when Saguy offered only the bland advice to "Ask their leaders," Draper abandoned the point and returned to his original argument. "The critical point for us is that everyone in the world believed us when we said that you wouldn't go into West Beirut, that you gave us your word on it. This is a crucial point for us."

"Circumstances changed, sir," Sharon said coldly.

"Once people believed that your word was good," Draper went on, hitting at what he presumed was the weak spot in the Israelis' shield of bland equanimity.

Finally he got a rise out of Sharon. "We went in because of the 2,000–3,000 terrorists who remained there," the defense minister exclaimed. "We even have their names!"

"I asked for those names, and you said there was an *enormous* list," Draper was goading him now, "but what you came up with is a minuscule one. . . . The Lebanese will take care of those who have remained behind. . . ."

"You know the Lebanese," Sharon retorted contemptuously. "We'll tend to our own affairs."

"You yourself said that the names were passed on to the Lebanese army and two men were arrested."

"May I say something," Eitan broke in on the increasingly pointless exchange. "They're not up to it. Let me explain to you. Lebanon is at a point of exploding into a frenzy of revenge. No one can stop them. Yesterday we spoke with the Phalange about their plans. They don't have a strong command. . . . They're obsessed with the idea of revenge. You have to know the Arabs well to sense something like that. If Amin tells the

Phalangists to wreak their vengeance, he'll legitimize what's going to happen. I'm telling you that some of their commanders visited me, and I could see in their eyes that it's going to be a relentless slaughter. A number of incidents already happened today, and it's a good thing we were there, rather than the Lebanese army, to prevent it from going further."

To hear Eitan tell it, the IDF was the last obstacle to a bloodthirsty rampage by the Phalange. Of course, he neglected to state that the Phalange forces were waiting outside Shatilla at that very moment because he, among others, had encouraged them to fight in the camps.

"How long will you stay?" Draper asked, as if finally resigned to the *fait accompli* and looking ahead to the next stage. But this time it was Lewis who grasped the initiative.

"You've taken over West Beirut!" the ambassador charged.

"That's right," Sharon said, just as belligerently, "after what happened."

"And that's contrary to what we agreed between us," Draper joined in. Now Sharon's annoyance flared.

"What did we agree about weapons being left behind?" he sneered. "Why portray *us* as the violators of the agreement. *They're* the ones who broke it!"

"You can't expect perfection," Draper objected. "You went in to take over there even though you pledged that you wouldn't."

"We're not sitting in a courtroom here, and don't you try to catch me on a technicality," the defense minister admonished. "You held your peace when there were cases of slaughter there in the past."

Draper seemed momentarily fazed by Sharon's barb, but Lewis picked up the slack. "How long will you stay in there? You still haven't answered the question?"

"I talked to Bashir, and he wanted us to go into Beirut and deal with the remaining terrorists."

"And that's what you're going to do now," Lewis stated.

"I'll tell you frankly," Sharon replied. "Of course that's what we intend to do, and we'll talk it over with the new president. . . ."

"And what if it's not in Lebanon's interest that you clean up Beirut, as you want to?" Lewis asked, still trying to back the minister into a corner. Sharon ducked the question by saying that he had to rush off to a Cabinet meeting in Jerusalem.

At the very time of this conversation in Tel Aviv, unbeknownst to the diplomats—and, once again, to the Israeli Cabinet—Elie Hobeika's men began to enter Sabra and Shatilla. Commanded by "Michel," "Maroun," and a third officer nicknamed "Paul," they broke into squads and penetrated Shatilla from the south and over the earth embankment in the west, storming forward behind a screen of continual fire. At first their movements were followed by Yaron's division intelligence officer from the roof of the forward command post, but the Phalangists dropped out of his sight the moment they entered the narrow alleyways. Nor had he any idea that at the same moment, without the knowledge or permission of the IDF, more of Hobeika's men were stealing into the camps from other directions. As the Palestinians' small-arms fire shifted toward the area in which the Phalangists had just made their appearance, one of the Phalangist liaison officers, Jesse Soker, asked for aid in the form of illumination, and a section of Israeli 81-mm mortars began to shoot off flares (later, illumination would also be provided by Israeli planes).

Sharon left the American diplomats at 6:50 P.M. and headed for a Cabinet meeting in Jerusalem. Ten minutes later the first hint of the butchery going on in the camps was picked up on the roof of the command post. Less than an hour had passed since the Phalangists entered the camps when one of the commanders of the force inside was heard to ask what he should do with the fifty women and children he had rounded up.

"That's the last time you're going to ask me," Hobeika snapped over the communications network. "You know what to do."

This brief exchange was heard by Lieutenant Elul, Yaron's adjutant, who immediately rushed to tell his commander. The latter responded by seeking out Hobeika and again warning him not to molest civilians.

During the inquiry commission's preliminary work, the father of one of the Phalangists involved in the massacre agreed to speak to a staff member on condition that his identity remain secret. He testified that Hobeika briefed his men before they entered the camps, and that according to what his son had told him an IDF officer had indeed made a point of saying that civilians were not to be harmed in any way. From their own commander, however, the men understood that their mission was to liquidate young Palestinians as a way of instigating a mass flight from the camps—in accordance with Bashir's vision of the final act of the war in West Beirut.

At 7:30 that Thursday evening, when the Cabinet convened in Jerusalem, Menachem Begin presented his ministers with a survey of events since Bashir's assassination, taking great pains to assuage their anger at not being consulted about the army's entry into West Beirut. Even if it was necessary to act quickly, charged Mordechai Zippori, the ministers could have been summoned in the morning, not thirty-six hours after the fact! Zevulun Hammer also gave vent to his anger. But by then there was no point in arguing the matter, and the Cabinet settled down to the business of the hour. Sharon reviewed the activity in West Beirut. In a presentation that lasted more than half an hour, he made no mention at all of the Phalangists' involvement.

While the ministers were thus being selectively briefed, in Beirut warning lights were flashed again when the man monitoring the Phalangists' communications network reported to Yaron's intelligence officer that he had just heard Soker being asked what to do with forty-five men caught inside the camp. "Do God's will," was the reply. Soon Soker turned up in the command post's improvised mess hall and told some of the officers there that 300 terrorists and civilians had been killed in the camp. But a short while later, coming back down from the roof, he must have thought better of that announcement, for he amended the number of casualties to 120. Yaron's response was to upbraid him about the civilian losses, and Soker assured him that from then on they would be contained as much as the fighting allowed.

This was the third time in the space of a few hours that Yaron had had to admonish a Phalangist officer against abusing civilians, so we can assume that the issue must have weighed heavily on his mind. Yet when he convened his officers for an update briefing at 8:40 that evening, he seemed reluctant to face up squarely to the problem.

"The Phalangists went in today," was how the division's intelligence officer opened the session, which was recorded by an officer from the IDF's History Department who happened to be present. "I don't know what level of combat they're exhibiting. It's hard to see it because it's dark. . . . One has the impression that the fighting is not particularly serious. They have suffered casualties, as you know: two wounded—one in the leg and one in the hand. . . . And it seems that they're trying to decide what to do with the people they find inside. On the one hand, there are evidently no terrorists in the camp; Sabra is empty. On the other, they've gathered up women, children, and probably old people and don't know quite what to do with them. Apparently some decision has been made to concentrate them together, and they're leading them off somewhere outside the camp. Yet I also heard [the remark] from Jesse, 'Do what your heart tells you because everything comes from God,' meaning I don't. . . ."

"Nothing," Yaron broke in at this point. "No, no. I went up to see him, and they're not having any problems."

"[There are] people left in the field? And there's no danger to their lives?" the intelligence officer asked.

"It won't . . . won't harm them," Yaron stammered.

In Jerusalem, the Cabinet was still in session. At 9:00 P.M., General Saguy asked to be excused. "I haven't slept for three nights," he told the understanding ministers and promptly left. He was therefore not present when the chief of staff received a note and broke the news that Phalangists were operating in two refugee camps. Eitan explained to the ministers that the IDF would see to it that the Lebanese troops carried out their task properly and that no Israeli soldiers would enter the camps, leaving the Phalangists to fight "according to their own methods." In emphasizing that the IDF could give the Phalangists their orders—which was emphatically not the case regarding the Lebanese army—Eitan implied that the force inside the camps was under firm Israeli control at all times.

When he came to analyze the possible repercussions of Bashir's murder, however, Eitan launched into a grisly forecast of mass carnage in Lebanon, not realizing the contradiction and the irony of what he was saying.

"Another thing that will happen—and it makes no difference whether we're there or not—is an outburst of vengeance that I don't know . . . I can imagine to myself how it will start, but I don't know how it will end. It will be between all of them, and neither the Americans nor anyone else can do anything about it. We can temper it, but they've already killed Druse there today . . . and one Druse casualty is [reason] enough for four Christian children to be killed tomorrow . . . and that's how it will start if we're not there. It will be a convulsion like no one has ever seen before. I can already see in their eyes what they're waiting for."

The head of the Mossad took a similar position. "When we learned of Bashir's death, we thought that two things could happen," he said. "First, that the whole city would erupt and that the Phalangist forces, suddenly bereft of their commander and itching for revenge, might go on a rampage. On the other hand, when the Palestinians and Lebanese organizations in West Beirut learned that the Phalangist leader was gone, *they* might start something, so that there was definitely a chance of a general flare up in the city."

The ministers took in these analyses quite matter-of-factly. The only one to comment on the paradox of wanting to prevent an outpouring of revenge but sending the Phalangists into the Palestinian refugee camps was David Levi. "When I hear that the Phalangists have already gone into certain quarters—and I know what vengeance means to them, the kind of slaughter [that would be involved], no one is going to belive that we went in there to maintain order, and we'll bear the blame. . . ."

Not a man in the room responded to Levi's comment. Perhaps no one heard it (the prime minister later testified that while Levi was speaking he himself had been immersed in drafting a Cabinet resolution), or more likely no one got the point. After all, for months the Israelis had been coaxing the Phalangists to join in the fighting in Beirut, and the Cabinet had been roundly criticized by the press for the acute passivity of Israel's supposed ally in Lebanon. Now that the Lebanese Forces had stepped forward to bear their share of the burden, relieving the IDF of the most dangerous and odious task of all (and a matter that the ministers had never been allowed to debate), the Cabinet found itself being warned that Israel's celebrated partners were little better than a gang of savage murderers who should be plucked out of the camps just when months of nagging, chiding, and cajoling had finally borne fruit. So if David Levi's message failed to sink in, it was undoubtedly because he had told his colleagues precisely what they least wanted to hear.

Failing to acknowledge an unpleasant fact does not change it, however. While the peeved ministers were deliberating in Jerusalem, the Phalangists were busy setting up their headquarters in a small grocery store and leading the civilians they had snared to a nearby garage. Throughout the night additional groups of women, children, and elderly people were escorted to other points in the camps. In addition to the wholesale slaughter of families, the Phalangists indulged in such sadistic horrors as hanging live grenades around their victims' necks. In one particularly vicious act of barbarity, an infant was trampled to death by a man wearing spiked shoes. The entire Phalangist action in Sabra and Shatilla seemed to be directed against civilians; whatever Palestinian fighters may have been in the area at the start had apparently fled northward. Only a dozen or so youngsters had continued firing after 6:00 P.M. on Thursday.

At 10:00 P.M., in a completely different sector of the front, Northern Command's intelligence officer was heard to comment that the Phalangists would be involved in the searches in West Beirut.

"There'll be a slaughter there!" predicted a major from Intelligence/Research in Tel Aviv who had been posted to Northern Command's forward headquarters in Aley. During the siege of Beirut this major, known among his colleagues as a vehement opponent of all collaboration with the Phalange, had assessed from his vantage point in Junieh that after the presidential election Bashir would turn his back on Israel. His reading now might therefore have been suspect as biased, but a few minutes after his outburst a phone call he happened to overhear in the next room convinced him that if anything his warning had been too mild. For at 10:30 P.M. Yaron's intelligence officer called Aley from the roof of the forward command post and reported what Jesse Soker had said about the casualties in the camps. Northern Command's intelligence officer asked him to check the matter out more thoroughly. The major, meanwhile, waited almost an hour for further information, then phoned his superiors at Intelligence Branch in Tel Aviv to pass on the item about the casualties, stressing that the report had aroused serious concern and should be brought to Saguy's attention. Seven hours would elapse before Saguy was apprised of the message.

Even so, on the night between Thursday and Friday, September 16–17, suspicions that atrocities were being committed in the camps had been aired in or passed on to four separate IDF headquarters: Yaron's command post just outside the camps, Northern Command's forward headquarters in Aley, Maj. Gen. Menachem Einan's headquarters in Behamdoun (which happened to receive a report written that evening by Yaron's intelligence officer), and Intelligence/Research in Tel Aviv. Yet in every one of these places, the information was treated as specious rumor. No one took any steps to alert General Drori. The report of the major from Intelligence/Research, as it turned out, was held up for a number of hours by a junior officer in the General Staff who deemed it of little importance. Saguy's subordinates decided to let him get a good night's sleep. And by the next morning, Friday, both Yaron's intelligence officer and the major from Intelligence/Research left on a tour of West Beirut. Thus two clarions of alarm were gone from the scene.

That night, while the two intelligence officers fretted and Saguy slept, at least two sharp exchanges took place on the roof of Yaron's command post. The first occurred when Jesse Soker asked to have the illumination of the camps renewed and Yaron's operations officer, Lt. Col. Bezalel Treiber, turned him down on the grounds that the Phalangists were killing civilians. Yaron, meanwhile, had lost his temper with Elie Hobeika because the search of the camps was not being carried out properly, and for the third time saw fit to address Hobeika harshly about ensuring the safety of civilians. On top of these explicit and implicit accusations, Israeli officers witnessed a heated exchange between Soker and some of his own comrades, which gave them the distinct impression that the Phalangist officers were divided among themselves about the course the operation was taking. Soker swore to Amos Yaron that all acts of murder would cease forthwith—thereby confirming fears that they were going on—and the Israelis present on the roof noticed that the Phalangist liaison was very perturbed. Apparently Hobeika likewise took Yaron's reprimand to heart —or at least wanted to create that impression—because he quickly went down into Shatilla to talk with his men (though we have no record of what he told them).

The most incredible thing about the whole ghastly business in Sabra and Shatilla was that the residents of the camps were themselves unaware of the slaughter going on around them. Hundreds of Palestinians who lived in the crowded alleys near the section of Shatilla where the Phalangists were at work failed to notice any signs of a harrowing bloodbath. Most of them went to sleep in their shelters or boarded themselves up in their homes as soon as they heard shooting nearby. Speaking to reporters a few days later, dozens of the camp's residents insisted that they had had no inkling of what was taking place just a few meters away, either on that first night or over the following two days. "If we had known that there were Phalangists inside, we would have fled!" one man explained reasonably. A *mukhtar* in Sabra was sure the IDF was going to take over the camp, so he preferred to hole up at home. "We saw the Israeli soldiers on the rooftops surrounding the camps and the tanks driving along the road," he explained, "but there was no sign of Phalangists."

Shortly after midnight Thursday, another equally inexplicable phenomenon occurred when a correspondent for the IDF radio station broke the story that the mop-up in the camps had been assigned to the Phalange. One would have thought it would be received as the most remarkable scoop, yet even though thousands of listeners throughout Israel and Lebanon heard that midnight news broadcast over the very popular and highly credited army station, the item didn't seem to register.

So another five hours passed before the communiqué from the intelligence major in Aley finally got to Saguy's adjutant, Lt. Col. Moshe Hevroni. At 6:15 that Friday morning Hevroni conveyed the report about "300 dead" to Saguy at his home. Saguy ordered that the report be checked out, but no further details were available, and the head of Intelligence/Research said that he had no information at all. Saguy's main contention before the Kahan Commission was that even on that Friday morning he was not yet aware that the Phalangists had been let into the refugee camps, but the judges could not credit that claim—if only because Saguy had been present on three occasions when the matter was discussed. In any event, early that afternoon Intelligence/Research informed Saguy that it was retracting its report about killings going on in the camps. The first leak out of the military establishment that something serious was amiss in Sabra and Shatilla came at 7:50 Friday morning, when Ze'ev Schiff, military correspondent for the daily *Haaretz,* heard of a *dabah* (Arabic for slaughter) from one of his contacts in the General Staff. Schiff immediately called several other sources in the offices of the General Staff, but each denied any knowledge of the rumor or belittled its veracity. The journalist weighed his next step carefully. Here he was with a rumor he could neither verify through his regular channels nor drop cold, it was so deeply disturbing. He decided to raise the matter before Communications Minister Mordechai Zippori, an old friend with his own network of reliable sources in the defense establishment and the clout to get through to the highest level of the political establishment, if necessary. But when Schiff phoned Zippori, he was told that the minister had spent the night in the north and would not be back until later that morning. Schiff reviewed his options again and decided to wait.

At about the same time, but much closer to the scene, Lt. Avi Grabowsky, the commander of a tank company stationed alongside one of the camps, noticed a squad of Phalangists leading groups of civilians to the sports stadium near Fakahani. A few minutes later he saw two Phalangists escorting a couple of men back into the camp, after which shots rang out and the two Phalangists reappeared alone. At first Grabowsky did not realize that a murder had taken place practically in front of his eyes. Only later did curiousity cause him to drive his tank up to the high earth embankment, from which vantage point he witnessed the murder of five women and children. As he was about to report the incident, members of his tank crew mentioned having already heard incidents of murder being reported over the network, and pointed out that the battalion commander, while replying that "it's not to our liking," had ordered his men not to intervene. Grabowsky continued his personal watch until 4:00 P.M., during which time he saw one other case of murder, when a Palestinian tried to resist his captors and was shot. When a militiaman passed within shouting distance of Grabowsky's tank and the Israelis asked him why his people were killing women and children, the Phalangist replied, "Women give birth to children, and children grow up into terrorists."

By this time most of the killing was over, though still unknown outside of Sabra and Shatilla, the Phalangists having prevented their prey from fleeing the camps by posting guards at the exits. A Danish TV cameraman who happened by the area that Friday caught sight of Phalangist militiamen stopping hysterical women who were trying to escape, but it didn't occur to him that corpses might lie rotting just a few dozen meters from where he stood. Also obscuring the situation was the fact that some of the people who had initially fled the camps were trying to return to their homes on Friday morning. One man who went back into Shatilla to bring his children milk lost his life before he could reach them. A young woman on her way to visit her mother was raped by four Phalangists. Furthermore, those going in the other direction and managing to get out safely did not complain of a massacre. One woman emerging from the area told Israeli soldiers that she had been beaten in the face with a rifle butt, and a man came running up to an Israeli officer shouting frantically that his son had been kidnapped, but no one so much as hinted at wholesale slaughter.

Neither were the foreign nationals in the vicinity of Sabra and Shatilla speaking in such terms. At 9:00 A.M. the ranking Red Cross representative in Beirut, Peter Cume, phoned Bruce Kashdan, his liaison with the Israeli Foreign Ministry in Beirut, to report that a Red Cross convoy that had driven into the area of the camps the previous evening had found about a thousand refugees and eighty wounded people in the Gaza Hospital. He also passed on the rumor that Phalangists had entered the hospital and removed the foreign medical personnnel. Later, Cume called back to say that most of the Palestinians had fled the Gaza Hospital (thirty-seven wounded and four doctors remained), while the other Palestinian hospital in the sector (the Acre Hospital) was deserted altogether. There was no intimation of a massacre in either of these conversations.

As Cume was holding his first conversation with Kashdan, the Phalange's operations officer, Fuad Abu Nader, strode into Yaron's forward headquarters and announced that he had put together a second force to go to work in the camps. Yaron took to the idea, having learned that the force then operating in Sabra and Shatilla was made up entirely of Hobeika's "elite" rather than regular Phalangist units. As Yaron later testified, he was, by then, already suffering from "an uneasy feeling" because of what he described as "the buzzing" about civilians being beaten and his impression of Hobeika's men and their predispositions. Welcoming the prospect of a more responsible force, Yaron supplied Abu Nader with a map and aerial photographs of the camps and marked how the relief force should continue the mop-up. The Phalangist was told to return that afternoon to present a coordinated plan.

At eleven o'clock General Drori arrived at the forward command post. It was then, as they huddled behind a wall from the sniper fire still coming out of the camps, that Yaron finally told Drori about his qualms and recommended that they call the whole operation off and stop the reinforcements from going in. Even though this was Drori's first awareness of Yaron's misgivings, his response was immediate and emphatic: he approved the request, then picked up the phone to the chief of staff and reported, among other things, that the Phalangists had "gone too far." By the time he had completed the call and told Yaron that Eitan was coming to Beirut, the division commander had already ordered the Phalangists to cease all activity and remain confined to the buildings already captured.

Around the same time, Ze'ev Schiff was seated in Mordechai Zippori's Tel Aviv office telling the minister what he had heard about a *dabah* and urging him to inquire whether there was anything to the rumor. Zippori tried to get through to a number of officers in intelligence and the security services. Failing to locate them, he changed directions and put through a call to Foreign Minister Yitzhak Shamir, who was scheduled to meet early that afternoon with Sharon, the Israeli intelligence chiefs, and Morris

Draper. Zippori told Shamir about Schiff's report and suggested that it was worth pursuing through his own contacts. Then the minister and the journalist passed the time waiting for Shamir's return call. They waited in vain. For Shamir, it transpired, never asked his staff to check out the rumor, and in his testimony before the inquiry commission he denied that Zippori had described in any dire way what was allegedly happening in the camps. When he appeared before the commission, however, Shamir was unaware that Schiff had been in the room when Zippori called him, and the journalist's testimony corroborated Zippori's version of their talk. In any event, the first attempt to circumvent the usual channels of command and communication reached a dead end in Yitzhak Shamir's office.

Some time after 1:00 P.M. Amos Yaron, concerned about what might still be going on in the camps, reversed his earlier order and allowed the Phalangists to relieve Hobeika's force with a unit detached from the regular battalion waiting at Khalde airport. Jeeps carrying 150 men drove into Shatilla, and Hobeika's men were supposed to come out. Yet it is all but certain that most if not all of Hobeika's fighters remained in the camp, so that instead of replacing troops, as Yaron had intended, the Phalangists had essentially reinforced their contingent.

As a consequence of his earlier talk with Yaron, at 3:00 P.M. Drori made yet another attempt to get the Lebanese army on its feet and into the camps. Speaking again to the Lebanese deputy chief of staff, Brig. Gen. Abbas Hamdan, at his headquarters within sight of the spot where the Phalangists were massed at the airport, Drori tried to appeal to the man's nobler instincts. "You know what the Lebanese are capable of doing to each other," he said, a note of genuine urgency in his voice. "When you go to [Prime Minister] Wazzan now, tell him again—you can see what's happening out here—and perhaps the time has come for you to do something. You're going to see Draper. Ask him for some *good* advice this time, that he agree to your going into the camps. It's important. It's about time you did it."

While Drori was addressing this plea to Hamdan, Rafael Eitan's plane landed at Khalde airport. Drori joined him soon thereafter and, together with Amos Yaron and their respective aides, continued on by car to the Phalange headquarters in Qarantina.

Meanwhile a second effort to secure information outside regular channels was set in motion when Israel Television's military correspondent, Ron Ben-Yishai, arrived at the airport to send some footage out on an Israeli military flight. As he boarded the plane, a battalion commander stopped him and asked, "Have you heard about the havoc going on in Shatilla and Sabra?"

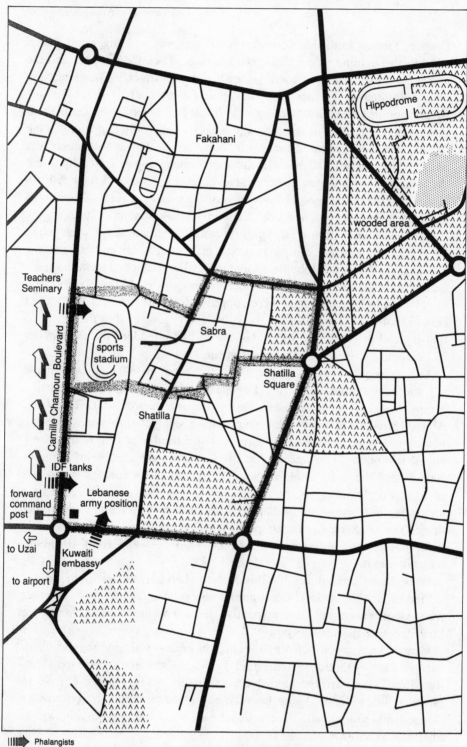

SABRA AND SHATILLA

"No," Ben-Yishai said, his professional instincts aroused. "Did you see it yourself?"

The officer shook his head but repeated, "I heard the Phalangists are doing awful things there."

The reporter decided not to press the man and quickly left to pursue his tip in the field. On the tarmac he saw the regular Phalangist force still waiting for the signal to go into the camps, and his curiosity was piqued even further. Here is how Ben-Yishai described his experiences tracking down the story in a private letter written to Prime Minister Begin three days later:

> The officers and men of that force told us candidly that, in coordination with the IDF, they were on their way in to drive the terrorists out of the refugee camps. Some of the soldiers made it quite clear to the other journalists and myself that they intended to kill the inhabitants of the camps without mercy, and they resorted to certain idioms and hand gestures that left no room for doubt.
>
> What I heard from our officer [in the plane] and from the Christian militiamen aroused my curiosity and left me feeling uneasy. I decided to drive toward the refugee camps, and on the way, still within the airport, I met another officer—one of [Amir Drori's] aides—and asked him whether he too had heard about the "nasty business" the Phalangists were up to in the camps. He patted my arm through the open window of his car but said nothing. I asked him again, and again I was rewarded with silence. I tried to ask other officers in the field; most of them knew nothing or had heard something very vague and unfounded . . .

But word of something wrong was definitely getting around, because at 4:00 P.M. three American journalists arrived at their embassy in Beirut and told one of the senior diplomats that they had heard the Phalangists were in the refugee camps. The diplomat phoned the local chargé d'affaires, Robert Barrett, who passed the report on to Draper. Meanwhile, a member of the embassy's political section telephoned the highest source in the Phalange, Amin Gemayel, and asked him to confirm or deny the report. Amin replied that he knew nothing about it but would check the matter out, and shortly thereafter he returned the call to say that the Phalangists were indeed in the camps but would soon be leaving.

Half an hour later, a most cordial meeting began at the Phalangists' barracks in Qarantina, with Fadi Fraem, Zahi Bustani, Fuad Abu Nader, Josef Abu Halil, and Elie Hobeika in the company of the Israeli chief of staff, his deputy, Moshe Levi, Drori, Yaron, and a number of aides. The one subject conspicuously absent from the agenda was the departure of the Lebanese Forces from Sabra and Shatilla. In reporting on the action completed so far, Elie Hobeika spoke of a tough battle in which his forces had suffered two dead and some forty wounded. He claimed that there were hardly any civilians left in the camps and gave no indication of his troops having killed any noncombatants—certainly not of having perpetrated an all-out massacre. Fadi Frem raised the problem of the American pressure being exerted on the Phalange to pull out of the camps, and in almost the same breath asked for additional arms, command cars, and medical equipment. It was his way of expressing the resolve to go on with the action anyway.

Nor did any of the Israelis touch upon the rumors about the killing of civilians. Despite the previous night's scenes on the roof of the forward command post and Yaron's discreet talk with Drori that morning, the whole meeting remained geared toward beefing up the Phalangist presence in the camps. Eitan gave the Phalangists permission to remain in the camps until dawn the next morning. When the Israelis were asked to supply bulldozers for the purpose of razing "illegal structures," Moshe Levi protested that such a move had political implications and should first be taken up with the higher-ups in the Phalange. But the Mossad supported the request, and Eitan acquiesced. Second thoughts caught up with him afterward in the corridor when Yaron advised him to furnish only one bulldozer and Drori ordered that its identifying IDF marks be removed. (In the end, the Phalangists couldn't use this bulldozer, not being trained to operate it properly.) Moreover, as they left the building, the Israelis noticed two bulldozers already loaded onto trailers and apparently headed for West Beirut. When the truth about the killings was finally known, it became clear that this equipment had been requested to dispose of the hundreds of corpses scattered through the camps, not to demolish unsightly or unsanctioned buildings.

The free movement of militiamen in and out of the camps continued over the next hours, to the point where the Israelis lost track of the number of fighters inside. Rather than stabilize the situation, the fresh forces joined in the slaughter with alacrity. Indeed, they seemed far less concerned about concealing their deeds than their predecessors. Dozens of Palestinian women were bundled onto trucks and driven through the streets of East Beirut, their Phalange escorts gleefully introducing them to passersby as brand-new Palestinian widows courtesy of Phalangist guns. One such truck was driven as far as Bekfaya before returning to Uzai, from where the women fled into the city.

By now they were not the only ones running for their lives. At 6:00 P.M.,

Colonel Yair, commander of the IDF's paratroop brigade, told Yaron over the network that women and children fleeing north from the camps were spreading tales of atrocities and would have to be brought under control. When the commander of another brigade broke in on this transmission, Yaron promptly ordered them both to stop using the wireless and asked Yair to report to him personally. Then he convened his officers and told them to keep the Phalangists from circulating anywhere outside the camps until their planned withdrawal the following morning. His intentions were probably good: he wanted to contain both the danger and the damage. But rather than root out the source of the problem, all he effectively did was seal the murderers in with their victims.

At approximately that same hour, Morris Draper was on the phone to Amin Gemayel complaining about his breach of promise: the Phalangists had still not left the camps. An hour and a half later, the special ambassador phoned Bruce Kashdan, who represented the Israeli Foreign Ministry in Beirut, and passed on a complaint from Prime Minister Wazzan that murder was being committed by uniformed men in the Acre Hospital and that Phalangists were loose in Shatilla. To stiffen the impact of those charges, Draper added that American sources reported 200 Phalangists standing at the ready at Khalde airport. "Contriving to employ the Phalangists in West Beirut could lead to terrible consequences," he boomed into the receiver. The words must have been ringing in Kashdan's ears as he dialed David Kimche, the director-general of the Foreign Ministry, and reported on his conversation with Draper. Upon checking with IDF headquarters at Aley, however, Kashdan was told that Phalangists had infiltrated the camps via the checkpoints manned by the Lebanese army!

Enough pressure had built up inside the ranks of the IDF by that evening for unusual measures to be taken. At 8:30 a group of officers from the armored battalion stationed opposite Shatilla paid Ron Ben-Yishai an informal visit at the apartment he rented for the Israeli television crews in Beirut. "It was from the officers of this unit that I first heard something explicit," Ben-Yishai related in his letter to Begin. "Almost all [of them] had heard stories from their subordinates about residents of the refugee camps being placed up against the wall and shot . . . and similar tales that attested to something untoward going on in the camps." But when he asked his guests if they themselves had seen anything of this sort, the answer was negative. The senior officer among them, who impressed Ben-Yishai as the most upset, added indignantly that had he seen anything himself, he would immediately have reported it to the front commander and gone higher up, if need be.

While the officers were sharing their disquiet with Ben-Yishai on that eve of the Jewish New Year, bulldozers were feverishly working to cover up the evidence of Phalangist iniquity in Sabra and Shatilla. Rafael Eitan arrived home at his farm in the Galilee at 9:00 P.M. and picked up the phone to Ariel Sharon, who was spending the holiday eve on his ranch in the south. Eitan reported that the Phalangist operation had been halted and that the men would come out of the camps the next morning. "They overdid it," he said, according to Sharon's version of this talk, though Eitan denied that he made any reference at all to the Phalangists' behavior and implied that the action had stopped because it was completed. (This conversation would become the subject of a bitter clash between the two men during the Kahan Commission investigation.) Either way, however, at 11:30 Sharon received another phone call, this time from TV correspondent Ron Ben-Yishai, leaving no doubt about what was happening in the camps. Ben-Yishai reconstructed the conversation as follows:

> I apologized for calling at that hour, explained that I was phoning from Beirut, and told him everything I knew [instead of "Phalangists" I used the expression "our allies"]. I remember telling him, among other things, that something must be done to stop it, that IDF officers know about it, and we'll be in a terrible fix. . . . The defense minister, who had been awakened by the call, listened attentively. He asked if I knew any details, and I told him exactly where the Israeli soldiers had seen the murders and executions, explaining to him that the place wasn't far from the division headquarters south of Shatilla. The conversation lasted about four to five minutes, during which I did most of the talking. Minister Sharon hardly responded, and I refrained from asking him any questions. Finally, we wished one another a Happy New Year and hung up.

Thus on the night of September 17 a spate of reports about incidents of murder—or at least rumors and suspicions about atrocities in the camps—were known to more than a few officers in Beirut, to the chief of staff, the minister of defense, Northern Command, and Intelligence Branch. Sharon did not consider it necessary to ring the chief of staff after speaking with Ben-Yishai. As he stated before the Kahan Commission, he was satisfied with Eitan's earlier report that the Phalangists would be leaving the camps on the following morning. Eitan, Drori, Levi, Yaron, and other officers knew that the Phalangists would be in the camps all night and that they were using bulldozers; they also knew about the flight of panic-stricken civilians northward. Yet there was no attempt to get to the bottom of all "the buzzing"—whether out of sheer indifference or because the reports

were discredited or because the key men in the field were disc
their own problems (such as the search for three missing crew men
a tank that had overturned in downtown Beirut). Nor were steps taken to
hasten the departure of the Lebanese Forces or put an end to the wanton
bloodletting. And outside the army, the two attempts by journalists to get
around the usual channels by direct approaches to ministers had failed to
elicit the intervention that might have been expected, either by Shamir or
Sharon.

And so a second night of bloodshed and terror settled over the streets
and alleys of the two hapless camps. At 6:30 the next morning—an hour
and a half after the Phalangists were supposed to have come out—Amos
Yaron peered into Shatilla through binoculars and beheld the first of the
many dismal sights that would fill that day. Members of the Lebanese
Forces were conducting a group of about fifteen fair-complexioned people
dressed in white and green hospital coats in the direction of his headquarters. These "prisoners" were foreign doctors and nurses who had been
rounded up with the rest of the medical staff of Gaza Hospital and separated from their Lebanese and Palestinian colleagues, who had been ordered to sit up against the walls of a street in Sabra together with hundreds
of other civilians. As they were marched through the camp to the command
post, the foreign doctors and nurses could see corpses strewn about the
streets and bulldozers at work in the shadowed alleys.

Choked with anger, Yaron flew down the stairs accompanied by one of
his officers and an Israeli doctor. The commander of the Phalangist escort
met the Israelis and turned over his captives with the smug explanation
that they were "members of Baader-Meinhof"—the West German terrorist gang. Yaron rewarded him for his trouble by throwing him out of the
building. Meanwhile, the Israeli doctor debriefed his foreign colleagues
and sent them on their way. Three of these foreign nationals were later
brought from Lebanon by special car to testify before the Kahan Commission.

After that incident, Yaron began pressing the Phalangist officers to speed
up their exit from the camps. They were supposed to have been out by
5:00 A.M., now it was almost seven, and still they were loading the arms
and ammunition they had uncovered in the area as their fair share of booty.
Nor was there any sign of their exit at eight o'clock. That was about the
time Ron Ben-Yishai approached the camps with his film crew, and here
is how he described the scene in his letter to Begin:

> The Phalangists were driving a long line of women, children, and
> elderly people ahead of them at a run. Some of these people were

covered with blood, others were wailing and shouting, and some had their faces streaked with dirt. [The refugees] shouted at us that they had been separated from their menfolk, whom the Phalangists had marched off elsewhere. The members of the "Lebanese Forces" tried to prevent us from filming by shooing us away from the edge of the camp. While we were arguing with them, a senior IDF officer brought the procession to a halt. Through a loudspeaker mounted on one of the buildings, the women and children were told to return to their homes. The Christian militiamen were ordered to leave the area, and thus, essentially, the massacre was halted.

Hundreds of Palestinians from the two camps had been assembled in the sports stadium, where Israeli officers now distributed milk and cookies while investigators began to interrogate the men in their remaining search for members of the PLO. Of the forty-four men interrogated from this group, not one spoke of a massacre.

The full extent of the disaster began to emerge during the next hours, piece by harrowing piece. Some time before eight that morning, prior to his departure for synagogue, the prime minister had received a call from Sam Lewis complaining about the murder of patients and staff in Gaza Hospital. Begin contacted Eitan, told him of the call, and asked him to investigate. Eitan checked the matter through his own channels and was told that the report was untrue. (Begin could not recall having spoken to either man that morning and testified before the Kahan Commission that he had spent the entire morning in synagogue. Scores of fellow worshipers volunteered to corroborate that fact, but it proved irrelevant, for a further inquiry revealed that the conversations had taken place before the prime minister left for the holiday services. The incident also called attention to the fact that the prime minister's aides did not follow an orderly procedure in logging phone calls.)

The phone wires were crackling in Beirut that morning too. At 10:00 A.M. Morris Draper called Bruce Kashdan and asked him to relay an urgent message to Sharon. "You must stop the acts of slaughter," he dictated into the receiver in short, choppy sentences betraying the depth of his rage. "They are horrifying. I have a representative in the camp counting the bodies. You should be ashamed. The situation is absolutely appalling. They're killing children! You have the field completely under your control and are therefore responsible for that area." Kashdan relayed the message to David Kimche's office, and the defense minister replied at 1:00 P.M. that the Phalangist forces had been driven out of the camps. Then Sharon phoned the prime minister, but was told by Begin's son that he was still in synagogue. He did not try Begin again before 5:00 P.M., and the prime minister did not return Sharon's 1:00 P.M. call.

During these hours journalists and television crews began flocking to the camps, and it was from their descriptions that the Israeli officers began to apprehend the magnitude of the disaster. At 11:30, when Drori came to Yaron's headquarters and was told of the reports coming out of the camps, he issued strict orders forbidding any Israeli soldier to set foot inside Sabra or Shatilla, lest the IDF be implicated in the killing. This edict prevented the army from conducting its own assessment and left it wholly dependent on outside sources for information. As a result, as late as Saturday afternoon the men in Yaron's headquarters still believed that the toll of dead was a few dozen, and some high-placed Israelis in Beirut had yet to hear of the massacre at all. A senior Mossad officer, for example, first got word of the tragedy from his son, who phoned from Tel Aviv and asked caustically, "What have you been up to there, Dad?" To confound the situation even further for the chagrined Israelis, all of the Phalangist officers who had been in the sector promptly vanished; it was days before anyone in the IDF could locate and speak to them.

The prime minister of Israel heard about the massacre not from Sharon or Eitan or Kimche or any others of his officials but from the BBC. That was at 5:00 P.M.! Immediately he phoned Sharon, and the defense minister in turn demanded a detailed report from the army "because it was then," he later claimed, "I first had reason to suspect that the chief of staff's report on the extent of the killing and the measures adopted to prevent it did not faithfully reflect the situation."

Queried by the American embassy in Tel Aviv, Sharon adamantly denied that Israel had had any knowledge of or connection with the Phalangist action. It was a long holiday weekend; the Cabinet was scattered and the religious ministers were incommunicado because of Rosh Hashanah. From his ranch in the Negev, Sharon's instinctive reaction was to disassociate his country, and himself, from the whole bloody business—a political holding action until more hard information was available and the government could decide how to proceed. To those on the receiving end of this strategy, however, it smacked of a cover-up.

The Phalangists, meanwhile, were seizing the initiative by releasing their own version of events. At 6:30 the state-run Voice of Lebanon radio announced that "members of Haddad's militia" had entered Sabra and Shatilla, arrested young men, and killed a number of them, and at 10:45 the Phalangists' Radio Free Lebanon broadcast an emphatic denial that its forces had anything to do with the carnage in the camps. These were the opening gambits in a perfidious campaign to clear the Phalange and shift the blame onto Israel. The Israelis were to fight back with a countereffort to clear their army of any association with the slaughter by alleging that the Phalangists had infiltrated the camps from the east without prior coordination—meaning that they had sneaked in from one direction not covered by the IDF.

The next morning Rafael Eitan flew to Beirut for a showdown of sorts with Fadi Frem and the rest of the Phalangist commanders. His usual directness was now augmented by outrage as he demanded that they publicly own up to the crime committed by their men. All he could elicit from his shamefaced allies was silence. Frem averted his gaze and finally mumbled that the Phalange would not shirk responsibility for its deeds but that it could not admit culpability before the parliamentary vote that was expected to elect Amin Gemayel president. While that meeting was going on in Qarantina, the president-prospective issued a statement deploring the massacre without in any way indicating who was responsible for it.

Late that day the senior echelon of the Phalange was plunged into a bitter debate on how to contain the damage caused by the wanton killing. Some of the commanders feared that the massacre would destroy the hard-won alliance with Israel and proposed that the movement issue a new announcement ascribing the casualties to the bitter fighting between the terrorists and one Phalangist unit. But Elie Hobeika adamantly refused to consider the suggestion and warned that he would not stand for having his men turned into scapegoats. Finally, the movement's leader, Sheikh Pierre Gemayel, ruled that under no circumstances should the Phalange admit to any involvement in the massacre, lest such a confession wreck Amin's chances of gaining the presidency and embarrass the Moslem leadership into abandoning its efforts to reach at least a semblance of rapprochement with the Phalange. In private talks with Moslem statesmen, the elder Gemayel conceded that a few Phalangists had been in the camps during the massacre but characterized them as "Israeli agents" who were not following his orders. "Sharon had a good many Judas Iscariots in our ranks," he lamented—and he clung to this rendition for months. A whole year was to pass before Fadi Frem admitted publicly that the massacre was perpetrated by "Lebanese elements."

Oddly enough, up to the time of this writing, the PLO has carefully refrained from placing responsibility for the massacre on the Phalange. Arafat and his lieutenants insist that "at most the Israeli soldiers were assisted by a handful of guides from Haddad's militia." The Moslem leadership in Lebanon professes the same version. After he declared that "no members of the Phalange were in West Beirut during the massacre," Saeb Salam was asked why he was deliberately ignoring facts. "If one is permitted to kill for one's country, how much more admissible it is to lie for it," was his laconic reply. Thus a broad-based understanding was quickly forged in Lebanon to salvage the prospect of collaboration between the Moslem majority and Amin Gemayel's administration. It was simply convenient for all these parties to draw together behind the transparent lie that Israel alone was responsible for the bloodshed.

In a curious but telling coda to the massacre, there is a welter of fragmentary testimony to the effect that the murders kept on throughout Saturday and Sunday, after journalists and foreign diplomats had begun to enter the area. On Saturday a group of women emerged from Sabra and told a Mossad agent that the killing was continuing. On Sunday Israeli security agents encountered a number of women and children who had fled to the vicinity of the Abdel Nasser mosque on Corniche Mazraa and asked that the IDF enter the camps to protect them because the massacre had not stopped. Other women approached an Israeli officer on Rue de l'Université that morning with a similar tale, and one young woman told an Israeli investigator that on Sunday morning she witnessed Phalangists murdering women and children in one of the camps.

On Sunday morning, hundreds of angry women came streaming out of the camps shouting that "Haddad's men" had come back to kill. Colonel Yair drove his car into the heart of Sabra to find out the reason for the mass hysteria. He got all the way to the camp's main square but saw no sign of violence of any kind. On his way back out, Yair came upon Drori, who had arrived to investigate the reports personally. "I was in the thick of it," Yair told his commander, "and I didn't see a thing." The Kahan Commission was unable to reach an unequivocal verdict on whether or not the Phalangists remained in the camps after Saturday morning, but it is difficult to discount the possibility that bloodshed may have continued in houses and alleys at the very height of the furor, despite the fact that the area was already crawling with journalists and photographers!

On Sunday night, at the close of the Rosh Hashanah holiday, the Israeli Cabinet convened to get the full story of the massacre. They heard Sharon, Eitan, and Drori all confirm that, contrary to what they had been feeding the Americans and the media, the Phalangists had indeed entered the camps in coordination with the IDF. As to what went wrong, Eitan explained that the Phalangist command had simply lost control of its men. Yet they all swore that the minute they had discovered the misconduct they had intervened to drive the Phalangists out.

Once again the Cabinet seemed torn between the need to close ranks at a time of crisis and a natural pull toward mutual recrimination. When Yitzhak Moda'i remarked caustically to Begin that he had portrayed the aim of entering West Beirut as "protecting lives," the prime minister retorted, "That was our pure and genuine intent. That night I spoke to the chief of staff about it. I told him that we must take up positions to protect the Moslems from the vengeance of the Phalangists. I might have assumed that after the murder of Bashir, their beloved leader, they would wreak their vengeance on the Moslems."

"If we suspected they were planning to commit murder, we should have thought twice before letting them go in," Zevulun Hammer remarked in a gesture of collective self-reproach.

"It's been days since then," Begin snapped back. "What are you complaining about? That night I said [we have] to prevent it."

Evidently the Cabinet believed that the storm would blow hard for a while but then exhaust itself quickly—as furors tend to do in Israel—for the communiqué it issued at the close of the meeting said that the massacre was perpetrated by "a Lebanese unit" that entered the refugee camp "at a point far away from the IDF position." The ministers knew full well that the Phalangists had gone in with the IDF's knowledge and approval. Their communiqué can therefore be taken either as the height of self-delusion or, less charitably, as a deliberate attempt to suppress the truth. After three months of a war that, despite grumblings from the press and the parliamentary opposition, was accepted by a rather compliant if not altogether supportive public in Israel, the Cabinet chose to believe that the effects of the massacre would dissolve quickly as long as it was portrayed as a peculiarly Lebanese perversion—"*goyim* killing *goyim*," as Begin was reported to have dismissed the affair.

It was an understandable but severe miscalculation. For something snapped in Israel over that holiday weekend as hundreds of thousands of Israelis took the hideous pictures of slain children and piles of bloodstained bodies as confirmation of most of their suppressed fears. The war had not crowned their country with a great political and military victory but had dragged it down to the sordid depths of the Lebanese maelstrom and stained its honor indelibly. The growing shock and revulsion led the whole country to take a new, deeply sobered look at the aims of the war and the means used to achieve them, and gradually the entire enterprise was perceived in a different light; it seemed to have changed the face of Israel and debased its cherished rectitude to the point where the government and army were implicated in the commission of atrocities. Sabra and Shatilla had become synonymous with infamy.

The more the press disclosed in the days to come, the more the public clamored for an independent commission of inquiry into the circumstances surrounding the massacre, and the more Begin and members of his Cabinet arched their backs and bristled with indignation. One reason for the mounting uproar was the brazen but clumsy attempts to cover Israel's tracks in everything related to the hideous affair. The Kahan Commission commented on this phenomenon in extremely discreet language by noting that the IDF and the Foreign Ministry had issued "incorrect and imprecise statements" asserting, implicitly or explicitly, that the Phalangists had entered the camps without the knowledge of the IDF.

But there were many in the army who viewed all this concern about "protecting the IDF" as little more than a cynical attempt to shift the probing public spotlight away from their own responsibility and failings. Brig. Gen. Amram Metzna of the IDF's Staff College requested a leave from the army to protest Ariel Sharon's refusal to accept ministerial responsibility for everything related to the IDF; Colonel Yair asked for an audience with the prime minister to air his own store of grievances (Yair never did get to see Begin because Sharon intervened and told the prime minister, "I'll go see that officer from Hashomer Hatzair" *); and a conference of the IDF's senior command witnessed an unprecedented outpouring of resentment and remorse by some of the army's highest-ranking officers. "It was a matter of insensibility at every level," said Brig. Gen. Amos Yaron in the first honest IDF attempt to grapple with the significance of what had happened. "A case of callousness on everyone's part. As simple as that . . . I take myself to task. I admit here, from this rostrum, we were all numb. That's all there is to it."

Ariel Sharon did not go to Beirut to confront his irate officers, but on Wednesday, September 22, he did offer the Knesset the first statement officially confirming that the Phalangists had entered Sabra and Shatilla in coordination with Israel. Rather than placate the public, that admission only fueled the outcry for an investigation, and a week later—after a reported 400,000 people had gathered in Tel Aviv to demand an independent probe—Begin finally relented and appointed Chief Justice Yitzhak Kahan to head a state commission of inquiry. Ten turbulent days went by between the revelation of the massacre and the prime minister's surrender to the pressures—including the resignation of one minister (Yitzhak Berman) and unprecedented television appearances by such respected personalities as President Yitzhak Navon and Professor Ephraim Urbach, president of the Israel Academy of Sciences and Humanities, recommending that the episode be submitted to formal, judicial scrutiny. Spokesmen for Begin's Likud party argued fiercely that the appointment of an inquiry

---

* Left-wing faction of the Zionist Labor movement and all but anathema to a man of Begin's political outlook.

commission was tantamount to a confession of guilt; Begin's aides asserted (rather more feebly) that the prime minister was trying to protect the chief of staff—as if, under the circumstances, that was a noble gesture! No one but Berman seemed to realize that the more Begin resisted, the more it appeared that Israel had something monstrous to hide. Only when the ministers of the National Religious party saw that the Cabinet's position was morally untenable and began to hint at a coalition crisis—for the second time since June 6—did Begin yield.

The three members of the commission, Chief Justice Kahan, Supreme Court Justice Aharon Barak, and Maj. Gen. (Retired) Yonah Efrat, made a special effort to obtain testimony from non-Israelis. Not everyone was eager to cooperate; the Red Cross and the *New York Times* refused to have their Beirut representatives appear before the commission for fear of creating an undesirable precedent. But testimony was taken, albeit secretly, from the commander of the Lebanese Forces, Fadi Frem, and from some of his officers. The Phalangists confirmed their presence in the camps but claimed that the civilian deaths resulted not from a deliberate campaign of murder but from the heavy fighting with the remaining terrorists, and that the undeniable atrocities had been committed by Palestinian terrorists who liquidated the Lebanese for their identity cards.

To support this claim, the commission was provided with a copy of the report written by Assad Germanos, the Lebanese army's chief prosecutor, whom President Amin Gemayel had appointed to investigate the affair. Following orders from above, Germanos did not summon Lebanese witnesses. The Palestinians from the camps were afraid to appear before him, and the Phalangist fighters were expressly forbidden to give testimony. His report stopped short of reaching any conclusion about who had perpetrated the slaughter but determined that a total of 460 people had been killed in the camps, including fifteen women and twenty children. The remaining victims were 328 Palestinian men, 109 Lebanese men, seven Syrians, two Algerians, three Pakistanis, and twenty-one Iranians.

That account notwithstanding, there is no reliably documented figure of the number who died in the massacre. The Kahan Commission adopted the estimate of Israeli intelligence (700–800 dead), while the Palestinian Red Crescent put the number at over 2,000. Death certificates were issued for more than 1,200 people, but the accuracy of even this number is dubious, since the certificates were issued to anyone who could produce three witnesses prepared to swear that a member of his family had disappeared at the time of the massacre.

Not one of the Phalangists was punished for a role in the slayings. Hobeika has continued to fortify his position as the "strongman" of the movement's high command, backed by the other officers who worked under him in Sabra and Shatilla. Chastened by the experience, Jesse Soker left the Lebanese Forces and has turned his talents to importing condoms for sale to the Saudis (he once actually applied for a license to receive his goods in an Israeli port). On Saturday night, September 18, the Lebanese army took over supervision of the camps, and in the weeks that followed they went on to arrest and deport Palestinians without proper immigration papers. But most of the residents of Sabra, Shatilla, and the other camps of the area remain in Beirut, and many have restored their destroyed homes. Bashir's vision of a mass expulsion of Palestinians from Beirut may not have died with him, but it proved to be beyond the powers of his heirs.

The Kahan Commission published its findings and recommendations on February 9, 1983. Some were couched in mild terms, others were more pointed; some were followed to the letter, others were the object of controversy. One created a renewed public uproar that ultimately led to tragedy.

The commission ruled that Maj. Gen. Amir Drori, Maj. Gen. Yehoshua Saguy, and Brig. Gen. Amos Yaron had "committed a breach of the duty incumbent upon" them. Various recommendations were made about present and future postings for the latter two, but no conclusions were drawn as to Drori's future service. Saguy was dismissed as head of Intelligence Branch, in line with the commission's recommendation, and he retired from the army. Yaron was appointed head of Manpower Branch and promoted to major general over a year later. Drori completed his term as head of Northern Command and took a year's study leave in the United States pending a new appointment.

As for Lt. Gen. Rafael Eitan, the commission "arrived at grave conclusions regarding the acts and omissions of the chief of staff" and implied that under different circumstances they might recommend his dismissal, but since his term was about to expire anyway, they let the matter drop. They also found that the prime minister's "lack of involvement in the entire matter casts on him a certain degree of responsibility," and that Foreign Minister Shamir "erred in not taking any measures after the conversation with Minister Zippori." No specific recommendations were made beyond these judgments.

But the commission's findings and recommendations regarding the defense minister were considerably more drastic and thoroughly unequivocal:

> It is our view that responsibility is to be imputed to the minister of defense for having disregarded the prospect of acts of vengeance and bloodshed by the Phalangists against the population of the refugee

camps and for having failed to take this danger into account when he decided to have the Phalangists enter the camps. In addition, responsibility is to be imputed to the minister of defense for not ordering appropriate measures for preventing or reducing the chances of a massacre as a condition for the Phalangists' entry into the camps. . . .

We have found . . . that the minister of defense bears personal responsibility. In our opinion, it is fitting that the minister of defense draw the appropriate personal conclusions regarding the failings revealed in the manner in which he discharged the duties of his office and, if necessary, that the prime minister consider exercising his authority under [the law] according to which "the prime minister may, after informing the Cabinet of intention to do so, remove a minister from office."

Ariel Sharon refused to "draw the appropriate conclusions," and Menachem Begin agonized over his options but could not summon up the political and personal fortitude to fire him. The country seethed and roiled again, as in the days after the massacre, and when the group Peace Now organized a march to protest the outright contempt for the commission's findings, the explosion came—literally. A grenade was tossed into the dispersing crowd, killing Emil Grunzweig and injuring ten others (including Yosef Burg's son, Avraham). Yet, even perhaps especially, in the wake of that trauma Begin seemed unable to act. Finally a compromise was reached: Sharon agreed to forfeit the post of defense minister but stayed in the Cabinet as minister without portfolio. And so he remained after Begin resigned in September 1983, to be succeeded by Yitzhak Shamir.

Even before his resignation, Menachem Begin retired to his home and has been glimpsed only once since. Aides say that just before announcing his intention to retire in midterm, the prime minister had been engrossed in reading minutes of the General Staff meetings held in May and June 1982. Perhaps he discerned the many discrepancies and contradictions between what was being said to the Cabinet and to the General Staff during that critical period. In any event, as the casualties in Lebanon mounted over the months of occupation, with only the palest of compensating political achievements, and especially after the publication of the Kahan Commission's findings, Menachem Begin became steadily less strident in his defense of the war until he withdrew into isolation and complete silence.

The Kahan Report notwithstanding, it is difficult to say that Israel has truly and ultimately come to grips with the events at Sabra and Shatilla. In many ways the government is still treating the entire affair as a freak historical accident or a matter of abominable luck; not once has it been acknowledged that dispatching the Phalangists into West Beirut, and particularly into the refugee camps, was a cornerstone of the war policy from June 15 onward and that, in discussions at both the General Staff and more restricted forums, Ariel Sharon repeatedly urged his officers and aides to have the Phalangists "clean out" West Beirut. The odds of a slaughter resulting from this policy were never considered, despite the Phalange's infamous record at liquidating its enemies. And although it was never the intent of any Israeli that a massacre occur in Beirut, there definitely was a desire to see the city rid of every last trace of the PLO, and the defense minister hinted more than once that he would not object if the noncombatant Palestinians left Beirut as well.

Clearly, then, Israel courted disaster by inviting the Phalangists into the camps days after Bashir had been murdered. The officers in the field were slow to grasp and react to implications of the impressions and rumors— "the buzzing"—that piled up about the Phalangist action. Amos Yaron once spoke of a "gut feeling" that something was wrong but failed to act on it. And it was Amos Yaron who put his finger on what may really have been at the root of Israel's implication: after the long siege of Beirut and the relentless harm knowingly visited upon the civilian population of the city, the men in the field had become desensitized, hardened, inured to the suffering of the Palestinians; as soon as such outrageous ideas as the "purging" of Beirut began to be bandied about at the highest levels, the rank and file was invited to turn a blind eye to the harm inflicted upon innocent people.

The result was a chain reaction of negligence: the decision to send the Phalangists into the camps was made without the approval of the Cabinet or even the prime minister; there was no orderly examination and discussion of the issue within the military establishment; the heads of intelligence and the Mossad were not called in to offer their assessments; the supervision of the action was confined to sloppily improvised measures; there was no serious attempt to ascertain what was really going on even after rumors of a massacre were rife among the troops on the scene. And when it was all over and the terrible truth had come out, almost everyone scrambled to pass the blame as far as it would go rather than ask themselves what went wrong.

If there is a moral to the painful episode of Sabra and Shatilla, it has yet to be acknowledged.

14
Things Fall Apart

THE EVENTS IN SABRA AND SHATILLA completely overshadowed a concomitant political and diplomatic drama that would have a far more telling effect on Lebanon's future, on Israel's efforts to extricate itself from the Lebanese quagmire, and on the United States' standing in the Middle East. The next act of Israel's war in Lebanon opened with a question: Who would be the next man to inhabit the presidential palace in Ba'abda? It was an issue on which Israel and the United States, once again, did not agree.

Bashir was not yet interred in his tomb when the Israelis got wind that Amin Gemayel would make a bid to assume his slain brother's place. Amin's name did not stir up much enthusiasm in Israel, not least because Bashir had consistently warned the Israelis to steer clear of his brother on the grounds that Amin was a conduit who passed everything he knew on to Damascus. In his erratic contacts with the Israelis, Amin had always been very guarded and correct, taking pains not to say anything that could be construed as support for an Israeli operation in Lebanon. Some observers in Israel believed that such behavior was proof of a Gemayel division of labor: Bashir served as the link with Israel while Amin fulfilled a similar role vis-à-vis Syria and the PLO, leaving the family well covered on both flanks.

Amin was his brother's opposite in many ways—rigid where Bashir was wily, aloof where Bashir was magnetic—and strove to assume a completely different political image. He wanted to be perceived as a champion of compromise and conciliation (in contrast to Bashir's propensity to crush his opponents), as a statesman who preferred parley to force, and as an urbane man who had nothing but contempt for the vile behavior of the Phalangist thugs under Bashir's command. In an authorized biography written in 1983 by one of his close associates, Amin comes across as a Lebanese politician of the old school delivering himself of polished rhetoric rather than the crisp, crude slogans favored by his brother.

So prim and private a man was Amin Gemayel that he refused to divulge his birth date (although his wife, Joyce, ascribed that particular quirk more to Lebanese superstition than to reserve).

Amin's propriety in the midst of the war-racked Levant had a certain appeal to American observers, a certain appearance of solidity. On September 16, Morris Draper, feeling that he had to act quickly to restore a semblance of stability in Lebanon and, no less important, to get the Israelis out of Beirut, flew to Bekfaya (in an Israeli helicopter) to pay a condolence call on the bereaved family and took the opportunity to tell Amin that if his mind was set on running for president he could rely on full American backing. Amin seemed to have outdone his little brother: Bashir had had Israeli tanks behind him, but now Amin—who early in 1980 had confided to the Americans that, unlike Bashir, he didn't trust the Israelis because they were always bound to ask for more—had the clout of a superior delivered to him on a silver platter (and courtesy of the Israeli air force, at that). Or so it seemed at the time.

Ariel Sharon had paid his respects to the Gemayel family before Draper, on the day of Bashir's funeral, and found Amin solicitous. "I'll go beyond what Bashir promised!" the heir apparent volunteered in a reference to the understanding reached four days earlier about moving into West Beirut and establishing a joint committee of high-ranking figures to hammer out the terms of an agreement. Despite these assurances, however, the Israelis were left cold by the prospect of Amin in the palace at Ba'abda. They had quite another plan, one that postulated a stalemate: a new presidential election would not be held, and in its place would come the constitution of a military government under a prime minister appointed by Sarkis and granted emergency powers. Israel's candidate for the job was Col. Jonny Abdu, chief of military intelligence and one of the Americans' most trusted friends in the Lebanese establishment.

Over the previous six years, Abdu had become President Sarkis's right-hand man and, many believed his éminence grise. Serving as the president's primary contact with Bashir and the American diplomats in Beirut (whom he frequently hosted in his home), he was also well connected with the PLO and a personal friend of Walid Jumblatt. More than any other figure in wartime Lebanon, Abdu had the image of an honest broker between all sides to the conflict, to the point where he served as one of the main channels through which American intelligence operatives maintained contact with Yasser Arafat. (Knowledge of these contacts was kept from even the U.S. embassy in Beirut. They were orchestrated directly from the White House through Robert Ames, and only Arafat and his chief of staff, Abu Jihad, participated in them on the PLO side.) So the irony was that just when the Israelis, bereft of Bashir, were contemplating a break with the Phalange in favor of a middle-of-the-roader who might actually have managed to juggle all the elements of the Lebanese equation into an equilibrium of sorts, the Americans threw their support behind Gemayel rather than hold out for a president with a broader political base. They have paid dearly for that decision.

On September 21, the Lebanese parliament elected Amin Gemayel president of Lebanon by a majority of seventy-seven votes, including those of many of the Moslem delegates who had boycotted Bashir's election but now were willing to vote for Amin because they sensed that the United States, rather than Israel, was behind him. Within two days of his election, Amin had been sworn in and taken up residence in the presidential palace. Meanwhile the Israelis set to drawing up a "working paper" that would serve as a guideline for negotiations with Lebanon, while Secretary of State Shultz and his Middle East envoys began to draft their own outline of a settlement that would provide new impetus for the broader peace process—in effect, a grand design American-style.

The consensus in Washington was to dispose of the Israeli presence in Lebanon first, then proceed to deal with the Syrians on the assumption that the road to Damascus passed through Ba'abda. In broad strokes, the American strategy was to pull Assad down a notch or two by supplanting what was left of his hold over Lebanon. Amin led his American backers to believe that he had Assad's promise ("in writing") to withdraw his troops from Lebanon if the Israelis did the same. They took that commitment both at face value and as a sign of Syrian weakness. And it must be said that Assad never denied that he would play along with such a scheme. On the contrary, he professed a willingness to leave Lebanon as a matter of principle. In any case, whatever the actual purpose of such talk, it left the Americans convinced that they stood to achieve two coups for the price of one: by engineering an Israeli-Lebanese peace they would be able to sweep the Syrians out of the Soviet orbit and into their own, just as they had done with the Egyptians almost a decade earlier. In effect, they fell into the same pool of illusions that the Israelis had been splashing in for over a year. Just as Sharon had convinced himself that Lebanon's salvation lay in Bashir, Shultz and his subordinates now had a similar perception of Amin. As for Assad, the Americans repeated the Israeli mistake of underestimating his staying power in face of the trials they themselves had in store for him.

With Amin established in Ba'abda and the Americans enjoying a new, self-induced sense of "can do," the main concern in Jerusalem shifted back to the concrete question of security arrangements for Israel in South Lebanon. Two schools of thought contended over the issue. One believed that Israel should insist on the IDF's right to operate freely on Lebanese soil even if that meant conceding the parallel right of Syrian forces to remain in the Bekaa Valley. This was the approach taken by the pragmatists, those senior IDF officers who had never had much good to say for the Big Pines plan and now wanted to fall back on the practical propositions behind Little Pines. The opposing outlook was rooted in concepts left over from the more sanguine era of Bashir. It posited that Israel should turn full responsibility for the security zone over to the Lebanese, demonstrate its recognition of the sovereignty of the Beirut government by agreeing to withdraw its forces from Lebanon, and insist that the Syrians do likewise. As part of this scheme, the IDF's presence in Lebanon would be confined to contingents manning surveillance stations. (It later came out that Sharon intended to have it both ways by using these surveillance stations as a cover for direct Israeli control of the area.)

After deliberating the two options with his resident experts, Sharon ruled in favor of the second. On October 11 the Cabinet followed suit and endorsed a working paper that Foreign Minister Yitzhak Shamir took to Washington. Shultz praised it as "simple and logical." That description alone—against the far from simple background of the Lebanese arena—should have made its efficacy suspect. For what the document lacked was a grounding in reality, based as it was on the vain belief that Amin Gemayel would soon impose his rule on the whole of splintered and squabbling Lebanon. The distortions operative when Haig and Sharon had danced their pas de deux around the delicate subject of cleaning up South Lebanon returned to bedevil George Shultz.

As soon as the position paper received Shultz's blessings, a copy was passed on to Amin's envoy. The new Lebanese president studied the demands, agreed to a high-level standing committee to discuss the conditions for a peace treaty—even if it took years to reach an acceptable formula—and acquiesced in the establishment of three Israeli surveillance stations in South Lebanon, along with other military accommodations. The Israeli side of the plan stipulated a staged withdrawal in which the PLO would first be removed from the Bekaa Valley and the mountain areas farther to the east, an exchange of prisoners after that, and then an IDF pullback to a line forty or fifty kilometers from Israel's border. Meanwhile the Syrian army would withdraw from the Mount Lebanon area and be replaced by a multinational force in the zone commanding the Beirut-Damascus highway. The IDF would then remain in the security zone in South Lebanon until agreements on the demilitarization of the south and the normalization of relations between the two countries had been fulfilled. Only then would the Israeli and Syrian forces execute their final staged withdrawal, with each step attended by the realization of another of the negotiated security arrangements. On the political level, the document proposed the establishment of an Israeli representation in Lebanon that would enjoy diplomatic status and serve as the principle instrument for forging a "normalization" of relations on the basis of open borders.

Although creating the impression that he agreed in principle with most of the clauses of the draft, Amin objected from the outset to the term "normalization," so reminiscent of the American-guided peace process between Israel and Egypt. Encouraged and partially directed by Secretary of State Shultz, Defense Secretary Weinberger, Philip Habib, and Morris Draper, the negotiations would culminate in an American-crafted peace, the next stage of the Pax Americana that Washington envisioned for the Middle East under its own tutelage.

Nor was Ariel Sharon particularly happy about the American involvement. Having locked horns with Washington's envoys throughout the siege of Beirut, he now saw them elbowing in on negotiations that he wanted to handle himself. Thus while these official exchanges continued under America's benevolent gaze, a secret parley was going on between Amin Gemayel's personal envoy to Israel and the Israeli defense minister. At least that was what Sharon believed. But far from acting behind America's back, Gemayel threw himself into Ronald Reagan's arms, telling him during a trip to Washington in mid-October 1982, "You are president not only of the United States but of Lebanon as well, and I will not depart from your advice." The Lebanese president was also providing Habib and Draper with a steady stream of reports about the supposedly secret talks with Sharon. The first of these talks was held at Sharon's ranch. Subsequent sessions were conducted by three other Israelis, including David Kimche and Maj. Gen. Avraham Tamir. As Sharon saw it, these contacts were the materialization of the "high-level committee" promised by Bashir and confirmed by Amin on the day after his brother's death.

Together with the Israelis, Gemayel's envoy worked to forge a secret document that, in the Lebanese conception, would remain locked in a drawer as a confidential understanding between the two governments, while out in the open the negotiations shepherded by the Americans would proceed according to other rules. The document that finally emerged from this not-so-secret dialogue bore the date December 14, 1982, and stated in its preface that the two sides would make every effort to strike an agreement as quickly as possible in the form of a "package deal," meaning that the Israeli withdrawal would be conditional upon reaching a concomitant agreement on security arrangements and the normalization of relations. In the final draft, the term "normalization" was replaced by "mutual relations," and other stipulations were made about the makeup of the delegations to the official talks and the disposition of Major Haddad's militia.

Sharon rejoined the discussions on the final day, supposedly to stamp his imprimatur on their conclusions. The Lebanese envoy was prepared to sign the document, and Kimche and Tamir advised Sharon to do likewise. But the defense minister balked, saying that he must first clear the wording with Begin. As a result, the document was never signed. For when Amin Gemayel's envoy next met with Sharon in Beirut, the Lebanese refused to sign on the grounds that it was only a secret understanding drawn up as a guideline for the official negotiations, not a political accord in its own right.

On December 16, two days after Sharon had delayed putting his signature to the secret document, Philip Habib met with Begin and his leading ministers to discuss his own proposals for the official negotiations. Habib stressed their resemblance to the working paper that Shamir had brought to Washington a few weeks earlier. No sooner had he concluded his presentation than Sharon whipped out the three-page secret agreement. He read its clauses aloud as Habib's aides scribbled furiously to take down every word.

"Has President Gemayel confirmed this?" Habib asked at the end of the meeting.

"Yes, of course," Sharon replied.

"That's not the way I heard it from the Lebanese," the American said coolly.

The day after this conversation, with great fanfare, Sharon announced that he had achieved a "breakthrough" in direct contacts with Beirut, citing the achievement as proof that Israel and Lebanon could overcome their differences without the aid of the Americans. To his great disappointment, however, the Lebanese still refused to sign, and on December 23 Sharon went to Beirut to apply pressure in person. He took his case straight to Pierre Gemayel and threatened that his son would have a hard time ruling Lebanon, would in fact find himself reduced to lord of the palace in Ba'abda, if he did not order his envoy to sign forthwith. "If we open one gate to Israel," Gemayel replied drily, "we will lose twenty gates to the Arab world because of it." Even the proposed compromises— signing an abbreviated document, or simply making reference to the unsigned paper in an official letter attached to the full agreement—were spurned by the Lebanese. The Gemayels were nursing a king-size pique because the publicity had done Amin untold damage on the domestic front.

Predictably, Amin Gemayel did run into a string of difficulties establishing his rule in Lebanon, and predictably he blamed Sharon for them all. In November, when the Druse opened their offensive against the Christians in the Shouf, driving them into encircled enclaves, Gemayel complained that Sharon was attacking him through the back door by supplying arms and ammunition to the Druse militia while carrying on secret contacts with Jumblatt himself. His next affront came when Israel designated Haddad's militia a territorial brigade and deployed it with much flourish. But the worst occurred when Gemayel found himself in a head-on clash with the defiant Phalange over the proceeds from Pier 5 in the Port of Beirut. Amin was convinced that Sharon had put Fadi Frem up to it, an impression bolstered by Sharon's inviting Frem to his ranch at the height of the spat. Gemayel was determined to wrest the lucrative customs levies from Phalangist control, and, through intermediaries, told Sharon, "It's absurd that the Phalange enjoys a greater income from customs than the state does!"

The negotiations between Lebanon and Israel, conducted with American mediation, began on January 3, 1983. The Lebanese put together a delegation that reflected the political and ethnic makeup of their country. Heading the group was Dr. Antoine Fattal, a seasoned diplomat with a command of Hebrew and close ties to the president. Ambassador Ibrahim Harma represented the moderate Sunni Moslem leadership, and the head of the military team, Brig. Gen. Abbas Hamdan, was a Shiite accompanied by a Christian and a Sunni Moslem officer. The Israeli delegation was headed—against Sharon's wishes—by David Kimche, whose previous acquaintance with Amin now stood him in good stead. "You're the only one who has treated me fairly," Amin told him. Kimche was accompanied by General Tamir, who was responsible for handling the military issues. The American contingent, directed by Habib and Draper, tried to help the two sides bridge the gaps between them by forwarding proposals for compromise and forging understandings that would remain outside the official protocol. Through their mediation, the Americans hoped to fashion an agreement that would carry the momentum of the peace process on to negotiations with the Syrians.

Along general lines, the principles guiding the talks held alternately in Khalde, south of Beirut, and Kiryat Shmonah (later Netanya) resembled the Egyptian approach to the peace talks with Israel. For example, the Lebanese adopted as a sine qua non Sadat's opposition to any form of "sovereignty-within-sovereignty," which automatically disallowed the Israeli demands to maintain surveillance stations in the field, activate the IDF on Lebanese soil, and maintain Haddad's militia in its original form. Gemayel also refused to include in the agreement any element that might prejudice Lebanon's relations with the Arab world or oblige it to prefer an alliance with Israel over its association with the Arab League. The Lebanese further rebuffed all Israeli efforts to broaden the political scope of the agreement by squelching such ideas as the establishment of a standing committee to draw up a peace treaty, according diplomatic status to the two countries' representations, and embarking on an overt process of normalization. The drift of the negotiations was therefore quite different from Israel's expectations.

Throughout the talks, Amin Gemayel had an eye more to Washington than Jerusalem and, like Sadat before him, regarded as his primary goal not an accommodation with Israel but the attainment of American support for his regime. Calculating that only a deep American commitment would enable him to survive the pressures from both without and within Lebanon, Gemayel worked relentlessly to obtain President Reagan's guarantees of Lebanon's independence and territorial integrity, along with a semblance of deterrence against potential aggressors. These U.S. commitments translated into a token military presence as part of the multinational force, a two-year program to double the size and strength of the regular Lebanese army, and economic aid to the war-torn country.

The minutes of the negotiations show that Lebanon's fears of Syria hovered over the talks like a heavy mist that even the sun shining out of Washington could not dispel. The fact that the Syrian army had not been mauled in the fighting, that it had indeed maintained its hold over more than half of Lebanon's territory, was a decisive consideration for the Lebanese. For even though Israeli forces had reached a point twenty-five kilometers from Damascus, President Assad, apparently serene in the belief that he would emerge from the seeming debacle with the upper hand, had already proceeded to muster the antiestablishment Moslem factions in Lebanon for a war of attrition against the Gemayel regime.

But it was President Reagan's strategy to postpone dealing with Syria. When Yitzhak Shamir came to Washington in October with the Israeli working paper, the president summed up the American approach by telling Shamir almost mischievously, "Let's leave the Syrians on the outside looking in." Meanwhile, in Lebanon, the Syrian bugbear was so omnipresent that at one point the Phalangist leadership accused the Israelis of talking to Damascus behind the conferees' backs, with Sharon, according to the rumors, meeting secretly with either Rifat Assad or the Syrian chief of staff, Gen. Hikmat Shihabi. Dr. Fattal asked Kimche for a clarification on this point, and Kimche authorized him to publish a denial in his name. Other than that, the Israelis did nothing to dispel the rumors.

The Lebanese sensitivity on the subject of Syria came out particularly during the discussions about the surveillance stations. At one point Morris

Draper threw out the idea of having members of the Phalange man these stations. "They're your friends," he reminded the Israelis. But when Sharon declared in Beirut that the surveillance stations were so important to him that he was willing to "pay" for them by according similar rights to Syria, the voices in the negotiating room rose to a very undiplomatic level.

"Has Sharon joined the rejectionist front? Is that the kind of high-handed treatment we deserve?" Fattal asked the Israelis, genuinely offended.

"We have not come here to listen to attacks on a minister in the Israeli government," Tamir retorted just as sharply. "In all my experience in negotiations, I have never heard a speech like that!"

"Sharon is prepared to make a deal with the Syrians at my expense," Fattal charged, "with everyone dividing up the territory like spoils. How can we hold negotiations with outbursts like [Sharon's]?"

The Americans, meanwhile, pursued their plan to neutralize Assad as Lebanon's chief power broker by nailing down a Lebanese-Israeli-PLO peace that would leave Damascus out in the cold. The PLO was of course the touchiest subject to deal with from every possible angle. As far back as August 1982, Secretary Shultz had warned Ariel Sharon that Washington was determined that the destruction of the PLO's military power and its evacuation from Beirut must be followed by a resolution of the Palestinian problem. Without disclosing the Reagan Plan, then already in preparation, Shultz told the Israeli defense minister, "On the Palestinian question, I feel . . . the president feels . . . that it must be dealt with. The PLO must be scattered and its credibility destroyed. But unless the Palestinian problem is solved, a new PLO will arise. The Soviet Union will be glad to arm them and nurture their fantasies. . . ." Shultz also cautioned Sharon about taking the proper measure of the American president. "I know him well. . . . He is a decisive man and a winner by nature. He knows how to carry the country behind him, and the Congress. . . . Take him seriously," Shultz advised Sharon. "Remember that he is a friend of Israel, he thinks for himself, and he knows a lot about the Middle East. Don't underestimate him. . . ."

The Reagan Plan was announced on September 1, and for a short while it actually appeared that Yasser Arafat would reach an understanding with King Hussein about serving as his partner in peace talks to be held on the basis of the plan. But after the two men had worded a draft of their entente, Arafat flew to Kuwait to present the document to Fatah's Central Council, which vetoed it, and the chairman pulled out of the deal at the last minute. Israel and Syria, each on the defensive against the American initiative for reasons of its own, could now thank Arafat for getting them off the hook.

But then the Americans tried a new tack. In unprecedented secrecy two American envoys who had been instrumental in the evacuation from Beirut flew to Tunis—Arafat's temporary haven—in February 1983 to present a plan for evacuating the remaining PLO force in Lebanon via Tripoli, again under the protection of the multinational force. It was probably out of sheer spite for Assad, and not due to any sudden support of peace in the region, that the Iraqi government agreed to take in most of the fighters, while Jordan volunteered to absorb the rest. The American scenario postulated that, after this proposed evacuation, negotiations on a solution to the Palestinian problem would begin on the basis of the Reagan Plan. If they succeeded, the United States would walk off with the coup of the decade in the Middle East, spinning the straw of the Lebanese tragedy into pure gold. But having scotched an understanding with Hussein about the peace process, Arafat was not interested in evacuating the rest of his fighters from Lebanon. So the entire issue was dropped.

Perhaps the only result of this abortive American maneuver was to alert the Syrians to Washington's plot to isolate them. Not to be outdone by outsiders, Assad struck back with a show of his own political strength in the area. First he punished Arafat for his impudence in flirting with Hussein and the Americans by igniting a rebellion in Fatah, thereby raising the danger that Arafat's own power base and the PLO's largest constituent organization would fall into the hands of Syrian-backed hardliners. At the same time, he placed relentless pressure on Gemayel not to make any concessions to Israel. On one level this pressure took the form of Syrian aid to the Lebanese Druse, the most blatant threat to Gemayel's tenuous hold over the country. But lest that be too subtle a hint, Assad beefed up his own garrison in Lebanon to an unprecedented 1,200 tanks. He also signaled Jerusalem that he was not in the least dismayed by the prospect of renewed fighting in Lebanon and pointedly obtained a Soviet defensive umbrella for just such a contingency. The number of Soviet military advisers in Syria doubled to 5,000, and batteries of long-range SAM-5 missiles were stationed around Damascus, manned by Russian crews with a direct line to the control system in Moscow. Soviet officers even began to make rounds of positions in the Bekaa Valley.

In a word, the American scheme had backfired. Rather than bring Assad to his knees, it left him sitting pretty on the sidelines, building up his strength while the vision of a Pax Americana faded out of sight. The Lebanese-Israeli agreement was detached from the broader Middle East peace process. Secretary Shultz—reverting to a far simpler one-on-one approach that did not require the cooperation of a recalcitrant Arafat, Assad, or Hussein—came to the Middle East at the end of April 1983. His intention was to wind up the negotiations between Lebanon and Israel through classic shuttle diplomacy, and he came away from Beirut with the impression that the Lebanese were ripe for a new relationship with Israel. "I have talked with many Arabs in my life," Shultz told Begin upon arriving in Jerusalem, "and even when they spoke logically I sensed in them a deep animosity toward Israel. Not so with the Lebanese. I simply did not detect any feeling of hatred toward you."

Not that the absence of enmity made Shultz's job so much eaiser. Avoidance, not hatred, was the real issue. His main task was to shape a collection of secret understandings between Lebanon and Israel into the makings of an official agreement. Ariel Sharon loudly objected to this oblique approach of secret protocols and third-party letters confirming what the two sides would not say outright, but by then he was no longer defense minister and lacked his former clout. For weeks the talks were deadlocked. Something had to give. The turning point came when Israel dropped its insistence on a direct presence in South Lebanon and yielded even on the surveillance stations in favor of joint patrols. "Better to achieve an agreement than to live with the consequences, securitywise, of a situation in which none exist," was how General Tamir explained the turnabout. "There's more security with an agreement than in military control without one." On the political side, the Israelis also settled for considerably less than their original demands. The principle of a "package deal" had been whittled down to the so-called Iranian model of unofficial relations, in this case underwritten by American guarantees. Amin Gemayel was not required to commit himself publicly to an open border with Israel; a joint supervisory committee took the place of diplomatic missions; and the framework that was supposed to formulate a peace treaty vanished altogether. On the other hand, the agreement determined an end to the state of belligerency with the removal from Lebanon of all forces hostile to Israel—a promise that Gemayel was in no position to keep.

In shaping the final agreement, it was decided to leave in the open only those clauses that could be defended before Moslem public opinion in Lebanon and the criticism expected from Syria. Everything else was grouped into secret protocols and a "memorandum of understanding" with the United States. The need for absolute secrecy greatly troubled Shultz, who feared that the least indiscretion, unwitting or otherwise, could destroy the whole delicately balanced construct. So when the Israeli negotiating committee discussed the final form of the agreement, he did not hesitate to address the problem of leaks. "How am I to relate to this meeting?" Shultz asked the prime minister as he slowly took in the faces of the men around the table. "In Washington, when I walk into a room with so many people in it, I act as if the meeting were taking place in Madison Square Garden!'' To the embarrassment of many of the ministers, the secretary looked Begin hard in the eye and said, ''I want you to tell me how much to say forthrightly here. Because if I read about it in the paper, I don't care. But if [the Lebanese] read it in the papers, it will affect what they are prepared to say next time. . . .''

''I understand the difficulty,'' Begin told him. ''I often come up against it myself.''

As finally constituted, the May 17 agreement was merely the wrapping around a series of secret understandings, and it was in this format that the Lebanese parliament approved it by a majority of eighty votes. Yet even (or especially) in its watered-down form, no one seemed happy with the agreement. The Lebanese Druse protested that Israel had broken its promise to consult with Jumblatt before concluding any pact. President Assad promptly declared it ''a deal of capitulation,'' with many important Lebanese joining in his decrial. And in Israel everyone knew that the outcome bore only the faintest resemblance to the dreams that had fueled the whole foray into Lebanon a year earlier. Even before the ink on it was dry, the May 17 agreement had become a sterile, unenforceable document because it was conditional upon a Syrian withdrawal from Lebanon, and the Syrians did not regard themselves as obliged to uphold any terms that had been agreed upon without their prior consent. On the contrary, Assad immediately embarked on a resolute campaign to destroy the agreement with the active aid of Jumblatt's Druse forces. And nine months later, the most modest of political achievements was repudiated by Amin Gemayel in a desperate effort to save his beleaguered regime.

Just as Israeli military pressure had not been able to change the basic facts of life in Lebanon, neither could American political pressure. The ingrained fragmentation and volatile partnerships of Lebanon were no more responsive to position papers than they had been to bombs and shells. In the months following the birth of what Assad termed ''the still-born agreement,'' the tangled skein of alliances and rivalries in Lebanon often seemed to verge on the ludicrous, particularly when some of Syria's allies in the anti-Gemayel coalition sought to line up new backers to protect them from Assad's bear hug. The Lebanese Druse were willing to forgive Israel its ''perfidy'' and offer it security against a revitalized PLO as the price of support for a Druse canton in the Shouf and a modicum of independence from Syria. Arafat, pushed into a corner by the rebellion in Fatah, suddenly discovered new allies in the Phalange, who were only too happy to supply weapons and Israeli ammunition to his last stronghold in Tripoli, now that he dared to defy Damascus. And in the midst of all this shifting of alignments, the Israelis and Americans, like latter-day "innocents abroad," were left to maneuver as best they could.

Israel proved more adept, at first, than the United States. At the end of August 1983, the IDF unilaterally withdrew its forces from the Shouf Mountains to a new line along the Awali River. Accomplished despite American appeals—and though twice postponed so that Gemayel could send his army in to replace the IDF (he never did)—the Israeli pullback came in response to loud popular protests at home that the IDF had no business playing the thankless and wasteful part of policeman between the warring sects in the Shouf. The move was preceded by a series of futile attempts to coax Gemayel into reaching an accommodation with Jumblatt, and when the IDF left the area it was with full realization that Jumblatt's men would roll up the Phalange almost effortlessly, taking a great stride toward realizing the dream of a Druse canton (without Israeli help) and leaving the U.S. Marine position in Khalde airport an easy target. Meanwhile, on the anniversary of the massacre in Sabra and Shatilla, the sight of brutal carnage returned to the TV screens. Only this time the bodies were Maronite Christians slaughtered in the Shouf and Aley, now that the Israelis had gone. In a single stroke, the Maronites lost sixty villages, suffering 1,000 dead and 50,000 homeless, 15,000 of them besieged by the Druse in the town of Deir el-Kamar.

By now it was clear to Washington as well as Jerusalem that Amin Gemayel sorely lacked the political leverage and personal stature required to carry the role envisioned for him. Rather than draw the ends toward the center, he had a knack for alienating the people he needed most, all the while assuring the Americans that if only they continued supporting him everything else would fall into place: the Druse, the Shiites, and perhaps even Assad would come crawling to him in the end. It was truly a perverse fantasy, for Amin was caught in the bind of being damned if he did and even more if he didn't. If he agreed to reform the formal power structure in Lebanon, as the Shiites and Druse clamored he should, he was sure that such flexibility would be taken as a sign of weakness. On the other hand, if he hunkered down in Ba'abda and did not give at all, he was doomed to lose his country in the next round of fragmentation and violence.

Under these circumstances, a new negative alliance arose in Lebanon. It was based on Gemayel's flagrant weakness, the crumbling belief that a compromise could be reached under the aegis of American negotiation, and Israel's decision to act alone in a last-ditch effort to protect its own best interests. Together these factors encouraged the Syrians, through their proxies in Lebanon, to poke at the many soft spots of this very vulnerable trio of allies after Israel's withdrawal from the Shouf. By means of Shiite terror groups headquartered in the Bekaa Valley, they attacked first the American Marine position at Khalde, killing 241 men by the same truck-bomb technique that had been used against the American embassy in Beirut the previous April, and then the Israelis stationed in Tyre. At the close of 1983 the Syrians went one step further and moved to dispose of Yasser Arafat by sending the dissident Fatah forces under the command of Abu Moussa against Arafat's remaining loyalists in Tripoli, soon driving them into distant exile.

The leading force in Lebanon had now become the Syrian-backed Druse and Shiite front, with tacit support from the Sunni Moslems and Maronite rivals of the Gemayels in the north. Led by Walid Jumblatt and Nabih Berri, it pronounced Amin Gemayel president of a fascist party, not of Lebanon, and began to expose his impotence by shelling Beirut and the Ba'abda palace at will. Assad, established as king of the mountain, if not yet the coast, demanded that the multinational force be withdrawn from Lebanon forthwith and, to be doubly sure that he got his message across, set Shiite snipers and Druse artillery against the American contingent in Khalde. The American choice now was essentially to fight or to leave. Conciliation had failed and the charade of muscle-flexing in the form of air strikes on Syrian positions in the Bekaa and fire from the battleship *New Jersey* on the Shouf and beyond, deep into Syrian-occupied territory, had little practical effect. The only imaginable way to change the picture in Lebanon was through massive troop intervention, but neither the United States nor Israel could conceive of wading deeper into the mire.

In February 1984 a coalition of Druse and Shiite forces moved forward in a successful bid to open a corridor from the Shouf to the capital, take over West Beirut, and place Ba'abda directly under their guns. The Lebanese army disintegrated in a matter of days, half fleeing south to the Israeli-occupied zone, half deserting to the dissident front. Amin Gemayel was reduced to lord of the palace at Ba'abda, just as Ariel Sharon had predicted more than a year earlier. Abu Moussa's faction of the PLO reopened the organization's office on Corniche Mazraa, and Palestinians returned to Damour in triumph after the town fell to the Druse. Once again refugees streamed south in a sight painfully reminiscent of the last round of the civil war in the mid-1970s. Though many of the dramatis personae had changed, the situation in Lebanon was a close facsimile of the days in which a gawky Bashir and a frosty Amin had first boarded an Israeli missile boat in Junieh. The country was again racked by fighting. The Syrians were more deeply entrenched than ever. It was as if close to 600 Israeli and 250 American lives had been lost in Lebanon just to bring the situation full circle.

The Marines pulled out of Khalde airport in February 1984, much as the Israelis had left the Shouf six months earlier. That seemed to be the only way out of Lebanon—to pick up one fine day and stalk out without looking back. And with the Americans gone, the last of the Gemayels sat teetering on his shaky throne, left to brood on the fact that, although his family had invited the Syrians, the Israelis, the Americans into Lebanon in turn, never once had it savored the taste of victory. Israel was stuck in South Lebanon, hoist by its own petard. Still lacking security for its northern settlements, it could only hope that things would not get much worse than they were before the war.

Perhaps Lebanon's sole hope lies in the fact that Hafez Assad, having once bitten into the poison apple, will be wary of its lure a second time. After the disastrous experiences of Israel and the United States, who could possibly crave a stewardship over Lebanon now?

Afterword

BORN OF THE AMBITION of one willful, reckless man, Israel's 1982 invasion of Lebanon was anchored in delusion, propelled by deceit, and bound to end in calamity. It was a war for whose meager gains Israel has paid an enormous price that has yet to be altogether reckoned; a war whose defensive rationale belied far-reaching political aims and an unconscionably myopic policy. It drew Israel into a wasteful adventure that drained much of its inner strength, and cost the IDF the lives of over 500 of its finest men in a vain effort to fulfill a role it was never meant to play.

There is no consolation for this costly, senseless war. The best one can do now is to learn its lessons well.

The war in Lebanon unfolded as it did because of a sharp departure from the conventions and norms of government in Israel, a lapse that made it possible for the country to "slip" into an offensive military operation that a decisive majority of the Cabinet had rejected from the outset. One individual—Defense Minister Ariel Sharon—arrogated the authority to conduct a major military venture as he saw fit and encountered no effective opposition from his government colleagues until the nation hovered on the brink of disaster. Promising what he never meant to deliver, Sharon transformed the war in Lebanon into a personal campaign, even though the Cabinet had disqualified his approach, the country's intelligence community cautioned against it, and the senior ranks of the army—not to mention the political opposition and certain sectors of the press—forthrightly opposed it.

How did such a situation come to pass? Crudely put, one could say that just prior to the war an extraordinary kind of putsch occurred in Israel and persisted for the first two months or so of the conflict. It was a very subtle one-man coup whereby the Cabinet's decision-making powers were unilat-

301

erally assumed by the defense minister without setting off an alarm or activating the safeguards that were supposed to prevent just such a dangerous development. On the surface, Ariel Sharon was very careful to adapt his moves to Israel's accepted democratic and political conventions. He invested considerable energy in building the image of a reformed recalcitrant who wouldn't dream of embarking on any consequential action without first submitting a detailed report, receiving prior authority, and explaining himself to the public. The paradox is that exactly the opposite was true: the image of obedience and cooperation was a thin but effective veneer masking a highly original method of circumventing democratic procedures. Instead of trying to take over or disperse governmental institutions, as is the usual course of a coup d'etat, Sharon devised a formula for bypassing the decision-making process and evading the supervisory prerogatives of the country's parliamentary system. Through chinks in that system, he gained the freedom of maneuver necessary to implement his plan.

Primarily, Sharon exploited his command over information as a weapon with which to gain decision-making control. By blocking the flow of information from the General Staff to the Cabinet, he effectively isolated the political echelon from the military and made himself the sole link between the government and its army. Thus, he was able to impose his views on the General Staff without the misgivings expressed by most of his generals ever coming to the Cabinet's attention. As well, he managed to present the ministers with a series of selective and tendentious reports tailored to secure their approval. First he concealed his conviction that there was no way to avoid a clash with the Syrian garrison in Lebanon; then he described the army's advance beyond the 40-kilometer limit as an effort to deter the Syrians. On the eve of the war he sold the Cabinet on a 40-kilometer, 48-hour action, only to proceed to tell the ministers that it was imperative to take the Beirut-Damascus highway, knowing that it would mean a link-up with the Phalangist forces. And when that link-up brought the IDF into Beirut, he portrayed this next step as a spontaneous outcome of developments in the field. And so Ariel Sharon dragged the Israeli Cabinet behind him, step by step, into moves that he claimed were dictated by the situation on the ground but were in fact elements of his original grand design.

To ensure minimal resistance, Sharon devoted himself untiringly to procuring the prime minister's backing, kindling Begin's personal zeal to penetrate right down to "Arafat's bunker." Quite rightly Sharon assessed that few ministers were likely to defy Menachem Begin and risk incurring his wrath. Whenever a cabinet colleague tried to pin Sharon down on critical issues or warned of the grave ramifications of his plans, he was silenced by the prime minister. For his part, Begin seemed torn throughout the war between a desire to keep the operation within its declared limits (as he had pledged to the Knesset and to the United States), and a temptation to grasp the opportunities he imagined winking at him in Sharon's proposals. In most matters, including the plan to storm West Beirut, Begin gave Sharon his unqualified support and thereby became a full, if not always active, partner in the conduct of the war and its consequences. Even when angered by a tardy, ex-post-facto report, he remained faithful to Sharon's outlook and gave his defense minister a free hand to do as he pleased. Whether Sharon deliberately misled Begin about certain facts, we have not been able to determine. Nor can we say that Begin simply deluded himself. Either way, however, as prime minister his responsibility for the war is beyond question.

Even those men who suspected Sharon's true intentions bowed to Begin's will, so that hardly any of the defense minister's proposals were rejected until it came to the issue of storming West Beirut. The few who did offer resistance spoke out too softly or too late, and then voted for the very measures they had decried moments earlier. One minister resigned, but that was well after the worst of the damage had been done and the issue was whether or not to investigate how just one "mishap"—the massacre in Sabra and Shatilla—came about.

A similar paralysis seemed to have spread through the senior ranks of the IDF even though many of the commanders took a jaundiced view of Sharon's aims and opposed the broadening of the war. Some high-ranking officers did relay pointed warnings and fragments of information to Begin's office surreptitiously, but even they became resigned to the suppression of dissent within the General Staff, to their isolation from the political echelon and, when the time came, to the orders they received in the field. Like the Cabinet, the top brass of the IDF deferred to the defense minister's authority; few if any stood up to Sharon until it came to the issue of a costly ground assault on West Beirut. To avoid a collision with the defense minister, Chief of Staff Eitan, himself decidedly unenthusiastic about fighting the Syrians, was deliberately absent from Cabinet meetings throughout the first week of the war. The IDF's chief of intelligence, Maj. Gen. Yehoshua Saguy, sounded his warnings high and low within the defense establishment, until he saw that they were having no effect and withdrew into silence. The head of the Mossad did not endorse the war, but the Cabinet was never apprised of his negative views.

Sharon had partners by default not only in the Cabinet and the army but in the loyal opposition as well. Leading figures in the Labor Party could not help but have known about his plan, and some of them even talked about it quite openly, but they nevertheless took their time in speaking out against it—and a few Labor people accorded Sharon a measure of support. The incorrigible squabbling within the party and a fear of incurring the public's censure by breaking ranks in time of war prevented Labor from taking a coordinated stand against the aims of the war at the outset and thus further contributed to Sharon's freedom of action.

The same must be said for much of the Israeli press. In light of the early victories in the field, many of the papers abandoned themselves to jingoistic raptures and a festival of gloating at the enemy's undoing. To this day, the press has yet to ask itself why it lost its usually sharp critical sense just when it was most needed.

Very few members of Israel's political and military establishment are entitled to consider themselves exempt of responsibility for this war that almost all have come to rue. A hapless combination of mental laxity, opportunism, and diffidence in the face of an aggressive personality thwarted a system of checks and balances whose very purpose was to prevent the concentration of so much power in the hands of one man.

Ariel Sharon's grand design was a simplistic approach built on highly specious logic. The scheme posited that from the moment Israel struck a blow in Lebanon, a chain reaction would be set in motion and continue until it had forged a new balance of forces by (1) eliminating the PLO as an independent political factor (even if it retained nuisance value as a source of terrorism); (2) cutting Syria down to size and neutralizing the threat it posed to Israel; (3) installing an allied regime in rehabilitated Lebanon under the rule of Bashir Gemayel; and (4) heightening cooperation with the United States while further supplanting Soviet influence in the Middle East. In a single stroke, Sharon believed he would reap a historic yield and open glorious vistas before his country. A victory in Lebanon, so the theory went, would accord Israel absolute control over the West Bank by inaugurating an era of unchallenged Israeli domination and, at the same time, generate momentum for further initiatives to impose Israel's will on its neighbors.

On paper the plan held great promise as a military endeavor—traditionally Israel's forte—designed to achieve immediate political gains. Sharon, a gifted battlefield tactician, convinced himself and others that he was graced with the genius of an innovative strategist, but his undeniable flair for feint and manipulation served only to mask his true nature as a naive romantic. All too quickly it emerged that he had badly misjudged the conditions of the arena in which he had chosen to fight.

Sharon's plan was doomed from the start in its failure to appreciate the vehemence of the internal strife in Lebanon. That Bashir Gemayel would be able to impose a strong Christian regime on the country within weeks if only the IDF paved his way to the presidency was an outlandish assumption. Sharon's judgment regarding the enemy was no better, insofar as he failed to anticipate the resolve and perseverance of the PLO, or to presume a determined stand by the Syrians.

For this reason of consistent underestimation the war in practice differed sharply from how it was plotted on paper. The blitzkreig that should have carried the IDF through South Lebanon in a matter of hours turned into a slow, often gruelling trek that hit countless snags and repeatedly marked time until one obstacle or another could be removed. The Syrian army emphatically did not collapse, even when subjected to punishing blows. The PLO emphatically did not dissolve into helpless chaos, even at the height of the siege. On the other hand, the Phalangist chieftains were quick to divest themselves of all political and military association with the Israeli venture; and the United States, which had seemed prepared to countenance a swift "surgical" strike in Lebanon, changed course and prudently backed off from Israel's side.

Even Sharon's judgment of the mood of his own forces was found wanting. In clinging so determinedly to his vison of a new order in Lebanon, he lost sight of the cardinal rule of the IDF—a citizens' army par excellence —that honesty and mutual trust must abide between the troops and their leaders, especially in wartime. He abused that trust by using Israeli soldiers as pawns in a struggle that lacked national consensus, and was then baffled by anger in the ranks that lives were being squandered in a bootless cause. The cumulative effect of the drive toward the Beirut-Damascus highway, the assault on the Syrian army, the "creeping ceasefire," and the plan to storm West Beirut, capped by the affront of being stationed around Sabra and Shatilla when the Phalangists went in to do their execrable deeds, left deep cracks in the army's belief in its leaders and the justice of its cause.

Inexplicably, the defense minister believed that the IDF could be used like a golem, as a conditioned, compliant, and mute war machine wherever it might be sent. "Arik's War," as it came to be known among the troops, placed the officers of the Israel Defense Forces on the horns of a cruel dilemma: whether to loose the fury of massive firepower on civilians as a means to reduce losses within their own ranks, or to risk turning their men into cannon fodder in a cause not their own. After the siege of Beirut, many a weary veteran felt that the moral sensibility of the Israeli soldier had been blunted to the point where dozens of them could simply "stand aside" while the Phalangists did as they pleased in the Palestinian camps.

But sooner or later a reaction was bound to come from the ranks. Indeed, it was the agitation originating in the reserve units—particularly of the paratroops—that finally roused the press to confront Sharon. And that was the point where the Cabinet slowly began to reclaim its prerogatives as a decision-making and supervisory body. In essence, echoes of the grumblings in the field sparked the process that culminated in stripping Ariel Sharon of the sweeping authority he had arrogated to himself.

The major achievements of the war were and remain the destruction of the PLO's "state-within-a-state" in Lebanon, the elimination of the centers of command and supply for the network of international terrorism and, of course, the removal of the PLO's guns from range of the Galilee. Each of these aims was legitimate in itself, but they were achieved with significant qualifications. The PLO suffered a stunning blow from which it has yet to recover, especially as the war severely undermined Yasser Arafat's standing and led to a split and rebellion in the ranks of Fatah. Similarly, the PLO's tangible military threat to the Galilee has been lifted. However, the war has not changed the basic fact that a large concentration of Palestinian refugees remains in South Lebanon—not to mention the Shiite population of the area, already thoroughly antagonized by the Israeli occupation and radicalized by extremist elements—which could well become the seedbed of a new wave of terrorism. Moreover, the senior ranks of the PLO were not disabled during the fighting, so that a new center of terrorist activity could well arise in place of Beirut. To rid Lebanon of the PLO would require vigorous action by a strong central Lebanese government. But the constitution of such a government would itself require a rapprochement between the warring communities in Lebanon, and the experience of the period since the 1982 war does not justify any such optimism.

Above all, however, the war in Lebanon has in no way tempered the virulence of the Palestinian problem—which is hardly surprising, inasmuch as the roots of that problem do not lie in Lebanon. It was sheer folly to believe that any action there would ameliorate the political conflict between the Israeli and the Palestinian nations. If anything, the war has exacerbated the strife between the two peoples. Perhaps the greatest tragedy of the war, then, is that when it was over and the PLO had been whipped, Israel lacked the wisdom to choose a path to political compromise with the Palestinians, or at least with Jordan.

Another achievement initially claimed for the war in Lebanon—landing a devastating blow to the Syrians—has in the interim proved to be pure self-delusion. For despite the drubbing that the Syrian armed forces took at Israel's hands, especially in the air battles, President Assad has managed to upgrade his country's leverage as a factor to be reckoned with in any unraveling of the Lebanese knot. From the vantage of Damascus, the Syrian army foiled Israel's plan to drive it out of Lebanon by halting the IDF midway down the Beirut-Damascus highway in the area of Dahr el-Baidar. The Syrians are proud of this achievement and believe that for all its shortcomings—particularly the glaring inferiority of its air force—their army met the test of holding the Israelis at bay when it counted most.

Thus Syria is fully entitled to conclude that if it ever comes up with an antidote to Israel's superiority in the air, it can afford to be far more daring in tackling the Israelis on the ground. The experience in Lebanon has confirmed the Syrians' strategic assumption that any Israeli assault would be a relatively plodding affair in which the IDF would have to sustain heavy casualties and be limited to a slow timetable to make any progress at all, even under conditions of absolute advantage. The natural corollary of this judgment is to return to the long-standing Arab strategy of multi-front wars in which Israel must concentrate its main effort on one front at a time. Ironically, therefore, the Lebanese war, undertaken at least in part to enhance the credibility of Israel's deterrent power, may well have contributed to destroying it.

Another paradox of the controversial move against the Syrians is that the air force's stunning victory over the surface-to-air missiles came at the cost of disclosing the possession of technology that would have been better saved for the contingency of a genuine war of survival. Stung by the enormity of the defeat, the Soviet Union has invested an immense effort into improving its anti-aircraft systems, including the establishment of Soviet missile bases on Syrian soil; and in the next round, already being mooted, Israel may find itself up against a highly sophisticated missile network that can blanket most of its territory. And on yet another plane, the Soviet penetration of the Middle East has drawn momentum from the Lebanese venture, while the United States, in its desire to keep the Soviets out, seems newly prepared to use the Golan Heights and other territories occupied by Israel in 1967 as bargaining chips.

As to the Christian regime that Ariel Sharon and Bashir Gemayel wanted to impose on Lebanon, it was never really more than the figment of a callow political imagination. Obliged to choose between an alliance with Israel (which would inexorably lead to his downfall) and the icy distance now maintained by his brother, Bashir tried to have it both ways: he lured the Israelis into Lebanon, left them in the lurch on the battlefield, and then made short shrift of his promise to reward them for their pains by concluding a peace treaty. Now his political heirs—especially the commanders of the so-called Lebanese Forces—are paying dearly for the vain dream of Maronite hegemony. Their hopes of an Israeli invasion were indeed rewarded, but when the time came to move into the field and stake their claim to power, they proved helpless to take advantage of the IDF's presence and barely managed to defend the precincts they had held before the Israelis arrived. Consequently, they must now choose between holing up in a small Christian state surrounded by hostile neighbors or reconciling themselves to their status as a minority in Lebanon by striking a compromise with the country's Moslem majority. In one of the greatest ironies of the 1982 war, the Maronites have suffered the worst defeat in their history, losing some sixty villages in the Shouf Mountains and having to absorb tens of thousands of refugees driven out of that area by the Druse after the IDF's withdrawal.

One after another, the propositions underlying the Lebanese war collapsed under the weight of a very different reality, and out of its rude awakening Israel has had to face a string of unanticipated setbacks: the tarnishing of its image in world public opinion; unprecedented friction between many Jewish communities in the West and the Israel they perceived during the months of fighting; and yet another oppressive burden on the anemic Israeli economy. More than a year after the invasion, the IDF was still bogged down in the Lebanese quagmire. It was not until then that the government began to extricate its men by withdrawing from the Shouf Mountains. The area south of the Awali River, still occupied by Israel, has become a death trap for its soldiers. And during the IDF's second winter in Lebanon, the rest of that country plunged into a new round of civil war, with a coalition of Druse and Shiite forces assaulting the regime of Amin Gemayel. Of Ariel Sharon's grand design nothing remains.

The task now facing the Israeli government is to complete the IDF's withdrawal from Lebanon while seeing that it is not construed as an unqualified defeat, which would only invite further violence. At the same time, Israel must address itself to the work of rehabilitation—of its political life, its armed forces, its tattered sense of self and battered sense of purpose. Perhaps a misguided war is a stage that every nation goes through on its way to political maturity. If so, Israel has come out of its adolescence considerably sadder but wiser about the limits of what force can achieve and the illusions that power can breed.

About the Authors

Ze'ev Schiff is the military correspondent of *Haaretz*, Israel's most prestigious daily, and the author of *The Year of the Dove*, with Ehud Ya'ari. Ehud Ya'ari is the Middle East Affairs correspondent for Israeli television, and shared with Ze'ev Schiff the 1982 Journalist of the Year Award for their coverage of the Lebanon campaign.

10/96 Ø 4/96
12/97 1 12/96
3/01   5 4/00
1/03   6 10/01
1/05   11 7/04